Life in the *Spirit*

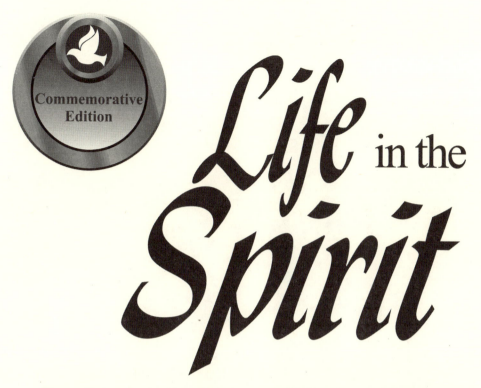

Commemorative Edition

Life in the Spirit

Devotions from the Pentecostal/Charismatic Revival

Compiled by

Robert White

Introduction by Bishop Charles Blake

Foreword by Marcus Lamb

Scripture Quotations are from the *New King James Version*. Copyright © 1979, 1980, 1982, Thomas Nelson Inc., Publishers. Used by Permission.

ISBN: 0-87148-539-7

Printed by Pathway Press

Cleveland, Tennessee 37311

Printed in the United States of America

Book Cover designed by Var White

DEDICATION

Usually a dedication is made to heroes or family members or role models in one's life. But the dedication of *Life In The Spirit* takes a different path.

First, *Life In The Spirit* is dedicated to the work and ministry of the Holy Spirit during the twentieth century which started in such a humble beginning and now impacts Christianity with over 620 million Christians claiming to be Spirit-filled.

Secondly, *Life In The Spirit* is dedicated to those men and women of this last century who had a hunger for more of God. These saints would not be denied; they would not settle for less than an enduement of power and a receiving of the outpouring of the Holy Spirit as they did on the day of Pentecost regardless of the persecution or sacrifice.

Thirdly, *Life In The Spirit* is dedicated to the unity of the Body of Christ and especially to those who have received an experience that classifies them as part of the Pentecostal/Charismatic Movement. Men and Women from various segments, communities, denominations and fellowships are contributors to this book. They might not share the same theology, dogma, polity, or liturgy, but they have experienced a similar experience and have all come together between the covers of this book to gather around the same table as the Body of Christ and the Family of God.

I trust that *Life In The Spirit* will underscore a fact written in the Blood of Jesus Christ that we are all One in the Body of Christ.

ACKNOWLEDGMENTS

I wish to acknowledge the hard work of a few key people without whose assistance this book would not be possible.

Var White has served as editor and has done the formatting, the rewrites, the book cover, and countless other services too numerous to mention.

Tom George has also assisted in communicating with many of the contributors, assisted with many of the rewrites, and given valuable insight into the formulation of the book.

H. Thomas Owens and Diane E. Willcocks-Owens have done most of the proofing as well as the finishing touches in completing *Life In The Spirit*.

I am indebted and deeply grateful to these people, and I leaned heavily upon them to make the compilation and publishing of this book a true masterpiece.

FOREWORD

Marcus D. Lamb

What a great honor it is for me to write the Foreword to this important book, *Life in the Spirit*, especially when I think about the Who's Who of the Pentecostal and Charismatic world, past and present, who have contributed to it.

Dr. Robert White is to be commended for the inspirational idea to put this great collection together into a devotional book. *Life in the Spirit* is a veritable treasure of spiritual insight and anointed ideas by some of God's greatest Generals.

As far as I know, there is no other book quite like it in the world today. It is destined to become a time-honored classic.

This book will inform, inspire, encourage, and bless everyone who reads it. *Life in the Spirit* is a must for every believer who wants to do just that, live his or her life in the Spirit!

In September of 1994, I went into a trance for about two hours on "live" television. While in the trance, the Lord spoke to me that if people really want to experience the glory of God in their lives they must do three things:

1) They must hunger and thirst for more of God. In other words, they must want God more than anything else to the point that they don't care what they look like, what they sound like, or what anybody thinks about them.

2) They must get into His presence. This comes through fasting and prayer and praise and worship and getting in the fire of Revival.

3) You can be in the presence of God, but if you do not completely yield, you will not receive all that God has for you.

God prophesied through Joel that in the last days "I will pour out My Spirit on all flesh." Surely, these are the last of the last days. Therefore, it is imperative that we keep our spiritual batteries charged and be keenly sensitive to the Holy Spirit. We must walk in the Spirit, talk in the Spirit, listen to the Spirit, and be led by the Spirit. This devotional book, *Life in the Spirit*, will help you do just that.

How practical of Dr. Robert White to have selected a different devotion for every day of the year. I encourage you to read one every day before you go to bed or when you first get up in the morning. You could say, "A devotion a day will help keep the devil away!"

Finally, I encourage you to obtain many copies of *Life in the Spirit* and pass them along to people on whom you want to make a lasting spiritual impact. They will thank you for it.

I, along with many thousands around the world, thank you, Dr. Robert White, for compiling these devotions.

INTRODUCTION

Bishop Charles Blake

Life in the Spirit is a testament to several aspects of the Pentecostal/Charismatic Movement. First, it testifies to its essential unity.

In Genesis 11:6, God said, "nothing will be restrained from them, which they have imagined to do," because He said they speak the same language. When the Body of Christ is united together, speaking the same language, with a common goal and purpose, they can accomplish beyond the imagination of humankind.

Jesus prayed to make the "disciples one as we are one." Bishop T. D. Jakes said in a private correspondence that he longed for the time when the entire family of God gathered around the Table. Bishop Earl Paulk in *Held in the Heavens Until* said, "Pentecost is the Spirit of unity. When we understand unity, we comprehend the heart of Pentecost."

When Pentecostalism burst onto the scene in a way that could no longer be ignored, it was called divisive, and speaking in tongues was considered chaotic. What was not seen by many was that the power of the Holy Spirit was *unifying* the believers in a common experience: they were no longer speaking simply their own words, no longer preaching simply their own interpretations of Scripture, but were speaking *as one* the language of God!

Life in the Spirit is a book honoring men and women of all walks of life and from every philosophical sector of the Pentecostal/Charismatic movement. Different perspectives, different life-experiences, different parts of the world, different cultures, different churches . . . but *one* in the Body of Christ, *one* in zeal for God, *one* in intention, *one* in power, and *one* in love.

Life in the Spirit also testifies to the *power* of the Pentecostal/Charismatic Movement. It is a book of miracles, testimonies to the absolute power of God working in the lives of believers. The Pentecostal/Charismatic Movement itself is not so much a doctrine (there are many perspectives represented), but an *experience* of God, a relation to God in which the believer is touched and empowered and in which God works through the believer.

The Movement hasn't grown to such a huge size (estimates as high as 600,000,000 people worldwide) because it formulated a doctrine that commanded assent, but because men and women hungry for God saw the *power of God* in its midst, because they witnessed God's touch and, more than that, they themselves *felt* God's touch. The revivals of the 18th and 19th centuries, known as the 1st and 2nd Great Awakening, shook the world and are the forerunners of the Pentecostal Awakening; but *Life in the Spirit* pays tribute to the special group of Holy Ghost-filled, fire-baptized, tongue-speaking body that brought new vigor, fresh anointing and power to the Church of the 20th century and continues to energize the Church today. Within these pages you will witness truly what God hath wrought.

Life in the Spirit, finally, testifies to the thoughtful spirituality of the Pentecostal/Charismatic Movement. Characterized often by its more extravagant aspects, the Movement is not limited to mere enthusiasm, nor is it only concerned with great events. Rather, it brings people into relation to God, whether seen in the exuberance of the whirlwind or in the quiet contemplation of God and God's Word, and in the tender communication of a child with his or her Father.

In these moments, perhaps more than in the exuberance of corporate worship, Pentecostals and Charismatics learn from God the importance of service. Here they learn God's heart. Here they realize their commission to go into all the world and preach the Gospel; to feed the sick; to clothe the naked; to provide shelter to the poor; to minister to the hurting, no matter the source of pain; to bring into the Kingdom of God whosoever will.

So we return to unity, for perhaps the essential mark of the Pentecostal/Charismatic Movement is that it seeks all who are lost to bring them to God. Empowered by the Holy Spirit, we love those whom God has created, we demonstrate God's power, and we accept all as brothers and sisters those who come to God in repentance.

So enter these pages, witness God's power, feel God's touch, read of God's love, and be one in God's Spirit.

Life in the Spirit . . . isn't it a wonderful gift?

TRIBUTE

Robert White

". . . of whom the world was not worthy." (Hebrews 11:38)

In Matthew 3:11, John the Baptist proclaimed regarding Jesus, "He will baptize you with the Holy Spirit and fire." Acts 1:8 says, "But you shall receive power when the Holy Spirit has come upon you; . . ." Acts 2:4 says, "And they were all filled with the Holy Spirit and began to speak with other tongues, as the Spirit gave them utterance." Peter reminds the onlookers in Jerusalem that "This is that which was spoken by the prophet Joel" in Joel 2:28. It is recorded in Acts 10:44 that "the Holy Spirit fell upon all those who heard the word." In Acts 15:15, James affirms that this event was a fulfillment of the words of the prophets (Amos 9:11).

For 2,000 years, God's church has enjoyed this wonderful outpouring of the Holy Spirit and dynamic enduement of power. There have been times when the flickering flame of revival and renewal would seem to die out, but then some prayer warrior would stay shut up in his or her prayer closet until heaven answered and the smoldering coals would be fanned until they would ignite again into a raging fire.

The Twentieth Century Encyclopedia of Religious Knowledge says: "The phenomenon of 'speaking with tongues as the Spirit gives utterance' (Acts 2:1-13) has appeared in all ages of the Church." G. B. Cutten states in *Speaking With Tongues* that ". . . in most cases the appearance of speaking with tongues has been connected with revival experiences."

John Wesley, the founder of Methodism, whose life spanned most of the l800s, said in a letter to a friend: "I must observe an historical mistake which occurs toward the bottom of your next page. Since the Reformation, you say: 'This gift (tongues) has never once been heard of, or pretended to, by the Romanist themselves.' (Page l22). But has it been pretended to (whether justly or not) by no others, though not by the Romanists? Has it 'never once been heard of' since that time? Sir, your memory fails you again. . . . It has been heard of more than once, no further off than the valleys of Dauphin (France)."

The world knows the names of John and Charles Wesley, John Fletcher, Jonathan Edwards, George Whitfield, James McCready,

Theodore Frelinghuysen, Gilbert Tennent, Barton W. Stoe, Phoebe Palmer, A. J. Gordo, Dwight L. Moody, Charles Finney and R. A. Torrey. These were they were the movers and shakers of the Methodist Revival of the 18th century, the first and second Great Awakenings. These mighty men and women spanned over 150 years of revival. In contrast, the early pioneers that birthed the Pentecostal Awakening are relatively unknown.

Around the turn of the 20th century there were those who, weary of dead, dry form, earnestly sought God for reality. They experienced the day of Pentecost according to Acts 2:4 all over again. These Spirit-filled believers would eventually birth the modern Pentecostal Movement, a revival without precedent in history. There were outpourings of the Holy Spirit Baptism in Rhode Island (1875), Arkansas (1879), Switzerland (1879), Ohio (1890), Minnesota (1895), Tennessee/North Carolina (1896), South Dakota (1896), Kansas (1901), and Texas (1904).

However, it was in Los Angeles in a small building on Azusa Street where a revival broke out that is recognized as the catalyst for the modern Pentecostal Movement. W. J. Seymour led the Azusa Street revival that eventually birthed the Assemblies of God. Charles Parham, Earnest S. Williams and Lucy Farrow are prominent names as well.

In Tennessee and North Carolina, another revival occurred involving key figures such as R. G. Spurling, Jr., William Martin, Joe M. Tipton, and Milton McNabb. These men were linked with the Christian Union which later became the Church of God (Cleveland, TN). A. J. Tomlinson was the first General Overseer of both the Church of God and the Church of God of Prophecy.

Aimee Semple McPherson was the key figure in establishing and founding the Foursquare Gospel Church.

The Pentecostal Holiness Church had its roots in the great revival in Iowa before the turn of the century. Three groups merged to form the present organization. Benjamin Hardin Irwin played a key role in its formation.

In the middle of the 20th century, T. L. Osborn, Oral Roberts, William Branham, Jack Coe, Gordon Lindsey, Kenneth Hagin, A. A. Allen, W. V. Grant, William Freeman, and, later, T. L. Lowery were the most prominent of the "healing evangelists" who conducted crusades and stirred America for God.

Then came the Charismatic renewal that breathed new life into Pentecostalism. Although the activities were initially primarily among the orthodox churches, the movement initially influenced the Pentecostals indirectly but then more directly. It brought a freshness and spontaneity to worship.

Now as the 21st century begins, the Pentecostal/Charismatic movement has impacted the world in an unprecedented manner. Mega churches are springing up all over the world. Dr. David Cho of South Korea has over three fourths of a million members. Dr. Alex Tanusaputra of Indonesia has over 50,000 members. The names of Rod Parsley, Benny Hinn, T. D. Jakes, Charles Blake, Jentezen Franklin, Paul Crouch, Marcus Lamb, Oral Roberts, Richard Roberts, Earl P. Paulk, John Osteen, John Hagee, Jack Hayford, Kenneth Copeland, Jimmy Swaggart, John Cherry, Joyce Meyer, Marilyn Hickey, Paul L. Walker, Bob Rodgers, and a host of others, are well known evangelists and/or pastors.

Pentecostal denominations and charismatic fellowships such as Church of God, Assemblies of God, Church of God of Prophecy, Pentecostal Holiness, Open Bible, Foursquare, Pentecostal Church of God, Christ for the Nations, Church on the Rock, and others are touching people in a powerful way.

These men and women are heroes of the faith who have indeed made a difference. The revivals of the 18th and 19th centuries incurred persecution but none greater than the persecution at the turn of the century endured by those who experienced the baptism of the Holy Spirit. But because their lives were not their own and, like the early church they rejoiced because they were counted worthy to suffer for His Name's sake, the Pentecostal/Charismatic flames burn brightest today.

In this book are devotions by great men and women of whom the world was not worthy. Although not all names are well known generally, they are well known to me. They are faithful, Godly men and women who represent a multitude of devoted followers of Christ. They have touched my life. I truly know them to be men and women of "Whom The World Was Not Worthy."

January 1

GOD'S POWER IS SUFFICIENT

Blessed be the God and Father of our Lord Jesus Christ, who according to His abundant mercy has begotten us again to a living hope through the resurrection of Jesus Christ from the dead, to an inheritance incorruptible and undefiled and that does not fade away, reserved in heaven for you, who are kept by the power of God through faith for salvation ready to be revealed in the last time. (1 Peter 1:3-5)

I was ministering at a church in Canada where the pastor is a good friend of mine. We began discussing the rise of devil worship and the occult in North America and how the devil is out to destroy every Pentecostal church.

My friend related to me a powerful story of how the might of God is sufficient in every situation. He said a lady hairdresser in his church was called to a woman's home to fix her hair. In their conversation, the hairdresser told the woman she attended the Church of God. The woman became enraged and admitted to being a witch. She told the hairdresser she and her followers would soon close the church.

Immediately following this incident, the pastor and congregation saw signs of visits by the witches in the church parking lot. The pastor called the church to prayer. They covenanted to fast and pray for one week. Following the week of prayer, the pastor saw the woman who claimed to be a witch on television. She said she had seen a vision of destruction coming to the city. She and all her followers were leaving town. They sold their homes at reduced prices to get out of town quickly. The church rejoiced because they knew God had heard their prayers and had delivered them from the satanic attack.

The Lord reigns supreme. He has all power in heaven and in earth. Greater is He that is in you than he that is in the world. God's power is sufficient!

. . . PRAYER . . .

Father, Your power is sufficient to give us victory in any circumstance of life. I am thankful we are kept by the power of God.

. . . TODAY'S THOUGHT . . .

We don't have to fear Satan. Christ is in control of our lives. He lives! And because He lives, we live and will live forever more.

—Dr. Robert White

International Evangelist, Author, Cumming, GA

January 2

GOD MAKES A WAY

For with God nothing will be impossible. (Luke 1:37)

There is a song that says, "Got any rivers you think are uncrossable, got any mountains you cannot tunnel through? God specializes in things thought impossible, and He will do for you what no other power can do."

To illustrate this, let me share a beautiful story about a pastor friend in our church. His church had outgrown their facilities and, at great sacrifice, the congregation had raised funds and purchased a new church site. However, when they applied for a building permit they discovered their land had been re-zoned and churches were not permitted to build in the area.

The pastor called the church to prayer. When a church prays, miracles take place. A short time later, the pastor was driving from church when he saw a boy lying in the median alongside a bicycle. The pastor stopped and discovered the boy was unconscious. He rushed the boy to the hospital.

After a while, the doctor came out and told the pastor he had saved the boy's life. The 10-year-old boy had juvenile diabetes and was in a coma. In another five minutes he would have died, but thanks to the pastor's quick action in getting him to medical attention the boy was already revived. His parents were on the way to the hospital and had requested the pastor remain until they could meet him.

When the parents arrived, the pastor was surprised to see that the boy's father was the mayor who had refused his building permit. After the mayor thanked the pastor for saving his son's life, he told him to be at the courthouse the next morning and assured him he would get the permit.

Isn't the power of prayer wonderful? Amazing things happen when people pray.

. . . PRAYER . . .

Father, thank You for Your miraculous power that bridges uncrossable rivers and moves mountains of opposition.

. . . TODAY'S THOUGHT . . .

When God's people pray, nothing is impossible, for with God all things are possible if we believe.

—Kathy White

President, International Ladies Ministries, Cleveland, TN (former)

January 3

FAITH—A SPIRITUAL GIFT

". . . to another faith by the same Spirit. (1 Corinthians 12:9)

My wife experienced a partial paralysis in the right side of her body and was hospitalized for some tests. The neurosurgeon suspected a tumor or some other abnormality of the brain. The testing procedures included a spinal tap, which produced a headache that seemed unbearable. After I brought my wife home, she was confined to bed. Attempts to raise her head, even to put a pillow under it, caused excruciating pain.

Over the years we had experienced definite healings in our family through prayer; so, many prayers were prayed for my wife to find relief from her severe suffering. Yet, the pain persisted day after day without any relief.

One night our three children had gone out with some friends. I was sitting by my wife's bed, praying silently for her healing. Suddenly she said, "Billy, put your hand on my head and pray for me. The Lord is about to heal me." I gladly responded. After my prayer she said, "The pain is still there, but it's going to leave." Within perhaps 30 seconds she sat up in the bed, saying, "Thank the Lord, it's gone." The headache never returned, nor did her paralysis. Was this a manifestation of the gift of faith? I believe it was.

Such an impartation by the Holy Spirit leaves no room for boasting about the greatness of one's faith. None of us should ever glory in the faith he possesses, or in his capacity for the exercise of faith. This would be to place faith in one's faith. Jesus said, "Have faith in God" (Mark 11:22).

. . . PRAYER . . .

Thank You, Lord, for Your marvelous grace, whereby we experience the richness of Your presence in unmistakable ways.

. . . TODAY'S THOUGHT . . .

Faith is much more than positive thinking. Paul designates it to be both the fruit of the Spirit and a gift of the Spirit. There are times when the Holy Spirit breaks in suddenly upon us to perform miracles that altogether bring glory to God.

—Billy Murray
General Overseer, COGOP (former)

January 4

THE NIGHT VISITOR

It is good to give thanks to the Lord, and to sing praises to Your name, O Most High; To declare Your lovingkindness in the morning, and Your faithfulness every night. (Psalm 92: 1-2)

Dawn, my sister-in-law, had just said good-bye to her family. Alone and exhausted, her thoughts remained riveted on Susan, her newborn baby fighting for her life in an incubator just down the hall. Suddenly, waves of grief and fear swept over her. The midnight hour had arrived—both literally and figuratively. Reaching out in desperation for the only solace she could find, Dawn opened her Bible at random and placed it on her lap. Because of her tears it was a long time before she was able to focus. The first words she read were "Weeping may endure for a night, but joy comes in the morning" (Psalm 30:5). The last thing she remembered was smelling a beautiful fragrance and falling into a deep sleep.

In the morning, long before the sun would rise, Dawn was awakened by an excited nurse. "Wake up, Mrs. Crabtree. Something wonderful has happened. It's a miracle! Susan is going to be all right!" After nearly 40 years, Susan is still all right. She is a beautiful Christian lady.

There is no question Christians will continue to face heartache and sorrow. It rains on the just and the unjust. Two kinds of people have trouble—the believer and the unbeliever. Then why serve God? Because when the storm rages and passes by, the believer is left to live with a testimony, not a tragedy.

Many believers have a tendency to fixate on the problems of the moment and not the eternal promises of God which endure. In other words, they live by reaction to the process of living and not the principles of spiritual life. Look to God and then trust Him. We are saved by hope, a hope that provokes songs in the night.

. . . PRAYER . . .

Father, thank You for Your presence in the darkness of my circumstances and Your guiding light in the night.

. . . TODAY'S THOUGHT . . .

In the middle of your night, God is working on a new dawn. In the middle of your winter, God is working on a new spring.

—Charles T. Crabtree
Assistant General Overseer, COGOP

January 5

UNREASONABLE FAITH

Blessed are those who keep His testimonies, Who seek Him with the whole heart! (Psalm 119:2)

I arrived late at the Shingle Hollow Camp Meeting in Rutherfordton, North Carolina. Upon my arrival the superintendent of the West Carolina District asked me to speak the next morning. Having consented, I went to my room to study. Tired from the labor of the day and the long trip, I fell asleep. During the night I had a dream in which I saw a hand posting a notice on a bulletin board in heaven. After the hand departed, I approached the bulletin board and read, "Wanted, unreasonable men with unreasonable faith in these unreasonable times."

Abel was unreasonable in worship in that he worshipped by faith and offered up a sacrifice that pleased God. Cain worshipped in self-will and offered an unacceptable sacrifice to God. God wants worshippers to keep His testimonies, seek Him with their whole heart, and zealously hold to the truth.

Noah worked uncompromisingly while building the ark. Days of tedious hard labor turned into months and then years. In spite of mocking and derision, this preacher of righteousness continued to build. God had spoken! Noah must not quit. He must be unreasonable.

Abraham was unreasonable in his walk with God. God appeared to Abraham and told him to leave his father's house and his relatives and journey to a strange land. No amount of persuasion would change his mind. He heard voices of negativism calling for reason. Abraham knew God had spoken and he must obey. So began the odyssey of a man who did not know where he was going but knew God had spoken to him.

. . . PRAYER . . .

God, let me be a man unreasonable in my worship, my work and my walk for You. Let me keep Your testimonies and serve You with my whole heart.

. . . TODAY'S THOUGHT . . .

The totally committed Christian will not allow the opinions of this world to change the direction of his feet. He will not compromise the message given him from God. He will be totally unreasonable.

—Bishop Chet Smith
General Superintendent, CHC, Inc.

January 6

GODLY INFLUENCE

Brethren, join in following my example, and note those who so walk, as you have us for a pattern. (Philippians 3:17)

Growing up as a boy in the backwoods of Louisiana, our family did not have many of the riches of this world. However, the possessions of this world could never compare with the riches imparted to me through Christian parents and grandparents who established a love for the Word of God in my heart. Their daily walk with God was a living testimony to their convictions and commitment to God.

At about the age of 15, I became very sick with an abscess in my left lung. One night while the fever was very high, my mother, father, pastor and his wife (Brother and Sister J. P. Sims) prayed for me. God in His mercy miraculously healed me and placed His call upon my life.

Not willing to accept the call of God into the ministry, it was another four years before I dedicated my life to the Lord. After receiving the baptism in the Holy Spirit in a revival at the Monroe Church of God in January 1955, I surrendered to the Lord and accepted His will for my life.

I feel very fortunate to have had ministers around me who were loving but firm and had a tremendous influence on my philosophy of ministry—men like Horace Taylor, Ed Cox, C. W. Kendall, Homer Smith, Lester Beasley and overseers such as John L. Byrd, T. M. McClendon, Y. W. Kidd, and V. D. Combs. These men helped me to realize that God's love and forgiveness is for everyone and that I should continue to love people, regardless of circumstances. They established in me a loving and caring heart which I think is very important in the pastoral ministry today. In my *35* years of ministry, I have tried to pass these godly attributes on to new Christians. If we will continue this process, their ministry will live on in the lives of others.

. . . PRAYER . . .

O God, help us to pass Your loving, caring, kind Spirit on to others as we go through life.

. . . TODAY'S THOUGHT . . .

We pass through this life but once—the influence we have on others is for eternity.

—Wayne Chelette
Pastor, Lake Orion, MI

January 7

THE GOD WHO ANSWERS

"Then you call on the name of your gods, and I will call on the name of the Lord; and the God who answers by fire, He is God." So all the people answered and said, "It is well spoken." (1 Kings 18:24).

I was saved in 1943 while visiting an older brother who was married and lived in a small South Georgia town some distance from where I lived on a farm with my parents and another brother. My brother had been deferred from the military draft because he was needed at home to help on the farm. My father was not physically able to do the necessary farm work. Having been won to Christ under the influence of Pentecostals, I desired the fellowship of other Christians of like precious faith but there was no Holiness or Pentecostal church in the area where I lived. I began to sincerely pray and petition God for a Pentecostal church to attend.

About that time, a series of unexpected things began to happen which, I am convinced, were direct answers to my prayers. The draft board refused to grant my brother another deferment, making it necessary for our family to leave the farm. We moved into a neighboring state and my brother was drafted into the military. To my amazement, we moved within walking distance of a Pentecostal church. The Lord knew we did not own an automobile! I received the baptism in the Holy Spirit a few days after finding the church.

Though my brother went into the military during wartime and was stationed with the 5th Army in Italy during the war, God answered prayer and brought him safely home without ever seeing combat.

Yes, the Lord is "the God who answers".

. . . PRAYER . . .

Thank You, Lord, for Your faithfulness to Your Word which declares that You are a rewarder of them that diligently seek You.

. . . TODAY'S THOUGHT . . .

To remember the thrilling experience of answered prayer in the past gives us great encouragement and should incite us to continue a life of prayer in the future. "Call to Me, and I will answer you, and show you great and mighty things, which you do not know" (Jeremiah 33:3).

—Bishop Cullen L. Hicks
District Superintendent, Western NC, CHC

January 8

KEEP YOUR EYE ON THE GOAL

And Terah took his son Abram . . . to go to the land of Canaan; and they came to Haran and dwelt there. . . . and Terah died in Haran. (Genesis 11: 31-32)

Gathering his possessions, cattle, herdsmen, and family, Terah took Abram and left Ur of the Chaldees to start his trip to Canaan, the Promised Land. After 600 miles of rough traveling, they came to Haran. Though this was not his destination, Terah remained too long among the conveniences of Haran and died there. He was almost to his goal, but missed it because of the attraction of the city.

God has called many people whose journey, like Terah's, was one of labor and tears, but who at a twist in the road discovered the pleasures of life at Haran. Camping too long in the pleasures of this world, they began dying spiritually and never completed their journey. Camping in the valley of Baca is not God's plan—we are only passing through this valley of weeping.

The story of the tortoise and the hare shows it's not as important how you start the race as how you finish it. Paul stated, concerning his fight to the finish, "I have fought the good fight, I have finished the race, I have kept the faith" (2 Timothy 4:7).

Quitters never win. Camping at a spiritual Haran can have deadly effects. If we continue the course God has set before us, we may not win every fight but we will win the battle and we can say, like Paul, "I fought the good fight, I have finished the race." Then we will hear the Lord say, "Well done, good and faithful servant" (Matthew 25:23).

. . . PRAYER . . .

Father, thank You for the road map You have supplied for us—Your holy Word. May we continue to grow in Your knowledge daily, as we devote time to studying the Word.

. . . TODAY'S THOUGHT . . .

This Scripture lesson has been effective in my life when I felt the road under me getting somewhat rough. Life's journey is not a picnic, but a warfare we are in until our journey's end. These Scriptures have given me purpose to work toward reaching my goal.

—Dr. Chester P. Jenkins
Executive Secretary, FGFCM (former)

January 9

DON'T PRAY UNLESS YOU WANT GOD TO ANSWER

If any of you lacks wisdom, let him ask of God, who gives to all liberally and without reproach, and it will be given to him. (James 1:5)

The revival crusade had continued for three weeks when several people began asking me to become the church's pastor. My immediate response was *no.* My calling from God was that of an evangelist. Nothing about being a pastor appealed to me. I had seen too many pastors being hurt and becoming discouraged.

The people continued to speak to me as the revival progressed into the fourth and fifth week. Finally, with a purpose of ending this matter, I agreed to pray about it. I knew better than to play games with the Lord, so I prayed sincerely.

To my surprise, God spoke to me so vividly I could not deny what He was telling me. His response to my prayer was "Feed my sheep"—the same thing Jesus told Peter in John 21. *That prayer was prayed almost 27 years ago.* I am still doing my best to feed His sheep in the same church and in the same city.

They have been the most joyous and fruitful years of my life. The Lord graciously placed within me a pastor's heart and a special love for people. He has given me grace to abide in my calling, and has faithfully given promotion and success, both spiritually and numerically. God's ways are not always our ways, but His ways are always best.

"Your seed I will establish forever, And build up your throne to all generations. Selah And the heavens will praise Your wonders, O Lord; Your faithfulness also in the assembly of the saints. For who in the heavens can be compared to the Lord? Who among the sons of the mighty can be likened to the Lord? God is greatly to be feared in the assembly of the saints, And to be held in reverence by all those around Him" (Psalm 89: 4-7).

. . . PRAYER . . .

Father, help me to lean not unto mine own understanding, but ask for Your ways in every decision of my life.

. . . TODAY'S THOUGHT . . .

When we sincerely call, He will always answer and show us great and mighty things, which we know not.

—Dr. Don Arnold

President, Full Gospel Fellowship of Churches and Ministries

January 10

A FAITHFUL FRIEND

No one will be able to stand up against you all the days of your life. As I was with Moses, so I will be with you; I will never leave you nor forsake you. (Joshua 1:5)

I was on the hospital X-ray table when I regained consciousness. My face hurt but I didn't know the extent of my injuries.

I was a high school senior. I had been playing second base on the varsity baseball team when a ball was hit over my head, just out of reach. As I dove to catch the ball my left cheek collided with the right fielder's shoulder. He, too, was making a valiant attempt to catch the ball.

The doctor's prognosis concluded that I had a severely fractured cheekbone that subsequently caused the collapse of my sinus cavity.

While riding to Denver for surgery, I heard a song on the radio:

What a friend we have in Jesus, All our sins and griefs to bear. What a privilege to carry, Everything to God in prayer. Oh, what peace we often forfeit, Oh, what needless pain we bear! All because we do not carry Everything to God in prayer (Joseph Scriven).

The Holy Spirit made me aware Jesus was with me to heal me and give me peace. I knew everything would turn out all right.

Within a week, I had surgery and returned home to celebrate the resurrection power of Jesus on Easter Sunday. I wore sun glasses to church to hide my "shiner," but I was feeling great!

Since that experience I have learned that Jesus sticks closer than a brother (Proverbs 18:24). He is a faithful friend who will never leave me nor forsake me. He never sleeps nor slumbers when I need His assistance (Psalm 121:3, 4). When I am too weak to believe, He abides trustworthy (2 Timothy 2:13). Yes, "What a friend we have in Jesus!"

. . . PRAYER . . .

Thank You, Lord Jesus, for staying with me through the good times and the bad, for always being there to cheer me up, and not being ashamed to acknowledge me as Your friend.

. . . TODAY'S THOUGHT . . .

Never consider yourself alone or helpless. Jesus, the Almighty One, our Friend, is with us.

—Dr. Don Long
Supervisor, Southwest District, ICFG

January 11

WE CAN EITHER "FREAK" OR WE CAN "PEAK"

I can do all things through Christ who strengthens me. (Philippians 4:13)

Hardly a day goes by in the life of born-again believers where we are not confronted with situations that challenge our stand and faith in Christ. When these situations arise, the devil comes immediately to attack our minds with fear-filled thoughts of defeat and failure. Sound familiar? It's at such times we must decide which way we will go. We can either 'Freak' by giving in to the devil or we can 'Peak' by allowing the Holy Spirit to bring us rest through God's Word.

God's Word tells us that the devil abides not in the truth because there is no truth in him: and he is a liar and the father of it (John 8:44). But God's Word also says that it is **impossible** for God to lie (Titus 1:2; Hebrews 6:18).

In John 10:10, Jesus tells us that the devil is the thief that comes to steal, kill and destroy. The devil tells us we're going to lose and fail. God tells us that through Him we not only have life, but we have it more abundantly and that "in all these things we are more than conquerors through Him who loved us" (Romans 8:37). I choose to believe God!

We must establish that if the devil said it, that can only mean one thing: It's a lie! No matter how the situation looks, God has a way of escape, to put us on top, to lift us above our circumstances. According to Webster's Dictionary, 'Peak' is "the highest or utmost point of anything." God's will is that we 'Peak' in times of trouble; He wants to raise us to "the highest or utmost point" above our circumstances.

Our Father tells us to cast the *whole* of our care (anxieties, concerns) once and for all on Him. He cares for us affectionately (1 Peter 5:7). God's Will is to see us victorious in all areas of our lives. It's our choice whether we will 'Freak' or 'Peak'.

. . . PRAYER . . .

Father, we thank You that Your Word is Truth. We ask that through our obedience and the leading of the Holy Spirit, You will show Your Word true in our lives. We claim it, we receive it, we call it done and give You praise.

. . . TODAY'S THOUGHT . . .

There is nothing greater than the sweet taste of victory we have when, with peace and confidence, we allow the Holy Spirit to take us to the "Peak" of our victory!

—H. Thomas Owens

Co-Director, Life Through Faith Ministries Intl, Dawsonville, GA

January 12

I'M GOING ON

"Let us go on to perfection". (Hebrews 6:1)

It was 2 a.m. and the California night seemed darker than normal! I searched for my key to unlock the back door. I had just returned from a Navy summer cruise. I climbed the stairs to my attic bedroom, took off my uniform, laid down, and tried to sleep. In the stillness of the night I could hear mother's prayers rising from her room below.

Mom was an old-time Holiness mother who ran a tight ship! Mom had been baptized in the Holy Spirit in the early days of the Pentecostal revival. All eight of her children were taught about Jesus by this Holiness mom.

That night I said yes to the call of God.

What would I do with my life now? I went to see the pastor and he said, "Go to Bible school." I had an old car and mother gave me all the money she had to make the trip from California to Oklahoma. I started east on Route 66. When I stopped for gas, I bought a package of cigarettes by force of habit. Once in the car, I lit one up. "See, I told you that you did not get saved. Go on back home," Satan said.

Then I heard another voice. "Just ask and I'll forgive you and help you get to Bible school," the Lord said. My eyes filled with tears. I pulled off the road, got on my knees by the side of the car, and cried out to God. "Help me! Forgive me," I prayed.

A truck stopped. The driver came to help me with the flat tire he thought I had. With tears streaming down, I cried, "I'm going on! I'm going on!"

"OK," he replied, as he got back into his truck.

I got into my car and drove to Oklahoma City to Bible school. After 40 years I'm still going on with God.

. . . PRAYER . . .

Father, forgive me when I fail. Give me strength to get up and go on, in the name of Jesus.

. . . TODAY'S THOUGHT . . .

"As I was with Moses, so I will be with you. I will not leave you nor forsake you" (Joshua 1:5).

—E. Leroy Baker
Conference Superintendent, TX, IPHC

January 13

CISCO IS DEAD

Weeping may endure for a night, But joy comes in the morning. (Psalm 30:5)

It was our grandson's sixth birthday. I called him to sing happy birthday. His mother answered in a low whisper, "Cisco has just died. We are getting ready to have his funeral now." I talked to Kyle for just a moment. "Today is my birthday, and Cisco died," he sobbed.

Cisco, his cockatiel, had been their pet for almost six years. Both he and his brother, Stuart, had awakened to his calls every morning. Cisco would whistle and call to get their attention. To them, a precious friend had died.

On this 6th birthday, Mom, Dad, and two brothers placed a little bird in a shoe box and had a funeral service. Our grandsons had their first experience with grief. Their hearts were broken.

What about grief? How do you handle it when life must go on for those who are left behind? First, we must allow time to grieve. It is both healthy and healing.

After my father's funeral, the Fisher children gathered at my mother's home. She pulled out the family albums and as we looked through them, she recalled many memories of meeting my father. We all cried together, then began to laugh at the funny things that had happened in their lifetime. Grief was taking its proper place and healing had begun its process. My parents had been married for 62 years. When I later visited with her, she said, "Oh, how I miss your daddy." Grief is real. When we work through it, peace and calm reassurance that after death, comes life.

The griever must allow the Holy Spirit to do His work within by going on with life. When a parent, friend or companion departs this life it brings grief. But you can reflect on the memories and allow the Holy Spirit to give comfort and restore joy.

. . . PRAYER . . .

Dear Lord, thank You for the joy and peace that comes from only You. Even when grief comes, we can recall Your life in our hearts.

. . . TODAY'S THOUGHT . . .

My grief may be heavy and my heart may be sad, but when I think of God's love, my heart becomes glad.

—Fred S. Fisher, Sr.
General Overseer, COGOP

January 14

GOD'S MINISTERING SPIRITS

And of the angels He says: "Who makes His angels spirits And His ministers a flame of fire". (Hebrews 1:7)

One cold, predawn morning I was in the intensive care waiting room of White Memorial Hospital in Los Angeles keeping vigil with the family of a sainted parishioner. We were told it was just a matter of hours.

The daughter left her mother's bedside: "Mother is asking for you."

Entering, I took her feeble hand and said, "It's your pastor." She nodded her head and drifted back into semi-consciousness. I quietly began to pray for God's perfect will for this saint, incorporating Psalm 91:4 in my prayer: "He will cover you with his feathers, and under his wings you will find refuge; his faithfulness will be your shield and rampart." I felt an awesome presence of the Holy Spirit. I felt a gentle breeze sweep over my shoulder and neck. Assuming a nurse had entered the room, I turned and was amazed to find no one had entered.

Confident in the power of the Holy Spirit's anointing, I walked into the waiting room and declared, "Your mother is going to live."

The startled children asked, "What happened?"

"Nothing," I said. "However, the Holy Spirit assured me she will live."

A few days later this dear lady was home. We were rejoicing, praising God for her miraculous recovery. She said, "Pastor, I had the most wonderful dream in intensive care. You were standing by my bed holding my hand praying and an awesome presence of the Holy Spirit filled my room. An angel of the Lord stood behind you gently waving his wings. I could feel the breeze from the angel's wings."

We began to cry and rejoice as I related to her what occurred that bleak, dark night in the intensive care unit of White Memorial Hospital.

. . . PRAYER . . .

Thank You, God, for Your never-failing promises. Thank You for ever-present watchfulness, for covering us with the ministering presence of the Holy Spirit to guard and protect us.

. . . TODAY'S THOUGHT . . .

I am confident God's angels have been commissioned to watch over me. Therefore, I will trust and not be afraid.

—Dr. Norman Fortenberry
Assistant General Superintendent, PCOG

January 15

THE HOLY SPIRIT'S PHENOMENAL PROVISION

The things which God has prepared for those who love Him . . . God has revealed them to us through His Spirit . . . no one knows the things of God except the Spirit of God. (1 Corinthians 2:9-11)

Standing in the airport of a foreign country and saying goodbye to God's missionary was not a panic experience. Although the country was experiencing invading troops, there was no reason to worry. We were getting ready to board our plane and fly on to other destinations. Boarding the plane and taking our seats would have been the final episode, but they could not start the motors, and we were asked to deplane and return to the airport.

The missionary was already gone. There was no way to contact him. My flight and connection was to a country I had no visa to enter, and the connection would be gone if I was delayed.

"Peace I leave with you" (John 14:27) is one of the promises of Christ the Holy Spirit provides for us. The Holy Spirit who knows the mind of God was in the process of preparing a provision for me. We boarded the plane, the motors started, and we lifted off.

A diplomat from the country, who was called out to another country on an emergency, boarded the plane also. During a conversation with him, he found out my destination and my dilemma and communicated with the personnel of the plane.

He told me that arrangements had been made. The commuting plane was still there. Upon landing someone would come to the plane and escort me, and I would be on my way to my proper destination.

The Holy Spirit continually makes phenomenal provision through both our prayers and His prayers through us with unutterable groanings. Protection is ours because the Holy Spirit, knowing the mind of God for future events in our experience, shields us from the enemy's snares.

. . . PRAYER . . .

Our Father, help us to be keenly sensitive to Your will revealed to us by the Holy Spirit.

. . . TODAY'S THOUGHT . . .

Nothing will be able to separate us from God, nor divert us from His Will as long as our will is under the control of the Holy Spirit.

—Garland Griffis

World Missions Representative, Cleveland, TN

January 16

A NEW THING

Therefore, if the Son makes you free, you shall be free indeed. (John 8:36)

For 10 years, drug addiction and crime was my thing. It cost me four years of my life in prison. My thing caused me to lose my identity, my pride, and, above all, my desire to live. Many of my friends had left the scene behind an overdose of heroin, and I had many close calls myself. Desperate, I tried doctors, psychiatrists and various rehabilitation programs, but nothing helped. Life was a merry-go-round, except it wasn't merry anymore; it was just a go-around. A force greater than I was enslaving my mind and eating away at me physically, mentally, and spiritually.

My mother, however, was persistent in her campaign to get me out of this bag, but I was stubborn and rebellious. Finally she succeeded in getting me to at least talk with a friend of hers who told me about the new thing that God was doing. In the Bible, God promises through one of His prophets, "Behold, I will do a new thing" (Isaiah 43:19).

Jesus Christ is God's new thing. The angel said to Mary, "That Holy One who is to be born will be called the Son of God" (Luke 1:35).

At the time I heard the good news, I was paying my habit dues, which means I was sick, frustrated, and in desperate need of a fix. My drug habit was costing me between $25 and $100 a day. While I was in this miserable condition I fell upon my knees, repented of my sins, and asked God to do a new thing in my life.

I had spent many hours waiting to make connections with a drug pusher, or waiting to get high, or waiting to be sentenced. But I did not need to wait this day, for God was waiting for me. Instantaneously, God did something new in my life. The pains and craving for narcotics left me, and I became a different person. Jesus Christ, God's Son, said, "And you shall know the truth, and the truth shall make you free" (John 8:32).

. . . PRAYER . . .

Father, thank You for Your love and faithfulness.

. . . TODAY'S THOUGHT . . .

He became what He made, that what He made might become what He is.

—Herb Green
Assemblies of God International Fellowship, San Diego, CA

January 17

BALANCE

Jesus answered and said to them, "You are mistaken, not knowing the Scriptures nor the power of God." (Matthew 22:29)

What an unusual dialogue! The Sadducees, rationalists of that day, had confronted Jesus with a bizarre tale concerning seven brothers who had married the same woman and had all subsequently died! Each one, pressed by tradition, felt obligated to perpetuate his dead brother's property. By this dubious story, these schemers attacked the doctrine of the Resurrection: "In the resurrection, whose wife shall she be of the seven?"

Jesus reveals the root of their agnosticism—they did not know the Scriptures, nor the power of God.

Some people know the Scripture but do not know the power; others know the power but do not know the Scripture. We all need a beautiful balance of a working knowledge of the Word and a practical experience of the power.

The one who only wants to know the Scripture may be a perpetual student, ever learning but never doing; orthodox, but dead; doctrinally straight, but walking straight into extinction; theologically sound, but sound asleep. Why be theologically strong, but powerless? God's response to needs is not based on our flawless theology, but on faith.

While one saint may be on an intellectual trip, another may only want the power. He wants an emotional trip, a thrill, a spiritual picnic.

Though some people deny both the Scripture and the power, ideally Pentecostals seek to walk in the light of the Word and in the dynamic of the power. The Scripture and the power of God complement each other. Holiness of heart is only realized by a knowledge of the Word and an enablement of the power.

. . . PRAYER . . .

Father, let my life reflect a healthy balance of the Scripture and the power of God. Transform me by Your Word and Your Spirit.

. . . TODAY'S THOUGHT . . .

"And the Spirit of God was hovering . . . Then God said" (Genesis 1:2, 3); "And they were all filled with the Holy Spirit . . . Peter . . . raised his voice and said" (Acts 2:4, 14). The Scripture and the power in harmony!

—Dr. Harold E. Helms
Angelus Temple, Los Angeles, CA

January 18

IN THE NAME OF JESUS

Therefore God also has highly exalted Him and given Him the name which is above every name, that at the name of Jesus every knee should bow, of those in heaven, and of those on earth, and of those under the earth. (Philippians 2:9-10)

When Jesus went back to Heaven, He left us with the power of His name. He told us to use it. This means that we operate on His behalf. Through the use of His name, the devil himself is subject to us.

I had just completed the manuscript for my book, *Healing Through Spiritual Warfare*, when I slipped on a sheet of ice in a parking lot. In a few weeks, a lump appeared on a bone near my elbow. The enemy taunted, "You have bone cancer. You have been through breast cancer and it often moves to the bones. I've got you! You have cancer!"

The doctor said it had to be removed: "It probably isn't cancer, but with your history, it has to come off." He scheduled outpatient surgery for the following Monday, but I headed for my prayer park. I walked the hiking trail and talked to the Lord.

Then I verbally resisted the lump. "In the name of Jesus, lump, you are shrinking." For three miles I battled, using the name of Jesus as my weapon. When I went home, I asked my husband if the lump was going down. "No, I don't think so," he laughed. I went back to the park the next day. "Lump, you are not going to frighten me. In the name of Jesus I command you to leave my body without surgery!" My husband said, "No, sweetheart, that lump is not getting any smaller."

On the third day, the lump appeared smaller. On the fourth, it was only half the previous size. On Sunday, the day before surgery, the lump was almost gone! On Monday morning, there was no lump to remove!

There is power and authority in Jesus' name!

. . . PRAYER . . .

Father, I stand against spiritual enemies, not in my own power or holiness, but in the power given to me by Jesus Himself. I ask You to meet my need in the name of Your Son, Jesus Christ.

. . . TODAY'S THOUGHT . . .

All problems—physical, material, psychological, and spiritual—must yield at the name of Jesus!

—Peggy Scarborough
Author, Ladies Conference Speaker

January 19

SURRENDER TO THE SPIRIT

For as many as are led by the Spirit of God, these are the sons of God. (Romans 8:14)

People often ask me, "Can everyone experience the Holy Spirit like you do? Can everyone see the Holy Spirit do the things that you've experienced?" The answer is absolutely yes! There is no special gift involved, only brokenness and surrender. So the question is not, "Do I have the gift?" The question is, "Can I surrender all to Him?" Surrender is only possible through prayer and brokenness before the Lord.

Here's how the process begins. As you get to know the Lord, it is then that He begins to manifest Himself and His love to you. A fellowship begins that grows and intensifies until you get to the place where you will say, "Lord Jesus, I give You my life, my mind, my heart, my dreams, my emotions, my thoughts; I give them all to You. I surrender spirit, soul and body. Do with me as You will."

And as you surrender to Him, it is then that the Holy Spirit begins to teach you, not just about yourself, but about all that the Father has for you (John 14:26). It is then that He imparts to you His strength and His living faith. For as Isaiah declared, "In quietness and in confidence shall be your strength" (Isaiah 30:15).

Everything about the Word now becomes stronger and everything about prayer now becomes richer. A passage of Scripture you have read 10,000 times becomes more powerful than ever because of the presence of the Holy Spirit. Your communion with God is richer than you've ever known, all because of the presence of the Holy Spirit. A peace and a tranquility will come into your life, and for the first time you will understand what the Lord Jesus meant when He said, "My peace I give to you" (John 14:27). All that becomes yours because of the Spirit.

. . . PRAYER . . .

Holy Spirit, I welcome You into every area of my daily life. Come in today and work in me and through me.

. . . TODAY'S THOUGHT . . .

The Holy Spirit longs to become your closest companion and helper. It's up to you to extend the invitation. He is waiting for you to say, "Welcome, Holy Spirit."

—Benny Hinn
President, Benny Hinn Ministries

January 20

SOVEREIGNLY BAPTIZED

And when they had prayed, the place where they were assembled together was shaken; and they were all filled with the Holy Spirit, and they spoke the word of God with boldness. (Acts 4:31)

I came from a hardworking, tenant farmer family in south Georgia, but none of us were Christians. Then, as my little 7-year-old brother lay on his deathbed, he called my father to his bedside and said, "Pa, I want to hear you pray one time before I die."

With tears in his eyes, Pa rose from the bedside and walked out to the porch. Sadly, he didn't know how to pray. A neighbor said to him, "Elisha, I'd go back in there and get on my knees beside that boy and pray if I said nothing but 'Lord, be merciful to me a sinner.'" *And* that's exactly what Pa did. He was gloriously saved at the bedside of a dying child and later became a Freewill Baptist preacher.

Shortly after Pa's conversion, I went with some friends to a brush arbor meeting. Suddenly, I found myself stretched out on my back in the sawdust shavings, praising God to the top of my voice! At that moment I told God that from that day on I was His and I would preach His gospel.

I began to preach wherever anyone would listen to an excited farm boy. But somehow, I knew there was more; there must be a deeper experience with God. We had never heard of the "Pentecostal experience."

Then S. J. Heath came to south Georgia preaching about this *phenomenon.* I was anxious to receive whatever was available from God.

I took an unsaved friend to a home prayer meeting, hoping he would be converted. My friend sat in a chair with all of us gathered around him, praying for his salvation. Suddenly, I began speaking in a strange language. I had been sovereignly baptized in the Holy Spirit!

. . . PRAYER . . .

Lord God, help persons everywhere to know that it is their privilege to be baptized in the Holy Spirit and to experience His enabling power

. . . TODAY'S THOUGHT . . .

Each Christian should prepare himself as well as possible for Christian service but should understand that the ultimate preparation is to be baptized in the Holy Spirit.

—Earl P. Paulk, Sr. (Reprinted from *SpiritWalk: Daily Devotions on the Holy Spirit* by permission of Pathway Press)
Assistant General Overseer, COG (former)

January 21

JESUS CAME

And after eight days His disciples were again inside, and Thomas with them. Jesus came, the doors being shut, and stood in the midst, and said, "Peace to you." (John 20:26)

While pastoring in Detroit, Michigan, our church was flourishing with young people, including our three children. We were blessed with grace and peace. But our feeling of blessedness crumbled one July afternoon when two police officers came to inform us that an accidental drowning had claimed the life of our 10-year-old son, Kenneth.

With the shocking news came many disturbing questions: Could we have done anything different? How could this be happening? How can we cope with the trauma? To whom can we turn? Then Jesus came.

Jesus first spoke peace to my wife, Dorothy, on the day of the funeral. She described her experience: "As we approached the church my grief intensified and my spirit was crying, 'Oh, how I wish I could escape this hour.' I just wanted to run away from this dreadful event, but as we entered the sanctuary where Kenneth lay in state, Jesus came in the Spirit and power of the Scripture illuminating my mind with 'the Lord gave, and the Lord has taken away; blessed be the name of the Lord.' Then and there a sweet peace beyond description enveloped me. It became clear to me that the Lord gave us a son for a little while but had now taken him to help populate heaven."

It was obvious Dorothy had received peace of mind I did not have. Then Jesus came, ministering to me in a dream or night vision. In the vision, my wife, our two daughters, and I had just entered the gates of heaven when I heard Dorothy saying, "Come on, Son." When I turned, I saw Kenneth waiting for us just inside the gate. The vision passed with my waking but that preview of heaven ministered comfort and peace to me that lives forever!

. . . PRAYER . . .

Thank You, Father, for grace and peace through our Lord Jesus Christ to calm troubled souls.

. . . TODAY'S THOUGHT . . .

A friend put things in perspective when he asked me, "After all, what would heaven be like without children?"

—J. C. Cagle
State Overseer, MD, COGOP

January 22

POWER TO PROTECT AND PRESERVE

"No weapon formed against you shall prosper, And every tongue which rises against you in judgment You shall condemn. This is the heritage of the servants of the Lord, And their righteousness is from Me," Says the Lord. (Isaiah 54:17)

He walked briskly up the outside aisle of the church carrying a loaded pistol, screaming obscenities as he approached the pulpit. He stopped a mere eight feet from me, pointed the pistol at my head and screamed for all to hear, "Get on your knees, Preacher, and beg for your life or I will kill you where you stand!"

I looked him in the eye and quoted Isaiah 54:17. It enraged him.

"I'm going to kill you on the count of three!"

The congregation reacted in different ways based on their spiritual maturity. Some were pointing at the shooter, binding the demon powers in his life. Some were hiding under the pews, screaming in terror. Others ran out the back doors in a stampede for safety.

He raised the gun toward my head and started counting. "One . . . two . . ." and then he emptied his gun trying to assassinate me before the congregation. He was a devout follower of witchcraft and openly confessed his hatred for Christ.

Every shot missed!

The police traced the bullets from where the man was standing to where they entered the wall. Three were to the right of my head and three were to the left as the angel of the Lord parried the shots.

The shooter was arrested and sent to a hospital for the criminally insane. Ninety days later he was released by a board of psychiatrists who pronounced him well. He went home and hanged himself.

I am alive today because the power of God can protect and preserve.

. . . PRAYER . . .

Father, thank Your for Your power that is greater than any adversity or adversary Satan may send to destroy us.

. . . TODAY'S THOUGHT . . .

God is greater than any trial you presently endure or ever will face. God's promise is true. He will not forsake you. He's the God who cannot fail.

—John C. Hagee
Pastor, Cornerstone Church, San Antonio, TX

January 23

MOVING OUT OF THE COMFORT ZONE

And when Peter had come down out of the boat, he walked on the water to go to Jesus. (Matthew 14:29)

How many of us have been called to a task by the Lord? We have commenced to walk in our calling, but then have taken our eyes off Jesus and begun to fail. Today, Jesus wants us to start trusting Him again in the midst of the difficulties in which we find ourselves and begin to walk on the water of life with our eyes firmly fixed on Jesus.

He will never allow us to fail or to go under in defeat. God has told us, "I will never leave you nor forsake you" (Hebrews 13:5).

Peter probably wished that he had never responded to the call of Jesus, but he *did* respond. He stepped out on faith and was successful while his eyes remained on the Lord.

As I stood looking at a group of fearful, lonely, hungry, orphaned street children in Zambia, God challenged my heart to begin to care for and support these children, to get out of my *comfort zone* and to begin trusting God to meet their needs. The Lord has told us, "Commit your works to the Lord, And your thoughts will be established" (Proverbs 16:3). Sharing the needs with our ladies' Bible study groups and other friends, I was reminded of Peter and his situation.

Two years on and from that first day, children are being clothed, fed, educated, and, most importantly, saved. At a recent children's crusade, there were 417 decisions to follow the Lord in salvation.

When Jesus called me at 12 years of age, I said, "Here I am, wholly available." Now, at an age when most people are thinking of retiring, God has said again to me, "Follow me, and I will make you fishers of men" (Matthew 4:19). I am so glad that I listened to His voice and was obedient to His command.

. . . PRAYER . . .

Father, may we always be willing to listen to Your voice and be obedient to Your commands.

. . . TODAY'S THOUGHT . . .

"Only one life, soon it will pass. / Only what's done for Christ will last." (Lanny Wolfe).

—Carol A. Evans
Co-Director, Emmanuel International Ministries, Wales, UK

January 24

BOLDNESS TO SPEAK

But you shall receive power when the Holy Spirit has come upon you; and you shall be witnesses to Me in Jerusalem, and in all Judea and Samaria, and to the end of the earth. (Acts 1:8)

I will always remember the first time I became aware of the Holy Spirit stirring my spirit and making me conscious of my need of God. I was a very young boy and even though I had never had such an experience, there was not one ounce of resistance to the wooing Spirit of God. Though it was very difficult for me because of my shyness, nevertheless, I responded to the pastor's invitation and made my way forward to accept the Lord into my life.

Even as a Christian I found it difficult to communicate Christ to others. I would read of the boldness of the first century believers and compare their ability to witness to my inferiority complex and realize something was missing in my experience.

What a wonderful truth to find out that God had already made provision for my weakness and inability. A faithful pastor taught me that the same Christ who had saved me would baptize me with the Holy Spirit and fire (Matthew 3:11), and that baptism in the Holy Spirit would give me power and boldness to be a witness for my Lord Jesus Christ (Acts 1:8).

What a difference the infilling of the Holy Spirit has made in my life! As a teenager I began witnessing for Christ on the streets of Houston where I was born and reared. I could never have fulfilled the call to preach, which I have now cherished for more than 40 years, had it not been for the mighty anointing of the Holy Spirit who gave me the boldness to speak.

. . . PRAYER . . .

Lord Jesus, thank You for the empowerment of the Holy Spirit that energizes an ordinary person to become a witness to the good news of God's love and salvation.

. . . TODAY'S THOUGHT . . .

Acts 1:8 is a promise of divine energy to fulfill a divine mission which involves delivering a divine message. And the promise is just as valid today as it was when it was first offered.

—James K. Bridges
General Treasurer/Executive Director, AG

January 25

SINCE I WAS A CHILD

. . . and that from childhood you have known the Holy Scriptures, which are able to make you wise for salvation through faith which is in Christ Jesus. (2 Timothy 3:15)

My father was a Pentecostal minister. In the early 1940's, he served as pastor of a church in Beloit, Wisconsin. His annual church plan usually included a summer revival. During the revival of 1943, I became a Christian. That touch by God has proven unequivocally to be the most wondrous experience of my life.

I didn't concern myself with where to sit during meetings. I would have preferred to sit in the back of the church with my friends; however, my mother insisted my brother and I sit with her. Had she done otherwise, I might have missed the greatest experience of my life.

Though only 5, I knew I needed Jesus as my Savior. Romans 3:23 reads, "For all have sinned and fall short of the glory of God." Jesus said, "Most assuredly, I say to you, unless one is born again, he cannot see the kingdom of God" (John 3:3).

As I sat next to Mom, the Holy Spirit's conviction enveloped me, drawing me with great love to Him. I could not resist nor was I afraid. He left me with no room to doubt that He had come for me to make my commitment to Him.

I nudged my mother and said, "I can't sit in my seat any longer. I've got to get saved."

She gently gave me an affirmative nod.

Never before or since have I felt such a powerful, compelling, and yet loving wave of conviction. God's Word pierced my heart and He made it new.

He saved me; He called me; He equipped me; He energized me for my journey. My commitment to Him and His call have remained firm.

. . . PRAYER . . .

I thank You, Father, for Your drawing and sustaining presence. Thank You for Your power to free all of us from sin and to keep us from sin.

. . . TODAY'S THOUGHT . . .

"Ask," He promised, "and it [salvation] will be given to you; seek, and you will find; knock, and it will be opened to you" (Matthew 7:7).

—James B. Keiller
Director, Global Missions, IPCC, Atlanta, GA

January 26

MY SINS ARE GONE

As far as the east is from the west, So far has He removed our transgressions from us. (Psalm 103:12)

I trembled, my heart pounded, I had trouble breathing normally. Only 10 years old, I didn't know what was happening, but I was certain the only relief for me was to be found at the altar. In later years, I came to realize what I felt that cold November night was the warmth of holy conviction. The Holy Spirit had seized me and confronted me with my need of a savior.

All I remember of that service is a song we sang that continued to echo in my mind until I finally knelt in godly sorrow and repentance and surrendered myself to Christ.

You ask why I am happy so I'll just tell you why, Because my sins are gone.

I wanted to find the joy that flowed from those who sang that song. The working of the Holy Spirit helped me to realize I must repent to find such joy. And so, I went forward, found a place of prayer in the left-hand amen corner and cried out to God for forgiveness.

'Twas at the old-time altar where God came in my heart, And now my sins are gone; The Lord took full possession, the devil did depart, the devil did depart, I'm glad my sins are gone.

Although I have occasionally stumbled since that night, I have never let go of that song; and God, in His continued mercy, has never let go of me.

When Satan comes to tempt me and tries to make me doubt, I say, my sins are gone. You got me into trouble, but Jesus got me out, I'm glad my sins are gone.

I'm living now for Jesus, I'm happy night and day, Because my sins are gone. My soul is filled with music, with all my heart I say, I know my sins are gone.

. . . PRAYER . . .

God, thank You for reaching down to me as a young child and drawing me to Your loving self. Thank You that my sins are gone!

. . . TODAY'S THOUGHT . . .

They're underneath the blood on the cross of Calvary, As far removed as darkness is from dawn; In the sea of God's forgetfulness, that's good enough for me, Praise God, my sins are gone.

—Larry T. Duncan

Ministry Director, Leadership Development/Discipleship, COGOP

January 27

YOURS FOR THE ASKING

Yet you do not have because you do not ask. (James 4:2)

When I was just a boy, one Christmas my parents gave me an Erector Set, that toy with varying lengths of steel bands and hundreds of bolts. I was so excited when I tore open my present!

Upon opening the box, I dumped all the contents on the floor and scrambled to find the instruction book. As I studied the guidebook, I spotted the diagram of a bridge I wanted to build. I went to work, following the instructions the best I could.

Before long the steps of instruction became far too complicated for my 8-year-old mind to comprehend. I was at my wit's end. I threw down my small wrench and screwdriver and blurted out, "I quit! There's no way I can do this. I've tried everything."

My father overheard my frustration and softly said, "Son, you've not tried *everything*. You didn't ask my help. And I know how to put those pieces together." Soon the bridge was completed.

What a parable of the way our lives can go! The world is a pressure cooker. Tempers flare. Stomachs churn. Hearts break. Nerves unravel.

At this moment it's time to let the words from our verse sink into your heart: "You do not have because you do not ask." What's the Spirit saying to you through His Word? "When the pressures of your life build up and circumstances get so complicated that you just don't know how to put it all together, be sure you don't forget to ask for My help, for I can handle *anything*." Your heavenly Father is telling you what my earthly father told me when I was totally frustrated: "You've not tried everything. You haven't asked for My help."

You did not read this by accident today. God wants to help you. His help is yours for the asking.

. . . PRAYER . . .

Lord, You are bigger than any situation I face. I praise You that I am in You and that You are in me. I'm grateful I have nothing to fear.

. . . TODAY'S THOUGHT . . .

Yesterday God helped me; today He'll do the same. How long will this continue? Forever, praise His name.

—Thomas Lindberg
Pastor, First Assemblies of God, Memphis, TN

January 28

WHAT ARE YOU CONSIDERING TODAY?

For consider Him who endured such hostility from sinners against Himself, lest you become weary and discouraged in your souls. (Hebrews 12:3)

Notice the Word of God said, "For consider Him." Your life depends on what you consider. When the Word says "consider Him," it is talking about Jesus. The Gospel of John reads, "In the beginning was the Word, and the Word was with God, and the Word was God" (1:1). Verse 14 says, "And the Word became flesh and dwelt among us." The Word that dwelt among us was Jesus. Jesus and the Word are the same. Jesus preached His Word to the people. He preached the Word of God as you and I know it today. We must go to His Word when we are facing battles in life. What we consider is going to cause us to be victorious or to worry and walk defeated.

Many Christians live in fear, with torment and worry. You can hear them talking, "I am worrying about that and I am afraid this is going to happen." You can tell they have not been considering the Word. If you consider the Word, it is going to put you over. "If God is for us, who can be against us?" (Romans 8:31).

It is time we start considering what the Word says about our situation and then stand on those promises. All God in Heaven has ever wanted you to do as one of His children is to take Him at His Word. No weapon formed against you will prosper. That alone should put you in a win-win situation. Refuse to worry or have fear about what you are facing. God is there for you all the time.

. . . PRAYER . . .

Heavenly Father, I thank You that You always hear our prayers. I thank You in Jesus' name that You are going to comfort Your children today who read and understand that we absolutely can take You at Your Word as it says in Hebrews 6:12-13.

. . . TODAY'S THOUGHT . . .

The Lord wants you to take Him at His Word today. The promises of God are for all believers, they are claimed by those with faith, but they are obtained by those with patience.

—Mac Gober

Canaan Land Ministries, Autaugauville, AL

January 29

BUSYNESS

"While your servant was busy here and there, he was gone". (1 Kings 20:40)

There is an interesting incident in 1 Kings 20. A prophet was given custody of a prisoner. During the night he escaped, and the prophet was called before the king. In his own defense he said, "While your servant was busy here and there, he was gone."

What an excuse! But, it is not really so uncommon, is it? Have you ever been so "busy here and there" that the really important things just slipped away? I recall a special day during which I forgot to buy my wife an appropriate card. I was so "busy here and there" that the person most dear to me was forgotten. How I regretted it!

In the busyness of life, things that God has entrusted to us are often overlooked and forgotten. Not intentionally! But, "while your servant was busy here and there, he was gone." For example, it is so easy to rush to work without kissing your spouse or telling your children that they are loved. It is so easy to bury yourself in layers of newspaper at the end of the day. It is so easy to remain silent when a compliment would bring that needed blessing. Oh, we would never willfully hurt those we love. Yet during our *busyness* precious relationships slip away. Suddenly they are gone while we have been "busy here and there."

If you are reading this in the morning, why not, before you go to work, make sure the bonds of love are holding strong? If you are reading this after the day has passed, you know what to do, don't you? A phone call! A good night kiss! A warm hug! Just do it!

. . . PRAYER . . .

Father, I thank You for the faithfulness of Your Spirit Who breaks into my schedule reminding me that the love shed abroad in my heart is there to enable me to love. Grant me the power to love as I ought to love.

. . . TODAY'S THOUGHT . . .

George Matheson (1842-1906) wrote, "O Love that wilt not let me go, I rest my weary soul in Thee; I give Thee back the life I owe, That in Thine ocean depths its flow May richer, fuller be."

—Garry E. Milley

Eastern Pentecostal Bible College, Peterborough, Ontario, Canada

January 30

GRACE FOR GRACE

And of His fullness we have all received, and grace for grace. (John 1:16)

When one becomes a child of God through the convicting ministry of the Holy Spirit he does not receive a full amount of grace with which to go on for the rest of his life. He has sufficient grace for that day, but he must receive additional grace on each passing day. Our Lord is the source from which we draw every blanket of grace as the need arises. No matter what the circumstances are, by His divine grace God infuses into the Christian a sufficiency of supernatural strength through the indwelling presence of the Holy Spirit.

His grace is clearly evident—

When we are weak. "Let us therefore come boldly to the throne of grace. . ." (Hebrews 4:16). The Holy Spirit understands what we are going through. No other strength in the universe can sustain us in time of need as He can.

When we are hurting. "My grace is sufficient for you" (2 Corinthians 12:9). The thorn pierced Paul deeply, constantly reminding him of his inadequacy. It certainly caused pain, doubts, and fear. Yet grace was sufficient in the midst of pain. The Holy Spirit is our Comforter when we face trials. Problems and perplexities always confront us causing concern. They often come on us when we least expect them. Troubles touch every area of our life—soul, body, and spirit. But the supply of sustaining grace corresponds exactly with the need: never too much, never too little, never too soon, and never too late. "But may the God of all grace, who called us to His eternal glory by Christ Jesus, after you have suffered a while, perfect, establish, strengthen, and settle you" (1 Peter 5:10). Praise be to God for the wonderful ministry of the Holy Spirit in us by His grace!

. . . PRAYER . . .

Thank You, God, for being so faithful and sharing with us Your Spirit and grace through faith in Christ Jesus.

. . . TODAY'S THOUGHT . . .

A long time ago the psalmist said: "He also brought me up out of a horrible pit, Out of the miry clay, And set my feet upon a rock, And established my steps " (Psalm 40:2). Stability is a free gift through His grace.

—David J. Mortelliti

Pastor, Fabre Street Pentecostal Church, Montreal, Quebec, Canada

January 31

THE DOVE HAS ARRIVED

And being assembled together with them, He commanded them not to depart from Jerusalem, but to wait for the Promise of the Father, "which," He said, "you have heard from Me." (Acts 1:4)

Arctic explorer Nansen felt ill-equipped without his carrier dove, the messenger with wings which linked his expedition to a waiting world. He released his winged messenger to travel 2,000 miles to his home in Norway with a message to his beloved wife.

The tiny dove, knowing his destination by instinct, traveled over ice, frigid water, and grassy land; then, at last, rested his wings. Nansen's anxious wife knew by the arrival of the carrier dove that it was all right with her husband in the frigid far north.

So it was for the apostles and the other disciples. The coming of the dove (Holy Spirit) was the fulfillment of the promise given by God through Christ to his family in the Upper Room. Jesus had directed them to remain there until they received the promise of the Father.

These chosen servants of the Lord went to the appointed place and awaited the promise of the Father. Suddenly, a noise of a mighty wind filled the house and the disciples, in one mind and one accord, witnessed the descending of the Spirit, tongues, and fire. The heavenly dove had arrived! The promise was fulfilled!

I recall when the heavenly dove arrived for me. I was a very young man worshipping in a small church in Fresno, California, when I was caught away in the Spirit for more than two hours. My body, during this experience, seemed to float from the floor to the ceiling of this cottage church. It was as if the whole world was reconciled to Christ. There were no earthly moorings as the Holy Spirit carried my spirit beyond this earth's gravity.

. . . PRAYER . . .

Father, thank You for the power to be Your witness. Your Word has confirmed to us a divine promise: "But those who wait on the Lord Shall renew their strength; They shall mount up with wings like eagles, They shall run and not be weary, They shall walk and not faint."

. . . TODAY'S THOUGHT . . .

Today I rest in God's Spirit; indeed, the Dove has arrived for me.

—Perry Gillum
General Presbyter, COGOP (former)

February 1

TO HONOR OR NOT TO HONOR, THAT IS THE QUESTION

What shall be done for the man whom the king delights to honor? (Esther 6:6)

I learned one of the greatest lessons on the subject of honor during a visit to Jamaica in 1980. Henry, an aged black brother, was given the task of looking after me during my stay as the visiting evangelist. He brought me water, furnished me with a towel, brought a dry shirt to change into, opened and closed the door for me, and did many other things to ensure my comfort.

I said, "Henry, I can manage, thank you."

"No, Brother Morgan," he said, "I cannot preach, you can preach; I cannot conduct a crusade, but you can. The one thing I can do is to serve you, for in serving you, I serve the Lord through you."

That comment touched my heart and has left an indelible impression upon my life. I've never forgotten that lesson on honor.

Webster's Dictionary defines honor: "Honor is manifested esteem. Something that is visible, obvious, and evident." This tells us that honor is not secret admiration but something that can be seen.

God tells us in His Word, "those who honor Me I will honor" (1 Samuel 2:30). To honor someone does not mean the person has to be greater than you; otherwise, God could honor no man. Let honor be a godly characteristic in our lives as we serve one another. The Scriptures teach us to honor parents, authorities, the aged, and the servants of the Lord, but first of all to honor God.

The world has honor for its own. In a court of law we address the presiding judge as "Your Honor." In 1953, I had the privilege of being part of the Guard of Honor for Her Majesty, Queen Elizabeth II, in the year of her coronation. If the world knows how to honor, Christians ought to be examples of giving honor to God and other people.

. . . PRAYER . . .

Dear Lord, thank You for honoring us by giving us Your Son. Let us honor You by serving You.

. . . TODAY'S THOUGHT . . .

Honor is not honor until it is given away. God made us to be stewards of honor; we are to give loving preference to each other freely.

—Dr. Peter B. Morgan
General Overseer, OBSCC

February 2

OUR WONDERFUL COUNSELOR

Counsel in the heart of man is like deep water, But a man of understanding will draw it out. (Proverbs 20:5)

As a young pastor of a fast-growing pioneer work, it appeared I was God's man of faith and power. However, there was a growing concern within me about a lack of manifested fruits of the Spirit. As I looked into my heart, I saw a man dominated by fear of rejection. I saw someone willing to sacrifice respect at the altar of gaining approval. I saw a man who would tell people what they wanted to hear rather than what they needed to hear. I knew the congregation needed to change, but it became obvious Jesus wanted to begin with me.

"Holy Spirit," I said, kneeling in front of my sofa, "please show me my heart." Instantly, I saw in my mind's eye a 10-year-old boy I recognized immediately. He was involved in a scene that I had confessed scores of times to the Lord while asking forgiveness. My neighbor friend had a little sister with whom I played "doctor." I had become involved and the defilement had stained my soul. Had Jesus forgiven me? Yes, the first time I had asked. It was my self-judgment that bound me to this shame. Jesus asked me to get down off the throne of judgment and forgive this 10-year-old boy He loved. I looked into that picture and spoke forgiveness to little Paul. Psalm 4 became real to me as I exchanged Jesus' glory for my shame. What a relief!

Many other pictures arose from the Counselor through the next years. Each time the Holy Spirit would encourage me to forgive others and myself, repent of sin, and cry out for the Spirit of Grace to change me. Childhood rejections began to give way to the Father-heart of God.

"You are accepted in the beloved," reverberated in my soul. I was no longer the "tolerated" but, rather, the beloved, thanks to the Holy Spirit—the Wonderful Counselor.

. . . PRAYER . . .

Thank You, Jesus, for our Counselor who knows every circumstance of our life, and sends the Word to heal us and deliver us from our destruction.

. . . TODAY'S THOUGHT . . .

Denial has never won a battle. God desires truth in the inward parts (Psalm 51:6).

—Paul R. Parker
Superintendent, Mountain Plains Region, OBSC

February 3

BE ANXIOUS FOR NOTHING

Therefore humble yourselves under the mighty hand of God, that He may exalt you in due time, casting all your care upon Him, for He cares for you. (1 Peter 5: 6-7)

Anxiety is a disturbed state of mind produced by real or imaginary fears. Mine was real! It was June, 1981. Our school board was facing a financial crisis. Bankruptcy seemed imminent. We needed a miracle.

With no solution in sight, it was an anxious chairman who got behind the wheel. Alone in my car and barely into the 250-mile journey home, I felt a presence shatter the tense solitude. I was arrested by the word, "Son." Whether the summons for attention was audible, I do not know. A moment passed. A sweet sense of calmness flooded my spirit. Then I heard in a gentle, reassuring tone, "Everything is going to be all right." I blinked to keep my vision clear as tears filled my eyes. My car was filled with a holy presence such as I had not experienced before. The Holy Spirit had spoken. "Son, everything is going to be all right."

The remainder of the journey was spent in a sanctuary of sweet communion. The ensuing weeks and months were free of anxiety as the situation unfolded. And, that moment was so sacred that it was not to be shared, nor was the promise of the Lord to be doubted.

Within 18 months the miracle emerged. The $9.3 million owed the bank by the board was reduced to $2.3 million. A mountainous obstacle had become manageable. The divine intervention endured in the years that followed and to the present. We operate on a balanced budget.

In life's trying moments we learn our most valuable lessons. Our tragedy becomes His triumph! "Be anxious for nothing, but in everything by prayer and supplication, with thanksgiving, let your requests be made known to God" (Philippians 4:6).

. . . PRAYER . . .

Heavenly Father, Your kindness and grace are greater than our burdens and care. Remind us we are never abandoned nor forsaken. Help us to be anxious for nothing.

. . . TODAY'S THOUGHT . . .

God invites us to trust Him and joins us to change our circumstance. His will is done. We are comforted. He is glorified!

—Roy D. King

General Superintendent, Pentecostal Assemblies of Newfoundland

February 4

THE COMFORT OF THE SPIRIT

I will pray the Father, and He will give you another Helper, that He may abide with you forever -- the Spirit of truth, whom the world cannot receive, because it neither sees Him nor knows Him; but you know Him, for He dwells with you and will be in you (John 14:16, 17).

In my darkest hour I came to know the reality of the Holy Spirit's abiding presence as Comforter and friend.

After a dynamic service in Georgia, I joined the pastor at the parsonage for a time of warm, pleasant fellowship. The telephone rang and after a brief conversation, the pastor walked straight to me. Kneeling before my chair, he looked me straight in the eyes and with trembling voice spoke words that would change my life forever:

"Steve . . . there's been an accident. David's dead!"

It felt as though my heart had been ripped from my chest. "Oh, God, not my boy, David," I cried, over and over. Despair and agony filled the next long, lonely hours, and the darkness of the night seemed to hold me captive for an eternity.

Darkness gave way to dawn the next day and I realized that this terrible nightmare was real. Returning home to Ohio that morning, I did not go alone, however. The Holy Spirit was with me, comforting me, helping me through the pain and grief.

The Holy Spirit is aware of our pain in times of need. He is our Paraclete, "one called alongside to help." When we are grieving or overwhelmed with the trials of life, He is our Helper, our buckler, our shield. He is the One who goes before us to overcome whatever would try to steal our peace and joy.

. . . PRAYER . . .

Precious Holy Spirit, I thank You in Jesus Christ for being there every time I have needed You. Help me to be a comfort to others, as You are to me.

. . . TODAY'S THOUGHT . . .

God's Word promises the Comforter will abide forever. No matter what you're facing, remember that you are not alone!

—Steve Brock (Reprinted from *SpiritWalk: Daily Devotions on the Holy Spirit* by permission of Pathway Press)
Minister, Benny Hinn Crusades

February 5

THE DAY OF REJOICING

Finally, there is laid up for me the crown of righteousness, which the Lord, the righteous Judge, will give to me on that Day, and not to me only but also to all who have loved His appearing. (2 Timothy 4:8)

The church door opened on Sunday night and in walked a visitor who motioned for one of my brothers to come to the back of the building. The word had come to our family that my dad had passed away. Being the oldest of the five boys, I felt the responsibility of bringing comfort to the family. The church service was now focused on expressing joy rather than sorrow because a child of God had been called to his eternal home.

My dad was a Christian. He was saved under my ministry. I knew his faith in God was strong. He had taken a backward glance at his past years of blindness caused by diabetes, and now with high anticipation he could see the future with the hope of a crown of righteousness.

His yesterday was a day of labor and service to his community in business. His achievements were made amid struggles and hard work.

Of his today he could say, "The time of my departure is at hand. I have fought the good fight, I have finished the race, I have kept the faith" (2 Timothy 4:6-7).

These words came from the lips of a man whose life was filled with a great past. At the time of his departing, Dad's attention was on the immediate view. With penetrating eyes, he gazed forward as though beholding something out of this world. He looked into the future and saw a day of rejoicing.

I have learned that the Word of God brings peace and tranquility at the parting of a loved one. This is best expressed by Psalm 119:105, "Your word is a lamp to my feet And a light to my path."

. . . PRAYER . . .

Thank You, Lord, for the peace that comes from Your Word to sustain us and abide in us. I am forever made to rejoice in it.

. . .TODAY'S THOUGHT . . .

My yesterdays were filled with excitement, my present is lived with great expectation, my future is viewed with sure hope of a crown of righteousness.

—Reynolds Smith
Assistant General Overseer, PFWB

February 6

THROUGH THE FIERY TRIALS OF LIFE

. . . that the genuineness of your faith, being much more precious than gold that perishes, though it is tested by fire, may be found to praise, honor, and glory at the revelation of Jesus Christ. (1 Peter 1:7)

It had the appearance of another normal day. We had recently built our home, and the yard needed much work. As I was burning some brush, suddenly I found my body engulfed in flames. Being an Eagle Scout, I knew not to run. However, when it's your body on fire, putting into practice what you know is not easy. Fortunately, my panic was brief, and within a few feet I regained my composure. With no one to help, I tore the burning clothes from my body. My first thoughts carried me to my childhood, to a woman whose clothes caught fire. Frightened, she ran until someone caught her. By then it was too late. When I saw the severe damage done to my body, and the melted flesh, I wondered if it were too late for me as well.

My parents lived next door, but my mom was not home. As my dad was rushing me to the hospital, I felt the presence of God settle upon me and bring the most incredible peace I had ever experienced. Live or die, I knew everything was going to be all right. When we pulled into the entrance of the emergency room, a nurse was standing outside with a clipboard that contained my name. They had a room and doctors waiting for me. We had not stopped to call, but Someone who knew my need had prepared everything.

Today, no sign of the damage the flames inflicted on my body can be found, except one small scar underneath my left wrist, which is not visible unless pointed out: a scar to remind me how God is always with us, and how miraculous feats that defy anyone's understanding still happen.

. . . PRAYER . . .

Heavenly Father, thank You that whether through the waters or through the fire, I have learned Your hand is not too short to touch and meet my need.

. . . TODAY'S THOUGHT . . .

We often learn the greatest lessons in life in the midst of adverse circumstances. When Satan tempts us to think God is far away, it is then that He is very near.

—Ronald Wilson
General Treasurer, CHC

February 7

AN UNFAILING PROMISE

So you shall serve the Lord your God, and He will bless your bread and your water. And I will take sickness away from the midst of you. (Exodus 23:25)

Thirty-three years ago this promise was given to my wife, Carole, and me as we began our ministry. It also became our sustenance in 1973 while serving as missionaries in Hong Kong. Our 12-year-old son fell down a flight of stairs, was seriously injured, and faced losing at least one kidney. We decided to wait until we returned to California on furlough in late 1974 before proceeding with any further major medical steps. In California, a urologist confirmed the diagnosis. Exploratory surgery was set for January 4, 1975. With the unknown before us, we could only hold to God's promise.

On January 4 God spoke to the urologist (a believer) to take one further X-ray. The results clearly showed that between 6 a.m. (when the first X-ray was taken) and 6:30 a.m., God had given our son two brand-new kidneys. Our son returned with us to Hong Kong and later played goalie on the colony's field hockey team. He is now a minister and the father of two children.

Healing is not new with God. In his book, *Healing*, Francis MacNutt writes: "Every time you meet Jesus in the Gospels, He is either healing someone, or has just come from healing someone, or is on His way to do it." One-fifth of the Gospels is devoted to Jesus' healing ministry.

Jesus healed for many reasons: to confirm His mission as the Messiah, to keep His Word and reveal God's will, to manifest the works of God and destroy the work of the devil, and to lead people to repentance. But the most evident purpose was to show how much He cared about people—His compassion. Jesus is still the same yesterday, today, and forever.

. . . PRAYER . . .

Lord, You are our source of life and health. We will rejoice in Your compassion and minister the same with others.

. . . TODAY'S THOUGHT . . .

God so loved the world He sent His Son. Jesus so loved us He took our burdens upon Himself. By His stripes we are healed (1 Peter 2:24).

—Dr. Ronald D. Williams
Communications Officer, ICFG

February 8

BURNING HEARTS

And they continued steadfastly in the apostles' doctrine and fellowship, in the breaking of bread, and in prayers. Then fear came upon every soul, and many wonders and signs were done through the apostles. (Acts 2:42-43)

Two early disciples, after breaking bread with Jesus, said, "Did not our hearts burn within us as we walked and talked with Him in the Way?" God's purpose for us is to discover that in Him we live and move and have being. Every breath expresses praise and thankfulness for His oversight of our thoughts and movements. I am not my own, I am bought with a price . .. . the precious blood of Christ.

The communion of the cup opens the celebration of being one with God. Thereby, we progress into a communion (fellowship) to be at one with each other. We are at a loss to have one without the other. The communion of the cup united the early Christians in spiritual things; the second communion made possible a larger realm and sphere.

The quality of New Testament fellowship was determined by the quality of the saints, who had *burning hearts* and were intoxicated with the Holy Spirit. Their lives were Christ-centered; emulating His image; becoming channels of God's redemptive, free-giving love; helping the needy, the lost, the unfortunate and the unhappy. They volunteered to bear the burdens of their fellow men, fulfilling the spiritual laws of Christ.

The New Testament saint sees Christianity as a practical way of life. He believes the kingdom of God has come into history and must continue in him as it began in Christ. The Christian knows that he must purify the springs of history within his own heart, with true humility, always decreasing while Christ increases.

All persons of every race, creed, color, or nation become an object of our wistful gaze as we search for individuals to enlarge our fellowship of burning hearts.

. . . PRAYER . . .

Father, thank You for Your indwelling Spirit guiding me in the Way, the Truth, and Life.

. . . TODAY'S THOUGHT . . .

The same Spirit that raised up Christ from the dead quickens my mortal body today.

—Theodore A. Lanes
Executive Director, AGIF

February 9

JOY IN HEAVEN

I say to you that likewise there will be more joy in heaven over one sinner who repents than over ninety-nine just persons who need no repentance.
(Luke 15:7)

I glanced at the clock as I lay down. It was almost midnight. This had been a long, wonderful day in my life. My mind was full of the activities that had taken place. I knew there would be no sleep immediately. As I settled into bed, I began to reflect on the special events I had experienced. My first grandchild was born today, and the joy I was feeling could not be expressed in words.

I began to pray, thanking the Lord for bringing this special promise into my life, and for helping my daughter with little Emily's birth. During the prayer I made this statement to the Lord, "Holding this baby causes me to feel as though my daughter has been born all over again." Suddenly, from deep within my inner man, the Holy Spirit spoke to my heart saying, "This is the same joy I feel when an individual is born again and enters into my family."

I cannot begin to express the sensation that flooded my being. I did not think anything could bring more joy than holding my new granddaughter. However, the joy and the presence of the Lord I was experiencing at that moment was greater than all the joys of the previous day.

Perhaps you feel you are not loved. You may feel no one cares if you exist. God loves all His children with a love that surpasses our human understanding. It is yours for the asking. Allow Him to bring His light and His warmth into your heart today. You will experience His overwhelming joy.

Help someone else find His joy. You will find a new purpose for your life, and a depth of joy you never knew was possible.

. . . PRAYER . . .

Father, thank You for loving us with a love beyond our comprehension. Give each person today the joy that comes as we live our lives in Your care.

. . . TODAY'S THOUGHT . . .

My joy does not depend upon the physical conditions around me, for the joy of the Lord comes from within.

—Terry J. Fowler, Sr.
Pastor, West Sunnyside, Griffin, GA CHC

February 10

THREE APPEARANCES OF CHRIST

For Christ has not entered the holy places made with hands, which are copies of the true, but into heaven itself, now to appear in the presence of God for us . . . He then would have had to suffer often since the foundation of the world; but now, once at the end of the ages, He has appeared to put away sin by the sacrifice of Himself. . . so Christ was offered once to bear the sins of many. To those who eagerly wait for Him He will appear a second time, apart from sin, for salvation. (Hebrews 9:24, 26, 28)

These Scriptures from Hebrews deal with the past, present, and future, as well as the purpose, place, and person of Christ. The past is spoken of in verse 26 when He appeared to put away sin by the sacrifice of Himself. His first appearance was to redeem mankind from sin. He cast our sins in the depths of the deepest sea, never to be remembered against us. Past sins are put away, not temporarily, but permanently. This appearance of putting away sin deals with the past.

His second appearance, Hebrews 9:24, deals with the present. Christ Jesus is at the right hand of the Father to make intercession for us. He is our advocate with God the Father. We have a place because He is in the presence of God for us. We have a great High Priest in the heavens who was tempted like as we are, yet without sin. Because of His present appearance, we can come boldly to the throne of grace. He is touched with the feelings of our infirmities.

The third appearance is found in verse 28, dealing with the person and the future. The next great event on Earth will be the reappearance of Jesus. The promise is given for the future. He shall come! Oh, what a day that will be!

. . . PRAYER . . .

Thank You, Father, for the hope of our past, present and future. Help us keep ourselves clean and pure as we await Christ's next appearance.

. . . TODAY'S THOUGHT . . .

Christ appeared in the past to put away sin. He appears in the present at the throne of God for us. In the future He will return for us. That is His promise.

—Thomas E. Trask
General Superintendent, AG

February 11

AS I HAVE LOVED

A new commandment I give to you, that you love one another; as I have loved you, that you also love one another. (John 13:34)

Guidelines for living are anxiously sought by multitudes. What are the rules? What applies to me? Religion provides some answers as we cling to the Ten Commandments despite the balance of our religious faith. Yet there is nothing more captivating and challenging than the new commandment—to love as God has loved us. Nothing more needs to be added. It is clear. It is direct.

If one were to look at God's love list, the names of the worst offenders, by any man's description, would be found. From every walk of life, God has the ability to love. He does! That's all right for God, but the commandment is that I do the same. This requires that my mental and personal attitude must reflect love in such a measure that in spite of the actions of an individual, love from my experience with God is extended to them—not to their sin or their unclean way, but to the person.

One cannot help but wonder what would happen in the church if this commandment were treated as it should be—unbreakable and binding in every way. It must be in this light that Paul writes in Romans 1:14, "I am a debtor both to Greeks and to barbarians, both to wise and to unwise." God loved me regardless of what I was. He still does. In turn, as a recipient of that love, I owe to every man an expression of love that comes from the God-nature in me as a result of my new birth.

This new commandment is the guideline for Christian living. Without it, we are incomplete as Christians.

. . . PRAYER . . .

Father, let it be that I am so involved in the marvel of Your love in my life that I may be able to love others as You would love them.

. . . TODAY'S THOUGHT . . .

"To the weak I became as weak, that I might win the weak. I have become all things to all men, that I might by all means save some" (1 Corinthians 9:22).

—Harry O. "Pat" Wilson
Director, Home Missions/Evangelism Department, PCOG

February 12

THE HOLY SPIRIT IS A GIFT

Then Peter said to them, "Repent, and let every one of you be baptized in the name of Jesus Christ for the remission of sins; and you shall receive the gift of the Holy Spirit" (Acts 2:38).

Although I was raised in a Pentecostal pastor's home and was saved at the age of nine, eleven years passed before I received the gift of the Holy Spirit. I wanted this gift desperately. Service after service, I sought relentlessly to be filled with the Holy Spirit. After each altar service, my arms were tired and my voice raspy from going through what I thought was the correct ritual for receiving this priceless gift.

I questioned pastors, teachers, college professors, and evangelists; their formulas were given, yet none of them worked. I wondered if the Holy Spirit was for me. Yet I knew the Scripture said the gift was "to all who are afar off, as many as the Lord our God will call" (Acts 2:39).

Many years later, I attended a tent meeting in Cleveland, Tennessee, where John D. Nichols was the featured evangelist. One night, while I tarried at the altar, a minister prayed for me, "Lord increase his faith and help him to worship You." It revolutionized my praying. For years, I had been rehearsing formulas, "Make love to Jesus," or "Lose yourself in Jesus." My mind was occupied with phrases and not with praises.

The next night, Jesus was the focus of my worship. It seemed as though He and I were alone on a deserted island. Suddenly, my words of worship changed into tongues of angels. I had received the gift of the Holy Spirit with the initial evidence of speaking in tongues. I was endued with power that would revolutionize my life. That same power is available to you today.

. . . PRAYER . . .

Lord, with this new millennium let us realize that the gift of the Holy Spirit has not diminished in importance, but has rather increased in significance in the lives of all believers.

. . . TODAY'S THOUGHT . . .

Holy Spirit baptism is a gift for all who will receive it through prayerful obedience. "Thanks be to God for His indescribable gift!" (2 Corinthians 9:15).

—V. R. LeBuhn
Pastor, COG, Florence, SC

February 13

THE SONG OF THE SOUL SET FREE

By the rivers of Babylon, There we sat down, yea, we wept . . . For there those who carried us away captive asked of us a song . . . How shall we sing the Lord's song In a foreign land? (Psalm 137:1, 3-4)

As an orchestra prepares to play, the musicians are free to play or not to play. All it takes is one note out of harmony to ruin the musical composition. Music comes from the heart of God. When man sinned he died not only physically, but also spiritually. Jesus through His atoning death took the note of sin and death and turned it into a note of victory.

Israel, because of sin, was captive in Babylon. Their captors wanted a song from them. They replied, "How can we sing the Lord's song in a foreign land?"

I was born in Puerto Rico into the family of a Church of God minister. By the time I was 15 years old, I was living in New York City and had turned my back on the church. I joined a gang, used drugs, and signed a contract to box professionally.

I felt miserable in my life of sin. A pastor invited me to a small storefront church. I promised to go, but I went dancing the night before. Soon I was in a gang fight. I was sent to the hospital with knife wounds and then to jail.

The pastor invited me to church again. That night my father was the speaker and he preached on the subject, "How can you sing to the Lord from a strange land?" He said, "When the dark cloud of sin covers our soul we lose all sense of the presence of God."

That night I gave my life to the Lord. Up to that time I did not know what to do with my life. A year later I was a student at Lee College. Since that day I have a song of joy in my heart. It is the song of the soul set free.

. . . PRAYER . . .

Eternal Father, thank You for filling our tongues with songs of joy.

. . . TODAY'S THOUGHT . . .

"What gave so much value to the old violin? . . . The touch of the Master's hand."

—Esdras Betancourt
Director, COG Hispanic Ministries

February 14

HE RIDES UPON THE STORM

Fire and hail, snow and clouds; Stormy wind, fulfilling His word. (Psalm 148:8)

Sledge-hammering stopped. Tent erectors shook their heads. If rain flooded this ground, it would be too spongy to anchor the steel pegs. The masts would crash. Yet, the tens of thousands expected at our Green Valley Gospel Crusade in South Africa must have shelter. What now? Give up this rare opportunity?

We consulted together and with the Lord. The direction was to "Go ahead!" Night after night, the canvas cathedral was crowded. One afternoon the face of the western sky glared with black belligerence. Satan held in his fist a wind and water catastrophe to hurl at us.

Then God smiled and whispered, "Point at the clouds and rebuke the devil." I pointed at that churning fury. "Satan, in the name of Jesus, if you destroy this tent I will build one three times bigger!" At that very moment Satan was unsaddled, and God took the reins of the galloping storm. It rushed on, but the Lord of heaven and earth and sky divided it north and south to pass us by. Not even one raindrop came our way.

For over 20 years in demon-infested territories He has pulled off impossible and spectacular triumphs. Every hostile circumstance is a stage for His glory. The clouds are His chariot. He rides upon the wings of the wind. His ambush springs the final surprise against His opponents.

Decisive issues for history were settled in the hearts of men like Abraham, Moses, Peter, and Paul. Every battle begins in the human spirit. Faith resists wrong, but not always on a grand scale. The lowliest of God's children do exploits. God chooses nobodies to display the splendors of triumphant trust before Satan. Our captain never lost a ship.

. . . PRAYER . . .

Lord Jesus, You hold all power on our behalf. By faith I draw upon it to be more than a conqueror. Sin and Satan shall not have dominion over me. Thank You, Lord!

. . . TODAY'S THOUGHT . . .

Christ leaves us here as weak mortals to prevail against the onslaughts of God's own enemy. Our heart-faith is the victory. Whether the world sees or fails to see, the outcome shakes hell and brings joy to heaven.

—Reinhard Bonnke

International Evangelist, Reinhard Bonnke Ministries

February 15

BUT PRAYER

Peter was therefore kept in prison, but constant prayer was offered to God for him by the church. (Acts 12:5)

It cannot go unnoticed in Scripture that God most often intervenes when men intervene. A wrong is righted, a sickness is cured, a foe is vanquished, or death becomes life when earthly intercession takes place. Of course, we know that the omniscient God of Heaven does not need our pleading to be aware of the situation. He knows all and sees all. Even the Scripture declares, "Now to Him who is able to do exceedingly abundantly above all that we ask or think, according to the power that works in us" (Ephesians 3:20). When we have thought but not yet verbalized the need, God is already aware of it and has the answer. And yet, in the midst of these profound truths, God listens for us to pray, and more often than not, begins His marvelous work commensurate with our prayers.

In this passage of Acts 12, we find one of the most dramatic stories of the Bible. Powerful prayer and evil despot, a confident apostle and an angelic rescue all combine to demonstrate the providential power of God. Herod, the evil king, had demonstrated his ruthlessness by killing the beloved James. He then imprisoned Simon Peter, and his execution seemed imminent. It is here that Peter's soon-coming death comes to an abrupt halt with the words "but prayer." Ah, there's the difference. "But prayer" and the Red Sea parts; "but prayer" and fire falls on Mt. Carmel; "but prayer" and Bartimaeus sees; "but prayer" and Jairus' daughter is alive. Prayer gets heaven's attention and, more than that, gets heaven's action. The church prayed, Peter was rescued, Herod lost, and God was glorified.

Your circumstances may seem impossible. Perhaps no easy answers are to be found. Remember Acts 12:5 and the phrase "but prayer." God is listening.

. . . PRAYER . . .

Father, may we learn to pray without ceasing until prayer is our natural reaction to everything.

. . . TODAY'S THOUGHT . . .

Faith stands on the shoulders of prayer and touches hope from above.

—David M. Griffis
Administrative Bishop, COG in WVA

February 16

WIT'S END

They reel to and fro, and stagger like a drunken man, And are at their wits' end. (Psalm 107:27)

Wit's end . . . this junction is on everyone's schedule. Sooner or later we all arrive at "Wit's End Corner." It's a well-known situation. It is the moment when you have exhausted every means at hand and do not know what to do next.

In this Psalm the writer describes a storm at sea and how the mariners came to the end of their resources, and then what they did in desperation. The remedy is in verse 28: "Then they cry out to the Lord in their trouble, And He brings them out of their distresses."

There are many different kinds of storms. You may be caught up in one this week. What should you do? To whom should your turn? Is there an answer?

"Wit's End Corner" means that all hope is gone. It means you have reached a place of despair. It means all human help has failed. Are you at this point in your marriage? . . . in your health? . . . in your finances? . . . in your soul? Do you feel desolate, alone, and helpless? Hold on! I have a message for you.

Spread your trouble and difficulty out before the Lord. That is where to go from "Wit's End Corner." The living God hears and answers. I love these words found in Isaiah 26:3: "You will keep him in perfect peace, Whose mind is stayed on You, Because he trusts in You." I ask you to rest your soul, your circumstances, and your business on Jesus Christ. The winds and the waves still obey His voice.

There is a human limit, but there is no limit with God. Ask yourself in this moment, "Am I at 'Wit's End Corner' for a purpose?" Now turn to God! He will *not* fail you!

. . . PRAYER . . .

Father, thank You for Your love and care for me even in the midst of difficulties. By the power of the Holy Spirit, I know Your grace is sufficient.

. . . TODAY'S THOUGHT . . .

Only in life's storms is our faith stretched far enough to hear the music of God's everlasting love; only then do we approach our real potential.

—Dr. Paula Boyer
Board Member, FGFCM

February 17

SHORT BEDS AND NARROW BLANKETS

For the bed is too short to stretch out on, And the covering so narrow that one cannot wrap himself in it. (Isaiah 28:20)

Have you ever tried to sleep on a bed that was too short or one with a blanket that was too small to cover you? It is an uncomfortable situation to say the least and certainly makes for a miserable night.

Isaiah used this illustration to demonstrate the insufficiency of Israel's attempts to escape destruction by the Assyrians. Isaiah 28 begins with a word of impending judgment as Isaiah prophesied war with Assyria and the removal of God's people to a distant land. He warned them that false refuges would be of no avail; all human attempts at safety and security would fail, like trying to enjoy a good night's sleep on a bed too short with a blanket too narrow to cover you.

Many people today try to find a religion that fits their personal preferences and allows for the lifestyle they want to lead. Their religion is just as discomforting and insufficient as a short bed with a narrow blanket. Some try to find spiritual rest by doing good works, but works in themselves are insufficient to guarantee salvation. Others try to find spiritual rest in a partial commitment to God and the church while clinging to material things and pet sins. This, too, is insufficient as God calls us to total commitment.

There is only one sufficient spiritual bed for the person who wants real rest. The Savior's invitation in Matthew 11:28 is "Come to Me, all you who labor and are heavy laden, and I will give you rest." The writer of Hebrews declares, "There remains therefore a rest for the people of God" (4:9).

Is your religion sufficient to guarantee your soul's salvation? Or is it just enough to make you miserable like a short bed with a narrow blanket?

. . . PRAYER . . .

Father, help us never to settle for a substitute of genuine salvation that comes only by faith in Christ and His atoning blood.

. . . TODAY'S THOUGHT . . .

We do not show the life of Christ by the multitude of things from which we abstain, but by the consistent presence in our lives of the fruit of the Spirit.

—Kenneth R. Bell

Administrative Liaison, General Overseer, COG

February 18

BIRTHPLACE OF MIRACLES

If you ask anything in My name, I will do it. (John 14:14)

Storms breed fear. Faith dispels fear. God gives faith.

A storm is an awesome thing. It has no respect for life or property . . . until God intervenes.

Some years ago, as summer slipped into autumn, Hurricane Hugo unleashed its terrifying forces against our home. From the Carolina coast, family members and friends came to seek safety with us. But Hugo changed its course. None of us was free from danger.

As the storm raged, we huddled together for support. Prayer was on everyone's lips. By midnight electrical power was gone, and the ensuing darkness gave us an even deeper sense of helplessness. Without the basic comfort of light, it is impossible to feel in control.

All night the storm seethed with unrelenting fury. Eventually, prayers brought Scriptures to mind, and we felt ourselves move into the circle of God's presence. The Scriptures God gave us reminded us how He delivered His chosen ones in Bible times. Then we were reminded of the many times He had intervened in our own lives and brought us through—and out of—situations that had once seemed hopeless.

Despite the wind's roar we learned to listen for God's whisper, "Be not afraid, I am in control." With bolstered faith and a renewed trust in the Master, we lifted our hands in confidence and said to the wind, "Be still!" Danger was abated; my home and family were unharmed.

A miracle happened in my home that night . . . a miracle that had its beginning in a wild, angry storm. With the right perspective of God, a storm can be the birthplace of a miracle rather than the breeding ground of fear.

. . . PRAYER . .

Thank You, Father, for Your all-sufficient grace in every situation and for Your power to lift us above the storm into miraculous victory.

. . . TODAY'S THOUGHT . . .

"I trust in God wherever I may be, upon the land or on the rolling sea. For come what may, from day to day, my heavenly Father watches over me."—From the hymn, "My Father Watches Over Me"

—M. Donald Duncan
Director of Missions, IPHC

February 19

ENCOURAGEMENT THAT NEVER FAILS

My righteousness is near, My salvation has gone forth, And My arms will judge the peoples; The coastlands will wait upon Me, And on My arm they will trust. (Isaiah 51:5)

Crashing waves from the Gulf of Mexico continued to break on sandy shores. Their rhythmic flow was soothing to my troubled soul. I was struggling with the pastoral problems of a stagnant church, disappointing results, and plaguing doubts about my adequacies and God's faithfulness.

Regular walks along the beach had become my refuge. I could read Scripture in solitude and cry out to God as loudly as I wanted knowing that those cries would be swallowed up in the sounds of the waves.

One day I sat and watched the waves as they would roll in . . . flow out . . . roll in . . . flow out. The Holy Spirit began to speak to me. "Do you see how those waves continually rush in and drift out? Your heavenly Father made them do that and they have done so without fail for thousands of years."

That Spirit proclamation pierced my despair and revealed a life-changing truth. Life has a rhythm, an ebb and flow. There is a time of high tide and a time of low tide; a time when the waves are roaring in with force and power, a time when the waters are quietly receding. But rising or falling, God has set the boundaries and is in control. Solomon said, "To everything there is a season, A time for every purpose under heaven" (Ecclesiastes 3:1).

Live in the flow of God. Rejoice and move forward when events are cresting. Remain constant when life is receding. God is as constant and faithful as the continuously breaking waves upon the shore. Just as the rhythm of those waters will not cease, so God's watchful care and clear direction will not cease. He will not fail.

. . . PRAYER . . .

Father, help me to be at rest in Your unfailing love and confident in Your purpose for my life.

. . . TODAY'S THOUGHT . . .

The God who created and controls the waves of the sea will remain constant in our lives in spite of circumstances.

—David A. Stephens
Superintendent of Alpha Conference, AL, IPHC

February 20

GOD HEARS US WHEN WE PRAY

Now this is the confidence that we have in Him, that if we ask anything according to His will, He hears us. And if we know that He hears us, whatever we ask, we know that we have the petitions that we have asked of Him. (1 John 5:14-15)

I accepted Jesus as my Lord and Savior in 1963. One of the things that led to this decision was the testimonies of a group of youth who had been born again while attending a Methodist church youth camp. As they were sharing about how real and alive God is, one of them said, "You can pray and God will hear you when you pray."

I had suffered with hay fever for a number of years and on the Monday morning after my salvation experience on Sunday, I awoke with a head cold in addition to the hay fever. I was so congested I could hardly talk. I was a certified public accountant and on this particular day I was to help a client obtain a bank loan. As I walked toward my vehicle I was thinking about how bad I felt and how I did not feel like meeting with bankers or clients. As I was about to start my car, it was as if I heard the testimony of that young person the night before saying, "You can pray and God will hear you when you pray." So I prayed a simple prayer, "Dear God, please give me some relief from this head cold." As I backed my car out of the driveway into the street, it suddenly occurred to me that I was totally healed, not only from a cold but also hay fever. That was in 1963 . . . and 33 years later I am still healed. Through the years I have discovered that what those young people shared that Sunday is still true. God does hear us when we pray.

. . . PRAYER . . .

Father, thank You for Your healing power working in my body. I receive it now in Jesus' name.

. . . TODAY'S THOUGHT . . .

James 4:2 says, "Yet you do not have because you do not ask." Find out what His will is and ask of Him. He will do exceedingly, abundantly, above all you could ask or think.

—Gene H. Evans
Treasurer, FGFCM

February 21

PRAYER WORKS MIRACLES

"The effective fervent prayer of a righteous man avails much." James 5:16b

The day started out as usual for our family. Joshua, our four-year-old was his normal, quiet self, while Jeremy, our three-year-old was talking non-stop about everything. We three climbed in the truck and started down the driveway. Reaching the main road, we made a left turn toward our destination. The sun was rising and was very bright.

Suddenly, the emergency stop light from the fire station came on. Two cars in front of us stopped, and I managed to stop. However, a truck was approaching fast from the rear, and the driver, blinded by the intense morning sun, was not stopping. Looking into the rearview mirror a second before impact, I yelled "JESUS" at the top of my lungs while reaching for my boys. The impact was bone shattering! Our vehicle was thrown into the one in front of us which dislodged the seat, throwing both boys into the windshield, breaking their noses on impact.

We were rushed to the hospital only to discover that Jeremy had severe back injuries also. The hospital said they were unable to handle his injury, and sent us immediately with the x-rays to Scottish Rite Children's Hospital in Atlanta. The impact had twisted his spine so much they believed he had spinal cord damage.

Leaving the hospital, we went to our church where the prayer team was praying. We anointed Jeremy, calling on Jesus' healing power. A calmness and peace came over my wife and I as we prayed.

At Scottish Rite a thorough evaluation was made. The doctors came out puzzled and ordered new x-rays. The new x-rays were compared with the old ones. The second set showed no signs of spine injury or any indication the spine was ever damaged! We give God the glory for a healing miracle through Jesus' Name! God still hears and answers the prayers of His people.

. . . PRAYER . . .

Father, increase my faith to believe regardless of my circumstances and human limitations. I pray I may understand that You desire to do wonders and miracles in my life and in Your church today. I give You all praise, honor, and glory as the Lord of my life. Amen.

. . . TODAY'S THOUGHT . . .

God still moves in miracles and healings today. It is not for us to decide what the miracle will be or when it will take place. However, it is left to us to believe God for the miracle.

—Spencer T. Selph
Pastor, New Covenant COG, McDonough, GA

February 22

IN GOD'S BACK POCKET

And do not be conformed to this world, but be transformed by the renewing of your mind, that you may prove what is that good and acceptable and perfect will of God. (Romans 12:2)

After my first conversation with Joe, I questioned in my heart if he would ever be able to lead a normal life again. I was pastoring a church in Concord, a bedroom community of San Francisco. Joe's brother-in-law had brought Joe to our church for help. Joe's history included years of drug addiction and financing his habit through burglaries. As a result of years of a self-destructive lifestyle, he could not even put a sentence together to express himself properly. I wondered, *Have too many brain cells been destroyed? Can he ever carry on a meaningful conversation?*

It was apparent from our first meeting that Joe truly wanted help and knew God was his only hope. With encouragement, he made a commitment to God and committed to reading the Bible. It was a struggle for Joe, but good things began to happen. His improved clear thinking was evidenced by his ability to verbalize entire sentences.

Joe had found a way to renew his mind—reading God's Word. The Word was true: "but be transformed by the renewing of your mind." God was renewing and healing Joe's mind.

Leading a Bible study at a men's prayer breakfast, I shared from 1 Peter 2:9. Emphasizing the meaning of "a peculiar people" (KJV), I explained that we are God's special possession, much like a purse or wallet is a person's private possession. Joe exuberantly responded, "Wow, does that mean I'm in God's back pocket?" Yes, Joe, you are in God's back pocket; you are His possession.

Today Joe shares Christ with a clear mind, declaring that God is willing to give "whosoever will" a new beginning.

. . . PRAYER . . .

Thank You, Father, for Your holy Word which has power to renew our mind, transforming us, giving us a new beginning.

. . . TODAY'S THOUGHT . . .

Transformation indicates we can have a spiritual metamorphosis from failure to success, from death to new life in Christ. Truly we are God's special possession.

—James D. Gee
General Superintendent, PCOG

February 23

A LIFE WORTH LIVING

But none of these things move me; nor do I count my life dear to myself, so that I may finish my race with joy, and the ministry which I received from the Lord Jesus, to testify to the gospel of the grace of God. (Acts 20:24)

When I gave my heart to Jesus a few days before my 18th birthday, I was a high school dropout, going to nightclubs and working in a movie theater. I had given the devil 100 percent of my life up to that time, and I determined I was going to give Jesus 100 percent. I never had to worry about backsliding because I made up my mind that day to live a life pleasing to the Lord Jesus Christ.

I often tell my congregation that I live for the day when I will meet Jesus face to face and hear Him say, "Well done, good and faithful servant." Nothing else in life matters to me as much as pleasing Jesus.

My focus in life is on "all the world" and "every creature" that Jesus came to redeem from sin, sickness, fear, and death. Jesus said, "Do you not say, 'There are still four months and then comes the harvest'? Behold, I say to you, lift up your eyes and look at the fields, for they are already white for harvest!" (John 4:35). God, as a husbandman, waits with long patience for the precious fruit of the earth that He wishes not to perish (Matthew 9:38; 2 Peter 3:9).

I wish there weren't a hell. I wish no one would die and be lost forever. John 3:16 says, "For God so loved the world that He gave His only begotten Son, that whoever believes in Him should not perish but have everlasting life." Jesus said, "I am the way, the truth, and the life. No one comes to the Father except through Me" (14:6). A life worth living is one that shares the good news with sinners that they can have eternal life through the Lord Jesus Christ.

. . . PRAYER . . .

Heavenly Father, I ask You to make my life count for eternity. Help me to share with others this good news about Your love and kindness to sinners.

. . . TODAY'S THOUGHT . . .

"Only one life, soon it will pass. / Only what's done for Christ will last." (Lanny Wolfe).

—John Osteen
Pastor, Lakewood Church, Houston, TX

February 24

GENERATIONAL LEGACY

"As for Me," says the Lord, "this is My covenant with them: My Spirit who is upon you, and My words which I have put in your mouth, shall not depart from your mouth, nor from the mouth of your descendants, nor from the mouth of your descendants' descendants," says the Lord, "from this time and forevermore." (Isaiah 59:21)

When I was a small boy, I was sure that my dad was probably the strongest man in the world. He was not only physically strong, but also morally and spiritually stalwart. I never knew my dad to lie to me or try to deceive me in any way. He was not only a man of faith, but he was filled with hope.

I was convinced that God did whatever my dad asked in prayer. Through Dad I came to understand God's omnipotence, His omniscience, and His tenderness and love. I saw my dad weep before it was acceptable for real men to cry. I felt his strong arms draw me to his chest as he would kiss me on the cheek. My dad was indeed God personified to this son.

My dad's hands were hands of blessing. Some of the keen memories of my dad concern those hands. Whenever I had a pain, a broken bone, a toothache, or looked like I was running on less than all cylinders, I could count on Dad saying, "Son, we need to pray about that." Suddenly Dad's hands would come down on my head with all the glory of an Abraham blessing Isaac, or David turning over his kingdom to Solomon. I could actually sense a spirit of blessing and the presence of God. Even today I revel in those memories of my father's touch and coming to know the presence and power of the Holy Spirit.

How I thank God for the blessing Dad gave me. He left me a legacy of strength and a marvelous sense of inheritance. I truly believe that from all those blessings, my father gave me a tremendous sense of identity and destiny.

. . . PRAYER . . .

Thank You, Lord, for a generational blessing that has been such a sustaining force in my life.

. . . TODAY'S THOUGHT . . .

When one begins to understand God's perspective of generations, it then becomes imperative to bless your children.

—C. Dan LeLaCheur
Eugene Bible College, Eugene, OR

February 25

ONE SMOOTH STONE

David . . . took out a stone; and he slung it. (1 Samuel 17:49)

A most unwelcome lawsuit was thrust upon my husband, Bob. He felt he had no choice but to defend the position of the church. He spent many hours poring over volumes of legal briefs and documents, memorizing sections of the *Church of God Minutes* that dealt with conferences, deeds, and properties.

One morning as I began my devotions, the Spirit directed me to 1 Samuel 17. I recognized the old Sunday school story of David and Goliath. My mind asked, "This? You want me to study this?" Again, I was impressed to study this Scripture not for a day or week only but for the duration of this legal battle. Every morning for over a year I read, reread, and gleaned nuggets of hope and courage from David's account of his deliverance. The process proceeded and often events played out to parallel 1 Samuel 17 so that I couldn't tell if it was David's story or mine. I did know this: I had found a place to anchor my hope!

On the day of the trial, our lawyer began his appeal before the Superior Court judge and was able to keep the hearing focused on one single point of law rather than a dispute of facts and accusations which would have necessitated a lengthy trial or one by a jury. As the young attorney got into the heart of his presentation, it became clear that this was more than a brilliant mind at work; the Spirit was touching his mind so that he could cite verbatim from the *Book of Minutes* and state laws from memory.

A moment in this trial will be forever etched in my heart and memory. Through all the tension in that courtroom, the Holy Spirit so sweetly whispered to me, "There's your one smooth stone—it's now heading for its mark!" The judge ruled in favor of the Church of God.

. . . PRAYER . . .

Thank You, Lord of Hosts, that You still bring deliverance to your people!

. . . TODAY'S THOUGHT . . .

When you face off with the giants in your life and you know you are out of your element in the circumstance, it's better to trust not in what you know but in whom you have believed!

—Pat Daugherty
COG World Missions

February 26

GLANCING BACK AND LOOKING AHEAD

You shall rise before the gray headed and honor the presence of an old man, and fear your God: I am the Lord (Leviticus 19:32). And He took them [children] up in His arms, put His hands on them, and blessed them. (Mark 10:16)

These two verses, from the Old and New Testaments, describe how the Lord sees those who have preceded us and those who follow us. An important benefit that comes from being middle-aged, as I am, is the view we have upon arriving at the halfway point of our journey. Part of my time is spent looking back at what used to be, while other moments are given to seeing what lies ahead. In those times of reflection and projection, the pictures in my mind are usually focused on older and younger people who hold places of special significance to me. They often teach lessons that put the present into proper balance.

I remember the day—more than 20 years ago—when my little daughter crawled up on my chest while we were playing together on the carpet. With her curly head turned sideways, just below my chin, it was clear she was listening to my heartbeat. I said, "What do you hear, Andi?" She looked up with surprise in her eyes and replied, "I hear Jesus in there and I think He's eating breakfast!"

Then there was the time, late in my Dad's life, when we talked about the qualities that were part of the ministry of his pastor. Dad said, "He loves God, he loves God's Word, and he loves God's people." In one sentence I came to understand what needed to be true for my future days in the pastorate.

Glancing back and looking ahead . . . both views reveal simple truths that help define what is important, like, "Jesus is in my heart" and "the greatest thing is love." Our memories and imaginations are God's tools for helping us put the present into perspective.

. . . PRAYER . . .

Father, thank You for the lessons You teach us about life each day as we glance back and look ahead.

. . . TODAY'S THOUGHT . . .

By embracing the Lord's viewpoint of seniors and children—and the role they have in teaching us about life—our vision can be expanded far beyond our immediate needs and ourselves.

—Tim Peterson
Superintendent, FGC

February 27

LIBERATED FROM COMPARISONS

Peter, seeing him, said to Jesus, "But Lord, what about this man?" (John 21:21)

Why does God seem to hold me to one standard while applying another to others? Three times Christ asked Peter, "Do you love me?" Three times He followed Peter's response with an admonition to feed His sheep. Peter was frustrated and then sobered as Jesus revealed His plan for Peter's life. Peter couldn't resist wondering how his life's destiny compared with his friend's, John, as he queried, "What about this man?"

The enemy would love to cause us confusion about our identity. Comparison with others can cause us to sag with the discouragement of inferiority or be puffed up with an air of superiority, both of which impair our spiritual growth. Paul said, "For we dare not class ourselves or compare ourselves with those who commend themselves. But they, measuring themselves by themselves, and comparing themselves, among themselves, are not wise" (2 Corinthians 10:12).

I can always find someone who, by comparison, makes me feel proud and confident. There are also people whose talents, gifts, and favor with others can make me feel low and empty. The measurement of my life can't be public opinion, appearance, talent, or even charismatic appeal. Paul experienced the extremes of measurement. His Roman citizenship, education, and position of authority permitted him to assume a proud superiority. It justified his vain and contemptuous torment of Christians. Paul also knew the humiliation of having to blindly lean on the very people he had persecuted. By the measuring stick of human comparison, Paul went from being a somebody to a nobody. But he discovered freedom in Christ. "But what things were gain to me, these I have counted loss for Christ" (Philippians 3:7).

Focus on God's grace at work in your life. Humbly rejoice in your walk with Him. Release others to their own accountability before God. Build your life and identity on the solid rock of Jesus.

. . . PRAYER . . .

Jesus, I know that if I keep my eyes on You I don't have to worry about comparisons with people.

. . . TODAY'S THOUGHT . . .

". . . for in Him we live and move and have our being" (Acts 17:28).

—Randall A. Bach

Executive Director, Church Ministries, OBSC

February 28

GOD HAS A PLAN FOR YOU AND ME

. . . that you may prove what is that good and acceptable and perfect will of God. (Romans 12:2)

Soon after the Korean War began, I arrived in Okinawa as a soldier in the 29th Infantry Regiment. A few weeks later, my regiment was sent to Korea where many of my friends were wounded or killed. Headquarters stipulated that ten of us were to remain in Okinawa as instructors. My name was on the list, but at the time I had no idea why. During the two years I spent in Okinawa my mother began attending a Pentecostal church. After I was discharged, she invited me to revival services. I was wondrously saved, filled with the Spirit, and called to preach the gospel.

As I look back on my military experience and my life since then, I am keenly aware God has a plan for each of us. God has planned not only for our spiritual welfare but also for our home life, our work, and our adversities and victories. He doesn't want us to miss any part of His great plan for our lives. He knows about our circumstances and the paths we are walking. Many of us ask God to change our circumstances to suit our desires. Instead of pursuing our will, we should expect God's will to be revealed in and through our circumstances as we conform our will to His will.

We have this assurance: God knows what is best for us and makes all things work together for our good and for his purpose (Romans 8:28). We need His constant guidance and help to receive all the benefits and blessings He has planned for us. If we live in constant fellowship with God, the Holy Spirit will lead us to fulfill God's plan for our lives. We can have great influence when we are in the will of God.

. . . PRAYER . . .

Father, help me to lean not on my own understanding but to be sensitive to the gentle voice of the Holy Spirit so I may live in the center of Your plan.

. . . TODAY'S THOUGHT . . .

To know the plan of God is the highest of all wisdom and to fulfill it is to follow our Savior—"not My will, but Yours, be done" (Luke 22:42).

—French Arrington
Professor, COG School of Theology

February 29

THE POWER OF PRAISE

But at midnight Paul and Silas were praying and singing hymns to God, and the prisoners were listening to them. Suddenly there was a great earthquake, so that the foundations of the prison were shaken; and immediately all the doors were opened and everyone's chains were loosed. (Acts 16:25, 26)

When we praise God from our hearts, the power of praise rearranges even the most contrary circumstances of life. This is vividly illustrated in Acts 16:16-35. Paul and Silas had been cruelly beaten and thrown into a dungeon. Their offense? They had cast a spirit of divination out of a slave girl! They found themselves in a pathetic situation. Their cuts and bruises were excruciatingly painful; they were forced to sit with their feet in stocks; no light penetrated the darkness of their dank cell. Did these men of God give up hope and blame their plight on God? No! Instead, they turned to their only source of comfort and aid. With their thoughts focused on God, there burst forth from their lips resounding praises which at the midnight hour kept the other prisoners awake. As Paul and Silas praised God from their jail cell, suddenly there was a great earthquake and the foundations of the prison were shaken. Immediately all the doors were opened and the chains binding the prisoners fell loose.

Not only were Paul and Silas released by the astonishing miracle which the Lord wrought, but every other prisoner was also freed, and the jailer and his entire household were brought to Christ – all because men praised the Lord! Paul and Silas had a secret weapon that was unknown to those who persecuted them. By praising God they tapped a reservoir of dynamic Pentecostal power that brought positive victory and deliverance.

. . . PRAYER . . .

Father, help me to follow the example of David, who said, "I will bless the Lord at all times; His praise shall continually be in my mouth." (Psalm 34:1)

. . . TODAY'S THOUGHT . . .

Regularly and consistently expressing praises to the Lord brings a fuller, more joyous and more powerful Christian life.

—Dr. T. L. Lowery
Second Assistant General Overseer, COG

March 1

LET HIM HEAR

He who has an ear, let him hear . . . (Revelation 2:7)

Everyone thought I was reckless to travel to the prayer conference in the dead of winter and that I was foolhardy to drag my wife and new baby out with me. The meeting was to be held in Champaign, Illinois, in the center of the cornfields of the great prairies of the Midwest. The frigid winds were whipping the temperatures to record lows of sub zero in the double digits. But I had to go for I had heard from God about my son who could not hear.

Allan had a difficult birth with breathing problems. When he survived, we were joyous, but our joy was reserved because he could not hear. His eyes were dull to our voices as we cooed at him. When set before blaring stereo speakers, he made no response. The doctor banged a pan to evoke a frightened gesture, but again there was no response.

As I prayed for God to heal Allan, He whispered to me, "I will heal your son." I told my wife we were going to the prayer conference, and God was going to heal Allan. She rolled her eyes and started packing. I called my mother and said, "Mom, God told me He is going to heal Allan." She admonished me, "Well, if He doesn't, don't get bitter." Neither my wife's incredulity nor my mother's doubt discouraged me. I knew God was going to heal Allan.

During the message the Spirit said, "Now . . . now I will heal the boy." Embarrassment overcame me. I did not want to argue with God about propriety and the order of service, nor did I want to interrupt the minister's message. I was desperate enough to obey the Spirit's voice. I carried Allan to the altar. The minister stopped preaching, placed his fingers in Allan's ears and declared them open, then resumed preaching.

That night I called to Allan from across our motel room and for the first time he turned his head toward the sound of my voice!

. . . PRAYER . . .

God, help me to hear Your voice over the voices of doubt and fear.

. . . TODAY'S THOUGHT . . .

Your voice in my ear/your Word as my mirror/my purpose is clear/I'll walk without fear.

—Dan R. Dempsey
Pastor, Tampa People's Church, Tampa, FL

March 2

GOD IS FOR YOU

When I cry out to You, Then my enemies will turn back; This I know, because God is for me. (Psalm 56:9)

It is a most wonderful thing to know that the Lord God, the Commander of the armies of heaven, never slumbers or sleeps; that He cares for His children and their needs; that He hears us when we pray; that He never loses a battle; and that we, through Him, will do valiantly because He will cause our enemies to be trodden down!

Sometimes when we pray, it seems the answer will never come. We wait and often become discouraged and distressed thinking that we will lose the battle. But when we prayed according to the will of God, the day we prayed in faith believing, God heard and began to move on our behalf.

Sometimes we give up just before the answer comes. Battle fatigue sets in and our spirit begins to faint. But even if our mind faints, if our spirit man is full of God's Word, we will still be the winner. Hebrews 10:23 says: "Let us hold fast the confession of our hope without wavering, for He who promised is faithful." Our mind may say that it won't come to pass, but all the time our heart or spirit is saying, "The answer is on the way!"

My husband used a sermon illustration about setting a thermostat on a heating unit. Turn the thermostat in an extremely cold house to 75 degrees, and the house will not immediately get warm. But if the thermostat isn't touched, soon the house will be warm as toast. If you believe for something from God, pray in faith according to the will of God. Set your thermostat to "On" and don't touch the dial again because the very day you prayed and called for help, the process of providing your answer began.

. . . PRAYER . . .

Lord, I am thankful that You are for me and that You will turn back my enemies when I cry out to You.

. . . TODAY'S THOUGHT . . .

No matter what your circumstance today, rejoice in the truth that God is for you. When you cry out to Him, you can be assured the answer is on the way.

—Dodie Osteen
Pastor, Lakewood Church, Houston, TX

March 3

GOD PROTECTS US

For He shall give His angels charge over you, To keep you in all your ways. In their hands they shall bear you up, Lest you dash your foot against a stone. (Psalm 91:11-12)

It was the climax of a glorious week of gospel meetings held in a remote village of Dominica. After resting for a part of the night, I arose at dawn and prayed for traveling mercies. I then started to drive the 40-mile country road to the airport to catch my flight to another destination. It was a dark, misty morning, and driving was somewhat hazardous. About three miles into the journey I suddenly lost control of the vehicle. I can remember nothing that took place immediately after.

About an hour later, I regained consciousness as two officers were lifting me from the porch of a house into an ambulance. They explained the car had crashed into a wall some distance away and I was thrown through the windshield. I landed several feet from the wreckage. I sustained major concussions, broken ribs, and my face was badly disfigured with cuts and bruises from the broken windshield.

How did I get to this house? Physically it was impossible for me to have traveled the distance from the wrecked car to the house. There was no traffic or activity this early in the morning. The homeowner who called the authorities explained that she was awakened by a knocking on her door. When she opened the door, she was shocked to see me collapsed on her porch, wounded and bleeding profusely. I have no recollection as to how I got there. I believe it was a miracle! The Lord rescued me from death and carried me to a place of refuge! In spite of much pain, the process of healing continued. I also continue to thank the Lord for His protection.

. . . PRAYER . . .

Thank You, Lord, for journeying mercies. You have promised to protect us as we travel on the busy highways of life, and we are grateful for Your constant presence in all circumstances of life.

. . . TODAY'S THOUGHT . . .

"Yea, though I walk through the valley of the shadow of death, I will fear no evil; For You are with me; Your rod and Your staff, they comfort me" (*Psalm* 23:4).

—Rufus R. Rogers
Regional Overseer, Northeast Region, COGOP

March 4

THE SPIRIT FLOWS

Do not quench the Spirit. (1 Thessalonians 5:19)

The Christian life is really very simple. Often, we try to make the Christian life complicated. If we cannot understand a teacher or his teachings, we label them "profound." But the Spirit walk is so simple, many don't believe it. We think we must produce something or accomplish something to walk in the Spirit. But, no—the price has already been paid. Although that seems too simple, we finally accept it. At that very moment the Holy Spirit moves into our house to live.

When He comes in, several things begin to happen. First, He comes in to lead us according to the Bible. He leads us by His book because, after all, He wrote it. That's why I don't understand why some people are always looking for men to lead them. Of course, God does use people, but why take second-best. The Holy Spirit-inspired Bible provides all the guidance we will ever need. But that's not all. The Holy Spirit comes to teach us. This wonderful Holy Spirit comes in to comfort, to strengthen, to fill, and to cleanse.

No one has to tell a river to flow. If no one blocks it, it will flow automatically. No one has to tell the Holy Spirit to do His work. If we quit bothering and blocking Him, He will do His work. It's the natural thing, just as it is natural for birds to fly and fish to swim and the sun to shine and the river to flow. No one needs to encourage Him; we just must not discourage Him.

It is the natural thing for the new nature that comes in with the Holy Spirit to receive the work of the Holy Spirit, so let Him who is now within you do what He will.

. . . PRAYER . . .

Holy Spirit, I yield myself to You and I pray that You will allow my path to cross the paths of those whom Jesus would help if He walked in the shoes I walk in today.

. . . TODAY'S THOUGHT . . .

I have found that all God wants is for us to yield ourselves. He will do the work if we just get out of the way and let Him.

—Tommy Barnett (Reprinted from *SpiritWalk: Daily Devotions on the Holy Spirit* by permission of Pathway Press)
Pastor, First Assemblies of God, Phoenix, AZ

March 5

THE SPIRIT COMES

Be still, and know that I am God. (Psalm 46:10)

I'm so thankful for the Holy Spirit in my life! I was not raised in a Pentecostal church but was introduced to its worship when my father received the Holy Spirit and was not allowed to stay in our denomination and openly share his testimony. Today, after 30 years, I continue to marvel and rejoice when the Holy Spirit comes to minister in a roaring, mighty, refreshing wind or when wave after wave of His power moves across a congregation. Yet it is also awesome to me when He comes in the still, small ways to speak peace to my heart and soul.

Our twin sons were born 10 weeks prematurely. Adam continued to see a pediatric heart specialist who told us several weeks after his release that he required surgery to correct a heart defect. Additional tests were done, the procedure was discussed, and the team of surgeons reached agreement. On the day Adam was to be admitted, my husband and I sat in the car and prayed for him one more time before entering the hospital. We prayed a sincere but simple prayer. We felt a powerful presence of the Spirit. A peace and a hope filled our hearts. It was not a mighty move of the Spirit, just a calm and reassuring peace.

Before his surgery, a nurse took Adam for a final series of x-rays to compare with the ones taken the day before. They marked his body with black markers for the surgical procedure. We waited and continued to pray. Later, the surgeon summoned us to his office and displayed the x-rays for my husband and me. He said he could not understand or explain but there was no longer a defect in Adam's heart! Praise God! We took our son home, healed and whole in his body.

. . . PRAYER . . .

Dear Heavenly Father, I praise You for the Holy Spirit that strengthens, directs, and makes a difference. Thank You for Your Spirit that comes to minister in the times of mighty and powerful outpourings as well as the times when the still, small, transforming touch of His presence makes the difference in my life.

. . . TODAY'S THOUGHT . . .

God's presence sometimes comes quietly, but with it comes His awesome power.

—Dee Cason
Administrative Assistant COG Executive Offices

March 6

STOP! LOOK! LONG ENOUGH TO SEE

But the Lord said to Samuel, "Do not look at his appearance or at the height of his stature, because I have refused him. For the Lord does not see as man sees; for man looks at the outward appearance, but the Lord looks at the heart." (1 Samuel 16:7)

John and Bill often walked a winding path in a forest. John would stop constantly to gaze at the beautiful surroundings. Bill would urge him to continue the journey. One day, John turned to Bill and said, "Stop! Look! Long enough until you really see."

Bill decided to stop and look. He saw for the first time two cottontail rabbits playing beneath a bush. He saw, high on a limb, a robin singing a lovely melody that could have only been taught by God. He saw the waters coming down from snowcapped mountains, cascading through the valley.

Do you stop and look long enough to see? When you look at a person, do you stop and look long enough or do you only see the color of his skin? Or the place from which he comes? Or the house in which he lives? Do you really realize you might be looking at a child of God?

Jesus gave a classic demonstration of the text when a woman of supposedly ill repute visited him. Simon had invited Jesus to his home for the purpose of deciding whether or not He was the Son of God. He omitted the usual custom of washing the feet of his guest. The woman rushed into this gathering of men and proceeded immediately to wash the feet of Jesus with grateful tears that fell from her eyes. The Bible records that she dried them with her hair.

Simon the Pharisee said to himself, "This man, if He were a prophet, would know who and what manner of woman this is who is touching Him, for she is a sinner" (Luke 7:39).

The Scripture says Jesus read his thoughts and said, in effect, "Stop! Look! Long enough until you really see."

. . . PRAYER . . .

Dear God, open our eyes that we might see You in everything and everybody.

. . . TODAY'S THOUGHT . . .

"Man looks at the outward appearance, but the Lord looks at the heart" (1 Samuel 16:7).

—Bishop Chandler D. Owens
Presiding Bishop, COGC

March 7

FINISH THE COURSE WITH JOY

"But none of these things move me; nor do I count my life dear to myself, so that I may finish my race with joy." (Acts 20:24)

This is one of the most powerful verses of scripture in the New Testament because it deals with how a person completes his life in the Spirit. It isn't how we start as it is how we finish this race. From the time we commit our life to Jesus Christ until we reach our final destination, the devil will do everything in his power to hinder our walk with Christ. He will try to destroy our faith, rob us of our joy, distract us from our service to the Master, and keep us from a productive, victorious, joyful journey in the Holy Spirit.

In Acts chapter 2, the 120 souls in the upper room received the promise of the Father which was the outpouring of the Holy Spirit. This was the fulfillment of Joel, chapter 2. The disciples would never be the same again. They lost their timidity and fear and boldly proclaimed the resurrection of Jesus and the enduement of power through the infilling of the Holy Spirit. They were persecuted, thrown into prison, and some gave their lives because of their testimony. But, listen to their testimony of victory in Acts 20:24. They were sold out to Christ. Everything they did pointed to their final reward. John 5:29 "And come forth-those who have done good, to the resurrection of life, and those who have done evil, to the resurrection of condemnation."

Listen to Paul's final testimony to Timothy in chapter 4, verses 7 and 8: "I have fought the good fight, I have finished the race, I have kept the faith. There is laid up for me the crown of righteousness, which the Lord, the righteous Judge, will give to me on that Day, and not to me only but also to all who have loved His appearing."

In a marathon in Chicago, a woman who had trained for the race finally had the opportunity to compete, but before she could cross the finish line, she had a heart attack and died. A sad ending to a beginning with great hope. Don't allow anything to affect your heart that would prevent you from crossing the finish line with great joy.

. . . PRAYER . . .

Lord help us to keep our eyes on You whereby we will not be distracted from the course set before us.

. . . TODAY'S THOUGHT . . .

Today and every day, I will focus upon the One Who saved me and Who is able to keep me in every situation of life.

—Dr. G. Dennis McGuire
First Assistant General Overseer, COG

March 8

LIVING ON A HIGHER PLANE

Though the fig tree may not blossom, Nor fruit be on the vines; Though the labor of the olive may fail, And the fields yield no food; Though the flock may be cut off from the fold, And there be no herd in the stalls—Yet I will rejoice in the Lord, I will joy in the God of my salvation. (Habakkuk 3:17-18)

My wife, Peggy, and I were on a World Missions tour visiting Haiti. For three days we had seen unbelievable poverty. Children with no clothing, families with no homes—not even a shelter. The hollow look on the faces of the poor people was a look of utter hopelessness.

There was a noticeable exception. The people of God! Even though most of them were also poor, they had smiles on their faces and purpose in their hearts. It was evident they were citizens of another country.

Wednesday night our group attended worship at the Rue-De-Centre Church in Port-au-Prince. We arrived about 15 minutes before scheduled service time, but they were already joyously worshipping God. The building was packed beyond intended capacity. Although we did not understand their language, we recognized the old song they were singing, "No One Ever Cared for Me Like Jesus." We were overwhelmed with the intensity of their worship, the pouring out of their hearts to God, the obvious loving relationship they had with God. A big lump came in my throat, and Peggy began to weep. One of the Haitian ladies, apparently thinking we did not understand how to worship, tapped Peggy on the shoulder and in broken English instructed, "No cry. Clap!"

We were so moved by their worship because for three days we had seen poverty, hunger, and desperation on every hand. It was their relationship with God that lifted them higher than life's conditions. They were living on a higher plane.

. . . PRAYER . . .

Thank You, Lord, for Your grace that lifts us higher than the circumstances of our lives.

. . . TODAY'S THOUGHT . . .

The Lord said to Paul, "My grace is sufficient for you, for My strength is made perfect in weakness" (2 Corinthians 12:9). Worship in times of uncertainty, need, or even fear, is an expression of faith in our loving heavenly Father.

—James A. Decanter
Pastor, Ruddle Rd, Blytheville, AR, COG

March 9

CHRIST IS MY HEALER!

He Himself took our infirmities and bore our sicknesses. (Matthew 8:17)

Alsop Street, on which I was born, ran through the middle of the poorest neighborhood in my hometown. In the dead of winter the doctor came to deliver me knowing he would never get paid. I had what was called "water head." I also had a hole in my heart. The doctor left no doubt thinking I would die; he never recorded my birth certificate.

My parents had 14 children. We lived in a three-room shack. My dad was a drunkard. The welfare lady would come and write my mother a note so she could go to the store and get food.

During my growing years, my head gradually became almost normal in size, but my heart still had a defect. I had spinal meningitis, diphtheria, and scarlet fever at different times. Three times I was given up to die.

When I started to school, I was told that if I didn't run, jump, laugh, cry, and get nervous or scared or too excited, I might live to be 16 years old. When I was 15, I was told my body had outgrown the ability of my heart to carry it and I had six months to live.

One Thursday night in August, 1951, I heard a lady singing at a Church of God tent revival three blocks from my home. She was singing "Something Got Hold of Me." Though I had never been to church, I went to the revival.

When I got there, the same thing that had hold of her got hold of me. Jesus saved me and healed me completely. Since then I have served three years in the U.S. Army, completed college, earned a doctorate, managed my own business, evangelized for eight years and pastored for 22 years. Today I pastor a large and growing church. From the day Christ healed me, I have never had another serious illness. Christ is my Healer!

. . . PRAYER . . .

Lord, You have a purpose for my life. You have borne my sicknesses, sins, sorrows, and burdens. I praise You today for salvation, healing, and deliverance. They are mine through the promise of Your Word.

. . . TODAY'S THOUGHT . . .

There is a purpose for every life! No matter what circumstances into which you were born, seek God until you find your purpose!

—Franklin Hunt
Pastor, COG, Fayetteville, NC

March 10

TRUSTING THE PATH

Jesus said to him, "I am the way, the truth, and the life. No one comes to the Father except through Me." (John 14:6)

My wife, Teri, and I were taking a few days to rest, relax, and regroup in the mountains of North Georgia. During one of our morning excursions we saw a sign: Dukes Creek Falls, two miles. We decided to take the two-mile hike to the falls.

Teri and I eagerly anticipated the moment we would see the falls. We had only traveled a few hundred yards down the winding path when I noticed that it turned sharply.

Although we could hear the falls to the right of us, the path took a sharp turn to the left, clearly leading us away from the falls. I convinced Teri to turn right and settle for a glimpse of the falls through the underbrush and trees. We read a devotion and prayed for the renewing of God's grace. After a few moments of meditation we began the steep incline back to the car. Then, God spoke to my spirit and told me that I did not trust the path.

What a sobering moment! I began to reflect on all the times I had settled for glimpses of God's grace and glory instead of trusting the path to the splendor of His fullness. Instead of seeing Him clearly, I had settled for "underbrush revelations." His grace was clouded by the twigs of my self-will. His peace was veiled by the branches of my cognition. His joy was seen only from a distance. Instead of trusting Him as the path, I set out on my own often becoming frustrated at the twists and turns in this Christian walk.

Once confronted by God, I repented, asked the Holy Spirit to be my guide, and began to trust God's grace to be my strength for the journey. Yes, I did return to Dukes Creek Falls, and by following the path I beheld the spectacular view in its fullness.

. . . PRAYER . . .

Father, enable me by Your grace to follow the path, knowing You will never leave me to find my way alone.

. . . TODAY'S THOUGHT . . .

"O Lord, I know the way of man is not in himself; It is not in man who walks to direct his own steps" (Jeremiah 10:23).

—Lanis Lewis
State Overseer, GA COGOP (former)

March 11

GOD'S WORD IS POWERFUL

For the word of God is living and powerful, and sharper than any two-edged sword, piercing even to the division of soul and spirit, and of joints and marrow, and is a discerner of the thoughts and intents of the heart. (Hebrews 4:12)

I was experiencing what seemed to be the worst trial of my life. The anxiety and emotional strain were taking their toll on my physical and spiritual being. Night after night, I lay down exhausted, yet sleep would not come to my eyes nor rest to my mind. My tears would run down the sides of my face, moistening my pillow. From one side to the other I would turn, trying to find comfort. My prayers were continual.

One night, as I turned toward the bedside table, the dim light of the digital alarm illuminated the cover of my Bible. I stared at its closed leather cover. As I reached for God's Word, Psalm 91:1-2 came to my mind. "He who dwells in the secret place of the Most High Shall abide under the shadow of the Almighty. I will say of the Lord, 'He is my refuge and my fortress; My God, in Him I will trust.'" Suddenly, God's Word became powerful to me.

I took my Bible and laid it on my chest. For the first time in many days, I began to relax as I felt the Word begin to penetrate my very being. Its words played over and over in my mind. The power of the Word of God became a reality to me for the first time in my life. I understood the words of the Psalmist: "I will both lie down in peace, and sleep; For You alone, O Lord, make me dwell in safety" (Psalm 4:8). God's Word can go deep into the hurting heart of man to bring peace and comfort.

. . . PRAYER . . .

Father, thank You for Your Word. May we learn to put our confidence in it as we lean on You.

. . . TODAY'S THOUGHT . . .

When God makes a promise, you can be sure it will be kept. God's Word is His promise to you.

—Reggie Powers
Assistant General Overseer, PFWB

March 12

GOD IS GOD AT MIDNIGHT

But at midnight Paul and Silas were praying and singing hymns to God. (Acts 16:25)

My first pastoral appointment was to a small, rural church. I was honored, excited, challenged, and scared. I was employed full time and drove 60 miles round-trip several times weekly to minister.

One of our faithful members became sick and was taken to Georgia Baptist Hospital in Atlanta. The diagnosis was that she would never again walk. Her husband needed her to help care for their several small children. Many people began to pray for a miracle of healing.

As I prayed one evening about 8:30 p.m., the Holy Spirit said I should go to Georgia Baptist and pray for Inez. It was almost 100 miles to the hospital, and I told the Lord I would go the next day immediately after work. I still felt a strong impulse to go and could find no relief until I finally said "yes" to the late evening divine directions.

My wife and I made the 100-mile journey. Arriving at midnight, I knew it would be difficult to get in with guards and nurses inquiring about our presence. I asked the Lord to make it possible. We parked and went to the fourth floor, never seeing one guard or nurse. I knew the Holy Spirit had sent us on this mission to this well-protected inner-city hospital.

We pushed the door open. Inez sat up in bed and said, "How did you know I prayed for the Lord to send someone to pray for me?" I didn't try to explain, but simply read a Scripture and calmly laid my hands on her as we prayed for her healing.

Suddenly, she leaped over the end of her bed and began dancing all over her room on both feet sounding out high praises to God. She was instantly healed! She went home soon, lived almost 30 more years, raised her children, and went home to be with the Lord. God is still God at midnight!

. . . PRAYER . . .

Dear Father, Help us to trust You . . . even at midnight.

. . . THOUGHT FOR THE DAY . . .

In Hebrews 11:6 we learn: "God . . . is a rewarder of those who diligently seek Him." He will come to you!

—R. Edward Davenport
Pastor, COG, Buford, GA

March 13

WAIT ON THE LORD

Wait on the Lord; Be of good courage, And He shall strengthen your heart; Wait, I say, on the Lord! (Psalm 27:14)

I received the baptism of the Holy Spirit when I was 10 years old. I am a third generation Pentecostal so I had some knowledge of the Holy Ghost and His workings in my life. After my Pentecostal baptism I became more aware of the Spirit's leading.

As I entered my teenage years, I realized I must become more dependent on the Holy Spirit. The pressures of my peers, society, and school were offering me choices I knew were not of God. I wanted to do right, but the enemy was there at every turn to tempt me to do wrong. During my devotions, my soul was fed and my cup was filled. Without these times with my Father and His precious Holy Spirit, I would never have survived spiritually.

All my friends were applying and being accepted to the colleges of their choice. I wanted to attend my church school, Lee College, but to do so I would have to have a financial miracle. I was a good student and I had done my best, but it seemed all my studying had been futile.

One evening after an incredibly hard week, I fell across my bed, my soul crying out to God for a solution to my problem. After literally crying until I was exhausted, I opened my eyes and saw my Bible lying open on the foot of my bed. My eyes were drawn to Psalm 27:14. There I found my answer: wait on God! I didn't need to work out the problem. All I had to do was wait.

Within one week God had provided my miracle. I had scholarships enough to cover an entire year of tuition and room and board. God had heard my cry and honored my petition.

. . . PRAYER . . .

Dear Father, help me to slow down and wait on You so I might have my heart strengthened and my life renewed.

. . . TODAY'S THOUGHT . . .

"But those who wait on the Lord Shall renew their strength; They shall mount up with wings like eagles, They shall run and not be weary, They shall walk and not faint" (Isaiah 40:31). Teach me, Lord, to wait.

—Barbara Fulbright
COG School of Ministry

March 14

OLD SOLDIERS NEVER DIE

"I have fought a good fight, I have finished the race. I have kept the faith."
(2 Timothy 4:7)

Douglas MacArthur became the ultimate soldier. He led the 42nd Rainbow Division during World War I, became Supreme Commander of the Southwest Pacific during World War II and was promoted to the rank of General of the Army, complete with five stars. As Supreme Commander of the Allied Powers, he accepted the surrender of Japan in 1945. Years later, he was Commander of the United Nations forces in Korea. Relieved of command in 1951, he returned to the U.S. to a hero's welcome. Announcing his retirement before Congress, he quoted the words of a ballad, "Old soldiers never die—they just fade away."

If ever there was a five star general in the army of Christ, it was Paul. He became one of the greatest champions for God and His cause, walking over the pagan world and lighting the lamp of the gospel. He turned every house into a chapel and every street corner into a pulpit. Under the inspiration of the Spirit, he wrote more than half of the New Testament and influenced more than 2,000 years of Church history.

See him, though, in Rome, not a hero, but a prisoner. He faces more than the end of a career: he faces the end of his life at Maritime Prison. From death row, he sends his last words to Timothy: "I have fought a good fight. I have finished the race. I have kept the faith."

The past? No regrets. The present? No fear. The future? Bright with faith. No "fading away" for this soldier. "Finally, there is laid up for me the crown of righteousness, which the Lord, the righteous Judge, will give me on that Day, and not to me only, but also to all who have loved His appearing" (2 Timothy 4:8).

Fighting, finishing, keeping. Is anything more important?

. . . PRAYER . . .

My heavenly father, help me to keep my priorities in order. Grant me the fullness of Your grace and power that I might fight the fight, finish the race, and keep the faith. For he that endures to the end shall be saved.

. . . TODAY'S THOUGHT . . .

"He is no fool who gives what he cannot keep to gain what he can never lose" (Jim Elliot).

—Mark L. Williams
Pastor, Riverhills COG, Tampa, FL

March 15

THE SPIRIT ABIDES WITH US

According to the word that I covenanted with you when you came out of Egypt, so My Spirit remains among you; do not fear! (Haggai 2:5)

At times in our Christian lives and ministry we feel overwhelmed. We wonder if we can do all that confronts us. Discouragement, fear, even anger, creep into our lives. But in desperate times we discover the reality of Jesus' promise to send the Comforter.

The prophet Haggai spoke to the people of Israel at a time when they felt overwhelmed. The people of Israel had returned from the Babylonian exile to a devastated homeland. Jerusalem had been destroyed by Nebuchadnezzar's army. Israel's resources were limited and the labor was hard. The rebuilding project had so many limitations it was evident that the new Temple would not be as beautiful as the former one built by Solomon. What a situation! The good news for Israel was that the glory of God's Temple was not dependent on their resources or abilities. God would do what they could not. Therefore, the prophet Haggai could declare God's word of hope, "My Spirit is abiding in your midst, do not fear!"

We have the same promise for today. In the face of challenging circumstances we have the promise of divine presence and power. Jesus said, "I am with you always, even to the end of the age" (Matthew 28:20). The promise of Jesus' abiding presence through the indwelling of the Spirit gives hope. The Spirit empowers us to do what God calls upon us to do. Despite limited resources and human abilities, the Spirit will accomplish the work of God.

We are not passive spectators in Kingdom work. We must have the courage to do our part with confidence that the Spirit of God will do the rest: "'Not by might nor by power, but by My Spirit,' says the Lord of hosts" (Zechariah 4:6).

. . . PRAYER . . .

Thank You, Lord, for the promise of Your abiding presence in the Spirit. As we submit our lives to You, let Your Spirit empower us for Your service.

. . . TODAY'S THOUGHT . . .

May God "grant you, according to the riches of His glory, to be strengthened with might through His Spirit in the inner man" (Ephesians 3:16).

—R. Jerome Boone
Professor, Lee University

March 16

NO MORE A FOREIGNER

Therefore remember that you, once Gentiles in the flesh—who are called Uncircumcision by what is called the Circumcision made in the flesh by hands—that at that time you were without Christ, being aliens from the commonwealth of Israel and strangers from the covenants of promise, having no hope and without God in the world. . . . Now, therefore, you are no longer strangers and foreigners, but fellow citizens with the saints and members of the household of God. (Ephesians 2:11-12, 19)

I had just returned from casting a ballot in my first presidential primary. Exercising my rights as a citizen of the United States of America was truly a privilege. However, I noticed the polling station was not busy and a 25% turnout was predicted! I can hear someone say, "Sure you're excited. It's your first time! It will wear off!" I hope not.

In the days before Christ, there were only two people groups—Jews and Gentiles. My being a Gentile excluded me from the Abrahamic covenant, Moses' tabernacle, and access to a priestly mediator. Gentiles were aliens, strangers from the covenant of promise, having no hope, and without God in the world—foreigners. But aren't you glad that due to the sacrifice of our Savior we are "no longer strangers and foreigners, but fellow citizens" (Ephesians 2:19)?

I can remember April 23, 1993, when I, along with 1,800 foreigners from 77 countries, received the privilege of becoming a citizen of the United States of America. Although I had been residing in America since 1973, I only then acquired citizenship.

However high that honor is, there is one higher. The day in Lucknow, India, at the age of seven, when my name was written in the Lamb's Book of Life, and my new citizenship was accompanied by the Holy Spirit himself with all the privileges of His kingdom, I was no longer a foreigner.

. . . PRAYER . . .

Thank You, Lord, for accepting and including me in Your kingdom as a joint heir—a pure manifestation of Your grace.

. . . TODAY'S THOUGHT . . .

There are privileges and responsibilities of citizenship. Both allow us to be what He wants us to be.

—Samuel R. Chand
President, Beulah Heights Bible College, Atlanta, GA

March 17

THE BLESSINGS KEEP ON COMIN'

And Jesus took the loaves, and when He had given thanks He distributed them. . . . So when they were filled, He said to His disciples, "Gather up the fragments that remain, so that nothing is lost." Therefore they gathered them up, and filled twelve baskets with the fragments of the five barley loaves which were left over by those who had eaten. (John 6:11-13)

When Peniel Residential Drug/Alcohol Center was little more than a year old, people were hesitant to support us financially. Dorms were filled and people came from everywhere for help, but we had no money.

We had a past due utility bill for $2,000 on non-insulated and drafty dorms. The serviceman came to disconnect the utilities. Responding to the pleas of a desperate staff, the man accepted all the money they could scrape together—$25—which guaranteed service until 5:00 p.m.

When my husband and I arrived, the staff met us in a panic and told us what had happened. How could we raise $2,000 in a few hours? I decided to spend time with the Lord. I went to my office, sat at my desk, and stared straight ahead as in a trance. It was as though I could hear the laughter of the devil, "You'll never do this!"

Then the most extraordinary feeling came over me. I knew that our bank balance held only a little more than $100, but the Lord urged me to tally the recent bank deposit slips again. Not understanding, I recalculated. To my surprise, the total was hundreds of dollars more than I had remembered. I added again. This figure was more than the previous balance. Astonished, I added again. Now the amount was even greater than the previous two totals! I called my secretary: "Add these figures!" Guess what? The figure was even higher! The only thing left to do was for the deposits to be entered. The total was well over $2,000! We were in the middle of a miracle! God had met our need plus baskets more!

. . . PRAYER . . .

Lord, do it again! Make a way out of no way. Lord, I know that you can. Manifest Your presence, manifest Your love. You've done it before. Please do it again (Song by Henry Mackenzie Davis).

. . . TODAY'S THOUGHT . . .

God is the absolute and on time source to meet your urgent need.

—Marion Spellman
Director, Peniel Drug/Alcohol Ministries

March 18

WAITING BEFORE GOD

But those who wait on the Lord Shall renew their strength; They shall mount up with wings like eagles, They shall run and not be weary, They shall walk and not faint. (Isaiah 40:31).

Who likes to wait? No one! Whether we are delayed in traffic, waiting to meet the doctor or waiting for an answer to prayer, most of us want to hear the report and move on to other things. We do not like to wait! In our work for God, there are times when we can do nothing else but wait.

I perceive that waiting is a part of God's divine plan, too. Actually, there is a beautiful facet of the communion and fellowship we enjoy with our Father that can only come through those times of waiting before God. Until we have learned this truth there will be times of restlessness and feelings of being unfulfilled. Waiting on the Lord in prayer, though, has produced great benefits for Christians.

Waiting before God will renew God's presence in your life. Mark 1:35 tells us about Jesus: "Now in the morning, having risen a long while before daylight, He went out and departed to a solitary place; and there He prayed." It is God's presence that motivates us and provides the aura that attracts people to Jesus!

Waiting before God will renew physical strength and help you to maintain your health, vitality, and vision. It's possible to finish one busy day and still feel the refreshing presence of God.

Waiting before God will reveal priorities. You will receive your heavenly orders for that day in the order of His importance.

Waiting in God's presence will enable you to be sensitive to God's voice. It's important to know God's direction and timing and to have insights for both.

. . . PRAYER . . .

Father, thank You for the renewal of Your presence, Your strength and Your love one day at a time as I wait before You.

. . . TODAY'S THOUGHT . . .

In today's rush-and-hurry living, inner strength comes from David's words, "Be still, and know that I am God" (Psalm 46:10)!

—David Yonggi Cho

Founder, President, and Chairman, Pastor Cho's International Ministries

March 19

GOD'S MIRACULOUS HEALING POWER

"For I am the Lord who heals you." (Exodus 15:26)

When our granddaughter, Kaitlyn, was only a few days old, she was admitted to T.C. Thompson Children's Hospital in Chattanooga, TN, because of a serious digestive problem. She cried in pain constantly and could not take regular baby formula. After extensive tests, it was concluded that Kaitlyn had a possible birth defect of the digestive system. The doctors put her on a special formula and sent her home. If she did not improve in time, they said, the only solution would be major surgery to correct the problem.

Our family has seen the power of prayer many times, so we asked the people to pray for Kaitlyn's healing. The retired ministers and their spouses who met for prayer every Wednesday morning at the Church of God International Offices in Cleveland, TN, put Kaitlyn on their prayer list. Many churches and individuals also prayed constantly for her. But, despite all their prayers, no improvement was seen.

On Friday, at 3pm, my office telephone rang. On the line was Dr. Robert White, who was then serving as General Overseer of the Church of God. He was driving to Florida for a church dedication and at the time was in southern Georgia, near the Florida state line. "Tom, Kathy and I have been praying," Dr. White said. "We felt impressed to call you and tell you Kaitlyn is going to be alright."

About 6pm that same day, I talked to my daughter. "Dad, I'm not sure what is happening, but Kaitlyn seems better," Letetia said. The next morning, Kaitlyn, the baby who had been so desperately ill and faced possible major surgery, awoke well and whole – completely healed overnight!

That was five years ago. Today Kaitlyn is still healed. So completely healed, in fact, that one of her favorite places to eat is a Mexican restaurant!

. . . PRAYER . . .

Father, thank You for the healing You provide for Your people. Help us to trust in You always. Amen.

. . . TODAY'S THOUGHT . . .

When God's people pray, He intervenes miraculously.

—Tom George
Superintendent, Romanians, COG

March 20

GOD WILL FORGIVE US

If we confess our sins, He is faithful and just to forgive us our sins and to cleanse us from all unrighteousness. (1 John 1:9)

It was October 19, 1941, one week before my 16th birthday. The Sunday evening message was directed at the unsaved students of Emmanuel College and Academy. A Pentecostal preacher's son, I had never been converted. A young man prayed in the Spirit, moved down the aisle, reached across several students, and laid his hand on mine. The gentle tug he gave me was clearly God's call. I followed him to the altar. I wept. I repented. I longed for the assurance of acceptance by God. But, still void of peace, I wondered why I didn't feel saved.

Harry Bartholf sat down beside me. "Are you saved?" he asked.

"No, I don't feel like I'm saved." My answer reflected confusion concerning the basis of salvation. I did not know how to be saved.

Harry was about to do me the greatest favor of my life. He turned to 1 John 1:9 and asked me to read it. As I read, "If we confess our sins . . ." he stopped me. "What does it say you are to do?" he asked.

"It says I am to confess my sins."

"Have you done that?" he probed.

"Yes, as far as I know how," I replied.

"Read on," he said.

". . . He is faithful and just to forgive us our sins, and to cleanse us from all unrighteousness."

"What does God say He will do?" he asked. I read it again. Then Harry asked a simple question, "Do you think God will do what He promised?" In that moment it dawned upon me that my salvation was not based on my feelings, but on God's unfailing Word.

. . . PRAYER . . .

God, You said You would forgive me if I would confess my sins. I believe Your promise, and I trust You for my salvation.

. . . TODAY'S THOUGHT . . .

An all-consuming peace filled my being once I understood that I was accepted by God. From that night 55 years ago until this day, I have walked in that assurance.

—B. E. Underwood
Presiding Bishop, IPHC (former)

March 21

GOD LOVES YOU

In this is love, not that we loved God, but that He loved us and sent His Son to be the propitiation for our sins. (1 John 4:10)

In 1978, at 21 years of age, and between my first and second years at Bible School, I won an all-expenses-paid trip to Russia. At that time, I was trying unsuccessfully to escape the call of God upon my life.

Arriving in Russia, well before the days of recent freedoms there, I was met by a maze of bureaucratic red tape: "We don't give free trips to our country," "You're entering our country illegally," "You're liable for a 10-year prison sentence," and so on.

One night, I was homesick, discouraged, disoriented, and feeling alienated from God. Bleakness enveloped me. In desperation, I dropped to my knees and cried out, "Where are You, God? Do You care for me? Do You even know where I am at this moment?" Suddenly, I felt an urge to go for a walk in downtown Moscow. Leaving my hotel, it seemed I was being directed towards an embankment. Reaching it, I stopped and wearily lifted my head. Looking across the ravine, my eyes focused on three words painted in white on a rock, "God Loves You." The chances of ending up there on my own were slim—the chance of seeing such an inscription in a godless country was even more remote.

These three simple words were sufficient to carry me through my remaining time in Russia, reinforcing God's personal care and concern for me. And they have been sufficient to carry me through the twists and turns of my own life since that time.

The Apostle John mentioned love 27 times in 1 John chapter 4. In a plastic world where love is often misunderstood, misdefined, and misappropriated, the greatest realization is the fact of God's unconditional love for us.

. . . PRAYER . . .

Father, Your love for the world is boundless. Help us to accept it and to live in its power and under its domain.

. . . TODAY'S THOUGHT . . .

If God loved us so much that He sent His Son to be the expiation for our sins, we would do Him the greatest disservice by rejecting that love.

—Burton K. Janes
Pastor, PAN, St. Johns, Newfoundland

March 22

THE GOD WHO REVEALS HIMSELF

Therefore that disciple whom Jesus loved said to Peter, "It is the Lord!" (John 21:7)

My mother developed Alzheimer's disease, and we placed her in a home for such patients. Either my wife or I would visit mum each week. On one visit Ruth found that my mother had been crying. She asked one of the staff what had caused her to cry. The nurse replied, "Flora does this sometimes. She is so confused and doesn't know where she is. But we cheer her up. We just tell her a dirty joke, and she laughs!" My mother had probably never laughed at a dirty joke. She was a committed Christian and loved the Lord Jesus deeply.

Ruth persuaded my mum to go to her lovely private room. After they sat down together, Ruth asked my mother if she could pray. My mum could not speak coherently, but a miracle happened. My mum was able to say, "Yes." There was something in the concept of prayer that unlocked her mind for a moment to understand what was being said to her.

Ruth prayed for my mother and asked, "Mum, would you like to pray?" My mum could not pray coherently, but a miracle occurred. She said, "Dear Lord, I don't know who I am, I don't know what I am and I don't know where I am, but please love me."

In our darkest moments the Lord reveals Himself. John said: "It is the Lord!" When John realized this fact, he didn't murmur the statement to Peter. He must have yelled in his excitement and delight that the Lord he loved was there on the beach.

The Lord is not remote. He comes to His people in the dark times of our grief and need—as much, if not more, than in the good times. The excitement John felt was shared by Simon Peter, so much so that Peter put his clothes on and leaped into the water to get to the Lord.

. . . PRAYER . . .

Father, thank You that You never leave us alone to cope without You. You come to us at all times.

. . . TODAY'S THOUGHT . . .

God's Spirit comes to you with His love and the knowledge of Himself. He is not hidden. He is here!

—Clive R. Calver
The Evangelical Alliance

March 23

HE WAS THERE ALL THE TIME

And I will pray the Father, and He will give you another Helper, that He may abide with you forever. (John 14:16)

It was the beginning of the worst week of my life. An infection had raised my temperature to 105°. My blood sugar shot up to an astronomical high. My condition was critical. I thought, *This could be the end of the road for me.* As I left for the hospital, my son touched my shoulder and said, "It will be OK, Dad."

I prayed for healing, but nothing happened. My condition worsened. The doctors and nurses applied their skills. I continued to pray, asking: "Where are You, Lord?" I heard no sound. There was no voice like the sound of many waters, no whisper like a soft gentle breeze. There was no response to my prayer. Only silence!

My situation seemed hopeless. It seemed as if my life were slipping away. Alone in my hospital room, it was dark. The needles in my arms added to my pain. I prayed again, "Where are You, Lord? Come to my rescue, Lord, for Your name's sake." Then I heard His voice deep within my mind, heart, spirit, and soul. He spoke kindly to me. He called me by my name. This is what He said: "And I will pray the Father, and He will give you another Helper, that He may abide with you forever—the Spirit of truth, whom the world cannot receive, because it neither sees Him nor knows Him; but you know Him, for He dwells with you and will be in you" (John 14:16-17).

Speaking my name ever so kindly, He said, "I live in you; therefore, you have never been alone." With assurance He said, "I have walked with you in each agonizing moment. You can always depend on Me. I will never leave you." My healing came in His abiding presence.

. . . PRAYER . . .

Thank You, Lord, for Your presence in every testing time. You are with us all the time.

. . . TODAY'S THOUGHT . . .

My son said it best when he said "It will be OK, Dad." He echoed the promise of the Father in Isaiah 43:2, "When you pass through the waters . . . they shall not overflow you."

—C. Russell Archer
Superintendent, Eastern Region, OBSC

March 24

WITH CHRIST . . . FAR BETTER

For I am hard pressed between the two, having a desire to depart and be with Christ, which is far better (Philippians 1:23).

"George, your dad has gone to be with Christ." I was shocked and speechless. Sadness engulfed me. I felt cheated and lonely. At the same time, I had assurance of God's peace. Dad was "with Christ."

The Apostle Paul had the same cherished hope. He longed to be "with Christ" in conscious fellowship (1 Corinthians 13:12), for conscious existence (2 Corinthians 5:1-4), and for conscious enjoyment (1 Corinthians 15:51-58). This intense yearning was not for death, but for what follows death—living "with Christ!"

This hope of being "with Christ" comes from a better covenant (Hebrews 9:15). By it, Christ satisfies His Father's interests and becomes our mediator (1 Timothy 2:5). In fact, His sacrificial blood speaks better things than Abel's (Hebrews 12:24). While Abel's blood shouts murder and calls for justice, Christ's blood speaks of cleansing, forgiveness, and peace.

The writer to the Hebrews confirms being "with Christ" to be better than being with angels and priests. Christ has a better name (Philippians 2:8-9), a better position (Hebrews 1:3-4; 1 Peter 3:22), and a better ministry (Hebrews 8:6). Christ remains a priest forever (Hebrews 7:21-28) to provide us a better hope for drawing near to God (Psalm 73:28). Consequently, being "with Christ" will give us better possessions (Hebrews 10:34), a permanent country (Hebrews 11:16), and a better resurrection (Hebrews 11:35). "With Christ" means a better citizenship. All the redeemed, including my dad, will be happy in the city of their God (Philippians 3:20).

Although I am happy to know Dad is "with Christ," at times I envy him. And because I have wonderful childhood memories, I often misunderstand his passing. It is then that my own lines bless my soul: "Someday, someday; I'll understand it all someday. When my body is redeemed, And God's glory is revealed, I'll understand it all someday."

. . . PRAYER . . .

Heavenly Father, thank You for the better life and better hope You have given us through Your Son, Jesus Christ.

. . . TODAY'S THOUGHT . . .

It is not far better to die; it is far better to be "with Christ."

—George H. Dawe
Pastor, St. Johns, Newfoundland

March 25

PERSISTENCE REALLY PAYS

Therefore, my beloved brethren, be steadfast, immovable, always abounding in the work of the Lord, knowing that your labor is not in vain in the Lord. (1 Corinthians 15:58)

A lot of things were going in the wrong direction in my life. In fact, every day was a very difficult day. To make matters worse, every single day Roy Mauldin would ask me to go to church with him.

Roy and I worked together at a huge plant in Pensacola, Florida. Every day I would tell Roy the same thing: "No, I have no interest."

It never seemed to stop him. The next day he would ask me again to go to any kind of church function—Wednesday night prayer meeting, Sunday services, men's prayer group. I always answered Roy with one word: "No!"

Finally, one day when I was angry at what was happening in my life, angry at the whole world, Roy asked me once again. With a great deal of emotional anger I said, "Roy, I will go to church with you one time, *if* you will promise to never, ever, as long as you live, mention church to me again." That was all Roy needed.

He was the happiest I had seen him in months. On a Wednesday night, I chose to go to Roy's church with him. The minister preached as if the house were filled when in fact there were only 10-20 people there. But halfway through his message I felt the most compelling urge to go down and kneel at the altar.

It was the greatest day of my life. With Roy and the others praying with me, I wept my way through to a wonderful experience of salvation.

Persistence really pays off.

. . . PRAYER . . .

Father, I thank You for the persistence of a man who would not stop until he won me to the Lord. Help me to have the same persistence in reaching out to lost people.

. . . TODAY'S THOUGHT . . .

Our labor for the Lord is never in vain. Let's determine to be persistent in our efforts to win the lost to the Lord.

—Joe E. Edwards
Pastor, COG, Cartersville, GA

March 26

GOD'S HOLY SPIRIT GUIDES US

However, when He, the Spirit of truth, has come, He will guide you into all truth; for He will not speak on His own authority, but whatever He hears He will speak; and He will tell you things to come. (John 16:13)

As we make our journey from earth to Heaven we need a guide. This we have in the Holy Spirit. There is not a person in the world who knows anything about the way to happiness and Heaven without the Holy Spirit. We have never traveled this way before. Because of our forwardness we are often rash, heady, and obstinate; therefore, we rush on heedless of consequences. It is essential that we have this Guide.

This Guide promised to us is excellent. He has perfect knowledge of the way. This Guide knows every step of the way. He knows all truth and He knows where truth leads. He is faithful and trustworthy. When we place our trust in a guide we surrender ourselves to His care. Since our Guide is so familiar, this will make him a pleasant companion. As we journey, He will describe to us the scenery and will enlighten us concerning the objects along the way. This will endear Him and make our pilgrimage easier. The Holy Spirit will reveal profound truths to us concerning the Father's everlasting love and of the Savior's finished work. He may also show us some dangerous snares and pitfalls of the enemy that we must avoid.

Gospel truth is a pleasant way to walk in (Proverbs 3:17). There is nothing in this way to cause grief or distress.

. . . PRAYER . . .

Thank You, Holy Spirit, for being my guide. You are always present when I need You, just as Jesus promised: ". . . that He may abide with you forever" (John 14:16).

. . . TODAY'S THOUGHT . . .

In Him we have perpetual guidance. "The Lord will guide you continually" (Isaiah 58:11).

—Bishop James Martin
District Superintendent, North AL, CHC

March 27

GRACE OF GIVING

Not that I seek the gift, but I seek the fruit that abounds to your account. (Philippians 4:17)

Many years ago I learned the joy of giving, especially to the cause of world missions. Soon after coming into the Pentecostal Movement, I was taught that the Holy Spirit was given to empower us to be effective witnesses. This gave me a love for evangelism that has continued to this day. Very early in my Christian life I made my first faith commitment to missions. Since that time I have renewed and increased it many times. This is one way all are able to help evangelize the world.

As the years have gone by, I have had a growing appreciation for the words of the Apostle Paul quoted above. While my giving has helped others, it has been a greater blessing to me.

It is difficult to convince people they should give to the Lord's work not only because it is worthy, but because of the blessings they receive in return. I suppose it is like explaining to a child why our Lord said, "It is more blessed to give than to receive." Normally there is a response of total disbelief. We have also heard the statement, "You cannot outgive God." While this sounds good, many people are reluctant actually to put it to the test even though we are challenged to do exactly that in Malachi 3:10: "'Try Me now in this,' says the Lord of hosts."

The Apostle Paul tells us there is fruit that abounds to our account. Maybe he had in mind the words he wrote to the Corinthians: "And God is able to make all grace abound toward you, that you, always having all sufficiency in all things, may have an abundance for every good work" (2 Corinthians 9:8). The message is clear: by giving we receive even greater blessings from God.

. . . PRAYER . . .

Father, thank You for the grace of giving. May my life continue to bear good fruit for Your name's sake.

. . . TODAY'S THOUGHT. . .

Today I will meet someone and have an influence on his or her life. This meeting will also have an impact on my own life. May the fruit of that encounter be to the glory of God!

—Jesse D. Simmons
Director of Missions, IPHC (retired)

March 28

HEALING FOR YOU

But He was wounded for our transgressions, He was bruised for our iniquities; The chastisement for our peace was upon Him, And by His stripes we are healed. (Isaiah 53:5)

From the beginning of my ministry I had experienced what many refer to as divine health. Also, I had preached what I believe to be a balanced message regarding divine healing. God is both capable and willing to heal His children today as much as ever. Jehovah's words to the Israelites: "I am the Lord who heals you" (Exodus 15:26) and "I will take sickness away from the midst of you" (Exodus 23:25) are God's own words. No one has ever been able to change them. Matthew 8:17 declares that Jesus took our infirmities and bore our sickness.

That message had worked through the years, but on a July day sitting in my doctor's office clutching my wife's hand, I felt like the world had fallen completely around me. I heard these words: "Melanoma cancer has metastasized and has spread to your right lung, to inside your rib cage and into the lymph passages, resulting in at least three known tumors—all malignant. All of them have likely increased in size 1 million times in the past six months." He knew this because I had a chest X-ray just six months earlier.

I had several X-rays, CT scans, and blood tests that determined I tested positive for terminal cancer. To make matters worse, this type of cancer cells would respond to no known treatment.

After a few weeks, it was determined that I had perhaps one year left to live. I called the elders of the church and was anointed and prayed for according to James 5:14. One dear brother visited me daily for about 100 days and rebuked the cancers in my body.

Prayer and fasting followed, and in a few months I was declared to be completely cancer free without any medication whatsoever.

. . . PRAYER . . .

Father, thank You for forgiving all our sin and healing all our diseases.

. . . TODAY'S THOUGHT . . .

As the Lord increased the life of King Hezekiah 15 years, so He added years also to mine. He is not a respecter of persons (Romans 2:11). Trust in Him to do the same for you.

—Lee Roy I. Maxey

Assemblies of God International Fellowship, San Diego, CA

March 29

A SONG IN MY DARKEST NIGHT

I call to remembrance my song in the night. (Psalm 77:6)

I met Jesus at an altar in Memphis when I was 19 years old. I accepted the call to preach and attended Central Bible Institute in Springfield, Missouri, for a year. I began to evangelize, and for six months I devoted my life to fasting, praying, and preaching. But success eluded me. I seemed to preach too long or not long enough.

Going home for Christmas was a great relief. All the family was home. Everybody was happy. But in the midst of this happy family group, I was lonely, discouraged, and depressed. In my mind I decided to abandon preaching and pursue a secular profession. After Christmas dinner I went to the bedroom to take a nap. Feeling too unworthy to even lie on the bed, I fell to my knees—a miserable, wretched soul—and cried out to God. Job 35:10 kept ringing in my ears and pounding in my heart: "Where is God my Maker, who gives songs in the night?"

In a state of exhaustion and desperation I fell asleep. I don't remember how long I lay there, but suddenly I was awakened. Half-asleep and half-awake, I was aware of brilliant white lights flooding the entire room. Far away I could hear a choir singing. The sopranos, altos, tenors, and basses were blending into one intense stream of harmony; but I didn't recognize the song. As I lay there, awed by this great happening, I was afraid to move.

In a moment the room reverberated with the sound of music. I could understand the words the heavenly choir was singing: "God is still on the throne, and He never forsaketh His own; When troubles oppress us and burdens distress us, He never will leave us alone."

God gave me a song in the midst of my darkest night! That song refreshed my spirit, renewed my strength, and reminded me that my calling from God had never left me.

. . . PRAYER . . .

Thank You, Father, for lifting my spirit with the presence of Your Spirit through dreams, songs, and spiritual insights.

. . . TODAY'S THOUGHT . . .

In our darkest and most trying circumstances, the Holy Spirit will give us a song of encouragement in the night.

—James L. Slay (Reprinted from *SpiritWalk: Daily Devotions on the Holy Spirit* by permission of Pathway Press)
Professor, Lee University (former)

March 30

AGAINST ALL HOPE

Likewise the Spirit also helps in our weaknesses. For we do not know what we should pray for as we ought, but the Spirit Himself makes intercession for us with groanings which cannot be uttered. (Romans 8:26)

Upon receiving a call that something was wrong at the home of a church elder, I arrived to find police cars and an ambulance in his front yard. I was greeted by another church elder coming out of the house holding the 8-month-old daughter of the couple who lived there. The baby was covered with it's mother's blood. Shocked and perplexed, I asked what had happened and the reply was, "Yvonne has been attacked and it is bad. Keith is around back." An armed burglar had broken into the home, beaten Yvonne, and left her for dead.

When I got to where Keith was I found him bent over weeping—unable to say anything. Not knowing what to say myself, the Spirit reminded me of this Scripture: "And the peace of God, which surpasses all understanding, will guard your hearts and minds through Christ Jesus" (Philippians 4:7). I put my arms around Keith and the Holy Spirit began to make intercession for us with groanings which cannot be uttered. Instantly the peace of the Lord settled over our spirits. We sat there holding on to each other, letting the Spirit pray for us.

The doctors told us it was hopeless, and Yvonne would not survive. Throughout the remainder of the day we held on to this Scripture, and against all hope we believed in hope. "Now hope does not disappoint, because the love of God has been poured out in our hearts by the Holy Spirit who was given to us" (Romans 5:5). Nine hours later, coming out of surgery, the doctors changed their prognosis. Four weeks later Yvonne was again in church, worshipping and praising the God who hears our prayers.

. . . PRAYER . . .

Father, thank You for Spirit-inspired intercession that brings peace in the midst of trials, hope into hopelessness, and faith into tragedy.

. . . TODAY'S THOUGHT . . .

No words of explanation could comfort my member that day, yet there were words uttered by the Holy Spirit, though not understandable in our language, which assured us of His presence.

—Mike Cowart
Pastor, Hinesville Live Oak, Hinesville, GA

March 31

GRACE TO DIE

And He said to me, "My grace is sufficient for you, for My strength is made perfect in weakness." Therefore most gladly I will rather boast in my infirmities, that the power of Christ may rest upon me. (2 Corinthians 12:9)

It was January 1968. My husband and I drove from New Jersey to Virginia to visit his brother. The room was quiet, the mood somber. A gray, wintry light streamed in through the windows. On the bed lay the 30-year-old, his tall frame stretching from pillow to foot board, his colorless complexion matched the day. He had just been told his illness was a recurrence of cancer. The gray face tried to smile but couldn't manage. "I'm having trouble praying for the first time in my life. I don't understand." A tear traced his jawline and he turned over so slightly so his younger brother wouldn't see him cry.

"We want to sing a new song for you. Do you feel like listening to the words?" Neil nodded his head, and Lynn lifted the old acoustic Gibson guitar Neil had taught him to play when they were both boys. We sang "His Grace Is Sufficient." The message came from 2 Corinthians 12:9. The apostle Paul had an illness that couldn't be treated. God chose not to heal him but gave Paul a valuable gift—sufficient grace.

The promise of grace struck home. Tears flowed freely as we approached the bed to pray. Romans 8:26 was demonstrated as Neil began to pray in an unknown tongue: "Likewise the Spirit also helps in our weaknesses. For we do not know what we should pray for as we ought, but the Spirit Himself makes intercession for us with groanings which cannot be uttered." Prayer in the Spirit ended, and a genuine smile covered the ashen face. Grace had been offered and accepted.

Three weeks later my husband sat alone by his brother in a Pittsburgh hospital as he went to be with the Lord. Never in the intervening weeks was Neil unable to talk to God. The gift of grace was sufficient for suffering and for dying.

. . . PRAYER . . .

Father, thank You for grace that is sufficient to live by and even better to die by.

. . . TODAY'S THOUGHT. . .

God's grace is always available. Through His Spirit, we can accept it.

—Mary Ruth Stone
State President Women's Ministries, COG in CA

April 1

THE FIRE OF GOD

I indeed baptize you with water unto repentance, but He who is coming after me is mightier than I, whose sandals I am not worthy to carry. He will baptize you with the Holy Spirit and fire. (Matthew 3:11)

I grew up in a preacher's home in southwest Missouri just a few miles from the location of a great outpouring of the Holy Spirit at the turn of the century. During my teen years, I saw firsthand many wonderful miracles of healing, deliverance, and victory.

Even though our church was small, the power of God was manifested in many ways. However, the church felt led of God to pray and believe for a great outpouring of the Spirit.

During one series of meetings there was an unusual outpouring of the Holy Spirit and many people began to receive the baptism in the Holy Spirit as they did on the Day of Pentecost. It was in the middle of summer. As we looked out of the open windows we saw a crowd of people standing together across the street from the church. Several of us went outside to see what was happening. The people pointed to the roof of the church. Flames of fire were dancing across the roof line of the church but the building did not burn. When the neighbors first saw it, they were prepared to call the fire department but then realized the building was not burning.

This became a sign that stirred the hearts of many. A great spiritual awakening occurred that brought many families into the church. Soon the building was filled to capacity. Many were saved and filled with the Holy Spirit; many were healed. But the greatest of all: many young people were called of God into service. From that one church, more than 75 people went into full-time Christian service.

The supernatural power of God is still important to reach this generation for God.

. . . PRAYER . . .

Father, I thank You for the past miracles, but today we open our hearts to see greater signs and wonders than we have ever witnessed.

. . . TODAY'S THOUGHT . . .

God is ready to meet His people again today with a mighty outpouring of the Spirit.

—S. K. "Bud" Biffle
Chief Financial Officer, IPHC

April 2

GRACE AND PEACE

To all who are in Rome, beloved of God, called to be saints: Grace to you and peace from God our Father and the Lord Jesus Christ. (Romans 1:7)

We can never know real peace until we discover the miracle of God's grace. Only then can we live in peace.

Paul "persecuted the church of God beyond measure and tried to destroy it" (Galatians 1:13). He said he did "many things contrary to the name of Jesus . . . many of the saints I shut up in prison . . . I punished them often in every synagogue and compelled them to blaspheme" (Acts 26:9-11).

Then Paul was converted. After he had "persecuted the church of God," Paul made a profound discovery: "God . . . called me through His grace, to reveal His Son in me, that I might preach Him among the Gentiles" (Galatians 1:15, 16).

Every letter that Paul wrote to the churches he began by speaking of God's grace and peace.

Grace means He wanted us before we knew to want Him; He believed in us before we knew to believe in Him; He came to us before we could come to Him; we were bought and paid for before we knew that He valued us. The price is fully paid for us to be restored as His friends.

Peace comes by knowing that He paid enough for our sins; that our sins have been punished; that He assumed our penalty, paid our debt, cleared our account, and endured our judgment. No debt can be paid twice. No sin can be punished twice. "He has brought us into the very presence of God, and we are standing there before Him with nothing left against us . . . this is the wonderful news . . . and we have the joy of telling it to others" (Colossians 1:22, 23 *TLB*).

. . . PRAYER . . .

Father, by Your grace I am what I am. Nothing I can do can improve my salvation. You did enough. I have peace and I rest confidently in Your love.

. . . TODAY'S THOUGHT . . .

During 54 years of ministry to millions in 74 nations, my passion has been, and is, to help people discover how much God values them, proven by the price He paid for them.

—T. L. Osborn
Missionary, T.L. Osborn Ministries, Tulsa, OK

April 3

HOPE IN OUR DARKEST HOUR

Likewise the Spirit also helps in our weaknesses. For we do not know what we should pray for as we ought, but the Spirit Himself makes intercession for us with groanings which cannot be uttered. (Romans 8:26)

I arrived in Clarksburg, West Virginia, September 1, 1976, to pastor a church with a rich background in the Pentecostal faith.

Among the many wonderful members was Martha Richards, who worked as a nurse in the United Hospital Center in Clarksburg. In the fall of 1977, she went for her annual physical required of all the employees. Soon after the initial exam, she was asked to return for further tests which revealed Hodgkin's disease, a cancer of the lymph nodes. The doctor told her she probably had six months left to live. How could this be? She was only 26 years old. She had grown up in the church, had been faithful, and had been trained to minister to others who were sick and hurting. Could it really be true? Sad, but true!

Sister DeHart and I visited her to try and bring comfort and hope. I have never felt more inadequate in my life. What could I say? She had already been told she had six months to live. After all my feeble efforts that day to comfort her, we went to prayer. Not long after we started praying, the Holy Spirit began praying and then a message in tongues came forth. The interpretation given was, "My child, I have seen your affliction, I will raise you up by my power." Nothing unusual seemed to happen that day, but Sister Richards soon realized something great had happened in her body. The doctor confirmed that her cancer was in remission.

She has resumed her role in the United Hospital Center where she serves as head nurse for the dialysis department. Sister Richards believes God healed her so she could, through the anointing of the Holy Spirit, minister to the many patients under her care.

. . . PRAYER . . .

Lord, teach us how to pray as we ought. We confess our need of the blessed Holy Spirit each time we approach Your throne.

. . . TODAY'S THOUGHT . . .

Jesus is a miracle worker. The Spirit discerns and knows our every need. Let us expect great things from the Lord.

—Wayne DeHart
Pastor, COG, Clarksburg, WVA

April 4

GOD'S PRESENCE SUSTAINS US

Have I not commanded you? Be strong and of good courage; do not be afraid, nor be dismayed, for the Lord your God is with you wherever you go. (Joshua 1:9)

It was a beautiful summer morning when I walked out of the attorney's office. I had just signed all the papers necessary to transfer ownership in several parcels of real estate to settle a business debt caused by unscrupulous business partners. Although I was innocent of their actions, it cost me the loss of all I had worked several years for.

I headed south on I-75, on my way to Starke, Florida, to begin my ministry as an evangelist. As I traveled, God spoke these words to my spirit: *Be strong and of good courage; do not be afraid, nor be dismayed, for the Lord your God is with you wherever you go. Now is a time for believing, for confidence, for involvement. I give to you the assurance of my presence, my guidance, and my commitment to you.*

Some people commit suicide because they cannot bear the thought of life going on one moment more. I too would have despaired that day if I were alone, if there were no God.

When the Scottish preacher John McNeil was a boy, he stayed too late playing with his friends. He started home in the dark. In dark, rocks looked like wild beasts and trees like giants waiting to scoop him up.

"My feet," he said, "felt as though they were buried in concrete. I could not move one step. My heart beat as though it would burst through my rib cage. Then in the darkness I heard a voice shout, 'John!,' and suddenly the trees were trees again, the rocks were rocks again, and the road was a road again, and my feet were feet again, and they could walk because this was my father's voice. He was coming over the hill. That made a difference."

Today the voice of our Father comes to us in our heartaches and problems as we hear it from the lips of Jesus: "I will be with you always, even until the end."

. . . PRAYER . . .

Thank You, Lord, for the promise of Your sustaining presence.

. . . TODAY'S THOUGHT . . .

God will calm our fears and meet our needs today and every day.

—William L. Lewis
First Assistant General Superintendent, CHC

April 5

STREET ECONOMICS: THE STORY OF BILLY BOB

God is our refuge and strength, A very present help in trouble. (Psalm 46:1)

One Spring afternoon, as I drove by the historic Oakland Cemetery in Atlanta, I saw a young boy make a hand gesture to me. I recognized the gesture as one made by male prostitutes to let men know that they are available. I pulled my car over and lectured the boy on making signals he did not understand. He listened patiently, then replied, "I'm just taking care of business! I live here in Cabbagetown, and my brother taught me the trade." In disbelief, I asked, "What's your name and how old are you?" "Billy Bob," he replied. "Eight years old."

Still in shock, I exclaimed, "Surely there are not many customers for a young boy like you!" That is when the little boy lectured *me.* "Let me teach you the economics of the streets. The younger the boy, the more money you get because there's less chance of AIDS, VD, or herpes. I get $200 a customer, but my burnt-out, diseased 13-year-old brother only gets $20. It's simple: supply and demand."

My heart broke as I tried to encourage Billy Bob to let me help him start a new life. Sadly, he refused: "I'm my family's ticket out of the ghetto." Weeks passed. I tried to reach Billy Bob with the good news of Jesus, but with no success.

Billy's body was found in a dumpster by the police. They believe that the little boy was murdered by one of his customers. The sad reality is that in street ministry not every story has a happy ending. The pain with which the people live is overwhelming. But one truth gives us hope: Jesus died for the Billy Bob's of the world just like He did for Philip Bray, Robert White, and you. Please support urban ministry in prayer as we serve in this spiritual oasis in the middle of satan's playground.

. . . PRAYER . . .

Father, let me not take for granted the grace of Jesus Christ is making salvation available to me and to all men, women, and children; and let me be Your instrument of healing in the midst of pain.

. . . TODAY'S THOUGHT . . .

Every person in pain is an opportunity waiting for God's grace.

—Philip Bray

Founder/Pastor, SafeHouse Ministries, Atlanta, GA

April 6

PROMISE FOR RENEWAL

Have you not known? Have you not heard? The everlasting God, the Lord, The Creator of the ends of the earth, Neither faints nor is weary. His understanding is unsearchable. He gives power to the weak, And to those who have no might He increases strength. Even the youths shall faint and be weary, And the young men shall utterly fall, But those who wait on the Lord Shall renew their strength; They shall mount up with wings like eagles, They shall run and not be weary, They shall walk and not faint. (Isaiah 40:28-31)

God wonderfully saved me and called me to ministry. Yet, it often appeared that I would faint from the doubt and fear that plagued me and robbed me of sleep. Many times I prayed into the night. My father, hearing my anguished prayers, would come to my room and pray with me. Often I prayed until the Holy Spirit witnessed and gave me peace. During those months of perplexity, God whispered to my spirit, "I will see you through."

I have never forgotten God's promise. He always keeps His word. He renews the strength of those who wait on Him. God was working in my life to renew my strength. I discovered a lesson for the rest of my spiritual journey. "The everlasting God . . . neither faints nor is weary. He gives power to the weak and to those who have no might He increases strength." The prophet used this expression to describe God giving His strength to the weary. Almighty God, who never lacks for strength, removes our cloak of weariness and weakness and replaces it with His glorious might.

God does not always renew in the same manner. In times of dramatic intervention we rise above the ordinary and "soar on wings like eagles." Other times, God enables us to run and not grow weary. God works through us to accomplish His purpose, and we are gloriously helped by His power. Sometimes God leaves us in a difficult situation while He works His grace in us. He inspires us to walk and not faint. He gives us grace to persist in seemingly impossible circumstances.

. . . PRAYER . . .

Lord, Your mercies are new every morning. Give me Your strength for today.

. . . TODAY'S THOUGHT . . .

God's promises are true. We can find renewal as we wait in His presence.

—Bishop James D. Leggett
General Superintendent, IPHC

April 7

THE FRAGRANCE OF LIFE

For we are to God the fragrance of Christ among those who are being saved and among those who are perishing. To the one we are the aroma of death leading to death, and to the other the aroma of life leading to life. And who is sufficient for these things? (2 Corinthians 2:15, 16)

I came to Christ as a teenager in the 1960's and quickly developed a spiritual thirst that led to my baptism in the Holy Spirit. It happened because I met Pentecostal young people and a Pentecostal pastor from whom the fragrance of Christ crept into the empty spaces of my life.

I was a typical young person of my generation. My parents were solid, moral, hard-working people, but they did not have a meaningful relationship with God and could not lead me in that direction. My need to be accepted by my peers led me into bad relationships and dangerous behavior. I was cool outside, but turmoil and emptiness were inside.

God brought across my path some young people from the Pentecostal church who quietly but forcefully impacted my life and caused me to consider the message of the gospel. They invited me to church and introduced me to their pastor who also exuded this godly character which I now know was the fragrance of Christ being produced in them by the Holy Spirit.

After a few weeks of exposure to Bible teaching and wrestling with conviction, I surrendered my life to Christ. After my conversion, the pastor led me through the Scriptures which teach about the infilling of the Spirit. My heart and mind were opened and I was baptized in the Holy Spirit a few days later.

When I'm asked how I became interested in becoming a Christian, I usually answer, "God quietly invaded my life through the fragrance of Christ in the lives of Pentecostal Christians."

. . . PRAYER . . .

Lord, may my life be so controlled by Your Spirit that the fragrance of Christ grows stronger and sweeter and others are drawn to Him.

. . . TODAY'S THOUGHT . . .

Fragrances attract or repel. The fragrance of Christ in our lives silently gains the attention and opens the hearts of those whom God has prepared to receive the gospel through us.

—Kenneth B. Birch
Regional Coordinator, Africa, PAC

April 8

THE EASTERN GATE

Then I heard a voice from heaven saying to me, "Write: 'Blessed are the dead who die in the Lord from now on.' " "Yes," says the Spirit, "that they may rest from their labors, and their works follow them." (Revelation 14:13)

The 20th-century Pentecostal revival has produced many heroes and heroines. Many we know by name. However, there are scores of Spirit-filled champions whose names are unknown, even to the church world. One such individual was Ida Porter. Her story is remarkable not only for the way she lived, but also for the way she died.

One of the early Pentecostal missionaries, Miss Porter spent 27 years working in China. Her return to America was almost as unnoticed as her departure had been, almost three decades earlier.

On January 25, 1939, her seventy-first birthday, Porter visited a service at the Pentecostal Church of God in Santa Rosa, California. The pastor recognized her and expressed his appreciation for her many years of sacrificial service. When asked to testify, this humble servant of the Lord said, "I am sorry that I haven't done more for the Master." She described the twelve gates in the new Jerusalem and said, "I expect to stand just inside the Eastern Gate and welcome my Chinese converts."

Her testimony was followed by an utterance in tongues accompanied by this interpretation, "You shall have the desire of your heart." No one realized how soon the Spirit's promise would be fulfilled.

Miss Porter joined the congregation singing one verse and the chorus of the hymn, "The Eastern Gate." As she finished the song, her lifeless body slumped in the chair. Her eternal soul had joined her Chinese converts, singing in heaven's choir.

Not all of us will have a home going as dramatic as Ida Porter's. Nevertheless, all of God's faithful children will someday be called into His presence to receive the reward of their labors.

. . . PRAYER . . .

Thank you, Father, that our labors are not in vain. You know our works and You will reward us when we enter Your presence.

. . . TODAY'S THOUGHT . . .

"If you hasten off to glory / Linger near the Eastern Gate, / For I'll be coming in the morning, / and you'll not have long to wait."

—Dr. Larry E. Martin
River of Life Ministries

April 9

ZEAL FOR SERVICE

My heart was hot within me; while I was musing, the fire burned. Then I spoke with my tongue. (Psalm 39:3)

Early in this century, the fire department in Biloxi, Mississippi, upgraded from horse-drawn equipment to gasoline powered vehicles. My grandfather purchased Fire Chief Barthes personal horse, a large black stallion. This horse, named Dan, was placed in a fenced pasture within the city limits.

Dan was a gentle horse until he heard a fire alarm sound. His training was to get to the fire and that's what he did! Dan didn't know he had been replaced by modernization. He would jump the fence or knock down the gate, go to where the alarm was sounding and stand there. It came to the point when the alarm sounded, my grandfather would head to the fire and lead Dan home. As far as Dan knew, he had just changed barns. He just went to the fire from a different pasture.

We are very familiar with Jeremiah 20:9: "Then I said, 'I will not make mention of Him, nor speak anymore in His name.' But His word was in my heart like a burning fire shut up in my bones; I was weary of holding it back, and I could not."

We may be less familiar with Jeremiah 4:19: "O my soul, my soul! I am pained in my very heart! My heart makes a noise in me; I cannot hold my peace, because you have heard, O my soul, the sound of the trumpet, the alarm of war."

Our neighborhoods are on fire with violence and addictions. Fires of unbelief are attacking God's Word. Our homes are filled with the conflagration of turmoil and strife.

Are we resting in the pasture or going to the fire? Are we stirred when we hear the prophetic calls of the gospel or has it become just an old, old story we have heard many times. Let us join David and say, "Zeal for Your house has eaten me up" (Psalm 69:9).

. . . PRAYER . . .

O, God, help us to not forget what we have been charged to do.

. . . TODAY'S THOUGHT . . .

A determined mind will find a way to get over the fence or through the gate to reach the place where the fire of God is burning.

—Paul O. Lombard, Jr.
Pastor, College Park, Huntsville, AL

April 10

GOD'S GUIDANCE SYSTEM

Trust in the Lord with all your heart, And lean not on your own understanding; In all your ways acknowledge Him, And He shall direct your paths. (Proverbs 3:5, 6)

Helen and I with our young daughter, René, got out of our car on a West Virginia mountain. The man loading pulpwood was John Triplett, my father, whom I had never seen in my life. I was 26 years old. There was no doubt who he was; we had the same nose, ears, hairline, height, and weight. We would have passed for twins had we been the same age. The only difference were his blue eyes; mine are brown. "You have your mother's eyes," he observed.

John hadn't known I existed. He left my mother seven months before I was born because of dire circumstances. After a brief and emotional visit, Helen and I headed for North Carolina, where I was preaching a revival. I called Pastor DeWitt Martin. "Tell the people God has answered our prayers. I have found my father. Tomorrow night I'll tell them all about it." My text was Proverbs 3:5, 6.

I had questioned God many times in those 26 years—being reared by foster grandparents to whom my mother was given when she was an infant, and being placed in an orphanage at age 10. The difference? Grandpa and Grandma Freeman were dedicated Christians and the orphanage was the Church of God Home for Children. God had more than taken care of me. There were no more questions after that West Virginia mountain-top experience.

Trust in, lean on, rely upon, put it all in God's hands. Don't allow other forces, temptations, circumstances, and pressures to take undue advantage. Allow God to take charge, and He will direct your paths.

. . . PRAYER . . .

Thank You, Father, for sending Your Son, Jesus, to be our Savior, Lord, and Elder Brother, to be our family when we have no family. Thank You also for our spiritual families, as well as our physical families.

. . . TODAY'S THOUGHT . . .

The dad stayed home; his son went to church. Upon his return, the dad asked, "What did they sing?" "There was one song—seems like it said, 'Trust and OK!'" And so it is—always, anytime, all of the time.

—Bennie S. Triplett

State Overseer/Songwriter, COG, Cleveland, TN (former)

April 11

OUR ETERNAL INHERITANCE

That having been justified by His grace we should become heirs according to the hope of eternal life. (Titus 3:7)

While ambling through a department store, I came across a table stacked high with books. I selected one, not expecting to find anything interesting. The preface stated the book contained names of missing heirs. Some had a few hundred dollars to claim, others a small fortune.

I turned to the D's, but found no Duncans. I checked for my mother's maiden name. Another disappointment. I looked under my wife's maiden name. Still no success. I exhausted the names even remotely connected to me. As soon as I discovered this book did not include me, I tossed it back on the counter.

Years ago I discovered a book of great worth, containing an inheritance of inestimable value. Unlike the book of missing heirs, this book addressed me personally. In a sense, it had my name in it because it declared, "Whoever calls on the name of the Lord shall be saved" (Romans 10:13).

The Bible assures the believer of an eternal inheritance. The Book of Life is the title deed to that inheritance. A title deed means nothing if a person is not a legal heir. But to one whose name is in the deed, it means everything. Paul said, "For you did not receive the spirit of bondage again to fear, but you received the Spirit of adoption by whom we cry out, 'Abba, Father.' The Spirit Himself bears witness with our spirit that we are children of God, and if children, then heirs—heirs of God and joint heirs with Christ, if indeed we suffer with Him, that we may also be glorified together" (Romans 8:15-17).

In a world of uncertainty and instability, it is good to know that "we have a building from God, a house not made with hands, eternal in the heavens" (2 Corinthians 5:1).

. . . PRAYER . . .

Thank You, Father, for making us Your sons and daughters and for assuring us of an eternal inheritance, a crown of life that fades not away. Lord, keep us strong as that day approaches.

. . . TODAY'S THOUGHT . . .

No earthly treasure could ever compare to the glory that will one day be revealed, not only to us, but also in us.

—Bobby G. Duncan
Pastor, Parma Park, Cleveland, OH, COG

April 12

SEALED WITH THE SPIRIT

In Him you also trusted, after you heard the word of truth, the gospel of your salvation; in whom also, having believed, you were sealed with the Holy Spirit of promise. (Ephesians 1:13)

As a young child, eight years old, my family and I were introduced to the Pentecostal experience at a tent revival in Bristol, Virginia, conducted by T. L. Lowery. After the revival we became members of the Shelby Street Church of God in Bristol, Tennessee. At almost every service, we heard someone speak of being filled with the Holy Spirit. That put a desire in me for the Spirit to live in my life. At age 10, in a revival service at our home church, I received the Holy Spirit with the initial evidence of speaking in tongues. Not only did I receive the Holy Spirit but that same night I accepted the call into the ministry. I have known from that time until now that I was chosen by God to preach the gospel.

The next day after receiving the Holy Spirit, I gathered the neighborhood boys and girls together in the backyard of our home and preached to them about what had happened to me. Two of the neighborhood boys were Catholic and when I told them I had received the Holy Spirit they ran home and told their mother that I had a ghost. She called my mother and told her I had scared her boys by telling them I had some kind of ghost. I am glad to report I still have the Holy Spirit and the desire to tell others is greater than it has ever been.

Have you received the Holy Spirit since you believed? He is available to be your constant companion and comforter. Jesus said, "Nevertheless I tell you the truth. It is to your advantage that I go away; for if I do not go away, the Helper will not come to you; but if I depart, I will send Him to you" (John 16:7).

. . . PRAYER . . .

Father, thank You for the Word of Truth, the gospel of salvation, and the faith to believe whereby we are sealed with the Spirit.

. . . TODAY'S THOUGHT . . .

Let truth be proclaimed, salvation be accepted, and the Holy Spirit of promise be received.

—Daniel W. Hampton
Administrative Bishop, COG in TX

April 13

HELP AVAILABLE

Let us therefore come boldly to the throne of grace, that we may obtain mercy and find grace to help in time of need. (Hebrews 4:16)

Harassed by life's pressures, baffled by its problems, depressed by its fears, and overwhelmed by its emergencies, limited, finite, frail, dependent man stands in need of help. Grasping the situation, the government, social agencies and friends offer assistance. After money spent, time consumed, and energy exhausted, man, a few pounds heavier and a few more dollars in the red, finds himself still frustrated. The cycle is repeated but man's situation is not improved. Why? Because human ingenuity only treats the symptoms, not the cause. But God, whose help transcends the combined resources of man in overall depth and power, stands ready to help. Those who understand this can appreciate the greatness of His provisions.

The Bible declares God will help us because His power is limitless (omnipotence). Man can never diminish nor deplete God's power.

God can and will help us for He is everywhere (omnipresence). Wherever we go we can find God.

God will help us because His knowledge is absolutely perfect. All facts, all causes, all relations, all operations, all motives, the past, the present, and the future are all known to Him. He knows what we need.

God will help us because He is holy. His holiness is infinite. All good reaches its maximum in God. This is sometimes referred to as His self-affirming purity. God's holiness guarantees us that He will use all His other attributes for our best interest.

Finally, God will help us because He loves us. His love is fathomless, eternal, boundless, matchless, unwavering and unchanging. His love is not mere sentiment but is the outgoing of His being. John said, "God is love." His love is never overindulgent and it never fails.

. . . PRAYER . . .

Father, thank You that the more we understand You, the more we understand You will help us.

. . . TODAY'S THOUGHT . . .

The Bible progressively from the first "In the beginning" to the last "Even so, come Lord Jesus," portrays how and why God will help us.

—E. C. Christenbury
Professor, Lee University

April 14

GRACE AND GUIDANCE

The Lord will guide you continually, And satisfy your soul in drought, And strengthen your bones; You shall be like a watered garden, And like a spring of water, whose waters do not fail. (Isaiah 58:11)

I had just preached at a church located an hour from where I lived. The Holy Spirit had anointed the giving and receiving of the Word. After the service, the pastor invited me to his home for a refreshment and visit. Ordinarily this kind gesture would have been received with appreciation but suddenly I felt a strong impression I should drive home immediately. I explained this to the pastor and was on my way.

When I entered our home, I understood the reason for the urgent message given to me by the Spirit. I smelled raw gas. Immediately, I turned off the furnace. I awakened my wife, Marie, and daughter, Dana, and led them outside to fresh air. We praised God they were safe and their lives were not taken by asphyxiation or a terrible fire.

The next morning we learned that the furnace had malfunctioned. The main burner had turned on even though the pilot light had gone out.

After this near tragedy, I realized the blessing of God's divine protection was given because of His grace and guidance. "Trust in the Lord with all your heart . . . And He shall direct your paths" (Proverbs 3:5, 6). I praised Him for saving the lives of my wife and daughter.

One meaning of grace is "getting what you do not deserve." Another is "a desired kindness which is granted without expectation or return (undeserved favor)." An Old Testament concept of grace is "to pause, to stop, to touch."

The Holy Spirit guides us into truth, from darkness to light, and even guides the blind. The word *guide* is used in 1 Timothy 5:14 to mean the management and direction of a household. We are promised God will deliver our household (Acts 16:31).

. . . PRAYER . . .

Father, thank You for Your grace to guide and protect us day by day through the leadership of the Holy Spirit.

. . . TODAY'S THOUGHT . . .

I will not depend upon my own words for God's protection and guidance but upon the redemptive work of Christ at Calvary.

—Dr. Dan Beller

Pastor, Evangelistic Temple, Tulsa, OK

April 15

BREAKING THE BONDAGE OF BRUISES

The Spirit of the Lord is upon Me, Because He has anointed Me To preach the gospel to the poor; He has sent Me to heal the brokenhearted, To proclaim liberty to the captives And recovery of sight to the blind, To set at liberty those who are oppressed. (Luke 4:18)

It happened on the tennis court. Running to return an excellent shot by my opponent, I fell, broke my arm, and badly bruised my leg. After surgery and a hand-to-shoulder cast, I began to mend.

Questions and comments about my broken arm were frequent. No one asked me about my bruises. Bruises are unseen pain. No gaping wound. No open sore. No obvious bandage. But the pain is real. Usually unseen, but, if seen, we pretend that we have neither bruises nor pain.

Some bruises are wounds of the heart—emotional welts, abused spirits, and battered feelings. Their causes are the multitude of negative experiences in life from which no one is exempt. Occasionally we forget them. Then someone touches them, and the pain starts again.

Jesus' words that promise liberty are like soothing ointment to those who have been bruised. Inner bruises bind us. We do not enjoy the freedom of wholeness. We are held captive by past wounds. The self-inflicted wound of sin holds us in chains. Rejection, grief, and depression are shackles from which we cannot free ourselves. But what we cannot do, Jesus can!

In His inaugural sermon, Jesus affirmed His intention to set at liberty those who are oppressed. He did not challenge us to free ourselves. He did not berate us because we were bruised. He promised release from the bondage of bruises.

How does He do it? By what means does liberation come? "The Spirit of the Lord is upon me." The liberating power of Christ released by the work of the Spirit breaks the chains forged by bruises.

. . . PRAYER . . .

Thank You, Lord, for freedom from the bondage of bruises. Help me to walk in the liberty of Your Spirit.

. . . TODAY'S THOUGHT . . .

You are the focus of Jesus' promise, not an exception to it. He had your release in mind before you were ever bruised. Be free!

—Warren D. Bullock

District Superintendent, Northwest District, AG, Everett, WA

April 16

TARRY UNTIL ENDUED

Behold, I send the Promise of My Father upon you; but tarry in the city of Jerusalem until you are endued with power from on high. (Luke 24:49)

As a young man wrestling for reality and a relationship with Jesus Christ, conviction had gripped my soul for weeks. Chest pains became so severe that I visited a doctor but the tests proved there were no physical problems. That evening I was still suffering from what I felt were chest pains. Betty, my wife, asked if she could call the pastor for prayer.

After meditating for several days upon the prayer the pastor prayed for me that night, I knew God was dealing with me. Nothing would suffice until I found the peace that comes through confessing, repenting, and believing.

The next Sunday night, as soon as the altar call was given, I rushed to the altar to recommit my life to Christ. After a short prayer, I knew I was forgiven. However, as I stood to go back to the pew the pastor's wife looked at me and asked if I was satisfied with what God had done in my life. My answer was yes and no. Yes, he had forgiven me; but no, I didn't have the experience I really wanted from the Lord. I will always be grateful for the words she spoke to me that night. She said, "You need to stay at the altar and tarry until you are endued with power. You need the Holy Ghost."

Now I know the tarrying was for me to personally prepare my temple for the person of the Holy Spirit. Thank God for saints that will tell new converts, "Tarry until you are endued with power." We need the power of the Holy Ghost today.

. . . PRAYER . . .

Father, I thank You for the Holy Spirit who convicts, teaches, guides, and comforts Your church today.

. . . TODAY'S THOUGHT . . .

As believers, we must wait upon the Lord and as we wait, our strength will certainly be renewed.

—Ray Garner
Administrative Bishop, COG in MS

April 17

HIS POWER IS REAL

But Jesus looked at them and said to them, "With men this is impossible, but with God all things are possible." (Matthew 19:26)

While serving as pastor of Tremont Avenue Church of God in Greenville, South Carolina, I became very sick. I was in much pain. I made an appointment to see our family physician. My doctor examined me and could not find a problem. He thought perhaps I had a kidney stone and made an appointment for me to see a urologist. I was thoroughly examined by the urologist and went through a series of tests. Though a stone was not found, the urologist said that did not mean one was not present. Some stones are only found by exploratory surgery. He gave me a prescription for pain medication and advised that if he was needed to call immediately. I could not sleep that night because of the intense pain. I finally told my wife to call the urologist and take me to the hospital.

At the hospital the doctor said, "We are going to put dye in you and give you another series of tests." When the tests were completed, he said, "We cannot find a kidney stone, but we must operate. If we find a stone, I will remove it."

Just before I was to be taken to surgery, my wife noticed a red spot on my side the size of a quarter. She told the nurse, "I want to see the surgeon." When the doctor arrived my wife showed him the spot on my lower right side and he exclaimed, "He has shingles! I am ecstatic! If we had operated it might have been fatal."

The Lord came to my rescue and spared me surgery almost at the point of being rolled to the operating room. My suffering of more than three weeks turned out to be shingles, but I was healed.

. . . PRAYER . . .

Now unto Him that is able to do exceeding abundantly above all we ask or think, according to the power that worketh in us. Unto Him be glory in the Church of Jesus Christ throughout all ages, world without end.

. . . TODAY'S THOUGHT . . .

May we present Christ our Lord in the world that men may love Him for what they see of His likeness in us.

—Thomas Grassano
State Overseer, COG (retired)

April 18

BAPTIZED IN THE HOLY GHOST

"The promise is to you and to your children, and to all who are afar off, as many as the Lord our God will call." (Acts 2:39)

On January 12, 1908, I prepared for Sunday school. A man baptized with the Holy Ghost and fire was to speak that day. I wondered how much different he would be from others. The sacredness seemed to increase as the moments galloped past.

On the way to Sunday school, I began to look over the congregation in my mind. Who would be the first to be baptized in the Holy Ghost? I knew it would take the best, most consecrated and spiritual of our sanctified brothers and sisters to receive such an experience. I singled them out one by one. I felt others in the congregation would enter right in and get the experience and be a help to me as pastor later on.

Sunday school was good and well attended. The song service ended, prayers were concluded, and the speaker was introduced. I sat on the platform in a chair. The speaker was going nicely, and I was catching every word. They were sacred to me. The atmosphere was exceedingly sacred.

At about 11:35, a flash struck me. Immediately, I was enshrouded with something I had never experienced. A spirit of weeping took possession of me. The chair disappeared and I was on the floor. I learned afterward that everyone in the house was affected by what was taking place on the platform. The minister closed the discourse and sat down. Other members I had picked out to be baptized in the Holy Ghost before myself were all present, but it was me the Holy Ghost fell on that day.

For three hours I was under the power and operated wholly by Him. From the time I fell to the floor to the time the power subsided and I came to myself I never moved or said a word except by the power.

. . . PRAYER . . .

Father, we thank You because the experience of our forefathers is also a contemporary experience today

. . . TODAY'S THOUGHT . . .

I appreciate my heritage and resolve to experience and share my faith as never before.

—A. J. Tomlinson (Reprinted from *SpiritWalk: Daily Devotions on the Holy Spirit* by permission of Pathway Press)
First General Overseer, COG and COGOP

April 19

GOD IS SELF-SUFFICIENT

Oh, the depth of the riches both of the wisdom and knowledge of God! How unsearchable are His judgments and His ways past finding out! "For who has known the mind of the Lord? Or who has become His counselor?" (Romans 11:33-34)

When God hovered over the waters in creation, man was not there to help. The sovereign God spoke and it was so (Genesis 1). He made the earth *for* man but without help *from man*! When the triune God designed the eternal plan of salvation before the foundation of the world, man did not have input. When Jesus offered one sacrifice for sin forever by His death, He did it alone. When the Holy Ghost was poured out on the Day of Pentecost, man did not help, but only obeyed, sitting, worshipping, and waiting to be "endued with power from on high" (Luke 24:49).

When man has a malady, does he have to present God with a diagnosis of his malady in order to receive the cure? ". . . the Spirit also helps in our weaknesses. For we do not know what we should pray for as we ought, but the Spirit Himself makes intercession for us with groanings which cannot be uttered" (Romans 8:26).

At the last trumpet, we will all be changed—in a flash—immortal! This change will come, not by the power of man, but by the Holy Spirit through the power of the resurrected Christ. When at last we shout, "Hallelujah!" with that great multitude, it will be only because God desired our worthless hearts, the Spirit drew us, and we accepted the invitation to the wedding supper of the Lamb.

. . . PRAYER . . .

Praise be to God "For of Him and through Him and to Him are all things, to whom be glory forever" (Romans 11:36).

. . . TODAY'S THOUGHT . . .

When we realize that God needs no help to perform that which He chooses to do, then we can offer perfect praise. He is truly God!

—Kenneth Dismukes
Academic Dean, West Coast Bible College (retired)

April 20

GOD IS FAITHFUL IN TIMES OF TRIALS

For in that He Himself has suffered, being tempted, He is able to aid those who are tempted. (Hebrews 2:18)

At the first church I pastored, a division arose and only four people remained faithful to the church. This caused my wife and me great emotional pain. During this trial, God visited me in a dream and told me He would bless me and multiply the numbers in our church. God directed me to read 1 Samuel 14:6: "For nothing restrains the Lord from saving by many or by few."

The second time the Lord visited me in a dream, He said, "I will truly bless you and multiply the number in your church, but I want you to know things first and experience things first. Then I will truly bless you and multiply the number in your church." As I awakened, God led me to read Job 42:10-12: "And the Lord restored Job's losses . . . Indeed the Lord gave Job twice as much as he had before. . . . the Lord blessed the latter days of Job more than his beginning." God truly blessed the number in our church and my days have been better than before.

The apostle James said, "My brethren, count it all joy when you fall into various trials, knowing that the testing of your faith produces patience" (James 1:2, 3). Let me encourage you with this word: God can only prove to you His faithfulness if you will allow Him to prove to you His saving power in time of trials.

Are you experiencing unusual trials in your life? Count it all joy, because God is coming to rescue you. "But thanks be to God, who gives us the victory through our Lord Jesus Christ" (1 Corinthians 15:57).

. . . PRAYER . . .

Lord, help me to look to You when storms seem to overwhelm me. Enable me through Your grace to stand and to endure until You come.

. . . TODAY'S THOUGHT . . .

"No temptation has overtaken you except such as is common to man; but God is faithful, who will not allow you to be tempted beyond what you are able, but with the temptation will also make the way of escape, that you may be able to bear it" (1 Corinthians 10:13).

—Jaime C. Buslon

Pastor, International Christian Assembly, Toronto, Ontario

April 21

THE UNCERTAIN FUTURE

Jehoshaphat made merchant ships to go to Ophir for gold; but they never sailed, for the ships were wrecked at Ezion Geber. (1 Kings 22:48)

In difficult times King Jehoshaphat turned to God for guidance and help. But towards the end of his life, he forgot to put God first in his life. The prophet Eliezer warned Jehoshaphat: "'Because you have allied yourself with Ahaziah, the Lord has destroyed your works.' Then the ships were wrecked, so that they were not able to go to Tarshish" (2 Chronicles 20:37). The king's plan to sail for gold was in vain; his unholy alliance brought the judgment of God.

We may have hopes, plans, preparations, and expectations for a good venture—a good life with great success. But will we even set sail? Only God knows our future. Our life needs to be lived in obedience to God.

Like Jehoshaphat, Christians often go for the gold of this world: worldly pursuits, pleasures, possessions, or wealth. But the gold will tarnish, fail us, and perish. Better to go with God than for gold.

God has a plan for our life, though it is often hidden from human view. The apostle James reminds us: "Come now, you who say, 'Today or tomorrow we will go to such and such a city, spend a year there, buy and sell, and make a profit;' whereas you do not know what will happen tomorrow. For what is your life? It is even a vapor that appears for a little time and then vanishes away. Instead you ought to say, 'If the Lord wills, we shall live and do this or that'" (James 4:13-15).

The future may be uncertain and veiled to us, yet if God has first place in our life and plans, He will see us through and we will say with the apostle Paul, "And we know that all things work together for good to those who love God, to those who are the called according to His purpose" (Romans 8:28).

. . . PRAYER . . .

Father, all my tomorrows are in Your hand. Help me to trust only in You for all things.

. . . TODAY'S THOUGHT . . .

I may not know what the future holds, but I know Who holds the future and if God be for me who can be against me.

—Daniel Ippolito
General Superintendent, IPCC

April 22

RECEIVING THE GIFT OF THE HOLY SPIRIT

If you then, being evil, know how to give good gifts to your children, how much more will your heavenly Father give the Holy Spirit to those who ask Him! (Luke 11:13)

My wife, Jean, and I were married in June of 1968. One fall day we were discussing our Christian experiences. I began sharing my conversion and Holy Spirit baptism experience with her. Even though Jean had been brought up in a Pentecostal church, she had never received the gift. So she began asking me questions about the Holy Spirit baptism that had taken place in my life. We began to pray that she would receive the Holy Spirit and this became our priority in our nightly devotion on a number of occasions. Our devotion would become a lengthy worship and praise time.

I began to hear my wife worship in another tongue, but because of her quiet and reserved nature, she did not make a public statement that she had received the gift of the Holy Spirit. Later in that year, we were attending a district meeting that was being held at Laurel Church of God in Laurel, Mississippi.

At that time, Reverend Frank Culpepper was the state overseer of Mississippi and he was the guest speaker. The subject he ministered on that night was the baptism of the Holy Ghost.

At the conclusion of the service, an invitation was given and Jean was one of the first to respond. Within minutes she began to speak in other tongues as the Spirit gave utterance. A very quiet and shy wife became a rejoicing worshipper of God.

. . . PRAYER . . .

Father, thank You that You give to those who ask the gift of the Holy Spirit.

. . . TODAY'S THOUGHT . . .

The promise of the Word was fulfilled according to Luke 11:9. So I say to you, ask and it will be given to you.

—Pettis E. Brewer
State Evangelism Director, COG in MS

April 23

THE FRAGRANCE OF HIS PRESENCE

Then Mary took a pound of very costly oil of spikenard, anointed the feet of Jesus, and wiped His feet with her hair. And the house was filled with the fragrance of the oil. (John 12:3)

After years of planning and preparation, my wife and I built a new house. When we moved in we found numerous details that required attention and the return of several of the sub-contractors. The vinyl floor covering in the kitchen needed a small repair. A service man came and while working said to my wife, "May I ask you something? I visit a lot of homes but there is something different about yours. There is a sense of peace and well being here. Why is your home different?" My wife proceeded to share with him that our home belonged to Jesus and more than anything else we wanted His presence to abide there.

Mary poured a fragrant oil on Jesus' feet. The fragrance filled the room. The sweet smelling perfume was released by a voluntary act of Mary's will. The presence of Jesus abides among those who willfully seek his presence.

Consider the depth of Mary's act. It was a expression of her profound love for the Master. The element of commitment is evident. She determined in her heart to serve Jesus. There was an obvious risk involved. How would Jesus respond and how would her sister Martha and brother Lazarus react as well as the other disciples? Then there was the cost of the fragrant oil, nearly a year's wages. But ultimately it was the woman's sincere expression of worship and devotion that touched Jesus and released His presence.

If we are to experience the presence of Jesus, it will surely be born of love for His person, commitment to His cause, and a willingness to risk all and pay the price that ultimately results in worship and releases His presence.

. . . PRAYER . . .

Lord, thank You for allowing the fragrance of Your presence to be manifest in every place through Your people.

. . . TODAY'S THOUGHT . . .

The peace and presence of Jesus will be released through us today as we focus upon His person and His purposes.

—Paul V. Canfield

Director, International Ministries, OBSC

April 24

FAITH AND THE GIFT OF THE SPIRIT

This only I want to learn from you: Did you receive the Spirit by the works of the law, or by the hearing of faith? (Galatians 3:2)

As a new Christian I longed to be filled with the Holy Spirit. The teaching on the baptism of the Spirit drew me into the Pentecostal Movement. I was raised in a nominal Christian home. Friends witnessed to me about the need to receive Christ. They spoke of a church where people spoke in tongues. I was intrigued about speaking in unlearned languages.

I attended a Pentecostal service because I thought I might hear someone speak in tongues. I was gloriously saved that night. Now my interest in the gift of the Spirit intensified. I wanted to be filled so I could effectively serve Christ. I sought God for Spirit baptism. Yet, while others received, I did not. The thought, "I'm not good enough," filled my mind. Then I learned the Spirit was not given on the basis of works but because of Christ's redemption.

Another problem still kept me from the Spirit's power. I felt I did not have enough faith. A sermon titled "Increase Our Faith" changed everything. The preacher said, "You do not need more faith, use the faith you have." My faith seemed small but Christ said faith the size of a tiny mustard seed could move mountains. Truth filled my heart with expectation. I thought, "I am going to receive now." I had only to believe what I had heard. I knew my faith, though weak, was sufficient. I began to joyfully praise God with the certainty of faith and received a mighty baptism in the Holy Spirit.

We need not search for more faith but only exercise the faith we already have. Jesus fills those who call upon Him in simple faith. This faith is released in words of thanksgiving and love to Jesus Christ. Nothing can prevent you from receiving this gift if you will put your faith in the One who promised to baptize us with His Holy Spirit.

. . . PRAYER . . .

Lord, thank You for the gift of Your Spirit to transform our service for Christ.

. . . TODAY'S THOUGHT . . .

The gift of the Spirit is our inheritance in Christ, and through faith we receive the gift.

—Ronald Osmond

Pastor, Elim Pentecostal Tabernacle, St. Johns, Newfoundland

April 25

GOD'S GIFTS

Every good gift and every perfect gift is from above, and comes down from the Father of lights, with whom there is no variation or shadow of turning. (James 1:17)

Both children and adults love special gifts and moments. Those gifts which aren't immediately recognizable seem to last longer. Such a gift was mine on a cold November night as I enjoyed a rare treat—an evening at home with my mother. As one of ten siblings, one-on-one time with our mother was a rarity. Daily responsibilities without modern appliances consumed her time.

Without dedicated effort and determination, other things crowd out a precious gift—our one-on-one time with God. We tell ourselves God will understand "no" better than man; He will wait more patiently.

Jesus walked as we must walk—under the control of the Spirit. How much more we need the power of the Holy Spirit! Reinhard Bonnke tells us there is a flame for every head and that this is our individual power station. Those who play with laser guns at amusement parks must have their power packs recharged. After shooting and being shot by the "enemy," they must return to the power source. In the game of life, returning to our power source is also necessary.

When my mother tucked me into bed on that cold November night, I didn't realize that that evening was a gift I would always remember. Before morning, my mother died of a heart attack. The rare one-on-one time we shared that night is a valued treasure. Having received God's gift of salvation as a six-year-old girl and the gift of the Holy Spirit at eleven, His hand kept me during the ensuing years. As He promises in His Word, He has been a mother to me. He laid His hand upon my life. He has never failed me. His special gifts are new each day.

. . . PRAYER . . .

Thank You for Your special gifts and the handsful on purpose You send our way. You know what is good for us. Thank You for loving and sustaining us.

. . . TODAY'S THOUGHT . . .

We fret about giving and receiving gifts. Many times we look to monetary value. No amount of money can buy His gifts. How blessed we are to be the children of God and the objects of His special love.

—Rebecca J. Jenkins
Director, COG, Women's Ministries

April 26

I'M NOT BACK THERE!

Indeed it was for my own peace That I had great bitterness; But You have lovingly delivered my soul from the pit of corruption, For You have cast all my sins behind Your back. (Isaiah 38:17)

The Scriptures use many different word pictures to teach us what happens to our sins once they have been forgiven through the blood of Jesus Christ. Our sins are removed as far as the east is from the west, forgotten, buried in the depths of the sea, covered by the blood, blotted out, and put behind God's back.

While I was preparing for Sunday services my three-year-old son, John, came to visit me in my office. Teasing him, I placed a sticker in the middle of his back. Around and around in circles he went, first to the right then to the left, trying to get at the sticker. Stretching his arms up over his shoulders and then hugging himself he tried every possible way to reach it.

"What's the matter?" I asked. "Got a sticker on my back, Dad," he said. "Why don't you take it off?" I inquired. "I can't reach it," said John. "Why can't you reach it, John?" I asked. "'Cause I'm not back there, Dad," he answered. The words of the Scripture came to my mind: "You have cast all my sins behind Your back."

That is just like our Heavenly Father. Our sins are gone never again to be remembered against us. We're not back there. Sins from our past are behind us. We cannot go back and relive those moments, but we can place them under the forgiveness of our Lord. Once we do that, our sins no longer separate us from the love and blessings of God. They are placed behind his back and He's not back there, just as we are not back there. God gives us a new start on life with a clean record. None of our past sins are laid to our charge.

. . . PRAYER . . .

I thank You, Father, that You forgave my sins through the blood of Jesus Christ.

. . . TODAY'S THOUGHT . . .

Today I will accept the new life Jesus gives, and from this day forward I will let old things pass away and all things become new (2 Corinthians 5:17).

—John W. Maglott
Overseer-at-Large, Southeast Region, OBSC

April 27

A REVELATION FOR TODAY

But without faith it is impossible to please Him, for he who comes to God must believe that He is, and that He is a rewarder of those who diligently seek Him. (Hebrews 11:6)

I sensed for days God was going to do something special in my life. Walking from my bedroom to my study early that morning, I was expectant! I could hardly wait to hear what He had to say. Sure enough, as I prayed the Holy Spirit spoke: "Jesse, if you stay in the boat you'll only meet disciples. But if you'll get out of the boat, you'll meet Jesus."

Faith is given to us in order that we might please God. When we use our faith and get out on the water with Jesus, we are showing God that we not only believe Him but we trust Him. And He will in no way take our trust lightly.

Oh, if people could only get beyond what faith will get them and see the real meaning of walking on the water! This awesome substance called faith will not only bless you with earthly blessings, it will take you on an adventure! With Jesus, you'll go places in the spirit-realm that you have never imagined!

Walking by faith is rewarding and fulfilling. Once you make that first step out of the boat, you're walking where Jesus walked! Think about that! You're following His footsteps and they lead to Glory!

People tell me, "Brother Jesse, you seem so happy all the time." That's because I don't see Christianity as a religion; it's my lifestyle. I don't see faith as a struggle; it's an adventure! I'm walking on the water with Jesus! I'm not sitting around in the boat saying, "Should I go? Should I stay? Which way, which way?"

Dare to believe the impossible is possible! Take the leap of faith and start walking on the water today!

. . . PRAYER . . .

Thank You, Lord, for preparing my path of adventure, for giving me the courage and faith I need to step out boldly in faith today.

. . . TODAY'S THOUGHT . . .

Never a man spoke like this man (John 7:46), because never a man lived like this man. In all your speaking, produce faith, and in all your living, faith will produce!

—Jesse Duplantis

International Evangelist, Jesse Duplantis Ministries, New Orleans, LA

April 28

GLORIOUSLY SAVED

And you will seek Me and find Me, when you search for Me with all your heart. (Jeremiah 29:13)

I was at the brink of despair. Some 80-plus persons of our small community of 225 had come to faith in Christ in two weeks during a Pentecostal revival—but not me. A 14-year-old "good boy," I had sought God intensely for three evenings in the old Methodist Schoolhouse, but had not experienced a "breakthrough." Discouraged, I went home to question God as to whether or not I could be saved. Several people thought I had been saved because of the fervency of my praying. But I knew the victory had not come. I was determined not to fake it.

I had made all the right responses, said all the right prayers, followed all the altar instructions I had received. Yet at the end of the fourth night of seeking, I stepped out of the building downcast and dejected. Just outside the door my old Methodist godmother put her arms around me and said, "Son, did you get saved tonight?" I hung my head in shame and replied, "No, ma'am." Suddenly it was as if a dam broke inside me and I was shattered in a million pieces. My tears flowed so freely that I could not see to walk. Supported by my two older sisters, I literally wept my way home and into the loving embrace of my waiting Lord. I had come to the end of myself in great despair and distress. God had brought me to this state of true helplessness and hopelessness before Him, then when all seemed lost, He lovingly stretched forth His hand, and gloriously saved me.

"But without faith it is impossible to please him: for he that cometh to God must believe that he is, and that he is a rewarder of them that diligently seek him" (Hebrews 11:6).

. . . PRAYER . . .

Our gracious heavenly Father, thank You for Your divine wisdom in dealing with our hearts, and for Your wonderful saving grace that brings us into full fellowship with You.

. . . TODAY'S THOUGHT . . .

Are you despairing in your search for God? Press on until you realize your helplessness, then watch God gloriously fill your shattered life with His holy presence.

—Adrian L. Varlack, Sr.
Director, World Missions, COGOP

April 29

MAINTAINING YOUR JOY

Now may the God of hope fill you with all joy and peace in believing, that you may abound in hope by the power of the Holy Spirit. (Romans 15:13)

The atmosphere of God's presence and creation is full of joy. God dwells among shouts of joy (Psalm 47:5). The heavens rejoice, the earth is glad, the fields are jubilant, and the trees shout for joy (Psalm 96:10-12).

All the major acts of God are accompanied by joy. At the coming of Jesus to earth, the angels sang tidings of great joy. Hebrews 12:2 says Jesus faced the cross with joy. At Christ's resurrection, the women who saw the risen Lord were filled with joy and ran to inform the disciples. Following the Ascension, the disciples returned to Jerusalem with great joy. The redeemed will return with singing; everlasting joy and gladness will overwhelm them (Isaiah 35:10).

It is God's desire for His people to be a people of joy. God promises, "Therefore with joy you will draw water from the wells of salvation" (Isaiah 12:3). He wants to impart to His people "the oil of joy for mourning, the garment of praise for the spirit of heaviness" (Isaiah 61:3). In John 15:11, Jesus instructed the disciples that His joy should be in them and that their joy should be complete. He then prayed that they would have the full measure of His joy (John 17:13).

Joy is one of those qualities (fruits) which the Holy Spirit will develop in our spiritual character. Our joy will be in direct proportion to our sense of forgiveness: "You will show me the path of life; in Your presence is fullness of joy" (Psalm 16:11). Joy is in direct proportion to our devotional life: "Your word was to me the joy and rejoicing of my heart" (Jeremiah 15:16). Joy is in direct proportion to our sacrificial service: "Those who sow in tears shall reap in joy" (Psalm 126:5).

. . . PRAYER . . .

Thank You that Your joy has become my strength. Thank You that "weeping may endure for a night, but joy comes in the morning" (Psalm 30:5).

. . . TODAY'S THOUGHT . . .

To know the true joy of the Lord is to have the capacity to triumphantly transcend all the turmoil of our times in profound, quiet, inner joy.

—John R. Holland
President, ICFG (retired)

April 30

WANTED: FOR CRIMES AGAINST SOCIETY

For God so loved the world that He gave His only begotten Son, that whoever believes in Him should not perish but have everlasting life. For God did not send His Son into the world to condemn the world, but that the world through Him might be saved. (John 3:16, 17)

The concrete beneath me was cold and wet. In the darkness I could hear the wheels of passing cars splashing through puddles a few feet from my head. I tried to open my eyes, but the effort was too much trouble. Suddenly I could sense someone bending over me. Methodically, he began going through my pockets. I wanted to get away from him, but my body seemed disconnected from my mind, unable to respond to commands. I groped for his hand, but couldn't find it. "Whaddya doing?" I managed to ask. "Shut up, you filthy junkie," he muttered, turning away and leaving me to lie there on the pavement. When I regained consciousness, I rolled over on my stomach and pounded the sidewalk. Tears poured down my swollen face. I was marked—either to die or to spend the rest of my life a hopeless addict.

Later in jail, one of my fellow prisoners told me about a church in the Bronx where addicts were getting "delivered." The day I was released from jail, I boarded a train, fell asleep, and missed my stop. I got off and began walking back. In the darkness I saw a cross brightly lit and the name of a church—the one I'd heard about. When I walked inside, a service had begun.

While I was there, they told me about a camp where the counselors prayed with addicts. I visited the camp and stayed two weeks. One night I walked outside. Looking up, I felt I could almost see God. I knelt and began to cry. I could sense something had to come out of me, and I began to weep from deep inside. I knew then that God had come into my life.

. . . PRAYER . . .

Thank You Lord for Your saving grace, Your outstretched hand, and Your undying love.

. . . TODAY'S THOUGHT . . .

It was like an explosion when I found Jesus. I found the *only* way out. Now, walking hand in hand with Christ, everyday is a new experience.

—John Gimenez

Pastor, The Rock Church, Virginia Beach, VA

May 1

GOD REWARDS FAITHFULNESS

"A faithful man will abound with blessings." (Proverbs 28:20)

My mother was in the hospital that year more than at home. My father was working in a textile factory for a meager salary. He paid more in hospital bills that year than he made. He depleted his savings and sold whatever he could to pay the bills.

One morning as my sister, Brenda, and I finished breakfast, Dad said, "There is nothing left to eat in the house. When you come in from school today, pack your clothes, and I'll take you to your grandparents until things get better." Then he reached in his pocket and pulled out a tithing envelope. "The only money I have is in this envelope," he said. "If I take it and buy groceries, you could probably stay home for a few more days until we see how things are going, but I don't want to make that decision on my own. I have never spent God's money, although I don't think He would mind this time."

Brenda and I protested, "No, Dad, we don't want you to do that. As much as we don't want to go away, we will do so." We prayed together, and then Dad went to work and Brenda and I went to school.

When we came in from school that afternoon, I was the first one in the house. When I walked into the kitchen, I saw groceries setting on the table and on the floor. On the back porch, groceries were stacked up in boxes. I had never seen so many groceries in one place outside a grocery store. To this day we don't know where the groceries came from, but I believe that God must have dispatched an angel from heaven and said, "That's a faithful man – go down to Number 1 Walker Avenue, Lauren, SC and be sure his family has something to eat."

. . . PRAYER . . .

Thank You for supplying our daily needs. Help us to remember that every good gift comes from above. Amen.

. . . TODAY'S THOUGHT . . .

Those who honor God with their tithe will be blessed abundantly.

—Dr. R. Lamar Vest
Presiding Bishop, COG

May 2

PEACE, BE STILL

For it is not you who speak, but the Spirit of your Father who speaks in you. (Matthew 10:20)

Shortly after my daughter, Bethany, turned two years old, she lay at the point of death. After repeated doctors visits and the simple diagnosis of a common virus, our daughter now was unconscious. As we raced toward the hospital, our hearts beat with the terror of our daughter never regaining consciousness.

Upon arrival at the local emergency room, we realized we were in for more of an ordeal than we ever dreamed. As the doors to the emergency room swung open, we were thrust into a world of screams, tears, and frantic parents. After signing our daughter in, we lined up behind the many sports fractures, fevers, and just plain nervous parents with newborns.

Tension in the waiting room grew and grew as parent after parent began to blast the solitary nurse with insult and complaint because of the chaos and extended wait. Feeling the life slip away from my daughter, my own frustration began to grow. Then, in the middle of the chaos, I heard a familiar voice from within: "Stop the nurse and tell her no matter what anyone else says, you think she is doing a good job." Ever since I was a child and had received the Holy Spirit at the age of 7, I knew that when He spoke, the best response was to obey. I followed His direction, stopped the nurse, complimented her efforts, and returned to my seat. The nurse rounded the corner and then returned past the line of others and came to our seat. She then escorted us to the much-needed care that saved my daughter's life.

Moments were all that were left for my daughter, without immediate care, according to the doctors. Moments that would have been wasted in an emergency room if not for the intercession of a trusted Friend.

. . . PRAYER . . .

Father, today teach me that You are present to guide me in every part of life; both small and great, You are in control.

. . . TODAY'S THOUGHT . . .

In the middle of life's storms, His voice echoes "Peace, be still."

—Don C. Allen

Pastor, War Hill Christian Fellowship, Dawsonville, GA

May 3

TRUST GOD'S FAITHFULNESS

He who calls you is faithful, who also will do it. (1 Thessalonians 5:24)

"I want you in full-time ministry." As God lovingly impressed these words upon my spirit, it produced a burning within my heart reminiscent of my original call many years earlier. Preparation, training, and attempted ministry had led me down a road of defiance, cynicism, and ostensible failure. Through loving discipline and brokenness, God restored my soul and renewed my spiritual fervor.

God blessed me in business, so by the time I sensed the prompting of the Holy Spirit to accept this fresh offer some serious questions had to be answered. My heart would fill with fear and doubt as I considered the consequences of leaving my comfortable lifestyle and free-falling into the beckoning arms of the One who had called me to service as a youth. Ironically, in the midst of my confusion, the voice of the Lord became more clear than ever before. The Lord of the Harvest consumed me each passing day with the burning passion of His call. Within six months, God answered every question as He orchestrated my comeback with meticulous detail. As I look back across the years to the decision to let go and let God, it becomes clear that trusting the Heavenly Father's faithfulness was the launching pad that thrust me into the greatest adventure of my life, an adventure that has not ended and affords me the highest privilege in life—conducting Kingdom business.

God has a plan for you in the operation of His Kingdom on earth. You may not be called to a ministerial career, but you are called to a career of service within the church of Jesus Christ. We are living in perhaps the most significant time of the church, a time of unprecedented growth. The saints who have gone before us longed to see this time. Jesus wants to launch you into the greatest adventure of your life. Trust His faithfulness! In Him you are safe (Proverbs 29:25).

. . . PRAYER . . .

Father, thank You for calling us to the great work of Your Spirit. We trust You to accomplish Your work in us.

. . . TODAY'S THOUGHT . . .

God is faithful to call us. Be faithful "to walk worthy of the calling with which you were called" (Ephesians 4:1).

—B.G. Turner
Assistant General Overseer, IPCC

May 4

ROSES IN THE SNOW

I am the rose of Sharon, And the lily of the valleys. (Song of Solomon 2:1)
I am the way, the truth, and the life. (John 14:6)

As I walked along a mountain road early in December, I saw through the falling snowflakes a rose bush with three crimson roses on it. The great soft flakes were clinging to the crimson velvet of the petals like white lace upon a royal robe. The leaves of the bush were completely covered with snow. I stood for a moment and watched as the roses stood out vividly on their background of white.

Yes, roses in the snow. Spiritually, we feel frost and the winter wind upon us. Iniquity abounds on every side. The love and spirituality of many is growing cold. The snows are upon us.

The true church, purchased by the precious blood of Jesus, has always been beautiful, lovely, and fragrant as the rose. We can see the true church still blushing warm and beautiful with the message of salvation from sin.

Roses in the snow! Do you see them? The Father. . . the Son. . . the Holy Spirit! They are still blooming, but the snows of unrighteousness are getting heavier and we are sometimes tempted to wonder if there is a way out?

Oh yes, there is a way! We can be lifted by God's power! This is the time when we more than ever need the Holy Spirit. To try to find our own way out is dangerous. We can be saved only by faith in Christ and by the power of the Holy Spirit that will lift us above the world and the pressures of life.

Focus on the roses in the snow. Christ, the Rose of Sharon, is coming back to lift us up out of this weary world. He will deliver His children. Though every road is seemingly covered with the snow of unbelief, the Holy Spirit is ever present to lift us up.

. . . PRAYER . . .

Father, help us to ever look to Jesus, the Rose of Sharon, and to fully yield ourselves to the presence and power of the Holy Spirit.

. . . TODAY'S THOUGHT . . .

I am not afraid of tomorrow, for I have seen yesterday and I know that God's love is with me today!

—Dr. Bebe Patten

Founder/Chancellor, Patten College, Oakland, CA

May 5

LISTENING TO GOD'S VOICE

Now the Lord came and stood and called as at other times, "Samuel! Samuel!" And Samuel answered, "Speak, for Your servant hears."
(1 Samuel 3:10)

I was startled out of my sleep by a bad dream. The dream had so jarred me that my spiritual sensibilities were at their keenest. I heard the voice of the Lord intuitively, yet as clear as Samuel had heard it that night when the Lord came and stood there before him in the temple. The Lord said, "Paul, gather some spiritual warriors who'll stand with you in prayer."

It is important for us to keep our hearts open to the voice of the Lord! It is not by mere chance that the word "boy" is used in reference to Samuel (vv. 1, 8). The Holy Spirit intended to highlight this fact in order to relate to us the importance of the development and the maintenance of a particular spiritual posture. That posture is a child-like openness, tenderness of heart, and availability to the Lord and His speaking to us. This openness is what the bride in the Songs of Solomon spoke of when she said: "I sleep, but my heart is awake" (5:2) the sensitivity a mother's ear has to the slightest whimper of her newborn.

It is sad indeed how some Christians can easily become less sensitive and discerning of the Lord's voice over the years, like Eli the priest, whose unfamiliarity to the Lord's voice is clearly revealed by the fact that only after the Lord called young Samuel the third time did he realize the Lord was calling the boy. His apparent dull perceptibilities were no doubt occasioned by his tolerance of sin. Others lose sensitivity to the Lord because they have allowed negative experiences with people or difficult circumstances of life to embitter them, thus calcifying their hearts. It is for this reason that Proverbs tells us: "Keep your heart with all diligence" (4:23).

. . . PRAYER . . .

Lord, help us to guard our hearts from those "little" compromises and from those things that render our hearts undiscerning and insensitive to Your voice.

. . . TODAY'S THOUGHT . . .

To maintain an openness to the still, small voice of the Lord, strive to keep our hearts tender by giving total control to the Holy Spirit.

—Paul Gallicchio
IPCC, Hamilton, Ontario

May 6

HIS GRACE IS SUFFICIENT

And He said to me, "My grace is sufficient for you, for My strength is made perfect in weakness." Therefore most gladly I will rather boast in my infirmities, that the power of Christ may rest upon me. (2 Corinthians 12:9)

I was attending college in southern California. I had been to my brother's house, completing a term paper for one of my college classes. The night was rainy and foggy.

A car was stalled on the road and I stopped to offer help. As I tried to push the stalled car with my car, the bumpers locked. I was in the process of trying to unhook the bumpers when an elderly man, driving in the rain and unable to see, ran into the rear of my car, driving it into the other car and pinning my legs in between.

My legs were crushed and felt as though they had been cut off. I can remember yelling, "Somebody help me." In the darkness I heard a still, small voice saying, "Do you believe what you preach?" I replied, "Yes." Then the Lord spoke again saying, "It is written, my grace is sufficient" I responded, "I accept your grace."

At that moment His presence covered me. I felt great peace and strength. I had the assurance I was in the Lord's hands and He would see me through. I survived a horrible ordeal with victory and praise.

You can have victory in any situation, because it is written, "My grace is sufficient."

. . . PRAYER . . .

Father, thank You for Your provisions for our lives. In this world we will have suffering, pain, and disappointment, but You have made provisions. Open my eyes, help me to see Your hand. Open my ears and help me to hear Your voice. Your hand and Your voice will guide me.

. . . TODAY'S THOUGHT . . .

It is encouraging to know that the Scripture states, "My grace is sufficient for you." There are no limits! Whatever comes into our lives, regardless of how severe: His grace is sufficient!

—John D. Nichols
Director, Department of Benevolence, COG

May 7

ENERGY FOR MELANIE

But you shall receive power when the Holy Spirit has come upon you. (Acts 1:8)

Melanie, the mother of three little boys was in a battle for her life with liver cancer. She was undergoing special treatments. Brenda and I were there for the same reason. Brenda was in a daily struggle with breast cancer. Brenda said, "I believe the Lord would have me to share a Scripture with Melanie and her mother." As Brenda read to them, they both wept profusely. Melanie, Doris (her mother), and Ray (her dad) were devout Christians. Our friendship was immediate, warm, and real.

Almost every day Brenda visited Melanie to share a Scripture. She also prepared a special message of encouragement which Melanie had taped to the wall beside her bed. Then we began singing worship songs to her at night. Soon we were all singing together. We were enjoying these little worship services with our new friends. When a minister visited us, we would take him over to pray for Melanie too. When a minister came to see them, they sent him over to pray for Brenda.

One evening after we had sung some hymns and choruses, Melanie began to exclaim loudly to her mother, "Mama, energy is pouring in me! Energy is all over me! God must be doing something!" Indeed, God was doing something. The color came back into Melanie's face immediately. The next morning she was out of bed and walking with a "walker." The next day her doctor did a series of tests. He gave Melanie the good news: "Your liver is functioning again. You can go home to your children."

We were witnesses to a miracle. How appropriate that Melanie described the divine touch upon her frail body as "energy". He is the source of all life and all energy. He is the Healer—our Great Physician.

. . . PRAYER . . .

Merciful heavenly Father, thank You in Jesus' name for our brothers and sisters in the family of faith. Thank You for the abiding presence of the Holy Spirit, and Your compassion toward us in our overwhelming needs.

. . . TODAY'S THOUGHT . . .

The Holy Spirit has come to us to make our lives a habitation of His presence. We are blessed to be a blessing. If you have received Him, share Him.

—Al Taylor
Director, Stewardship Department, Cleveland, TN

May 8

DETERMINED OBEDIENCE

Therefore, to him who knows to do good and does not do it, to him it is sin. (James 4:17)

I was preaching overseas when I received a call from my wife. She said, "You've received a letter asking you to go to India." Overwhelmed with my responsibilities at home, my pastorate, my schedule, I justified my decision not to go: "I never really had a desire to go to India."

Returning home, I read the letter. The Holy Spirit whispered, "You must go." I went into the kitchen where my wife was busy. Before I could speak, she said, "The Lord just spoke to me and said you must go."

After three days of preaching to curious Hindus, nothing happened. They listened, yet remained unresponsive. Returning to my room, I cried out: "Lord, I obeyed, now we need a breakthrough!"

The weather was sweltering the next evening when I stepped to the podium. The shade of sunset barely diminished the oven-like temperatures. I was physically weak. Mosquitoes buzzed furiously as if to suck what peace remained in me. Yet, the tent was packed.

As I began to preach my sermon on signs and wonders, suddenly the place became electrified by the presence of the Holy Spirit. People began to tremble with the power of God. Some were instantly filled with the Spirit. Some were instantly healed of debilitating diseases.

My sermon took a short version. All I had left to say was, "This is the God of signs and wonders. Do you want to serve Him?" All across the congregation Hindu people of every age thrust their hands into the air indicating their faith in Jesus Christ.

A few days later I was on the plane returning to my home, leaving those new children of God with the pastor in India. Obedience and dependence upon God honoring it had resulted in the birth of a new church in an obscure Indian village.

. . . PRAYER . . .

Lord, I know You will be with me when I obey You.

. . . TODAY'S THOUGHT . . .

Sometimes Jesus calls on us to do something special for Him. When we obey, we are assured of His favor.

—Alex T. Emes
Director, Operation Mercy and Freedom Village, NY

May 9

ABOUNDING IN HOPE

Now may the God of hope fill you with all joy and peace in believing, that you may abound in hope by the power of the Holy Spirit. (Romans 15:13)

As a strong-willed, sometimes rebellious teen of the late 1960's and early 1970's, my life was not taking the course I thought it would. I was reared in a Christian home that emphasized the importance of a personal relationship with Jesus Christ as well as the dynamics of the Holy Spirit. Unfortunately, somewhere along the way I lost or forgot that training. I was frustrated, bewildered, and hopeless. My thoughts began to lend themselves to the idea of running away from everything in an attempt to find a new hope for my life and perhaps "myself."

One day while sharing my troubles with a coworker, I was reminded of my upbringing. The co-worker was a Church of God pastor's daughter (whom I would later marry). She encouraged me to think of renewing my relationship with God. Obviously, the path I was taking wasn't working, so maybe I should give God a chance again.

Only a few weeks later, while attending a revival service, again at her urging, I received Christ back into my life and was baptized with the Holy Ghost. Immediately, the feelings of frustration, bewilderment, and hopelessness began to dissipate. These feelings were replaced by a renewed joy, an abiding peace, and an eternal home. A short time later I accepted a call into the ministry.

Since that earlier experience, I have come to understand the importance of the Holy Spirit as the means of maintaining that hope. This world does not offer us much in regard to hope. However, a life in Christ, immersed in the Holy Ghost, through the experience of faith, empowers us to move forward in joy, peace, and hope.

. . . PRAYER . . .

Dear God, thank You for the hope delivered by Your Son, the empowering of the Holy Spirit, and the motivation of hope for tomorrow in this hopeless world. Keep me sensitive to the remembrance of Christ's gift and saturated with this dynamic Holy Ghost that I may share Your hope with others.

. . . TODAY'S THOUGHT . . .

Live in the Spirit "that you may abound in hope by the power of the Holy Spirit" (Romans 15:13).

—J. Martin Taylor
Administrative Bishop, COG in DelMarVa-DC

May 10

MAMA'S MONUMENT

"Honor your father and mother," which is the first commandment with promise: "that it may be well with you and you may live long on the earth." (Ephesians 6:2, 3)

When I was a young evangelist, conducting a revival in Greensboro, North Carolina, I visited a battlefield of the Revolutionary War. The National Park Service maintains this battlefield which marks the events of the Battle of Guilford's Courthouse. Having a little free time and being a lover of history, I roamed through the park admiring the beautiful monuments and reading the markers which explained the events of the battle.

I came across one particular monument which seemed peculiar and misplaced on a battlefield. It was erected as a memorial to a mother, Mrs. Karen Turner. She had ridden on horseback from her home in Maryland to North Carolina in order to nurse her son, who had been wounded in the battle, back to health.

As I thought about this, I became more convinced that it was right and proper for this monument to be standing on a battlefield—a monument to a loving mother. As I stood viewing this site, I recalled memories of my own mother. I longed to build a monument to her.

As I pondered the matter, I was gripped with the realization that such an act was impossible. I was saddened by the thought, for surely my mother deserves such an honor. Suddenly a flash of inspiration came to me—I believe it was from God. "You may never be able to erect a monument out of stone or bronze for your mother, but you can so live and conduct yourself that you will bring honor to her." I proposed, again, there in the park, to live so my mother will never be ashamed to say I am her son.

. . . PRAYER . . .

Dear Father, thank You for my mother and father and for the love and care they have shown me. Help me to live my life so they will be proud of me and that You, heavenly Father, will be pleased also.

. . . TODAY'S THOUGHT . . .

What things can we do to honor our fathers and mothers? Do you feel your parents are proud of you? Why?

—Ronald B. Minor
General Secretary, PCOG

May 11

HOW TO OVERCOME

To him who overcomes I will grant to sit with Me on My throne, as I also overcame and sat down with My Father on His throne. (Revelation 3:21)

I would like to deal with two special ways for us to overcome. Perhaps there are many more, but only these two occupy our attention at the moment.

In Luke 11:1, "One of his disciples asked, Lord teach us to pray as John also taught his disciples." Notice the request is not *how* to pray. It was important for the Master's prayer to induce the request to pray and not how. No words have to be memorized, no form has to be followed; each one in his own way has the avenue of prayer opened to him.

In the promise of Jesus regarding our thrones, there is a required overcoming. Prayer is not given to coerce God to bring us through our battles, but we have some overcoming to do. It is not forced on us, but "to him that overcometh." Victory is on the other side of the conflict but the conflict is ours. Overcoming is not an automatic grace. It is our will to do battle and receive the reward of sitting with him in his throne.

Prayer and conflict are two things needed in the armor of the Christian. We are assured of victory through the prayers of Jesus. In Luke 22:32, he told Peter, "I have prayed for thee . . . ." In John 17:20, he has prayed for us. To fail would defeat the prayer of Jesus. We must not cause his prayer to be defeated. We must be victorious! If we do overcome, a special place is reserved in the throne of Jesus!

Failure will never occupy His throne—only overcomers. You need not know how to pray, but simply to pray. You need not expect the Lord to do your overcoming. He is there if you need Him: He promises to go with us "always, even to the end of the world" (Matthew 28:20).

. . . PRAYER . . .

O Lord, teach me that I must overcome today, and let tomorrow take care of itself. I cannot cross the river until I have reached it, and neither can I solve tomorrow's problems today. Teach me to pray as I should.

. . . TODAY'S THOUGHT . . .

There is no greater blessing than to look back and remember victories. If yesterday gave us victories, tomorrow is as bright as the promises of God. By His grace I will overcome whatever comes my way.

—A. A. Ledford

World Missions Representative, COG (retired)

May 12

HAVE YE RECEIVED THE HOLY GHOST SINCE YE BELIEVED?

". . .he said unto them, have you received the Holy Ghost since you believed?" (Acts 19:2a)

Christ's greatest gift to His followers was the mighty infilling of the Holy Spirit. As He stood with His little band of disciples on the Mount of Olives just before His departure for heaven, His words were "Wait for the promise of the Father which saith he, ye have heard of me. For John truly baptized with water; but ye shall be baptized with the Holy Ghost not many days hence" (Acts 1:4-5). After speaking these words, the Lord ascended to heaven, and the disciples returned to Jerusalem where they passed the next ten days in prayer and worship. Then suddenly the Holy Spirit fell. It came as tongues of fire and a mighty rushing wind. It filled all the house where they were sitting, and they all began to speak in tongues as the Spirit gave them utterance. This wonderful gift that they received revolutionized their lives, and set them afire for God. Though unlearned laymen, they went forth and preached a message that changed men's lives (Acts 4:13).

We need power to be able to witness effectively to others and carry out our chief function as Christians. The purpose of the baptism in the Holy Ghost is to give us this power.

The most amazing proof of the truth of Christianity lies in the fact that a band of lowly fishermen, who, according to the standards of religious leaders of that day, were "ignorant and unlearned men" (Acts 4:13), were able to go forth against the severest opposition and under God bring into existence the most powerful religious movement of all history.

The glorious Holy Spirit infilling is the only thing that can fully satisfy the human spirit. Man is so made that he is not complete in himself. In his soul there is a spiritual vacuum. If it is not occupied with God, it will eventually be filled with that which is evil (Luke 11:24-26).

When the full baptism in the Spirit comes, and we yield to it, we will find that the Spirit of God within us will intercede and help us to pray and get answers to the difficult problems. None of us knows how to pray as we ought, but if permitted, the Spirit of God will make "intercession for us with groanings which cannot be uttered."

. . . PRAYER . . .

Heavenly Father, fill, baptize, and saturate every believer with the Holy Spirit just as it happened in the upper room on the Day of Pentecost.

. . . TODAY'S THOUGHT . . .

I will be led and directed in all things by the Holy Spirit. I will seek to do the Will of God as revealed to me by His Spirit.

—Gordon and Freda Lindsey
Founders, Christ For The Nations, Dallas, TX

May 13

GOD'S PROTECTION

Put on the whole armor of God, that you may be able to stand against the wiles of the devil. (Ephesians 6:11)

I would be alarmed if I thought there was someone who was constantly trying to work out a plan to do my family or me bodily harm. We read reports of people who are stalked and they cry out to law enforcement people for protection. In some cases, nothing is done until it is too late.

According to Ephesians 6:11, the devil is constantly seeking our downfall. The devil is systematically looking for a way to destroy us spiritually or to bring us bodily harm so that we will be limited in our ministry. If he determines that we have an area of strong resistance, he moves to other methods. If we appear to be weak in an area, that is noted and he seeks to break down our resistance. So, methodically, he hammers away and never quits. Over and over, he seeks to accomplish his goal: our spiritual defeat or physical demise.

However, the devil is no match for our protector: God. Paul instructed us to put on the whole armor of God. In reality, the armor is Jesus Christ. Let the devil try his best shot. Protected by Jesus Christ, we have nothing to fear. Thank God for this protection.

Late one night I was traveling the West Virginia turnpike, not the best of highways. Suddenly, a car traveling in the opposite direction crossed the center line into my traffic lane. I swerved to the right. There was sufficient space for me to safely pass. Could it be, since God knows all things, He knew I would need extra space that night? So, when the road was constructed, He made sure enough space was there for me.

No matter what we are facing today, we can rest in the confidence that God is with us. We are secure in the armor—Jesus Christ—against the systematic, methodical attempts of the devil. It is impossible for the devil to destroy us. We are secure in the armor of God.

. . . PRAYER . . .

Thank You, God, for Your loving and protective care for me.

. . . TODAY'S THOUGHT . . .

I am safe and secure this day because of Jesus—the armor of God.

—Edward W. Wood

Superintendent, Appalachian Conference IPHC

May 14

GOD'S HOLY SPIRIT GIVES US POWER

But you shall receive power when the Holy Spirit has come upon you . . .
(Acts 1:8)

There comes a time in each of our lives, when there is no one else around, that we need the power of the Holy Spirit to pray.

My family and I were about 25 miles from Fort Worth on our way to a preaching appointment when a man in an approaching automobile had an epileptic seizure and hit our car head-on.

My car was complete demolished. I did not know if my wife and daughter were dead. My son was thrown from the car and suffered a broken leg.

I felt helpless and alone when the Spirit spoke this Scripture to me: "And I will pray the Father, and he shall give you another Comforter, that he may abide with you for ever" (John 14:16). As I began to pray, the Holy Ghost began to pray through me making intercession for us.

In the hospital the doctor told me that my wife could not live through the night. She remained unconscious for 18 hours, my daughter for 12 hours. He told me my son's thigh bone was crushed and his leg would wither away. The Spirit spoke to me again, "Have faith in God" (Mark 11:22).

We placed our faith in a God who never changes. God completely healed my wife, son and daughter.

This accident occurred December 20, 1950. These healings were complete miracles by faith in God.

. . . PRAYER . . .

Father, we thank You for the indwelling Holy Spirit, the Comforter who stands along side us.

. . . TODAY'S THOUGHT . . .

"I am the Lord God that healeth thee" (Exodus 15:26); "Jesus Christ the same yesterday, and today, and forever" (Hebrews 13:8); "Casting all your care upon Him; for He careth for you" (1 Peter 5:7). Now is the time to cast your every care on Him.

—Othoe Stegall
Pastor, COG in TX (retired)

May 15

STRENGTH TO OVERCOME OPPOSITION

No weapon formed against you shall prosper, And every tongue which rises against you in judgment You shall condemn. This is the heritage of the servants of the Lord, . . (Isaiah 54:17)

It was, judging by the things that had happened, just a routine Sunday morning. I dressed early for Sunday School and started to read from the book of Isaiah. When I came to 54:17, the words stood up on the page and began talking to me. It was as if God Himself had come into the room and said the words. I knew that the Holy Spirit had spoken to me and that I could rest in Him.

My wife and I were facing some very strong opposition and even some mild persecution. We were perplexed. The opposition did not go away. The persecution increased. But God had spoken and there was strength to overcome. This verse from Isaiah and a dream that my wife had increased our courage to the point that nothing could hinder us. My wife dreamed that the church was surrounded with muddy flood waters; the church, though, stood clean and white, untouched, above them.

This dream and one verse of Scripture gave us unwavering faith. God had sent us there to work for Him. The stress caused by the opposition immediately left. We were free to spend our time in productive labor. Even being strapped financially did not bother us. Each time that I began to worry about finances the Lord would remind me that He was taking care of everything. He did.

The words of the text above came to pass. The words that came against us, as promised, did not hurt us. Those people who were against us either became our friends or God took care of the situation in another way. We were triumphant over all negative re sistance.

. . . PRAYER . . .

God, help us always to triumph over our enemies through Your Word and through the Holy Spirit.

. . . TODAY'S THOUGHT . . .

Nehemiah 6:16 said it best: ". . . when all our enemies heard of it . . . they were very disheartened in their own eyes; for they perceived that this work was done by our God."

—E. L. Murphy
Pastor, Church Planter and Builder, COG

May 16

MAKING THE IMPOSSIBLE POSSIBLE

For God may speak in one way, or in another, Yet man does not perceive it. In a dream, in a vision of the night, When deep sleep falls upon men, While slumbering on their beds, Then He opens the ears of men, And seals their instruction. (Job 33:14-16)

God communicates with unsaved people through their human spirits. He sends the Holy Spirit to them in often supernatural ways, including dreams and visions, as a witness of His saving love and grace.

God communicated to Nebuchadnezzar's spirit through a dream. Daniel sought God and the dream and its interpretation were revealed to him. After Daniel told the king what he knew, Nebuchadnezzar acknowledged Daniel's God. But even though he acknowledged God, Nebuchadnezzar had not made Him the Lord of his life.

This is like the impossible people in your life, the unsaved loved ones who don't read the Bible or allow Christian witness. They see the miraculous works of God around them, yet fail to accept their source.

To get Nebuchadnezzar's attention, God spoke to him again in a dream, warning him to forsake his pride and worship the real God. He chose not to take heed, lost his mind and lived as an animal. God was after Nebuchadnezzar's heart. After Nebuchadnezzar acknowledged God, his full faculties were restored, and he was converted.

God still speaks to the unsaved through dreams. When their minds and bodies are asleep, their spirits are awake. Recently, in one area of the Muslim world, Jesus appeared in a dream to several men in a village and told them that He was the Savior. The next morning, when they shared their dreams, they realized that this type of miracle could only be from the true, living God. They have since become Christians.

If you think your unsaved loved ones are impossible, remember—God specializes in the impossible. God may reach them through a dream.

. . . PRAYER . . .

Father, send Your Holy Spirit to communicate the truth of who You are with our loved ones who don't know You in their waking and sleeping moments.

. . . TODAY'S THOUGHT . . .

Don't look at people as impossible, for then you limit God. See them as possibilities for God's kingdom. Allow His love to reign in their lives and give them the turnaround they so desperately need.

—Marilyn Hickey
President, Marilyn Hickey Ministries, Englewood, CO

May 17

ASSURANCE IN TIMES OF UNCERTAINTY

You did not choose Me, but I chose you and appointed you that you should go and bear fruit, and that your fruit should remain, that whatever you ask the Father in My name He may give you. (John 15:16)

Fear, doubt, or a sense of insecurity can strike even the strongest Christian at the most unexpected times. I have felt its gnawing pain and ensuing paralysis as I struggled with questions: *Did I do the right thing? Did I make the right choice? Is God going to come through for me one more time?*

Peace begins to return as I read again that God chose me rather than the reverse and that I am in His will. He did not call me to frustration and failure but to peace and fruitfulness. When I carefully check my bearings, I am reassured that I am in His will, placed there by the direct leading of the Holy Spirit. Faith then begins to rise in my heart once again. That flame of faith grows brighter as I recount how God has led me in the past through similar trials and has brought me out every time. He has never failed nor has He been late, although there were times when I thought He was both.

The phrase, "Whatever you ask the Father in my name He may give you," is the icing on the cake, the healing balm for the pain. Not only will there be relief, there will be victory—overwhelming victory that comes only from the hands of a loving Father as He heals, restores, and provides for His children. This victory is not earned; it is a gift directly from the mercy of God that we can receive without any guilt or hesitation.

Then, we are admonished to love one another. This is possible only when we have forgiven one another. Uncertainty and insecurity often spring from lack of forgiveness.

. . . PRAYER . . .

Thank You, Lord. You have totally forgiven me. I will do the same for all others so I can live in Your peace.

. . . TODAY'S THOUGHT . . .

I refuse to allow fear and doubt to rule my life. I will live in the victory that God has provided for me.

—Charles E. Hackett
Executive Director of Home Missions, AG

May 18

THE HOLY SPIRIT—GUIDE AT THE CROSSROADS

However, when He, the Spirit of truth, has come, He will guide you into all truth; for He will not speak on His own authority, but whatever He hears He will speak; and He will tell you things to come. (John 16:13)

I received my call to the ministry on July 13, 1936. Although I was young, the call was so definite Satan has never been able to make me doubt it. I spent three years in the U.S. Army during World War II. When I was discharged, I felt God's call to pastor. When I expressed my desire to the state overseer, he was gracious and kind, but nothing was available.

Soon after my discharge, the company I had worked for before going into the Army notified me that my former job, along with periodic raises, was available to me. However, I would have to return no later than a specified day. What a dilemma—I now had a family to support and no assurance of an immediate assignment with a church.

On the last day before the job offer expired, I felt I had no choice but to return to my former job. So I dressed in my best clothes and was almost ready to leave the house when the Holy Spirit convicted me in a very definite way that I was moving in the wrong direction. I had come to the crossroads. Should I listen to the voice of logic, or should I follow the guiding hand of the Holy Spirit? So convincing was the leading of the Holy Spirit that I decided not to return to my former job.

Did I move in the right direction? Yes! The Lord gave me a small church to pastor and wonderfully blessed my ministry there for nine months. Then I was appointed state Sunday school and youth director of the Church of God in Ohio—a position I held for eight years.

How thankful I am for the Holy Spirit's guidance at that crossroads experience in my life! Had I not followed His leading, how different my life and ministry would have been.

. . . PRAYER . . .

Holy Spirit, thank You for always being with us when we stand at the crossroads in our lives. Help us to listen to Your gentle voice.

. . . TODAY'S THOUGHT . . .

Among the many benefits that accompany our commitment to God is that we always have Him by our side and the Holy Spirit as our guide.

—O.W. Polen
Editor-in-Chief, COG Publications (retired)

May 19

THE GLORIOUS GOSPEL

For I am not ashamed of the gospel of Christ, for it is the power of God to salvation for everyone who believes. (Romans 1:16)

The gospel of God displays the wisdom of God, the power of God, the holiness of God, and the love of God. No wonder the devil has fought the gospel so hard and has tried to stop its spread throughout the world.

To the question "What do you think of the glorious gospel?" John Newton would respond:

Amazing grace! how sweet the sound,
That saved a wretch like me
I once was lost, but now am found,
Was blind, but now I see.

Ask William Cowper, "What do you think of this glorious Gospel?" His answer:

There is a fountain filled with blood
Drawn from Immanuel's veins;
And sinners, plunged beneath that flood,
Lose all their guilty stains.

I say to Fanny Crosby, "You have been blind all your life. What do you think of the gospel?"' As she speaks the words of her immortal hymn, her face glows with an inward joy. Confidence is expressed in every word she recites:

Blessed assurance, Jesus is mine!
Oh, what a foretaste of glory divine!
Heir of salvation, purchase of God,
Born of His Spirit, washed in his blood.

. . . PRAYER . . .

We are thankful, Father for the power of the Holy Spirit to bring the redeeming message of the glorious gospel into our lives.

. . . TODAY'S THOUGHT . . .

The Holy Spirit gives us the power to glow with the gospel, go with the gospel, and grow with the gospel.

—James A. Cross (Reprinted from *SpiritWalk: Daily Devotions on the Holy Spirit* by permission of Pathway Press)
General Overseer COG (former)

May 20

ENJOY BEING WHO YOU ARE

As the Father loved Me, I also have loved you; abide in My love. (John 15:9)

The Lord had told me to draw aside with Him for several days. I was to write a book from His heart to the heart of His children. Then, He did the unexpected. "First, you need to hear what is on My heart concerning yourself." His presence was very real, and a dialogue developed between us.

"I love you," He said. *I know*, I thought. "I love you, but you don't love yourself." He had hit a tender nerve. "I accept you," He said. *I know*, I said. "I know I am accepted in the beloved." "Yes, but you do not accept yourself.

"I like you," He said. That I didn't know. It was surely His divine job to love me, but how could He like me? He hit the nerve again. "I want you," He said, "for yourself." I sensed a pressure building within me. How could this be? I want to be useful to Him, but how could He want me for myself? "I enjoy you," He said.

I could stand no more of this. I did the only thing possible and went to make a cup of coffee. But God followed me.

"You have children and know their imperfections, yet you love them, accept them, like them, want them, enjoy them. They have done nothing to gain such a place in your heart. You feel all that because they are your children. Is not My love for you greater than your love for your children? Yes, I see all that is wrong and all that I need to sort out in you. But there is nothing you have to do to win My love or affection. I love you, My child. So I accept you, like you, want you, and enjoy you. Enjoy being you, despite your imperfections. And enjoy My love for you!"

. . . PRAYER . . .

Father, thank You for Your love and acceptance, and that You actually enjoy being in me by Your Spirit.

. . . TODAY'S THOUGHT . . .

If God loves me and enjoys me, I have no right not to accept myself and enjoy being me, despite all my imperfections.

—Colin Urquhart

Kingdom Faith Ministries, West Sussex, England, United Kingdom

May 21

THERE'S LIFE IN THE SON

The thief does not come except to steal, and to kill, and to destroy. I have come that they may have life, and that they may have it more abundantly. (John 10:10)

My Christianity was limited to attending mass at the Ethiopian Orthodox Church, conducted in Geeze, an old church language I did not understand. Kissing the cross on the priest's hand was all the "spiritual touch" I had. We were not encouraged to read or interpret the Bible which was the priest's job.

I came into contact with the Bible for the first time as a teenager. I had spent three fruitless months in hospital, then sent away to die of Leukemia. I trembled with fear as I held the Bible I had found in a library. I was not supposed to touch it, but, already on the death list, I didn't care. As I read the entire Bible, hope started rising in me. Fear fell off my eyes, and the Holy Spirit made the words alive. The Bible became my daily companion. John 10:10 became very vivid and meaningful to me. I thought, *If Jesus came to give me life, then I'm not going to die.* I had never associated life with Jesus Christ before then.

Hope gave way to faith which gave birth to life for my frail and ailing body. I was completely healed and have had good health for three decades since then. I also gave my life to God. No one had ever told me how to receive Jesus as Savior. I prayed, "God, this is my life; do whatever you want to do with it." I have served him joyously!

Jesus came to give us life but many have chosen death. As you hear His voice, do not harden your heart. If you take God's Word as it is and believe in Jesus, the Son, He'll bring life and meaning to your situation no matter how hopeless it may seem.

. . . PRAYER . . .

Lord, help me to go back to the Word as my only source of hope, comfort, success and spiritual renewal.

. . . TODAY'S THOUGHT . . .

"It is the Spirit who gives life; the flesh profits nothing. The words that I speak to you are spirit, and they are life" (John 6:63).

—Dr. Betta Mengistu
IBS-Africa, Nairobi, Africa

May 22

GOD IS SUFFICIENT

Whatever your hand finds to do, do it with your might; for there is no work or device or knowledge or wisdom in the grave where you are going. (Ecclesiastes 9:10)

Singing softly, I climbed the stairs to the schoolrooms above the church to ring the bell to summon the students to their classes. Our first missionary appointment, Utila Island, a small island off the north coast of the Republic of Honduras, had been our home for almost a year. I served officially as pastor of the local church, director-teacher of our elementary school, and unofficially as mechanic, doctor, and counselor.

I threw open the wooden window shutters. I saw the *Limon*, a small boat in the harbor, preparing for its first trip to the mainland after refurbishing. A plume of black smoke suddenly gushed from the hold. I stood transfixed as I watched the captain run to the hold and bend over the smoke and flame to pull out a young man. He then went to the bow with an ax and cut a hole in the hull at the water line to scuttle the boat.

Someone on the wharf shouted "Fire." Hundreds were gathered by the time the captain brought the man to the dock in a dory (a dugout canoe). They carried him to my porch, deposited him and stood back as if to say, "Here he is. Do what you can." My medical training consisted of a course in First Aid, so I prayed. The man was one big blister with his earlobes falling off. I had no medical supplies. I called to the crowd, "Go bring *Vaseline* from your houses." My wife tore a sheet into strips, and we coated him with petroleum jelly and wrapped him in the strips. The other boat from the island transported him to the hospital on the mainland. To our delight and God's glory, he made a complete recovery.

So often we are thrust into situations for which we are not prepared, but with our trust in God and a spirit willing to do what our hand finds hard to do, it is amazing what God can do through us.

. . . PRAYER . . .

Dear Lord, help us to prepare ourselves the best we can and to remember that we can do all things through Jesus Christ our Lord.

. . . TODAY'S THOUGHT . . .

Life is full of events that surprise us, but God is never surprised and is sufficient for every need.

—William R. McCall
Missionary Superintendent, COG

May 23

REVEALED BY THE HOLY SPIRIT

For the Holy Spirit had revealed to him . . . (Luke 2:26)

As a pastor I have ministered to many persons who were departing this life. But August 20, 1986, was a different day. It was the day my father, Reuben Miller, passed away. His demise is etched in my mind. The spiritual ramification was awesome.

The day before his death, my father entered the North Broward Hospital in Pompano Beach, Florida, because his doctor wanted to run tests. The test results were negative except for emphysema. The doctor said that his heart was "as strong as a bull" and he could live longer.

I was excited! I spent the night in the hospital. Up early for our devotional time, my father reported to me that the Holy Spirit revealed to him that he was "sealed for the kingdom." He also said that if I would "release him" he could go to be with the Lord. I had reservations about what he was saying. I went on with the devotion, quoting Scriptures and trying to encourage him. Before prayer, we sang the hymn "'Tis So Sweet to Trust in Jesus," his voice augmented with the words, "And I know that Thou art with me, wilt be with me to the end."

The Holy Spirit began to speak through him as if giving sanction to his words. After we finished our worship and prayer, he said again, "Son, release me. You are holding me here. I am ready to go home." I then said, "Pop, I release you this day in Jesus' name." He smiled.

I left the hospital to go home to change. When I returned later in the day, my oldest brother met me and said, "Dad is gone." I was literally in shock, then I remembered Simeon. After the Holy Spirit's revelation and seeing the Messiah, he said, "Now, lettest thou thy servant depart in peace" (Luke 2:29). I learned that God does reveal His will not for just the dying, but more so for the living.

. . . PRAYER . . .

Father, thank You for the power of the Holy Spirit that reveals to us Your will and purpose in this life as well as the life to come.

. . . TODAY'S THOUGHT . . .

The concealed will be revealed through the personhood of the Holy Spirit. Your life—past, present and future—is in God's hands.

—Quan L. Miller
Administrative Bishop, Cocoa COG, FL

May 24

THE MEANING OF JOY

. . . for the kingdom of God is not eating and drinking, but righteousness and peace and joy in the Holy Spirit. (Romans 14:17)

My father, Paul H. Walker, and Dr. David du Plessis drove around a West Virginia hairpin curve and they broadsided a locomotive parked across the road while coal cars were being loaded. Both men were severely injured, and my father's life was in jeopardy. He was in a West Virginia hospital.

In my father's hospital room, my mother took his hands in hers: "How do you feel?" His answer changed my life perspective. With his head swollen twice its normal size, his rib cage, breastbone, kneecap, and kneebone shattered, and his legs broken, he made a statement of joy: "I feel terrible pain in my body, but I am happy in my soul and spirit." In my father's words: "Sitting on the bench in the rain waiting for the ambulance, I told the Lord I was ready to go, but that I had preached for Him over 30 years and that I would like to live and raise my family if He would let me. Just then a bright and glorious light came, the same in appearance that I had seen at my conversion, only much larger. A great warmth of consolation came over me, and I had the assurance that my life would be spared."

My father died in 1975, 26 years after the accident, but the impact of that experience ignited an intense desire in me for the Christian life motivated through the power of spiritual joy. This was truly the Kingdom—joy in the Holy Spirit.

This is the essential work of the Holy Spirit—to infuse our lives with spiritual joy—regardless of circumstances. The meaning of joy is to be: "sealed with the Holy Spirit of promise" (Ephesians 1:13); "given access by one spirit to the Father" (2:18); "strengthened with might through His Spirit in the inner man" (3:16); "kept in the unity of the Spirit on the bond of peace" (4:3); "filled with the Spirit" (5:18); "praying always with all prayer and supplication in the Spirit" (6:18).

. . . PRAYER . . .

Father, thank You for the joy of Your Spirit which is always our strength to meet the challenging circumstances of life.

. . . TODAY'S THOUGHT . . .

Joy means that the Holy Spirit Who is in us is greater than any power that is in the world (based on 1 John 4:4).

—Dr. Paul L. Walker

Pastor, Mt. Paran Central, Atlanta, GA (former)

May 25

THE POWER OF PARENTAL INFLUENCE

But Esau ran to meet him, and embraced him, and fell on his neck and kissed him, and they wept (Genesis 33:4). "I am Joseph your brother, whom you sold into Egypt. But now, do not therefore be grieved or angry with yourselves because you sold me here; for God sent me before you to preserve life." (Genesis 45:4, 5)

Years after Jacob had deceived his father, Isaac, and at the same time violated his brother, Esau, by stealing his firstborn blessing, an event took place that would be remembered and repeated still years later. In Genesis 33, the frightening prospect of Jacob meeting up with Esau happened. Not knowing what Esau's reaction would be, Jacob arranged his clan so that his favorite son, Joseph, was placed in the rear so he would be protected in case Esau sought vengeance for the earlier deception. What Joseph and the rest of the two clans witnessed was two estranged brothers being reconciled to one another.

Years later, Joseph is in the land of Egypt having been sold into slavery by his jealous brothers. Through a long series of seeming unconnected and unfortunate events, Joseph's brothers travel to Egypt where they come face-to-face with Joseph. In Genesis 45 Joseph is no longer a slave, nor is he powerless. He immediately recognizes his brothers; the same brothers who had hated him and deceived him. Joseph was now faced with the decision of what he would do to those who had mistreated him like Esau, his uncle, once faced.

We do not know all the reasons for Joseph's reaction, but maybe it was in part due to the scene he had witnessed as a child. Maybe Joseph was so impressed by the experience of his uncle and dad that he followed the same course of action when faced by the same set of circumstances. The impact of family influence on Joseph as a child was so imperceptibly powerful that he instinctively followed the example. The result was forgiveness and reconciliation of an estranged family. How dynamic the impact of familial influence!

. . . PRAYER . . .

Father, help me ever so live that my life is influencing my family to live in a manner that will bring peace and restoration.

. . . TODAY'S THOUGHT . . .

Today's family experience will be tomorrow's family action.

—John Kie Vining
Director, Ministerial Care, Cleveland, TN

May 26

WHEN THE LIGHT GOES OUT

Who among you fears the Lord? Who obeys the voice of His Servant? Who walks in darkness And has no light? Let him trust in the name of the Lord And rely upon his God. Look, all you who kindle a fire, Who encircle yourselves with sparks: Walk in the light of your fire and in the sparks you have kindled— This you shall have from My hand: You shall lie down in torment. (Isaiah 50:10-11)

Darkness can be one of the most frightening experiences of life. Harmless shadows become "creatures of night." Active imaginations empower inanimate objects made impotent at the dawning of light.

Spiritual darkness has no less effect. The prophet Isaiah cautions that neither faith in God nor obedience to His Word insulates a believer from episodes of spiritual darkness. Such episodes can occur when feelings of hopelessness, loneliness and despair overwhelm believers. Overly active imaginations turn harmless words and thoughts into "creatures of the night."

What are we to do when the lights go out?

There have been numerous times in my spiritual walk when no bright shining light shows me the way. I have said to my wife, "I don't know what is going to happen, but I know that our trust is in God and He will not fail." In such times we are to stay, "Lean or rest on God."

Don't light your own path. There is always the temptation to take matters into our own hands. However, there is only one light that will lead us into all truth. Jesus said, "However, when He, the Spirit of truth, has come, He will guide you into all truth; . . (John 16:13).

Let the light of the Holy Spirit deliver you from the darkness of vain imaginations and cast down every thought that does not exalt Jesus. "For it is the God who commanded light to shine out of darkness, who has shone in our hearts to give the light of the knowledge of the glory of God in the face of Jesus Christ" (2 Corinthians 4:6).

. . . PRAYER . . .

Father, let the light of the Holy Spirit dispel the "creatures of the night" and illuminate my life that I may reflect the glory of Christ.

. . . TODAY'S THOUGHT . . .

Remember, God is God, even in the dark.

—Allen A. McCray
Pastor, Phoenix Parkway Community, Phoenix, AZ

May 27

THE WARM AND WONDERFUL HOLY SPIRIT

The Spirit Himself bears witness with our spirit that we are children of God. . . (Romans 8:16)

My wife and I have been blessed with three precious children. My oldest son calls me "Dad," my daughter "Daddy," and my youngest son "Pops." These are intimate expressions that mean much to them and me.

Scripture makes it clear that we can know God the Father even more intimately because we are told that by the Holy Spirit we are given "the spirit of adoption, whereby we cry Abba, Father" (Romans 8:15). We are brought into intimate contact with God as if the Father places us upon His knee as a little child and we look up into His face and say, "Abba, Father." This relationship with God is made possible through the warm and wonderful person of the Holy Spirit.

What else does the Holy Spirit do? Hundreds of verses describe the work of the Spirit. In believers He works in manifold ways.

The Spirit gives us new life in Christ.

The Spirit empowers us for service and gives us the ability to witness and to be fruitful.

The Spirit brings forth His fruit in our lives. "But the fruit of the Spirit is love, joy, peace, longsuffering, kindness, goodness, faithfulness, . ." (Galatians 5:22).

The Spirit leads us in our lives . "For as many as are led by the Spirit of God, these are sons of God" (Romans 8:14).

Pray every day for the Spirit of God to lead you. Ask Him daily to open the doors of your life.

Some Christians believe that all they need is to be filled with the Holy Spirit. The person who fills his or her car up once and never fills it again will soon be walking!

. . . PRAYER . . .

Grant me, O God, the fullness of Your Spirit daily so I may rejoice and sing.

. . . TODAY'S THOUGHT . . .

Claim His promise. Jesus said, "If you then, being evil, know how to give good gifts to your children, how much more will your heavenly Father give the Holy Spirit to those who ask Him!" (Luke 11:13).

—Fred G. Swank

Pastor, COG in MI (retired)

May 28

FOR SUCH A TIME AS THIS

Yet who knows whether you have come to the kingdom for such a time as this? (Esther 4:14)

Each day my agenda was the same. Wake up with the same wrenching knot located deep inside that reminded me I hadn't made any progress since the previous day. The long walks of prayer I had disciplined myself to take helped me temporarily, but the grind of life seemed all too overpowering. I needed relief, and I couldn't wait much longer.

For nine years I had been waiting on God to open the right doors for me. I knew I was called. I knew His hand was upon me. I just couldn't grasp the time element. My heart was right, and my motives were pure. What was taking so long?

Then, finally, the breakthrough I so needed came. "In all things God works for the good of those who love Him." A wonderful church invited me to be their pastor. I'm finally in the door! I've arrived! The waiting game is over! ". . . for such a time as this" is now reality. Although extremely grateful for the open door, it was a startling discovery to learn--there is not a final door to enter. There is no arriving point, only arrival points. The journey is the destination.

God's timing is so critical to us. Our natural desires insist we possess what we want without the pain of waiting. God is so faithful to reveal His plan only when it is best. May we always be reminded that ". . . for such a time as this" is in the hands of the master planner.

. . . PRAYER . . .

Lord, thank You for Your patience as I learn to trust You. In my rush, let me remember Your faithfulness.

. . . TODAY'S THOUGHT . . .

David wrote, "My times are in your hands . . ." (Psalm 31:15).

—Allen Skelton
Director, Spirit Vision Bible College, Gainesville, GA

May 29

MY HEART IS FIXED

My heart is steadfast, O God, my heart is steadfast; I will sing and give praise. (Psalm 57:7)

These were the words of the Psalmist speaking of his experiences of faith in God. He was established in the way. His mind was set on the goal—eternity. He faced the Creator and received strength daily from this great and wonderful God. Thank God for the day I was baptized in the Holy Spirit and spoke in other tongues as He gave me utterance!

I was converted as a young boy at the age of 11 and was baptized in the Holy Ghost a few weeks later. I was called to preach at age 13, but the advice of a good pastor urged me to finish high school before leaving for full-time ministry. I took his advice and later attended college. One college in particular had a life-long impact on me. It was the college where I received my bachelor's degree. At the school were several young professors that had at one time been Pentecostal. They had been influenced and turned away from Holiness doctrine. They were clever professors in teaching their doctrine, which was not at all the doctrine of Jesus Christ. They troubled me with the teachings I was receiving. There I was, a young pastor in a growing church (growing in numbers, finances and spiritual blessings). I did not want to appear ignorant, neither did I want to forsake the reality of the Holy Spirit.

One Monday morning after glorious Sunday services, the Holy Spirit had a talk with me. He asked me three pertinent questions: Did I not save You? Bring you faith? Baptize you and fill you with Myself and did you not speak in tongues? Of course He did! I could hear His voice as clear as a bell, and I could answer yes to each question.

After that night I never doubted His power again. I was fixed on the Lord. During my fifty-seven years in His service, I have never doubted God's presence.

. . . PRAYER . . .

Almighty God, Your sweet Holy Spirit is with us. We thank You for His presence and His administration in our churches around the world.

. . . TODAY'S THOUGHT . . .

By being fixed on the power of the Lord, you too can attest to others of the glorious power of the Holy Spirit.

—A.M. Stephens

Pastor, North Belmont, Belmont, NC

May 30

I CAN'T—HE CAN

For you see your calling, brethren, that not many wise according to the flesh, not many mighty, not many noble, are called. But God has chosen the foolish things of the world to put to shame the wise, and God has chosen the weak things of the world to put to shame the things which are mighty; and the base things of the world and the things which are despised God has chosen, and the things which are not, to bring to nothing the things that are, that no flesh should glory in His presence. (1 Corinthians 1: 26-29)

Just 20 years old and the Lord spoke clearly to me calling me to pastoral ministry. Being young and full of zeal, I concurred: "Yes, Lord, I can do this and will. I hope the denominational leaders will be as smart as you and I are. Give me a chance, and I'll turn a church into 'something.'" But nothing I did to get 'it' working worked.

Two years later I found myself quite by accident in a police station. I was in the construction industry at the time and thought I could get a job maintaining the building. Five days later they hired me to be a police officer. I had never considered this. I loved it!

At 30 years of age the same church I was in at age 20 asked me to be their pastor. I did not want to do it, but agreed to pray about it. The Lord spoke clearly to me, "I couldn't use you before because you didn't need me; now you don't want to do it, so if you will, I can use you." I admit that I did not like that response, but what I learned has taught me lessons that will last a lifetime. God does not need me—I need Him! He is simply looking for willing people to fill with His Holy Spirit to empower them to be His witnesses. "My message and my preaching were not with wise and persuasive words, but with the demonstration of the Spirit's power, so that your faith might not rest on men's wisdom, but on God's power" (1 Corinthians 2:4, 5).

. . . PRAYER . . .

Father, help us to always realize that You desire to fill us. It is Christ in us, the hope of glory. We are Yours, have Your way in us.

. . . TODAY'S THOUGHT . . .

Having spent over 11 years in the police force, and now 11 years as a pastor, I regularly am reminded that I can't do it, but His energy works powerfully in me, and He can!

—Arnie ter Mors
Pastor, FGCC, Calgary, Alberta

May 31

AUTHENTIC BIBLICAL SPIRITUAL CONVERSION

And you He made alive, who were dead in trespasses and sins, . . .
(Ephesians 2:1)

September 15, 1952—rendezvous with my spiritual destiny. The atmosphere in that revival meeting was supernaturally charged with the amazing and mysterious transforming power of God. I was brought face-to-face with the reality of my status before a holy and just God. My attempt to evade that power of conviction by leaving the church with a friend to indulge in my smoking habit proved futile. That which used to be my pleasurable experience made no sense to me. Returning to my seat, I experienced no break from this strange but real visitation.

Suddenly, I was carried away in a vision and found myself standing by a railroad track. A train passed by swiftly. On the last coach stood the friend with whom I had gone outside, waving good-bye. I asked about the train and its destination. "It's heaven's train" was the reply. "You are not on it; you are lost." Thoughts of being lost eternally shook me to the core of my being. I awoke only to find the service in its unabated electrifying tempo. Someone told me that my friend whom I saw in the vision was saved at the altar.

I recognized that God was calling me to repentance and eternal life. I made my way to the altar: "O God, help me not to leave the altar without being saved." He indicated to me what would hinder me. I responded obediently and was gloriously and wondrously saved.

I was incredibly recreated. I felt as if I had been taken out of my old body and placed into a new one. Glory to God who makes things new! Biblical, spiritual conversion is a reality and possibility.

. . . PRAYER . . .

I give You thanks, most gracious, loving heavenly Father. Through Jesus Christ, my Lord, You have retrieved me from the depth of my lostness and given me a new existence for time and eternity.

. . . TODAY'S THOUGHT . . .

"For one man (person) conversion means the slaying of the beast within him; in another it brings the calm of conviction to an unquiet mind; to a third it is the entrance into a larger liberty and a more abundant life . . ." (George Jackson).

—Bishop Aston R. Morrison
President, COGOP of Canada

June 1

WHEN YOU ARE ANOINTED

The Spirit of the Lord is upon Me, Because He has anointed Me to preach the gospel . . . (Luke 4:18)

Fatigued, my left arm was numb and would not respond. I felt a crushing weight on my chest. But at 35, I did not think anything could happen to me. After an hour of relaxing with my wife in the quiet of our home, I began feeling a strange sensation and lost consciousness. I regained consciousness hearing my wife and children crying and praying for me. My left side was paralyzed. Fear and uncertainty swept over me. It seemed my whole world had come to an end.

A heart attack! And the doctor said I would have to quit preaching! For two years I was on heavy medication for the heart condition and had major surgery for another problem. I still pastored my church and prayed for the healing of people with fewer problems than I had. One day while reading Luke 4:18, I stopped abruptly and said out loud, "If the Spirit of the Lord is upon me and I'm anointed to preach the gospel, then why is this happening to me?" At that moment, I told God I wanted to feel His Spirit and His anointing if I were to continue preaching His Word.

For the first time in two years, I felt the cleansing Holy Spirit come upon me and the anointing burn in my soul. I understood Romans 10:17: "So then faith comes by hearing, and hearing by the word of God." The Holy Spirit uses the Word to awaken a response of faith within us, and it is the reliability of the Word of God on which we rest our faith for salvation or healing. I experienced a gradual but complete healing, with the Stanford Heart Research Center confirming it.

All this happened 24 years ago, and today I walk in health, without any sign of heart problems. To God be the glory, for it was His Spirit and His anointing that made me whole.

. . . PRAYER . . .

Thank You, God, for letting me preach the gospel to the poor, to heal the brokenhearted, to preach deliverance to the captives, to set at liberty them that are bruised.

. . . TODAY'S THOUGHT . . .

Putting God's Word into action brings exciting results.

—Billy R. Phillips
Pastor, New Life Center, Redding, CA

June 2

GOD'S WORD IS TRUE

Therefore know that the Lord your God, He is God, the faithful God who keeps covenant and mercy for a thousand generations with those who love Him and keep His commandments; . . .(Deuteronomy 7:9)

In the late 60's and early 70's, I pastored a small, rural church called Happy Hill. We were struggling when, in October 1971, our missionary, Rev. Edgar Stone, from Mexico, came by for two nights of service. On the last night he gave an overwhelming prophecy concerning the future and growth of our church. One of the statements—"They will come from the north, south, east, and west." We were all blessed and enthused to hear from God.

On January 21, 1972, a car carrying six of our youth from a rally was hit head-on by an intoxicated man. Four of our youth and the driver of the other car were killed. One of those was our only daughter, 16 years of age, who loved God very much.

This was a long, cold night when we started home from the hospital knowing four out of eight of our youth group would no longer be with us, and two more left in the hospital not knowing their destiny. Since these young people were good friends and all loved God, their funerals were held together at the Ramona Ochelata High School. The very next service in our church, youth from the community came and filled the pews—revival started from that day. God never lets His Word fail. We were constantly reminded of His love for us through His Word and the Family of God.

It has been 24 years and today that little church in the country is a large church with attendance around 200. They just completed a family worship center that will seat 800, all paid for. God kept His Word; they have come—"From the North, South, East and West."

PRAYER

Thank You, Father for Your grace that is sufficient to keep us in time of sorrow, and for Your faithfulness to fulfill Your Promises.

. . . TODAY'S THOUGHT . . .

Discouragement may come, but be assured, God will keep His Word. "Jesus Christ is the same yesterday, today, and forever" (Hebrews 13:8).

—Charles R. Richey
Assistant Superintendent, COGoAF, Shidler, OK

June 3

A PASSION FOR GOD!

. . . if I have found grace in Your sight, show me now Your way, that I may know You . . . (Exodus 33:13)

Many people give up everything for an ideal, sacrificing themselves in order to reach the goal that is the passion of their lives. For example, an athlete preparing for a competition leads a rigorous life with severe privations. Such passion ought to characterize Christians as they seek God's face. We must burn with the spiritual fire that burned in Paul (Philippians 3:8-11), Jeremiah, Moses—men who did not feel satisfied with themselves regarding their own spiritual lives. They longed to know God intimately.

There was a time in my ministry when I would be told how tremendous the worship service was, but I was unsatisfied. I would pray: "Lord, I know there are rivers and springs overflowing with the Holy Spirit. I want to know You better." God put that thirst in me. When I sought Him passionately, I found what I needed.

When I understood that fellowship with the Spirit is more than addressing words to God, I was transformed. I reached a new stage in my life and ministry. Everything was fresh and renewed with no religious routine. Unable to sleep at night, I instead had fellowship with Him. My experience affected crowds.

We must seek God's face. The people of Israel wanted to witness God's great works, but they did not want God himself. How different was Moses' attitude! He witnessed the miracles, but he prayed to know God (Exodus 33:13, 18).

. . . PRAYER . . .

Lord Jesus, today more than ever I want to tell You that I love You and I need You. You are my absolute priority. Arouse my heart so I may worship You and hear Your voice daily. Show me Your glory.

. . . TODAY'S THOUGHT . . .

"Call to Me, and I will answer you, and show you great and mighty things. . . .'" (Jeremiah 33:3). His promise still holds good. If you have a real passion for God you will surely discover Him.

—Claudio J. Freidzon

Iglesia Rey de Reyes Ola Zaba, Republic of Argentina

June 4

DESPERATE TO SEE GOD WORK

But those who wait on the Lord Shall renew their strength; . . . (Isaiah 40:31)

What do you do when you have prayed with "all prayer and supplication," doing everything you know to do, and the mountain of your need still looms before you, seemingly as difficult to move as ever? When this happens simply stand still. Do not move. Do not try to bring about a solution in your own ability of strength. Allow your heart to be settled in quiet surrender as you wait silently before the Lord to hear the direction and answer that will come to you by the direction of the Holy Spirit. The time has come for trusting that the Lord will bring into existence 'all things' that work together for your good.

When you are physically, emotionally, and spiritually exhausted, the time has come to speak courage to yourself. By taking this small step of faith toward God, He takes one giant step of faith toward you. Then you can act as He enables you. Remind yourself of the promises of God to stand with you, uphold you, sustain you and to be with you. Remind yourself that He cares for the lilies of the field that last only for a short time and that He has declared that you are destined to be with Him forever. Philippians 1:6 states, "Being confident of this very thing, that He which hath begun a good work in you will complete it until the day of Jesus Christ."

When you stand by faith, knowing that you have done all you can do, God then only asks that you hold the door open for Him to move into your situation. You simply hold the door open for Him and do as He says in Ephesians 6:13,14. . . "Having done all to stand, stand therefore," God is working with you as you pray and stand in faith believing. God is bringing about His purposes in your life. Be renewed in every area of your life today.

. . . PRAYER . . .

Our Father, we thank You that when we wait upon the Lord, we are capable of walking without falling down, of running without becoming weary.

. . . TODAY'S THOUGHT . . .

When we stand in faith, the Lord not only acts, but He gives us an awareness of His presence as we are renewed.

—Daniel N. Sikes
Evangelist, Albany, GA

June 5

GOD'S GREATEST MIRACLE

I thank my God upon every remembrance of you . . . Philippians 1:3

From a sleepy little town in West Virginia to the screaming freeways and sidewalks of Los Angeles, the miracles of God's great grace have been too numerous to recount. How could I have known that the Lord would take me from my tiny hamlet, where everyone knew my name, to one of our country's biggest cities?

I reflect much on the places God has directed my life—ministry in three of our nation's largest cities, seeing the tragedy and hardships of people trying to fit into these mega urban areas where 80% of our population now resides. Heartbreak, poverty, and disaster are to be reckoned with each day. "The steps of a good man are ordered by the Lord, And He delights in his way. Though he fall, he shall not be utterly cast down; For the Lord upholds him with His hand" (Psalm 37:23,24).

My greatest source of comfort, God's greatest miracle, and my constant fount of strength have been the love and wonder of my family. My most valued compliments are not words, but experiences: Donna, a 30-year-old single mom, raised in foster care, told a friend about our family. She and her friend thumbed 300 miles from Boston to our home in New York just to prove what she had told the girl. "You see" she said, "they really do love each other." Midnight visits from teenagers in Chicago. "Pastor, could we stay here? We feel safe in your house." In L.A., a young lady who helps us around the house asked if she could just sit awhile after she finished her work. "I just feel at peace here." Amazing, isn't it, how we take the richest blessing of life for granted?

I thank God for Deb, my high school sweetheart and my strength. I thank God for my daughter, Charity, who loves and serves Jesus.

PRAYER

Thank You Lord, for the support and love of family in every situation and circumstance, good and bad. You have surrounded me by people who really care. Let me always be aware of Your blessings!

. . . TODAY'S THOUGHT . . .

The noblest miracles are found in companions, children, moms, dads, and brothers and sisters in the Lord. These are the people who will love you unselfishly and will give to you until the hurting stops!

—Dan Maynard
Pastor, Liberty Temple, Arleta, CA

June 6

SOUND FROM HEAVEN

And suddenly there came a sound from heaven, as of a rushing mighty wind, and it filled the whole house where they were sitting. (Acts 2:2)

About 120 men and women were gathered in a place of prayer and safety, expecting something from God, but not really knowing what God was about to do. All they knew for sure was that their Lord had told them to expect a visitation from the Holy Spirit, a visitation different from any that men had ever experienced—so intense that He called it a "baptism."

'Suddenly' is a description from the vantage point of the men and women in that place. In the heart and plan of God, it was anything but sudden, for it had been planned from the foundation of the world. There is an appointed time and place for the fulfillment of the promises of God, but they are not less sure because we have not seen them yet. 'Suddenly' the Lord comes and fulfills His Word to us, but His Word is already established in heaven.

"There came a sound from heaven." God did not need to clear this with any earthly magistrate. It did not need to be filtered through any philosophy or the Jewish religious system. Just as when the Word of the Lord came to John the Baptist in the wilderness, bypassing Tiberius Caesar, Pontius Pilate, Herod, Philip, Lysanias, Annas and Caiaphas, all of the civil and religious structure and fulfilled His Word to a group of common men and women.

The Lord had made the promise. They believed the promise and obeyed His Word. Suddenly, right on time, He fulfilled His promise, with a blessing from heaven that they received 'first hand', not watered down but exactly as He poured it out. It is through faith and patience that we inherit the promises of God.

. . . PRAYER . . .

Father, thank You that You will fulfill Your promise to me, right on time, in its fullness.

. . . TODAY'S THOUGHT . . .

The Lord is not slack concerning His promises. He will surely perform His Word in my life. I will trust and obey, and hold fast until the change comes.

—David Killingsworth
Pastor, COGoAF, Green Forest AR

June 7

HOLY SPIRIT BIRTHED ZEAL

. . . not lagging in diligence, fervent in spirit, serving the Lord; rejoicing in hope, patient in tribulation, continuing steadfastly in prayer; . . . (Romans 12:11, 12)

Laughter would always resonate off the paneled walls of the old Querandi Restaurant in downtown Buenos Aires when we would get together for our weekly lunch.

I have very happy memories of meeting with my mentor, Kenneth, as he would lead me, a young businessman who had recently given my life to Christ, in Bible study, prayer and a time of sharing. Kenneth was a successful and busy marketing director of large multinational corporation, yet he found time to meet with me.

Not only that, but he had a wonderful family who loved the Lord, he was a lay pastor, directed and taught Sunday school in our church, visited the sick in a local hospital each week, led many to Christ, and gave his testimony whenever the opportunity arose.

From my friend I learned a lot more than the Bible. His life was busy yet balanced. He served the Lord with a contagious joy, intense devotion, and a humble spirit. His life taught me more than his words. But the lesson from my friend I will never forget was that I must be zealous in serving the Lord, and that it is up to me, and me alone, to keep my own spiritual fervor.

May I pass on to you the same torch that was handed to me back in Argentina—keep on fire with Holy Spirit zeal as you serve Christ where you have been planted.

. . . PRAYER . . .

Lord, it is my heart's desire to keep my spiritual fervor. Help me today Holy Spirit to be filled with fresh zeal for knowing and serving You.

. . . TODAY'S THOUGHT . . .

Being on fire for Christ is catching. Joy is wonderfully contagious. Zeal is transferable. May you be a blessing to everyone you meet today.

—David A. MacFarlane
FGCC (retired)

June 8

GOD, MY FATHER

And because you are sons, God has sent forth the Spirit of His Son into your hearts, crying out, "Abba, Father!" (Galatians 4:6)

It was toward the end of a special time of consecration to which the Holy Spirit had called me, that I reached a place of emptiness and a sense of great personal need. I was finishing the fourth year of a pastorate when the Spirit called me to several weeks of intense daily prayer and frequent fasting.

During that time of emptying, God made me aware that a major change in the direction of my ministry was imminent. As a part of that change I was to resign my pastorate with nothing but the assurance of His sovereign Will to replace it. Like Abraham, I was to follow Him blindly.

My heart told me that God had never failed me and would not fail me this time. Yet my head experienced considerable anxieties and uncertainties over "starting over" at this stage of my life.

On a particular day I felt lonely and vulnerable. As I sat on the floor of the little Sunday school classroom, which was my favorite prayer room, I spoke aloud the feeling in my heart. "Although I am a father and a grandfather, I have no father to talk to about what I am going through. If I had, I know I would feel better."

At that moment the Holy Spirit said to me, "My son, you do have a father, a heavenly Father, and He waits to hear everything that is in your heart."

A peace suddenly came over me, and I have never hesitated, since then, to go to my Father with everything that concerns my life.

. . . PRAYER . . .

O, God, You are my Father, and a Father to all who are fatherless. I can talk to You about all my joys and pains. Thank You, Father.

. . . TODAY'S THOUGHT . . .

Jesus introduced God to us as a Father. The apostle Paul writes that the Holy Spirit in our hearts helps us to cry out, "My Father."

—Jack Smith

Minister, North Cleveland, Cleveland, TN

June 9

THE HOLY SPIRIT OUR HELPER

But the Helper, the Holy Spirit, whom the Father will send in My name, He will teach you all things. . . (John 14:26)

We are able to live the 'abundant life' promised by Christ through the gift of a helper—the Holy Spirit. The Spirit helps us in two ways: He helps us to *become* and He helps us to *overcome.*

As our helper, the Holy Spirit guides us in becoming a complete person in Christ. Columbus died with a limited knowledge of the beautiful mountains, rivers, forests, sea coasts, wealth, and minerals of the land he discovered. Likewise our discovery of Christ is the beginning of the walk. The Holy Spirit guides us in understanding our worth as a member of God's family—provisions, rich experiences, adventure.

As the Spirit bears witness with our spirit that we are children of God (Romans 8:16), several things happen. We receive confidence through *identity*—freedom to be, to do and to make big, beautiful plans. Condemnation is replaced by confidence (Romans 8:1). We receive confidence through *security*—we belong to God, sealed by the Spirit (Ephesians 1:13). This gives stability. We receive confidence through *productivity*—we have fire to make things happen (Matthew 3:11).

As our helper, the Holy Spirit stands by us and gives strength to *overcome.* He stands as an advocate, counsel for defense, defender, and companion. He walks by our side and during times of death, difficulty and disaster, He says to us, "There will be another day. God's Word is true. The devil will not win. There will be victory—hold on!"

The helper always lets us see what we have left, not what has been taken away. He lets us see hope, trust, faith, and the beauty of heaven.

. . . PRAYER . . .

As we begin each day, Holy Father, let us recognize the Helper is always beside us, equipping us to become total and complete in Christ, giving us guidance for ministry and assuring us that we will be victorious.

. . . TODAY'S THOUGHT . . .

When the Helper is on the inside, living water will flow from the heart to the outside, producing faith, fruit and fullness to live joyfully and successfully.

—Floyd D. Carey
Minister, Metropolitan Church, Birmingham, AL

June 10

THE PRINCIPLE OF THE ZERO FACTOR

I waited patiently for the Lord; and He inclined to me, and heard my cry. He also brought me up out of a horrible pit, out of a miry clay, and set my feet upon a rock, and established my steps. (Psalm 40:1,2)

Many face times of bitter hopelessness in their lives: a child is stricken with an incurable disease; a job is lost at a time when the household faces a mountain of debt; a son is hooked on cocaine; a divorce is pending in the judicial system.

In the Bible many turned to God when all hope was gone – when all their physical resources had been exhausted. In fact, when no banker, lawyer, or doctor can help, that's an excellent time to trust God!

Remember the woman with the issue of blood? For 12 long years she sought the help of doctors. She had spent her life's savings trying to get well. All hope was gone – until she caught sight of Jesus.

Something within her began to stir when she remembered that she had heard about the miracle worker. As she reached out in faith, grasping the hem of His garment, she was instantly made whole.

Are you at the point of hopelessness now? Get a glimpse of Jesus. He is still performing miracles.

Reach out and touch Him in faith.

Your miracle is on the way!

. . . PRAYER . . .

Thank You, Father, for the miracles You give us every day! Help us to always live worthy of Your love and grace.

. . . TODAY'S THOUGHT . . .

I am a miracle. I experience miracles daily. I will share God's miracles with others through the Holy Spirit.

—R. W. Schambach (Reprinted from *SpiritWalk: Daily Devotions on the Holy Spirit* by permission of Pathway Press)
International Evangelist, Schambach Revivals, Tyler, TX

June 11

REST AMIDST UNREST

Come to Me, all you who labor and are heavy laden, and I will give you rest. (Matthew 11:28)

At the age of 19 all my hopes and plans were toppled and crushed in the dust. Conviction seized me, and I became desperate to find God. The days of seeking day and night turned into weeks. After hearing restitution emphasized I, in desperation, had the horse hitched to the buggy and went over the community confessing and paid a farmer for stolen watermelons. I took my old phonograph records and sailed them away. Even these humiliating and humbling works did not bring rest.

After five months in deep despair, one night I prayed: "Lord, I have done all I can do. When I meet You I will point You to this night. I am going to leave it up to You. Here I am. I will trust You." A burden that was smothering me lifted off me as real as if a man had stepped off my chest. A heavenly peace that I had never known filled my soul! I had a Damascus Road experience.

I fear that in former years of my ministry, in relating my struggle with myself to find God, I may have led people to think it is hard to find salvation and that everyone a has Damascus Road experience. It is not to my credit it took me five months to do what I should have done the first day--trust Jesus! Rest is not found in denomination, creeds, rituals, or works. It is the depth of repentance and the totality of one's trust in Jesus that bring rest to a seeking soul.

"The Spirit Himself bears witness with our spirit that we are children of God. . . (Romans 8:16).

. . . PRAYER . . .

Thank You, Lord, for paying for our salvation and making a way we can have peace.

. . . TODAY'S THOUGHT . . .

The great creator God who created man can "sympathize with our weaknesses" (Hebrews 4:15). "For we who have believed do enter that rest, . ." (4:3). These truths are for our stress-filled lives today.

—George L. Britt
Bible Teacher/Prophecy Preacher, COG (Retired)

June 12

THE PRISONER

Let the groaning of the prisoner come before You; According to the greatness of Your power Preserve those who are appointed to die. . . (Psalm 79:11)

I have never been confined in a cramped jail. My wrists have never suffered the bites of steel. Since the time of my birth until now, I have walked in the outdoors. As a child I knew what it was to climb hills, roam woods, skate on frozen ponds, hike hills, and travel the length of the country roads.

Yet I was a person of despair in bonds of misery. A prisoner, my dungeon cell was my sinful self. Conceived in sin, shaped in iniquity; my transgressions were ever before me; in thought, word and deed I pulled the cord of captivity tighter. Conscience and memory stood as guards to remind me of my guilt and of impending judgment and doom. The power of the sun could not dispel the darkness within my heart.

Then one day I received my pardon. It came as a sunrise comes upon the darkened earth; as a pleasant rain upon thirsty plains. My fetters fell off; cords were loosed. The gates opened wide in sweet release.

One, in the form of God, made Himself of no reputation, took upon Himself the form of flesh, and became obedient unto death. In the presence of the Father, His garment dyed red in His holy agony, He provided payment—His own life. Jesus was condemned, scourged, and crucified. But the unfolding years have recorded the glory of His passion, and heaven has acclaimed His binding and our loosing; His condemnation, our justification; His bruising, our healing; His death, our life. Who is this Liberator? He is the same Who said the Spirit of the Lord God is upon Me to set the captives free and open the prison to them that are bound.

Yes, I was a prisoner, but I discovered God's power of forgiveness that brought me up from a horrible pit, out of the miry clay, and set my feet on a rock, and established my goings. He put a new song in my mouth and a praise unto God in my heart. Now indeed I find myself an heir of God and a joint heir with Christ.

. . . PRAYER . . .

Dear Lord, thank You for the power to be free!

. . . TODAY'S THOUGHT . . .

"If the Son shall make you free, ye shall be free indeed."

—L. Terrell Taylor

State Overseer, State Evangelism Director, COG (retired)

June 13

DOWNSIZING

Therefore we also, since we are surrounded by so great a cloud of witnesses, let us lay aside every weight, and the sin which so easily ensnares us, and let us run with endurance the race that is set before us. . . (Hebrews 12:1)

It has been said that Christianity has within itself the seeds of its own destruction. If we meet its conditions, we will be blessed, and the result of the blessings will draw our hearts away from that which attracted us in the first place.

One of the great blessings is the infilling of the Holy Spirit, which I experienced at the age of 15. The reality of this experience has been confirmed throughout my life by diminishing every other aspect of my life. At fifteen I cared only about sports and girls, but all my priorities were changed.

The major operational friend in the corporate world today is 'downsizing'. Survival in business means getting rid of excess, that which is not only unnecessary but also that which reduces the profit margin. The business world may be a step ahead of the church today, but the apostle Paul articulated the principle at the birth of Christianity.

In this church age, when wealth is often taken to be the ultimate approval of God upon a life, we should listen to one of the great Jewish sages, Maimonides. He said that the only purpose of obtaining wealth is to free the individual to have more time for the study of the Scriptures.

Wealth today is most often equated with a volume of our possessions, specific earmarks of affluence. The writer of Hebrews points to two things that hinder us from running with patience the race that is set before us: encumbrance and sin. Jesus asks, "What doth it profit a man if he gains the whole world and loses his own soul?"

. . . PRAYER . . .

Lord, may the great gift You have given be used to empower me this day to rid my life of the 'stuff' that hinders me from doing the perfect will.

. . . TODAY'S THOUGHT . . .

"It is extraordinary how things fall off from a man like autumn leaves once he comes to the place where there is no rule but that of the personal domination of the Holy Spirit" (Oswald Chambers).

—George Ekeroth
Assemblies of God International Fellowship

June 14

THE DAY THE CHURCH BLEW DOWN

And I will pray the Father, and He will give you another Helper, that He may abide with you forever. . . (John 14:16)

April 3, 1974, began as an ordinary day. However, ordinary became extraordinary as a killer tornado struck Xenia, Ohio, and my family and I witnessed the comfort of the Holy Spirit. Seeing the approaching tornado, we took shelter under the kitchen table. As the storm hit, the house quivered and shook—there was a tremendous roar as windows began breaking, the roof lifted, and concrete blocks from our church next door torpedoed through the windows and walls of the parsonage. Huddled under the table with our two sons, my wife and I prayed, and soon the Holy Spirit was praying through her. Something then hit me in the back causing me to look around. I saw what I thought was a white curtain, but later realized there were no white curtains, nor even a window, in our kitchen. I believe it was an angel. At the same time, I saw our large, heavy, dining room table roll up to the kitchen door and rest on its end across the doorway where it shielded us from concrete blocks and large pieces of dagger-like glass later found embedded in the underside of the table.

After the storm, I immediately thought of the glorious manner in which the Spirit had ministered to everyone who had attended the last worship service in the now-destroyed church building. The Spirit had prepared us for what we were to experience three days hence as we sang "If I Knew of a Land": "If I knew of a land where no dark clouds came, where the sky was always bright and there'd be no storm or rain, I would sell all I had and move that day." Thirty-two people lost their lives that day, most of whom were our neighbors, but we were spared.

Jesus' promise to send another Comforter became reality to my family and me the day the church and parsonage blew down.

. . . PRAYER . . .

Help us, Lord, to realize You are our Comforter in every circumstance.

. . . TODAY'S THOUGHT . . .

Comforter originally meant, "called along side to help in time of trouble," but later came to mean, "to help by doing for us what we cannot do for ourselves."

—Harold E. Stevens
Pastor, COG, Lebanon, OH

June 15

THE PHYSICIAN FOR LIFE'S CONDITIONS

". . . and they brought to Him all such people who were afflicted. . .and He healed them." (Matthew 4:24)

On December 22, 1998, God gave Teri and I a beautiful baby girl. Karley Hope came into the world with some complications. Her hips were not functioning properly. Our doctor recommended us to the Scottish Rite Children's Hospital in Dallas. This devastated us. We weren't sure if Karley was going to be able to walk, and that made us feel so helpless.

We took our daughter home with us and began praying for a miracle. We had churches and friends praying all over the world. After two weeks of waiting, the call finally came from Scottish Rite Hospital. We were greeted by all the physicians, and finally after several sonograms on her hips, we were given negative results. The doctor said she would have to be fitted with a special harness brace, and it was going to be an extensive process. However, two weeks later, we took Karley back to the same doctor, and the results were astonishing. I quote the doctor's words, "Her hips are perfectly normal."

Our Physician had done it again! This blessed Practitioner has prescribed an unfailing remedy for the hopeless, helpless, and useless of mankind; a remedy that is both effectual and eternal.

. . . PRAYER . . .

May every person who reads about this miracle also experience His healing power, spiritually, mentally, emotionally, psychologically, physically, and financially.

. . . TODAY'S THOUGHT . . .

Any time there is a condition, He will be the Physician Who gives a brand new position.

—Chris Moody

Pastor, Greywood Heights COG, Van Alstyne, TX

June 16

WOULD YOU LIKE TO ACCEPT CHRIST?

Therefore, if anyone is in Christ, he is a new creation; old things have passed away; behold, all things have become new. (2 Corinthians 5:17)

It was early summer. A revival meeting was in progress at our home church. The guest minister was a renowned revivalist. Just about 12 years of age and very interested in the Word of God and in observing people involved in worship, I was seated on one of the front pews. However, I fell asleep and missed most of the evangelists sermon. During the altar call I awakened and a kind, middle-aged lady seated behind me leaned over the pew and asked me if I would like to accept Christ into my heart. Having never been personally asked that question before, I replied, "Yes." The answer came from my heart. She led me in prayer and that night Jesus came into my heart as my personal Savior.

After the worship service, my mother and I walked up the street to a bus stop for our return trip home. It was not yet dark. I was exhilarated. It seemed to me the birds had never sounded more beautiful and the air had never been more sweet. Then I realized the change was not on the outside, but on the inside--inside my heart. I was a brand-new creature! This experience has lasted 41 years through the good and bad times. When I have sinned and failed God, He has forgiven and restored.

. . . PRAYER . . .

Father, thank You for Your redeeming and keeping grace. Help me live every day in such a way that my living is a praise to Your glory.

. . . TODAY'S THOUGHT . . .

God so loved the world that He sent His only Son to die for sinful man. He does not love His erring children any less. When His people call on Him, He will hear, heal, and forgive, then gather them once again into His strong arms of love and provision.

—Junus Fulbright
Director, Youth and Christian Education, COG (former)

June 17

ROOM FOR YOU

A man's gift makes room for him, And brings him before great men. (Proverbs 18:16)

It was a bright beautiful day filled with laughter and play as my sister and I enjoyed time outdoors with our mother. From nowhere, a policeman appeared and informed my mother that he was there to remove my sister and me from her care. I was 6 years old. Within hours we were made wards of the court and placed in an orphanage. During most of my growing-up years, my father was hospitalized with tuberculosis and my older brothers and sisters were in and out of juvenile hall. In my new home I was constantly reminded of the failures of my mother, the bad blood in my siblings, and the darkness of my future. I was taught to believe that I would never amount to anything.

One day while a teenager, I was reading the Bible (because my Sunday school teacher said I should) and Proverbs 18:16 caught my attention: "A man's gift makes room for him and brings him before great men." Like Mary, I wondered, "How can this be?" (Luke 1:34). Where were the great men in my small town? And I could not travel more than 20 miles from my home without court approval.

Years later, participating in a National Jesus March in New Zealand, my walking partner was the Prime Minister. As I was conversing with him, I was suddenly reminded of God's words spoken to my heart about a hope and future for me.

God's Word and faithfulness are available for you, and they are available now. Although you may, at this moment, feel trapped by your past and afraid of your tomorrows, or you are questioning the faithfulness of God's promises to you, stand assured that "there has never failed one word of all His good promises . . ." (1 Kings 8:56).

. . . PRAYER . . .

Father, thank You for the plans You have for my life. In You I have a future and I have hope. I trust in Your wise timing for my tomorrows, and I rest in Your love for me today.

. . . TODAY'S THOUGHT . . .

Listen and carry these words of Jesus with you throughout your day: "See, I have set before you an open door" (Revelation 3:8).

—Naomi Beard
Board Member, ICFG

June 18

THE POWER OF LOVE

. . . for love is as strong as death . . . (Song of Solomon 8:6)

Family and friends imprisoned during the persecution against Pentecostals in Italy were returning home after four years. Upon their arrest, believers had been sent to various parts of the region, far from their homes. It was an attempt to quench the fire of Pentecost . . . a failed attempt, for persecuted believers became torches that ignited spiritual fires in other hearts and cities. The church multiplied.

That night, in our home, the first meeting of believers began with tears of joy and singing of an old hymn, "L'amore de Dio" ("The Love of God"). The light of the moon paled to the love of God illuminating my heart for the first time. I was nearly four years old.

The love that surrounded me as a child and captured my heart has also kept me in close fellowship with God. It has brought me to love His Word, see the baptism of the Holy Spirit, and faithfully dedicate myself to the preaching of the Word and ministering in music. This love, superior to all others, is sublime, powerful and divine. It displaces indifference. It compels us to love Him, His work, His church, and those lost without Him. No one can sincerely and joyfully serve God and the church without the fire and zeal produced by this divine love.

If the first fruit of the Holy Spirit is love, then love is present where the Spirit is present. He who has the love of God, loves without difficulty. Adoration, praise, and service to God are a result of His love. Redemption's plan is based on love. "For God so loved the world . . . ."

Is this not what the world and, for that matter, the church is in need of? Do we possess the love? Does it possess us? With the songwriter I say: "Oh, love of God, How rich and pure! How measureless and strong!"

. . . PRAYER . . .

Father, I want to know You more. In knowing You more, to love You more. In loving You more, serve You better.

. . . TODAY'S THOUGHT . . .

My children love and serve God. After one month in Bible school, one came to me with tears in his eyes and said, "Oh Dad, this book [the Bible] is so wonderful. I love this book!" The power of love continues.

—Joseph Manafò

Pastor, Howard Park Pentecostal Church, Toronto, ON

June 19

THE SPIRIT'S VOICE

Now the Lord came and stood and called as at other times, "Samuel! Samuel!" And Samuel answered, "Speak, for Your servant hears."
(1 Samuel 3:10)

We were the first to arrive and the last to leave. Granddad was church custodian. He was the one responsible for making sure everything was ready for church. He liked to get there early to make sure no one had messed up anything. By the time the service was to begin, the church was comfortably full for a Sunday evening.

Sunday evening was always the evangelistic service. The preacher opened with an enthusiastic prayer, the opening choir sang and then there was special music. Each service had a certain "oomph" about it.

For an 8-year-old this was just another service. Just another time to tag along behind my granddad. Just another time to spend with my idol. But, this night turned out to be different.

The pastor concluded his message and gave the altar call. A few people responded to his request and then everybody went forward to pray. As usual, we were some of the last to kneel and pray. There was a hum of prayer as voices blended together. As the hum continued, something new happened to me: in the midst of the crowd, I felt the Spirit of God as He moved on my life. What an experience! The blessed Holy Spirit speaking to an 8-year-old boy! I have never forgotten that day as God spoke through His Spirit and I listened.

Since that night God has spoken to me again and again. At 15 I made the full commitment of my life to Jesus Christ. At 21 I heard His voice again and accepted the call to full-time ministry. Oh, how precious is His voice! He has spoken to me at the death of my mom, a crisis in my church, at the sickness of my wife and at the crossroads with one of my sons. God is still speaking today. We must listen! We must hear! We must obey!

. . . PRAYER . . .

Father, thank You for loving us enough to speak to us. Thank You for that still, small voice of Your Spirit.

. . . TODAY'S THOUGHT . . .

So often we look for God in the wind, fire or earthquake, but all the time He is speaking in a still, small voice. Listen, God is speaking!

—William A. Reid
Pastor, COG, Salisbury, MD

June 20

TRAGEDY AND TRIUMPH

So shall they fear The name of the Lord from the west, And His glory from the rising of the sun; When the enemy comes in like a flood, The Spirit of the Lord will lift up a standard against him. (Isaiah 59:19)

Northwest Bible College, Minot, North Dakota, had experienced 16 years of dramatic growth. On a beautiful Easter Sunday in 1969, word came that snow melt in the Canadian Rockies had produced massive flooding in the Souris Valley. Water which overflowed dams as it came was moving toward us. How could this be? Where was God?

The corps of engineers had built dikes to protect two-thirds of the city . . . but not us. With one truck, a few volunteers, and determination, we attempted to save major buildings. Water surrounded us for three weeks. Dikes were walked constantly because everything would be lost in a single break. Following my shift one night, I sat staring into the churning water and cried. God had not come. Had I believed a fable?

School opened with a reduced enrollment. Fridays became fasting and prayer days. Several weeks later, the major of Minot stood in the doorway of my office, his large Norwegian frame filling the door and his attitude of faith filling the room. Recognizing that the college had been hit hard and that Minot needed the school, he had a plan to appoint a committee of bank presidents and the local newspaper president to assist the school. He looked squarely into my eyes as if to ask whether his plan was all right . . . and I saw the messenger of God.

In the spring we broke ground with the city fathers in attendance. A dormitory with a long-needed dining facility was begun. The state's Governor spoke at commencement. In the following decade, the student body more than doubled and, with community backing, a million-dollar learning center was erected. The only Bible College for hundreds of miles could now continue to serve churches and expand its ministry.

. . . PRAYER . . .

Dear God, help us realize that things are not always what they seem and that true reality rests only in You.

. . . TODAY'S THOUGHT . . .

And we know that all things work together for good to those who love God, to those who are the called according to His purpose (Romans 8:28).

—Laud O. Vaught
President, Northwest Bible College (retired)

June 21

POWER TO ENDURE AND REMAIN FAITHFUL

But you shall receive power when the Holy Spirit has come upon you; . . (Acts 1:8)

As a draftee, my religious educational pursuits were interrupted by the Korean Conflict. A train of us left Maryland talking loudly and singing "I'm Alabama Bound." Smoke filled the car and inexperienced drinkers laughed and shouted. I was with them, but not of them.

Culture shock set in after being thrust into the Army from a peaceful, religious atmosphere. The first year was like being in prison; however, the Holy Ghost helped me rise to the occasion.

Attempts to witness were not well received. I became the object of persecution and ridicule. In a sporting attitude, some fellow soldiers sought to force cigarettes and whiskey on me. While I was at church, some poured glue on my laundered clothes; others played cards on my bed all night while I attempted to sleep.

The Lord helped me strive for excellence even with menial jobs. I was often named "Soldier of the Week" and earned weekend passes.

Tolerance and respect first came from my superiors, then from the platoon, and finally from my squad. I was given responsibility for training in chemical, biological and radiological warfare. Weary of menial tasks such as cleaning truck motors and KP, I volunteered for combat duty in Korea; instead, I was assigned as training cadre and retained as company barber. Many of the soldiers that left never returned to their beloved United States.

Two years after leaving Lee College, I returned to finish my course of study, a stronger believer than when I left. I look back and realize I would not have made it through successfully without the Baptism in the Holy Ghost.

. . . PRAYER . . .

Thank You, Lord, for the power to endure and remain faithful in an untoward situation.

. . . TODAY'S THOUGHT . . .

He is able to keep us in salvation which was committed unto us by the power of the Holy Ghost (2 Timothy 1:14).

—James Marshall
Historical Artist, COG

June 22

THE IMPELLING INFLUENCE OF THE HOLY SPIRIT

For You are my rock and my fortress; Therefore, for Your name's sake, Lead me and guide me. (Psalm 31:3)

When I was a child, my parents, who knew nothing of Pentecostal doctrine, began searching Scripture to learn more about receiving the Holy Spirit into their lives. Soon they embraced and joined a Pentecostal group of believers and, thereafter, our family found this joy in Christ for everyday living. In a few short years, under the impelling influence of the Holy Spirit, I received Christ as my Savior.

After my conversion, I had little interest in being filled with the Spirit. However, under the impelling influence of the Holy Spirit, certain Scriptures began to come to my mind (e.g., John 16:7, in which Jesus told His disciples that "if I do not go away, the Helper will not come to you; but if I depart, I will send Him to you").

I could not escape the urge of the Spirit to be filled. I knew if I responded to the call of God for my life, I must be filled with the Spirit. I sought advice from many people, but I soon discovered that advice, though good, was not the answer.

While attending a camp meeting, a minister who watched me in the altar approached me and said, "Young man, you will never receive the Holy Ghost in the manner you are seeking Him. You are fighting the Spirit, you are knocking Him off as fast as He comes upon you." After continued prayer and searching of the Word, I discovered that I did not need to help the Holy Spirit. Instead, the Holy Spirit wanted to help me. When I surrendered my will and mind with faith believing, I received the Holy Spirit as promised by the Father.

How wonderful it is when His power works in us, our hearts worship Him, and our lips praise Him as the impelling influence of the Holy Spirit flows through us.

. . . PRAYER . . .

Father, we thank You for the Holy Spirit that is ever present to help us in living a daily life of victory in Jesus Christ.

. . . TODAY'S THOUGHT . . .

The Holy Spirit is given to the believer, that he might be fully equipped for service in the Kingdom's work.

—T. Paul Patton
Pastor, COG (retired)

June 23

LED BY THE HOLY SPIRIT

For as many as are led by the Spirit of God, these are sons of God. (Romans 8:14)

In my early years I lived on a farm near Paris, Texas. I fell in love with and married a Church of God lady, Alma McCain. I did not know much about Pentecost, and I received a lot of persecution from friends and neighbors who tried to persuade me against the Holy Spirit baptism.

After moving to Electric, I'd take my wife to church and stay outside in the car. Since there was no air conditioning then, the windows were wide open. The singing and preaching came out loud and clear. I would put my fingers in my ears to keep from hearing the message.

Sometimes on Sunday we had the pastor come with us for dinner. My object in this was to argue the Scriptures, for I still was not convinced about the Holy Spirit. One Sunday in a discussion about the Holy Spirit, my wife joined the conversation. In a few minutes, the pastor's young daughter came to me and said, "She is right."

I finally decided the Holy Spirit was for me. After many times of seeking the Lord, the Spirit fell. I heard someone speaking in a language I did not understand, then realized it was coming from me.

I was farming and had to gather grain when it was ready. My neighbors would use the combine on Sunday to miss the rain. I would not gather my grain on Sunday, and the Lord always protected my crops. This made an impression on my neighbors.

The Spirit began dealing with me about preaching. I did not want to preach. I feared I might have to go to a foreign country as a missionary. I worried over this until I had a dream one night that I was preaching to a crowd out in the open by the courthouse. I was standing on the back of a truck. This was my witness that I should preach the gospel of Jesus Christ in my area.

. . . PRAYER . . .

Thank You, Lord, for the gift of the Holy Spirit and for His empowering presence throughout my many years of ministry

. . . TODAY'S THOUGHT . . .

My advice to everyone is to seek Him, for the power of Pentecost is real.

—W. L. Shires (Reprinted from *SpiritWalk: Daily Devotions on the Holy Spirit* by permission of Pathway Press)
Pastor, COG, TX (former)

June 24

THE MAIN POINT

On the same day, when evening had come, He said to them, "Let us cross over to the other side." (Mark 4:35)

As a senior seminary student, I was chosen to preach the last chapel service of the school year. I wanted my sermon to be a masterpiece. From my favorite miracle of Jesus, the stilling of the storm, I developed a message that focused upon "High Winds, Desperate Voices, and an Unexpected Word."

The high winds remind us how quickly our life situation can change from complete calm to total danger. In ordinary moments, we have no need to speak urgently or loudly. Others listen easily. But, in storm, even when we are shouting desperately, there is no one to hear our cry for help—except the Lord. The unexpected word is what Jesus speaks to the storm, "Be still." And, the rebuke He speaks to us, "Why are you so afraid? Do you still have not faith?"

For 20 minutes, I waxed eloquent, convinced that I had properly interpreted and applied it—throwing in enough dashes of verbiage to make my listeners a little seasick. I sat down smug with satisfaction.

My New Testament professor, Dr. Everett Harrison, greeted me saying, "That has always been a favorite passage of mine. Jesus rebuked them for not having faith because they had forgotten the word He spoke to them in the beginning, 'Let us go over to the other side.' And, when you forget the word of Jesus you will always be afraid."

In one tender diplomatic moment, Dr. Harrison had popped the bubble of my sermonic pride by showing me I had missed, with all my rhetoric, the main point in the story. But, I have never forgotten it since. In any storm, our faith will rise or fall upon remembering the word of Jesus. He is committed always to bringing us over to the other side.

. . . PRAYER . . .

Lord, too easily I forget Your promises when I am in need. Forgive me for my lack of faith. I will trust You in the storm.

. . . TODAY'S THOUGHT . . .

As no one falls in love with love, but with a person, so you cannot have faith in faith, but in the person of Jesus. It is His Word you must rely upon if you are to cross safely your own storm-filled sea.

—Dr. George O. Wood
General Secretary, AG

June 25

NOT BY MIGHT . . .

So he answered and said to me: "This is the word of the Lord to Zerubbabel: 'Not by might nor by power, but by My Spirit,' Says the Lord of hosts" (Zechariah 4:6)

I was at the end of my tether. Leading the church had become a mountain of impossibilities. People were leaving. Few had a vision for revival. No one, seemingly, wanted to go forward with a church extension project that would give us much needed facilities.

I had had enough and I was ready to leave. My wife and I made plans to move to a larger, livelier church.

Then on Saturday evening I was sitting in church. I opened the Bible to share a word with the congregation and it fell open at Zechariah 4. As I read, I knew God was speaking to me.

"I want you to rely on my Spirit, not on your own strength. If you do, the mighty mountain before you will be leveled, you will complete the building project, and you will hear my people proclaim, 'Beautiful is it! Beautiful is it!' In the meantime, do not despise the day of small things. Be faithful in the little I have given you."

My wife and I asked the Lord to confirm this word from the mouth of a respected witness. Ten days later, I was at a conference and a man of God spoke on this passage and exhorted weary leaders to take heart.

We have therefore chosen, like Zerubbabel, to stick with it, and to rely on God's Spirit, not on our own strength.

. . . PRAYER . . .

Father, You have seen our ministry. Now we'd like to see Yours. Help us to hand our churches back to You, that revival may come, and all may know it is Your work and not ours.

. . . TODAY'S THOUGHT . . .

Faith is: believing when you can't see it, obeying when you don't understand it, persevering when you don't feel like it, trusting when you don't receive it. Pray for more faith today. Remember, the world says, "I'll believe it when I see it." But the Word says, "I'll see it when I believe it."

—Mark Stibbe
St. Mark's Vicarage

June 26

THE BEST FOR THE WORST

For God so loved the world that He gave His only begotten Son, that whoever believes in Him should not perish but have everlasting life. (John 3:16)

O wretched man that I am! Who will deliver me . . . (Romans 7:24)

As a child I wanted to be a Christian, but I did not know how to change my ways. I hated the sinful life I lived every day.

I had just turned 19 years old when a revival began at the church I attended. The invitation to pray was given, and I responded by going forward and kneeling at the altar. I was told to believe that Jesus would forgive me and to allow Him into my heart. I followed the directions as best I knew how, and the best thing that heaven affords happened. Jesus took up residence in my heart! I was changed from a sinner to a Christian. Since that day, I have come to realize that heaven's best was given for the world's worst, and that we are kept daily from the enemy of our souls.

I was told there was more that God would do; so I began to seek God for a baptism in the Spirit. Approximately three months later, at an altar, I was filled with a spiritual power that was altogether different from the wonder saving grace that I had experienced earlier.

As I lay on my back, words that I did not know came forth from my vocal organs; the tongue and lips that once cursed, swore, lied, and blasphemed were now filled with praises to God who had given heaven's best for the world's worst.

That was more than 60 years ago, and the gift is still good today, with the way becoming clearer each day.

. . . PRAYER . . .

Thank You, Lord, for sending heaven's best and for keeping all who commit their way to You.

. . . TODAY'S THOUGHT . . .

Remember, when we were yet without strength, in due time Christ died for the ungodly (Romans 5:6).

—Louis A. Brannen
Pastor, COG (retired)

June 27

FOOTPRINTS IN THE SAND

Your word is a lamp to my feet And a light to my path. (Psalm 119:105)

Henry Wadsworth Longfellow once said, "Lives of great men all remind us we can make our lives sublime, and in departing, leave behind us footprints in the sand."

The footprints of many pioneers of Pentecost who have made a lasting impression on my life and ministry may not be literally visible in the sand, but they are evident in my heart.

Nearly 50 years ago, the Reverend J. L. Hathcock, one of our pioneers of Pentecost, brought the message of salvation and the importance of the baptism in the Holy Ghost to a young, impressionable heart.

This message of the Holy Ghost has burned like a refiner's fire in my heart, and, in turn, has given me the opportunity to ignite a fire in hundreds of precious lives.

. . . PRAYER . . .

May the great God of this universe cause us all to leave impressionable footprints in the sands of many lives.

. . . TODAY'S THOUGHT . . .

Remember, some little one might try to walk in your steps. May you leave a good impression in the sands of time.

—Raymond E. Pedigo
Evangelist, COG, Beckley, WVA

June 28

THERE IS A GOD OF MIRACLES

But Jesus looked at them and said to them, "With men this is impossible, but with God all things are possible." (Matthew 19:26)

I live on miracles. My life and breath is a miracle. Before God healed me of tuberculosis, every breath was a struggle. Now I breathe freely. Each time I speak it is a miracle for God healed my stammering tongue.

God first came into my life in the form of my sister, Jewel, when I lay dying with my lungs wasting away. She said, "Oral, God is going to heal you." It was like all the lights of the world were turned on in my soul. For the first time, I knew there was a God. And He cared for me. God's goodness caused me to repent of my sins and accept Him.

But God goes so much further than hearing our prayers and saving our souls and giving us new life. He speaks to us. Each, in his or her own way, hears the voice of God. I heard it inside me: "I'm going to heal you, and you are to take My healing power to your generation."

Later God spoke to my heart again. He said, "I want you to build Me a university. Put it under the authority of God, and build it on the Holy Spirit." Then He said something that really took my breath away: "*I want you to build it out of the same ingredient I used when I made the earth—nothing!*" It is good that God said that to me because I had no money, no land, no faculty, no students—just God's call.

Today, Oral Roberts University is a reality. But, I can honestly say I didn't build it. God built it! The only real virtue I have is that I was obedient. I came under God's authority and did what He told me to do.

The God who gave me a miracle in my lungs and my tongue and my soul and who raised me up from nothing is the God of the now. He's there with you to meet the impossibly tough situations you face. If He can perform miracles for me, He can perform miracles for anybody!

. . . PRAYER . . .

In the name of Jesus Christ of Nazareth, I expect a miracle for your life to begin today!

. . . TODAY'S THOUGHT . . .

Miracles are coming toward you every day. Don't let yours pass you by. Reach out and receive it.

—Oral Roberts
President, Oral Roberts University, Tulsa, OK

June 29

HE ABIDETH FAITHFUL

For He Himself has said, "I will never leave you nor forsake you." (Hebrews 13:5)

For 40 years neither my wife nor I had spent a night in the hospital, except when our children were born. So in 1990 when I had been feeling nauseated for about a week, I blamed my symptoms on a virus that was going around.

That Sunday I preached in both the morning and evening services. I was prayed for when we had prayer for the sick. At 4:00 a.m., after sitting in a chair all night because I couldn't lie down, I gave up and went to the emergency room. The doctor ruled out heart trouble, but while they were debating my condition I had a major heart attack.

Admitted to the hospital, there was a real battle raging within me. Why, after seeing probably thousands of people healed, was I here? This struggle was not an outward one, but an inner questioning of my spirit. God never did answer the "why" of the situation. But a voice, audible or silent, spoke gently and said, "Don't you think I am with you now?" I would like to report that I got right up and went home, but I didn't. I went through open-heart surgery that almost did not succeed. God's people prayed, and the problems that medicine could not resolve cleared up and I recovered.

I still don't understand why things happen like they do, but I am persuaded that He is there through sickness and through health, in joy or in grief. He abideth faithful (2 Timothy 2:13).

. . . PRAYER . . .

Heavenly Father, help my faith to claim Your promises; help my soul to trust You when the answer is delayed. Keep my spirit sweet in all of life's changing circumstances.

. . . TODAY'S THOUGHT . . .

Most of us know God from the chin up. But with the baptism in the Holy Spirit, our spirit is released to worship God fully. "Whom will he teach knowledge? And whom will he make to understand the message? Those just weaned from milk? Those just drawn from the breasts? For precept must be upon precept, precept upon precept, Line upon line, line upon line, Here a little, there a little" (Isaiah 28:9, 10).

—Mark G. Summers
State Overseer, COG (former)

June 30

GOD'S SOVEREIGN PLAN

The steps of a good man are ordered by the Lord, And He delights in his way. (Psalm 37:23)

There are times when we do not understand the circumstances that surround us, yet we can't seem to do anything about them. Everything seems to be against us. We are tempted to say with Jacob, "All these things are against me . . . Joseph is not . . . Simeon is not" (Genesis 42:36). Now he will loose Benjamin if he is to get corn from Egypt. If we look at his *now*, we will say Jacob has a right to be troubled. Things are dismal, discouraging and disappointing. However, as we see the total picture, God was working to turn Jacob's disappointment into His (God's) appointment.

We hear Joseph say, "For God did send me before you to preserve life" (Genesis 45:5). We often forget God has ordered our steps, and in Him is the power which enables us to make them. As King David said, "Even there shall thy hand lead . . ." (Psalm 139:10). Regardless of where or what, God will lead us. Even in the valley and shadow of death . . . you are with me."

Yes, God does have a plan for each of us. We may be overwhelmed by our present circumstances and feel there is no way out, but God is a "way maker" when we cry out to Him.

We, as Abraham's seed, are in training to exercise our faith in the Word. Even with our adversary whispering in our ear, "You will never make it," the Holy Spirit whispers, "I will never leave nor forsake you."

In moments such as this, we can draw from the wellspring within and be assured God has not forsaken us, and He is working out His divine plan for our life.

. . . PRAYER . . .

Father, I thank You for the strength I receive today from the wellspring of living water that You have given me.

. . . TODAY'S THOUGHT . . .

"But He knows the way that I take; When He has tested me, I shall come forth as gold" (Job 23:10).

—Thomas A. Perkins
State Overseer, COG (former)

July 1

HIDING PLACE, HIGH PLACE

Hear my cry, O God; Attend to my prayer. From the end of the earth I will cry to You, When my heart is overwhelmed; Lead me to the rock that is higher than I. (Psalm 61:1, 2)

I was born into a Pentecostal preacher's home. My great-grandfather was a shouting Methodist circuit preacher during the last turn of the century. My earliest memories are of my dad and mom singing and preaching. I surrendered my heart and will to Jesus during a Sunday night service, September 1967. At that moment I knew in my heart that I too had been called. Like Grandpa and Dad, I had been chosen to be a gospel preacher.

Twenty-one years later, after nine years of full-time ministry, I found myself bankrupt, without a ministry, in a strained marriage, a father of three children, jobless, and living a thousand miles from any familiar face. One Sunday morning, sitting in a strange church surrounded by strange people, this message came to me through the song that everyone was singing: "And when my heart is overwhelmed, lead me to the rock that is higher than I; that is higher than I. . ."

The Holy Spirit was singing to me.

My life had been so full of doing and providing for myself, that there was little room for God to have a part. It was not so much selfishness as it was self-sufficiency. I was despairing because I had run out of self and there was nothing left. Nothing until I realized that there was One who was higher, stronger, and more resourceful than I. I needed a new perspective. Not a different perspective, but a new one. Different does not always mean new. What others can give may be different, but what God gives is new. What I needed and what I got was a new view of my life from God's vantage point.

. . . PRAYER . . .

Father, thank You for Your vantage point. You are the pinnacle from which we can stand and see the meaning and purpose of our life's experiences.

. . . TODAY'S THOUGHT . . .

God is the Rock that provides clefts for a hiding place and mesas for a high place. With God you can hide in Him and stand on Him.

—Roderick Logan
Pastor, COG, Phoenix, AZ

July 2

GRACE TO REMEMBER

And I will pray the Father, and He will give you another Helper, that He may abide with you forever. (John 14:16)

Memory is an integral part of the human makeup. The brain is like a computer bank, storing every incident of our lives. It is possible, under certain circumstances, to bring these memories into focus and to enjoy the pleasant things that have slipped away. Sometimes these memories are painful and bringing them into focus causes remorse. Yet, there is loss if we fail to remember vital information. Losing focus, we become indifferent to the most important matters.

John 14:26 shows us that the Spirit will teach us the Word; not only this, but He will bring to our remembrance what we have been taught. Another ministry of the Holy Spirit is that of conviction of the world of righteousness, sin and the judgment to come (John 16:8-11).

In my youth, I was a successful businessman. The Lord delivered my wife-to-be and me from drowning miraculously. I made Him a promise, while desperately trying to save both of us from a torrential river, that I would serve Him if He would help us to safety. From nowhere, we were suddenly transported to a place of safety in the middle of the river and were saved. We were both without the Lord. Years later we married and had one son. I forgot the promise I had made to the Lord. Then one day, while viewing the body of a man who had drowned, the Holy Spirit reminded me of my promise—now was the time to fulfill my obligation. My wife and I gave our hearts to God, and have been actively in His work for the past 44 years. It was through the wonderful gift of memory and the prompting of the Holy Spirit that caused such a drastic and complete change in our lives. He will bring incidents to our memories that will make differences for our future.

. . . PRAYER . . .

So teach us to number our days, that we may apply our hearts unto wisdom. (Psalm 90:12)

. . . TODAY'S THOUGHT . . .

It has been aptly said that "the generation that forgets the mistakes of the past will be doomed to repeat them in the future." It is time for us to remember, and to return, and to take action!

—Walter D. Watkins
Pastor, Stratford Heights, Middletown, OH

July 3

OUR GOD OF HOPE

Now may the God of hope fill you with all joy and peace in believing, that you may abound in hope by the power of the Holy Spirit. (Romans 15:13)

Through the Holy Spirit hope in God was awakened and strengthened in my heart when I found myself in Miami alone, without my family, and without any assurance that I would ever see them again.

I left my country of origin, Cuba, in December, 1960. Along with other men who were under government threats by the Castro regime, we left in a small boat for the 90-mile journey to Florida. We had no adequate training to overcome the difficulties of such an odyssey. In a matter of hours, we found ourselves overwhelmed by a fierce winter storm. Colliding with a reef, our boat, belongings, and food supply were destroyed. We struggled for several days on the reef until we were rescued and brought to safety.

In Florida I found a job and initiated the laborious procedures to bring my family to the United States. Though encouraged by friends and churches, every door was being closed. There seemed to be no hope. For many months my struggle went on having no concrete indications that I would ever see my wife and children again.

At the lowest point of my life, going through endless nights of sorrow, loneliness and despair, the Spirit extended to me hope. He reminded me of my source and power of hope, of God who is the center of all true and worthy hope. The Holy Spirit is the divine agent who makes hope overflow in the life of the believer. Through the Spirit, we experience an abundant measure of joy and peace that is not affected by our weaknesses or limitations.

After God turned everything around, within a couple of months my family was in my arms again.

. . . PRAYER . . .

Holy Spirit, thank You for granting us hope in our times of despair.

. . . TODAY'S THOUGHT . . .

When we find ourselves without joy or peace, let us call on the Holy Spirit. He is the divine source of hope that warms us on chilly nights, dissipates our darkness in the endless night, and elevates our faith to put our trust in our God of hope.

—Lazaro Santana
National Evangelist, Hispanic Ministries COG

July 4

AN ENDANGERED SPECIES

But the hour is coming, and now is, when the true worshippers will worship the Father in spirit and truth; for the Father is seeking such to worship Him. (John 4:23)

As a young man, I was disturbed to think that the Father must seek worshippers. There should be an excess of worshippers!

Jesus told the woman at the well that there are few true worshippers even though the temples and synagogues were full of people. There are more people going to church today than ever before. Some people think that because they go to church they are worshippers or that physical manifestations of worship equal worshipping. Still, the Father seeks true worshippers.

The word Jesus used in this text means "one who prostrates." The Father seeks those who will prostrate themselves before His throne, giving Him total and true authority over their lives. The reason there are so few true worshippers is that most of us are too busy governing our lives according to our own will and desires. Singing the songs and expressing our worship physically, being faithful, tithing and giving should all be by-products of what a true worshipper is—a prostrate and obedient servant of the Most High. But somehow we have learned to do all of these actions without realizing that they have become ritualistic and meaningless expressions of people seated on the thrones of their own life. A true worshipper is someone who embraces the whole truth of God and lives his or her life according to His sovereign rule and not according to their own; someone who takes his or her crown off their head and throws it at His precious feet, in recognition that nothing that brings us glory compares to His great, majestic and powerful glory (Revelation 4:10). Total submission—this a true believer!

. . . PRAYER . . .

Lord Jesus, I'm sorry for not letting You be seated on the throne of my life. Please forgive me, and take the place that belongs to You. I relinquish all authority and turn it over to Your lordship. I want to be a true worshipper.

. . . TODAY'S THOUGHT . . .

There are so few people who live their lives prostrate before God's throne, that we can say *Handle with care: Endangered Species.*

—Marcos Witt
Can Zion Producciones, Houston, TX

July 5

VICTORY OVER DANGER

The angel of the Lord encamps all around those who fear Him, And delivers them. (Psalm 34:7)

It was a case of mistaken identity.

Evangelist Vincent Grassano closed a great revival at our local church. He had no means of transportation so I had taken him to a gospel singing in Fort Worth, Texas.

The hour was growing late as we passed through Azel, Texas. Leaving Azel, a car followed. A man, yelling and cursing, tried to run us off the road. I accelerated to speeds of 100 miles per hour. A cold fear gripped me as he hit the rear bumper, his bright lights blinding.

"I am afraid he has a gun," I told Rev. Grassano. "I must pull over."

As I pulled over, Brother Vincent bowed in prayer on the passenger side.

"Roll down the window or I will shoot!" the man screamed. As I rolled the glass down, I looked into the barrel of a large pistol.

"I'm going to kill you!" the man screamed.

Amid his vile language and threats, he related a story of how he had been looking for a car like mine that was driven by a man he had vowed to kill. I tried to explain that I did not know him or the circumstances of which he talked.

Brother Vincent continued to pray and plead the blood of Jesus. After approximately 1 hour and 45 minutes of holding us there, the man suddenly waved the gun and said, "Go on."

He could have killed both of us with no witnesses. But, thank God, He gave us victory over danger.

. . . PRAYER . . .

In this world with danger all around, we thank You, Lord, for divine protection and intervention.

. . . TODAY'S THOUGHT . . .

"When you pass through the waters, I will be with you; And through the rivers, they shall not overflow you. When you walk through the fire, you shall not be burned, Nor shall the flame scorch you" (Isaiah 43:2).

—O. D. Robertson
Pastor, COG, Paris, TX

July 6

GOD'S WAYS ARE ALWAYS BEST

"For My thoughts are not your thoughts, Nor are your ways My ways," says the Lord. "For as the heavens are higher than the earth, So are My ways higher than your ways, And My thoughts than your thoughts." (Isaiah 55:8-9)

Brandon and his grandmother drove along the road toward town on a frigid January day. "Granny," asked the three-year-old, "Why does Preacher God let it get so cold?" As the grandmother questioned the young boy about his statement concerning "Preacher God," he immediately let her know he was speaking of his pastor—of me.

The grandmother shared the story with me. Immediately I realized the seriousness of my office. Whether I realized it or not, that young man looked on me as more than just a preacher—he saw me as "God." The grandmother attempted to explain the difference to Brandon.

The past several months had been very difficult for my wife and me. We had resigned a very successful pastorate after 12 years of service. For several weeks, it seemed that God was very far away. Satan was constantly telling me my ministry was over after 30 years of preaching. Yet God was working in ways we could not see. His Spirit was probing my heart and causing me to search myself as never before. He let me know that my ministry had just begun and showed me what He desired for me to do. People let us know that we were their pastors! From that hurt and anguish came a brand-new work for God.

I needed to hear those words from Brandon. Someone was looking to me to help and guide him along life's way. Paul knew what he was talking about when he said, "And we know that all things work together for good to those who love God, to those who are the called according to His purpose" (Romans 8:28). Yes, God's ways are always best.

. . . PRAYER . . .

Oh God, help us to be mindful that You are ever with us and are in control of our lives no matter how difficult things appear at the time.

. . . TODAY'S THOUGHT . . .

The song states, "When you're feeling at your weakest, Jesus will be strong. He'll provide the answer when you've found all hope is gone. He'll find a way." That statement is so true. It may not be the way you would like, but it will be His way. And His way is always best.

—L. Wayne Hicks
Assistant General Superintendent, CHC

July 7

STANDING FIRM

He who dwells in the secret place of the Most High Shall abide under the shadow of the Almighty. I will say of the Lord, "He is my refuge and my fortress; My God, in Him I will trust." (Psalm 91:1-2)

My chest was so tight I could barely breathe. My soul was overwhelmed by the angry messages of a vengeful enemy. Worship vanished, prayer melted into cries of desperation. Despair was everywhere.

With a heart of cement, I stepped from the platform of a college chapel service. Questions and words of encouragement were more a bother than a blessing. Escape to an airplane for home was the only thing on my mind. As the auditorium finally emptied, a young girl handed me a nicely wrapped package from a local art shop. Her pastor asked her to give it to me. It was a gift of thanks for a favor I had done.

Weary appreciation turned to joy as I unrolled the photographic print of a man standing at the base of an offshore lighthouse. He stood calmly, hands in his pockets, as a 40-foot wave crashed all around him. The lighthouse and its rocky pedestal broke the fury of the crashing sea. Violent destruction loomed 6 feet in any direction, while standing still ensured unshakable security. God had sent me that poster. I knew he had heard my cry and promised the protection I so fearfully sought.

I remembered the word of the Lord to Israel on the day He piled up the waters of the Red Sea: "Do not be afraid. Stand still, and see the salvation of the Lord, which He will accomplish for you today. For the Egyptians whom you see today, you shall see again no more forever" (Exodus 14:13). Later I was led to Proverbs 12:7: "The wicked are overthrown and are no more, But the house of the righteous will stand."

Our part, like the man by the lighthouse is simply to stand still as He provides a faithful fortress against the enemy of our soul.

. . . PRAYER . . .

Lord, show me the security I have in You and Your willingness to make my needs Your own.

. . . TODAY'S THOUGHT . . .

Jesus said even a sparrow cannot fall without the Father's awareness. His reassurance still holds, "Fear not therefore: ye are of more value than many sparrows" (Luke 12:6, 7).

—Dr. Ralph Moore
Pastor, Hope Chapel, Kaneoke, HI

July 8

TRUST AND PATIENCE BRING RELIEF

In God (I will praise His word), In God I have put my trust; I will not fear. What can flesh do to me? (Psalm 56:4)

Saved the last night of a nine-week revival, I began preaching at every opportunity a year later after I received the Lord's call. For many weeks, though, I was depressed over the physical condition of my body. I would develop, every few weeks, a spell of pneumonia. It would weaken me so that it took a long time to regain my strength. The doctor told my wife and mother that if my resistance could not be built, I would be put in a tuberculosis hospital.

I thought about death and the lovely wife and little boy I would leave and I became more serious and sad.

Then a thought came to me: "Why would God call you to preach His Word and let you die before you have hardly started?" The Holy Ghost then urged me to "Trust in the Lord." The words of Job came to me, "Though he slay me, yet will I trust him" (13:15).

When I came in that Saturday, hot with pneumonia the sixth time, coughing blood from both lungs, I told my wife, "No medication." She didn't discourage me. She prayed with me for my healing.

From that Saturday until the next, I had no medicine, no food, just a glass of Pepsi in ice occasionally.

On the next Saturday, a few ladies who had gathered to pray came to my home after their prayer. I asked them to pray for me.

As these ladies and my wife prayed, the Holy Ghost moved in and I experienced a feeling like warm water being poured on my head to the bottom of my lungs. I felt better than I had for a long time. I raised my hands and praised God and when the ladies left, after shouting, I arose, put on my clothes and have never worried about pneumonia since.

. . . PRAYER . . .

Thank You, Lord, for the blessing we receive when we keep our trust in You.

. . . TODAY'S THOUGHT . . .

During my 57 years of ministering, the greatest joy I have is the souls I helped to win, and those they are winning.

—James L. Lombard
Pastor, Alabama/Mississippi, COG (former)

July 9

THE PENTECOSTAL REVIVAL

When the Day of Pentecost had fully come, . . . (Acts 2:1)

Praise the Lord for my part in it. It began for me when I was 13 in 1941. I was in my first Pentecostal service. I would have repented of my sins then, dad sat down by me and said, "Are you ready to go home?" I could tell by the tone of his voice that I was ready to go.

Two years later, I confessed my sins, and received the Lord Jesus as my Savior. I accepted Him as my sanctification while riding a horse home from a Pentecostal revival. I received the baptism in the Holy Spirit with the initial evidence of speaking in tongues as He gave me the utterance. In 1945, I received my call to preach this glorious full gospel of Christ. Down through the years I have found in the Savior a life that is simply wonderful and wonderfully simple. He's my all in all. He is the almighty mover of the Pentecostal Movement.

The Pentecostal Movement is a Book of Acts movement. It is a revival of prayer, praise, power, and progress.

Small was its beginning at the turn of the century when a few saints met for prayer. Now the Pentecostal revival is a mighty movement reaching around the world with the message of power that saves from vile habits, cleanses hearts, overcomes the devil, keeps us from all sin. Power to minister to the dying. Power to see the sick get well. Power to triumph over Satan. Power over sin and death and hell. So I say to all of us in the Pentecostal/Charismatic Movement, "Let us walk before this power, the Lord Jesus Christ, in humility of face and let us never cease to marvel at the wonders of His saving grace."

Let us know Him in all of His power, even in the power of His suffering so that we may also know Him in the power of Resurrection life. May we learn from His Spirit and from His Word till our lives are all complete, and, yonder, in that Holy City what a conference we will hold! Till then we'll walk in unity, and the grace of God we'll extol!

. . . PRAYER . . .

Father, please keep on drenching us with downpourings of the Holy Spirit.

. . . TODAY'S THOUGHT . . .

Praise God for this 20th century Pentecostal revival! If Jesus tarries may it ever increase!

—J. E. DeVore
State Overseer, COG (retired)

July 10

THE LIFE I NOW LIVE

I have been crucified with Christ; it is no longer I who live, but Christ lives in me; and the life which I now live in the flesh I live by faith in the Son of God, who loved me and gave Himself for me. (Galatians 2:20)

A five-hour emergency room visit . . . the unexpected death of two under-forty brothers in the Lord . . . poignant reminders of my mortality.

I thought of the '60 song that said: "Suddenly, I'm not half the man I used to be; There's a shadow hanging over me . . " But then I contrasted this pathetic but eloquent statement of the fear and despondency of the natural man with the boldness and near-reckless abandon of a Christian writer who declared, "I care not today what tomorrow may bring, if shadow or sunshine or rain. . . ."

I remembered events in my life that stand as cogent testimonies of the power of faith in Jesus Christ. One in particular is ever present. On a quiet country road late one summer evening, returning home with my wife and two children, a car hit us head on. The drunk driver was killed. The car, which had been traveling in excess of 100 miles per hour, burst into flames. My family and I were miraculously delivered with relatively minor injuries.

In that my faith in the Lord Jesus Christ proved more than sufficient for our protection enables me today to more conspicuously live the life of faith, thus facing each new reality with a perspective of a better future. And now, when disappointments come, or while facing a personal tragedy, there is no longing for yesterday, but a celebration of the amazing love of Jesus. Living by faith in Jesus Christ renders bad news from the doctor or the aftermath of a family split, not as the end of a better life, but the possibility of a closer relationship with the Lord Jesus.

. . . PRAYER . . .

Father, in a hurting world let the faith which Your people demonstrate in the common afflictions of life speak clearly to those who have no faith and hope.

. . . TODAY'S THOUGHT . . .

Living the life of faith in Christ brings peace and consolation as a consequence of accepting that life is not fair, but God is always good.

—Oswill E. Williams
Center for Biblical Leadership, COGOP

July 11

FAITH IN GOD

For we do not have a High Priest who cannot sympathize with our weaknesses, but was in all points tempted as we are, yet without sin. (Hebrews 4:15)

How can He who has a glorified body sympathize with our weaknesses? Because He was both perfect man and perfect God, the new Adam, combining the human nature of His mother with the divine nature of His father. This is a union that is impossible for us to comprehend. Don't try to define that which God has not defined.

After our first child was born, we discovered quickly that something was wrong with her eyes. She needed surgery, which would be done when she was three months old and would continue, until she was five years old. My wife did not consult me, but, instead, told the doctor that there would be no surgery. As we started the two-hour drive home, she said, "God will heal her!"

The Word came to me: "If only I may touch His garment, I shall be made well" (Matthew 9:21). When all else fails, you truly depend upon your faith in God. The Word He uttered to the woman, "your faith has made you well" (Matthew 9:22), will send virtue, comfort and consolation to you.

One Sunday evening—after I had ministered the Word and we were in our altar service—God spoke to me and said, "Anoint your daughter's eyes and I will heal them." I did not question but asked my wife to bring our daughter from the nursery to the altar. I anointed both eyes and prayed for her. There was no shouting and praising God, but I knew she was healed. At the next appointment with the doctor he stated, "I can find no problem with her eyes. No surgery required."

More than 20 years have passed and everything is still good. Today, our daughter has perfect dark brown eyes. She is our church pianist. To God be all the glory!

. . . PRAYER . . .

Jesus, thank You for healing our bodies—and purchasing our salvation along with our healing.

. . . TODAY'S THOUGHT . . .

Jesus is touched with the feeling of our infirmities.

—Randall L. Fuson
Pastor, COG, Byron, MI

July 12

ASSURANCE IN THE MIDST OF THE STORM

No temptation has overtaken you except such as is common to man; but God is faithful, who will not allow you to be tempted beyond what you are able, but with the temptation will also make the way of escape, that you may be able to bear it. (1 Corinthians 10:13)

The psalmist David was tested, but he was never left without a way out of the testing. David knew where his strength lay, so the testing turned him to God as he humbled himself before the Lord.

So many times in life, as a pastor, a shepherd, I have felt so alone —at times, forsaken, wondering if anyone cared or understood. But as I continued praying and walking with God, I was made to understand that God was allowing me to be tested, that I might prove Him.

David waited eight years before he became king of Judah and these were years of deep testing. It was during this time that he wrote many of the psalms. David was often in hiding and almost constantly in danger of his life. These were years when God was training his man to be Israel's shepherd.

God tests His servants and perfects them. We can see this in the life of Moses who for 40 years remained hidden away in a desert area as God prepared him for the task of delivering Israel. Moses thought he was ready when he was under the private hand of the Divine Teacher. Finally, Moses became the instrument God could use. David spent eight years of training through severe trials of various kinds before he was ready for the position to which God had appointed him.

There are times of great testing for the body of Christ. But the Word of God leaves us with the blessed assurance that in every temptation and test, He has made a way of escape.

. . . PRAYER . . .

Thank You, Father, for Your watchcare over us during those times of trials and testing. Thank You for the blessed assurance we have in knowing that in our moments of doubt and fear, You never give up on us.

. . . TODAY'S THOUGHT . . .

"It is God who arms me with strength, And makes my way perfect. He makes my feet like the feet of deer, And sets me on my high places" (Psalm 18:32, 33).

—Robert W. Clagg
Pastor, COG, Seaford, DE

July 13

THE SECRET OF IMMOVABILITY

Surely he will never be shaken; . . . He will not be afraid of evil tidings; His heart is steadfast, trusting in the Lord. (Psalm 112:6-7)

Painful silence. Eight months into the pregnancy. An eternity as the doctor searched for the sound of our unborn baby's heartbeat. We told him how we had prayed and waited for 17 years to be parents. We watched the sonograms together and smiled as we saw our son progress through each stage of the pregnancy. My wife, Donna, laughed when John Henry extended his tiny body and seemed to move to the camera.

Now there were no smiles. My mind wouldn't let me believe that the worst possible scenario was being played out. I struggled to speak, said only, "Doctor. . . ." He bowed his head, tears down his cheeks: "I'm sorry, he's gone." "Oh noooooooooo!" was the long, mournful shriek that erupted from Donna's lips and trailed off into a pitiful sob.

The steady drizzle falling outside when we stepped out the door was welcome. The rain on my face hid my tears. Besides, I didn't think the sun should be shining when my whole world had just fallen apart.

Two weeks later, Donna gave birth to a little brown-eyed corpse. We held him in our arms and counted his little fingers and toes. He was perfect in every way except there was no breath in his body. We kissed him good-bye and promised to see him in heaven. After the funeral, every day was eternal. Donna and I cried as we stored the unused toys.

The devil attacked my mind with tormenting fears of past and future. My life was a miserable failure. One morning as I knelt to pray, the Lord directed me to Psalm 112: the righteous are not afraid of bad news; his heart is firm, trusting in God. God began a healing work in me.

Not long after, Donna and I became the adoptive parents of a beautiful baby girl. God had set in motion a series of miracles that took us from the deepest sorrow in our lives to the greatest joy.

. . . PRAYER . . .

Thank You, Lord, for working all things together for good in my life. I will trust You and never fear because I know that even my trials work for me.

. . . TODAY'S THOUGHT . . .

Nothing can touch your life until it has been approved in heaven by your loving Father God.

—Sam Luke, Jr.
Pastor, Princeton Pike, Hamilton, OH

July 14

THE SPIRIT—ANOTHER HELPER

"I will pray the Father, and He will give you another Helper, that He may abide with you forever." (John 14:16)

At 16, I went to a Pentecostal revival in Oklahoma City. I felt convicted and vowed to go back. The next night I got on a streetcar and prayed for Jesus to lead me back to the church. I didn't know where to get off, but as the streetcar approached 32nd Street, a voice said, "Get off here and go left." I soon found myself at the brush arbor revival. I was saved and sanctified that night. Years later I was baptized in the Holy Spirit.

In 1932 we moved to Selman City, Texas, where I joined the Church of God. Through the years I had felt I was called to preach the gospel, but I was shy and timid. When I received the Holy Spirit, however, God took the fear away.

Left to raise three girls alone, I started a home laundry because I wanted to stay home with them. We always knelt down and prayed before they left for school each morning on the school bus that stopped in front of our house. One morning in March we were running late, but 1 said, "Come on, girls. Let's pray." I felt uneasy that day, and I will never forget my prayer: "Dear God, I'm not putting my children in the hands of the bus driver or the teachers but in Your hands. Please protect them and bring them home safely."

Ten minutes before the last bell that day, a gas leak caused an explosion, and the school blew up. Although 301 children and adults were killed in the terrible disaster, God spared my girls—Inez, 13; Louise, 12; and Lottie, 10. Inez crawled through the rubble, past the injured, mutilated, and dead to find her younger sisters. When I got to the school, they were waiting for me by the school bus.

. . . PRAYER . . .

Thank You, Father for Your protection. Your Holy Spirit abides with us always!

. . . TODAY'S THOUGHT . . .

Nothing is too small or too large for Jesus to do. We only have to pray and have faith in Him.

—Zoe Brown (Reprinted from *SpiritWalk: Daily Devotions on the Holy Spirit* by permission of Pathway Press)
Evangelist, Pastor, Church Planter, COG

July 15

EDIFICATION THROUGH PROPHECY

But he who prophesies speaks edification and exhortation and comfort to men. (1 Corinthians 14:3)

Like many other summer Saturday mornings in Southeast Tennessee, it was hot and humid. With the perspiration flowing, I methodically pushed my lawn mower. Though carefully making all the lines straight, I still meditated on the Lord. In that less than glamorous setting the Lord quietly spoke to my heart. I was to preach my father's funeral. He even shared the sermon text from 2 Timothy. Little did I realize the full impact of what would happen.

Twenty months later my brother and I, along with fellows ministers, led a congregation in worship to God as we paid respect to my dad, a minister who sacrificed physically and economically to pastor smaller churches.

As the final words of the benediction were about to be spoken the voice of a friend broke in. He began to prophesy: "Hear the word from the Lord. This is my servant that I have taken unto myself . . ."

In a few moments we understood the spiritual warfare which had caused my father to suffer several major health crises when taking small churches, remodeling the facilities and leading them in both spiritual and economic growth.

In a few moments a congregation comprised of many non-Pentecostals experienced the moving of the Holy Spirit in a new way. And for days they commented on the power and life of that service.

In a few moments we Pentecostals were reminded again of the edification which prophecy brings to the body—even in the funeral service of a believer.

. . . PRAYER . . .

Heavenly Father, help us to be open to the moving of Your Holy Spirit. May we be ready to use our spiritual gifts regardless of the situation or individuals present.

. . . TODAY'S THOUGHT . . .

Prophecy is for today's believers. It provides direction, comfort and edification for both individuals and the corporate church.

—Jerald J. Daffe
Professor, Lee University

July 16

THE WORKING OF HIS MIGHTY POWER

And from the days of John the Baptist until now the kingdom of heaven suffers violence, and the violent take it by force. (Matthew 11:12)

My wife, Faith, read Psalm 41:8, "An evil disease," they say, "clings to him. And now that he lies down, he will rise up no more." Then she remembered her dream: a threat of death, a child's life, the bite of a serpent, and a call from the hospital. But what did it mean?

A year later we remembered the dream after a satanic curse had been written on the wall of one of our church buildings and our fifteen-year-old son was diagnosed with cancer in six places. Faith rang me from the hospital: our son had perhaps three weeks to live.

Depressed, numbed, paralyzed with shock, I read Psalm 41:8 again, but, this time, also verse 11: "By this I know that You are well pleased with me, Because my enemy does not triumph over me." Hope began to rise. "So then faith comes by hearing, and hearing by the word of God" (Romans 10:17).

My wife, two ministers, and I prayed over my son. I threw everything I had—body, soul and spirit—into the prayer and at the enemy. I did not care that patients and hospital staff could hear. I was fighting as I had never fought before. *Win or lose*, I thought. With everything in me I drew on the energy that works within, and answers above all we ask or think. What did it matter what the other patients would think? This was my son we were fighting for.

That evening Chris felt better, the next day his glands had gone down, in a few days his lung X-ray was clear. The cancer had gone and has never returned. The enemy did not triumph in this situation.

. . . PRAYER . . .

Lord, thank You for the power that works in me/us mightily, and help me today to pray with all commitment and desire to see Your kingdom come and Your will be done on earth as it is in heaven.

. . . TODAY'S THOUGHT . . .

By force violent men take the Kingdom which comes violently; not against flesh and blood but spirit powers; so I wish to bring in an increasing percentage of God's heavenly kingdom every year until Jesus comes with it all.

—Roger Forster

Ichthus Fellowship, London, England, UK

July 17

THE HOLY SPIRIT IS A COMFORTER

And I will pray the Father, and He will give you another Helper, that He may abide with you forever. (John 14:16)

I was reared in a home where both parents believed in being filled with the Spirit. Consequently, following my conversion at age 15, I dedicated my life to Christ for His service and began praying to be filled with the Spirit . . . but nothing happened. However, the God who looks on the heart is faithful. One early morning when I was doing some of a country boy's chores, I knelt between two rows of corn to pray. The God who knew the hunger of my heart filled me then and there with the Holy Spirit. I didn't tear up the corn patch, but calmly arose and went my way. It was that morning that I realized where you are is not what is most important.

Some years later, at an army camp, I experienced the loneliness of being many miles from loved ones and home. One night while walking to my barracks, the Holy Spirit came upon me in a very special way. I began speaking in a language I had not learned, and my heavy load was lifted. The Spirit was my Defense and Comforter in time of need.

He is a Comforter when you are lonely. Always remember that you are not alone when He is by your side. As you lean on the everlasting arms, He'll whisper sweet peace to your soul.

He is a Comforter when you feel forsaken by family or friends. David said, "When my father and my mother forsake me, Then the Lord will take care of me." (Psalm 27:10). As you trust Him, you'll be able to sing, "He's all I need, all I need."

He is a Comforter when you feel that you are a failure. If you give the best of your service, He'll understand and say "well done." What man calls failure, God may call success.

. . . PRAYER . . .

Thank You for being my Comforter, and help me comfort others as You have comforted me.

. . . TODAY'S THOUGHT . . .

I will not allow myself to believe for the bad. If the worst comes, I can adjust at that time, but for now, I will rejoice and hope and believe that something good is coming my way.

—Thomas L. Dooley
General Secretary, IPCoC

July 18

THE WONDER OF HIS WAY

Who does great things, and unsearchable, Marvelous things without number. (Job 5:9)

It has been 44 years since, at the age of 19, I made an unconditional surrender of my life to the lordship of Jesus Christ. I never dreamed I could, or would, embark upon such a thrilling adventure with the God of all grace.

I had experienced divorce and its pain as a child and again as a teenager. It had left me broken, confused, with bitterness and hostility.

Scarlet fever had left me with leaking valves and epileptic seizures. It seemed, from the human standpoint, that my life was over before it had begun. Inside me was chaotic turmoil with no hope in sight, nothing to look forward to.

I was invited to attend divine healing services, and there I gave to the Lord the pieces of my life, saying, "If You can do anything with the broken pieces of my life, it's all I have to give, take it." He did! He gave the joy of His salvation. He delivered me from epilepsy! He healed my heart of the dreaded condition! I have had no heart problem since. He took me beyond healing deliverance to a wholeness that set me free from a haunting past and filled me with "the love of God [that] has been poured out in our hearts by the Holy Spirit" (Romans 5:5).

He challenged me to "seek first the kingdom of God and His righteousness," with the promise that "all these things shall be added to you" (Matthew 6:33). The many years since have held their challenge, but in it all and through it all He has remained the God who is able to do exceeding abundantly above all we ask or think or imagine. He is the Alpha and Omega, the beginning and the end. To Him belongs the glory!

. . . PRAYER . . .

Thank You, gracious Lord, for realizing in the experience of such a one as I, the wonder of Your abundant life with all its marvelous purpose. Touch each one who reads this truth today."

. . . TODAY'S THOUGHT . . .

"But seek first the kingdom of God and His righteousness, and all these things shall be added to you" (Matthew 6:33).

—Gerald A. Honey
General Moderator, FGCOG, South Africa

July 19

A WORTHY EPITAPH

I have fought the good fight, I have finished the race, I have kept the faith. (2 Timothy 4:7)

Recently, I asked myself how I wanted to be remembered. If I could answer this question, then I would know how to live my daily life. After giving this question much thought, I decided that 2 Timothy 4:7 was my choice for my epitaph. Each phrase in it has special meaning.

"I have fought the good fight." It's not my nature to fight. The Holy Spirit said to me, "If you don't embrace life as a spiritual battle learning to use faith, the Word of God, prayer and obedience, you will only know defeat."

"I have finished the race." The first morning following my arrival in California following a heavy schedule, I walked on the beach. A man slowly jogged out of the fog, passed me, and ran back into the fog. Inspired, I began to run in the same direction as the runner. Although I had waited a moment before beginning, I realized that I would soon overtake him. I slowed, but I couldn't run as slowly as him and soon passed him. Down the beach, though, I bent over with cramped legs and burning lungs. The runner again appeared out of the fog, passed me, and disappeared. The Holy Spirit spoke to me: "Life is a marathon, not a sprint. If you want to finish, you must change your pace." I know many people who have started, but who have never finished.

"I have kept the faith." Years ago, I compromised in my lifestyle. The generation before me had shown me holy living, but I had not guarded that life very well. To keep the faith doesn't mean to stand guard over what we believe, but, instead, to live a life that reveals our faith, to live a life of holy living. I decided if I was going to pass on to the next generation the life that Jesus wants us to live by faith, I could no longer compromise.

I want my epitaph to be the words of 2 Timothy 4:7.

. . . PRAYER . . .

Lord, by Your grace help me to be a fighter, a finisher, and faithful today.

. . . TODAY'S THOUGHT . . .

Our commitment to God isn't guaranteed by the strength of our will, but by the power of His grace. "His grace is sufficient."

—Dr. Roger A. Whitlow
Pastor, Valley Christian Center ICFG, Fresno, CA

July 20

DEVOTION FILLS OUR SPIRITUAL CISTERN

. . . be filled with the Spirit. (Ephesians 5:18)

We all ebb spiritually. We did not plan or anticipate it. Everything seemed to be going well. We were faithful in our church attendance. We participated in different programs of the church. We paid our tithes. Some of us diligently taught Sunday school classes. Some even held the office of pastor, teacher, or evangelist. But, the well ran dry.

I lived in an era when we depended on the cistern at the edge of the house for our drinking water. We had a trough to channel the water down from the eaves of the house to the cistern. When it rained we had plenty of water, but during the dry season there was always concern that the cistern would run dry. Anyone knows that the cistern is useless without rain.

Your body is the temple of the Holy Ghost. This temple could be compared with a cistern. In times of drought the cistern or well runs dry. How are we going to slake our thirst and minister the life-giving water to others if the well goes dry?

Jesus spoke of a man who went to his friend at midnight to get some bread. Another friend who was hungry had come to his house and he had nothing to set before him. He admitted he had nothing and went to the one who had an abundant supply. The prophet in the days of Elisha, who lost his axehead while felling a tree, refused to continue chopping until the axehead was retrieved. Let us confess we do not have what it takes to quench the thirst, nor to feed the hungry, and let us go to the right source for a supply.

When the well runs dry or the spiritual cupboard is bare, why don't we go to our heavenly Father for a replenishing? His address is the same and He does not have an answering service, nor call waiting. We have a hot line to the throne any time.

. . . PRAYER . . .

Heavenly Father, satisfy this longing heart of mine with thy fulness that I may share with others.

. . . TODAY'S THOUGHT . . .

"Here's my cup Lord, fill it up: Quench this thirsting of my soul."

—T. D. Mooneyham
Missionary, Overseer, COG (retired)

July 21

THE TUTOR

However, when He, the Spirit of truth, has come, He will guide you into all truth; . . . (John 16:13)

I always had trouble with math as a child. In grade school, arithmetic; in high school, algebra and geometry. I just couldn't get it. I needed a tutor. Webster defines a tutor as "a teacher who gives individual instruction to a student; a private teacher." But nobody had heard of such a thing where I grew up. Had I had someone with patience to sit beside me and spend time with me and explain things to me, I would have succeeded, I wouldn't have experienced such stress and failure.

Jesus said that the Holy Spirit is our very own private teacher. Our tutor. As the Spirit of truth, He guides us into all truth. As "the Helper," He comes alongside us in our distress and confusion. He patiently shows us truth about our past, about our present circumstances, and about "things to come." He can make things add up that never made sense.

What does this tutor teach us? He teaches us "the things of the Spirit" (Romans 8:5). He teaches us how to pray in the Spirit when we don't even know what to say (8:26). He teaches us to wield the sword of the Spirit, to contend for new territory and to defend ourselves from attack (Ephesians 6:17, 18). He instructs us concerning the gifts of the Spirit, so we can think like God thinks, act like God acts, and speak like God speaks (1 Corinthians 12). He teaches us the fruit of the Spirit, so we may gain a godly character (Galatians 5:22). He teaches us to worship in the Spirit (John 4: 23, 24), for the Father seeks such worshipers.

The Spirit is a tutor who never takes a break. He not only spends time with us, He is in us, and will be with us forever!

. . . PRAYER . . .

Father, thank You for the Spirit of truth, our own private teacher, who so lovingly and patiently guides us, defends us, teaches us, and gifts us.

. . . TODAY'S THOUGHT . . .

God has given us His Spirit to be our teacher and companion. He is ready to teach . . . but am I ready to listen, learn, yield, and respond?

—Dr. Ron Mehl

Pastor, Beaverton Foursquare Church, Beaverton, OR

July 22

THE PRICE OF A FRIEND

As iron sharpens iron, So a man sharpens the countenance of his friend. (Proverbs 27:17)

As I walked away from the grave that hot July day, my mind traveled back through the many years he had been my friend. We had been in school together, and there our friendship had its beginnings. As the years passed by, he had assisted me in pastoring churches. We had ministered together in many times in many ways.

Now he was gone. No more counseling together. No more singing together to magnify the Lord. No more uniting our voices together, praying in the Spirit. I cannot describe the emptiness I felt that day.

As I drove away from the graveyard, the Holy Spirit brought to my mind Proverbs 17:17: "A friend loves at all times." I began to think about the real value of a friend, a friend who had stuck by me through thick and thin, through good times and bad, a friend who could look me right in the eye and disagree without judgment. Just how much was this friend worth? How much would I be willing to pay? He was priceless. I could never have bought a friend like him. No amount of money, nothing could have bought the friendship we had.

Today I cherish the memory of this wonder friend. I realize too that our friendship has not ended. It has only been suspended for a little while. Soon we'll be reunited to never part, pain or hurting will never come again, tears will never fall from our eyes. In heaven our friendship is forever.

. . . PRAYER . . .

And so I pray, dear Lord today You who died, my debts to pay

Keep Lord in Your tender care My friend who now has joined You there.

Fill our hearts with love so sweet Until we sit together at Your feet,

For Lord, You have said that I'm Your friend That You'll be with me to the end

Help me to always faithful be Until Your wondrous face I see.

. . . TODAY'S THOUGHT . . .

"Greater love has no one than this, than to lay down one's life for his friends. You are My friends if you do whatever I command you" (John 15: 13, 14).

—Roland L. Keith
Presbyter Board, COGoAF

July 23

REPAIRERS AND RESTORERS

Those from among you Shall build the old waste places; You shall raise up the foundations of many generations; And you shall be called the Repairer of the Breach, The Restorer of Streets to Dwell In. (Isaiah 58:12)

When Hurricane Andrew swept across South Florida in August, 1992, it left debris everywhere. Streets were impassable and whole neighborhoods were unrecognizable. Families' lives were shattered.

Isaiah 58 speaks of a similar situation dealing with a nation's spiritual life. Our lives are filled with the same destruction and debris that a hurricane brings. We must deal with the hurts and wounds the world inflicts. Often the same hurts are placed upon us by the church that tells us it is more about what we do than about who we are in Christ Jesus.

We are called to be the Red Cross, National Guard, emergency personnel, and relief agencies to come in after the storm. We repair what has been swept away, restore the lives that have been filled with the debris of life's hurts, and clear away the garbage, twisted metal, and piles of wood to restore mobility.

Through the Holy Spirit, we can be Jesus to these people. We show them in tangible ways that God has not abandoned them. But this ministry requires sacrifice. We must roll up our sleeves, put on our work boots, and make the commitment to spend hours of sharing, caring, loving, and praying with people whose lives have been devastated. The rewards on the other hand are eternal.

In Homestead, Florida, remain only a few reminders of the hurricane that destroyed a city. People from all over the country sent help to repair and restore. We can make a difference by doing the same for the hurting people of this world. Jesus promised He will not only begin the process, He will also bring it to completion (Philippians 1:6).

. . . PRAYER . . .

Father, thank You for promising to repair and restore my life. Use me to reach out and touch someone else with the same message of hope.

. . . TODAY'S THOUGHT . . .

God's promise to rebuild and restore a nation is a glimpse of what He has done in the heart of man through the sending of His Son, Jesus.

—Roy A. Van Berkum

Superintendent-at-Large, Mountain Plains Region, OBSC

July 24

A PENTECOSTAL MOTHER'S PRAYERS

. . . a woman who fears the Lord, she shall be praised. (Proverbs 31:30)

After years of nonattendance, on Easter Sunday 1954, at the invitation of my aunt, my father took his family to the Flowing Wells Congregational Holiness Church. Within weeks a spiritual awakening took place in our home. As I pored over every page of a little Gideon New Testament that I owned, I soon became convinced of my need for salvation. Nevertheless, because of doubts, I just could not seem to accept Christ.

In August our church began a two-week revival. I was still struggling with the assurance of salvation. One night after a lengthy altar service, we were traveling home in my Father's truck. I was riding in the back of the truck with my brothers and sister. That night, in prayer, I turned everything over to Christ. Then I promised God I would seek the infilling of the Holy Spirit, no matter how long it took me to receive. Suddenly I felt as if I were having a hard chill. I shook uncontrollably. Our route home was the famous Tobacco Road near Augusta, Georgia. When I felt the jarring of the truck as it crossed the railroad tracks on Tobacco Road, it seemed as if a hand took the tip of my tongue and shook it for a full minute. When my tongue was released, I began to speak fluently in tongues.

Five months later, at the age of 14, I received my call into the ministry. Later my aunt confided that my mother, who died when I was six prayed from the time I was born until her death that God would save me, fill me with the Holy Spirit and call me into the Pentecostal ministry. It was an incident where a godly Pentecostal mother's prayers and influence continued even after her death.

. . . PRAYER . . .

I thank You, Lord Jesus, for a Pentecostal mother who knew how to pray. Lord, I ask You to bless praying mothers everywhere.

. . . TODAY'S THOUGHT . . .

"No one ever escapes the embrace of a loving mother. Long after she has gone from this life, even though we may wander carelessly for a time, her memory and her training bring us back to the path we should follow" (Dan Betzer).

—Jesse L. Wiggins
Pastor, COG, Bethalto, IL

July 25

ACCEPTING NO SUBSTITUTES

So Shishak king of Egypt came up against Jerusalem, and took away the treasures of the house of the Lord. . . . He also carried away the gold shields which Solomon had made. 12:10 Then King Rehoboam made bronze shields in their place. . ." (2 Chronicles 12:9-10)

Rehoboam substituted brass shields for the gold ones, endeavoring to deceive the people into believing he still possessed the real. The devil has always been in the substitution business. Since he cannot produce what Calvary provides, he offers inferior, fake experiences.

In the spring of 1608, the settlers in Jamestown, Virginia, discovered gold—or so they thought. They abandoned most efforts at planting crops, erecting buildings and preparing for winter. They devoted themselves to digging out and washing the precious "gold." Fortunately, the Indians fed them. They eventually sent a ship to England with a heavy load of metal for which they'd labored . . . but their gold turned out to be iron pyrite, also called "fools gold." They had given most of their time and energies to a worthless substitute.

An uncle of mine had tried fortune-tellers, crystal-ball gazers, etc., to fulfill the spiritual hunger in his heart, but found no satisfaction. When his oldest daughter contracted a rare malady for which doctors offered no hope or cure, a neighbor told him about a Pentecostal preacher who was praying for the sick in Los Angeles. In desperation he took little Sharon to be prayed for. She was healed! This resulted in the Ferraris family finding Jesus as Savior. Charlie aggressively went after other family members to go to church and be saved. In a short time more than 20 were saved, including me. We discarded all of our ineffective substitutes and accepted Christ.

. . . PRAYER . . .

Father, in Christ's name, give us a discerning spirit and an understanding mind to accept no substitutes for Your divine grace and gifts.

. . . TODAY'S THOUGHT . . .

"Instead of bronze I will bring you gold . . . I will make peace your governor and righteousness your ruler" (Isaiah 60:17). Reconstruction of shattered lives is highly advertised. Rebirth is not—but nothing has been produced that equals Calvary's provisions. Accept no substitutes!

—Robert G. Graham
Pastor, Maineville-Kingspoint, Maineville, OH

July 26

HIS EVERLASTING ARMS

The eternal God is your refuge, And underneath are the everlasting arms . . . (Deuteronomy 33:27)

Excitement mounted as we waited for the news. A boy or little girl? As long as the baby was healthy, it didn't matter. But then the phone rang and we heard our daughter: "There's something wrong. Please come to the hospital."

Hurriedly we rushed to the hospital where the doctor's office was located. In a few moment's time our joyful spirits had evaporated. The ultra-sound indicate a little boy with a diaphragmatic hernia. What were the alternatives? Abortion or a new surgical procedure!

Karla and Greg immediately responded: "We want to give our baby every opportunity to live." This meant moving to San Francisco.

Six weeks after arriving at the University of California, S.F. Hospital, little Andrew (meaning strong) was born. For four months he exhibited an unusual desire to live. With much anticipation the family looked forward to having him home in Florida . . . but the home celebration was interrupted by the doctor's word that Andrew had taken a turn for the worse and was dying. He had fought back before. Surely he would do so now.

We had expected Andrew in Orlando, but God planned a different destination. On the evening of June 23, 1995, our daughter held him and sang, "Jesus loves me this I know . . ." Our "strong one" smiled several times as if to say, "Mom, Dad, I love you! I will see you later." The Lord then took Andrew home.

This doesn't seem like a storybook ending, but in his four short months he gave us a lifetime of memories. Through this experience we learned to "trust in the Lord with all our hearts." We learned that "our ways are not always God's ways." And, we learned that "God is our refuge and underneath are his everlasting arms."

. . . PRAYER . . .

Lord, thank You for sustaining us in our most difficult times. Your comfort is always evident to the child of God.

. . . TODAY'S THOUGHT . . .

"Weeping may endure for a night, But joy comes in the morning" (Psalm 30:5).

—Ken Houck

Pastor, The Sanctuary, Orlando, FL

July 27

LITTLE CHILDREN

At that time Jesus was filled with joy by the Holy Spirit and said, "Father, Lord of heaven and earth! I thank you because you have shown to the unlearned what you have hidden from the wise and learned. Yes, Father, this was how you were pleased to have it happen." (Luke 10:21)

I am glad that our Lord has made the riches of heaven accessible to little children. Jesus used a metaphor to describe the qualification of those who are eligible to receive all that the Father has in store. Notice that the Father is the one who reveals the eternal riches of His kingdom to His children, and it is His good pleasure to reveal these riches. The riches of the kingdom are seen in the healing of the sick (v. 9), authority and power to overcome the enemy (v. 19) and most importantly, the proclamation that the "kingdom of God is near" (v. 9).

But for a moment consider the metaphor "little children." Jesus was not referring to the position of a person's heart. A childlike attitude coupled, with a simplicity to receive, joined with a teachable spirit, qualify an honest seeker to be in this category. Therefore, it's not surprising that God the Father would bypass the wise and learned (of this world) because simply accepting and being teachable goes against the grain of a man's pride, and the Bible says that "God opposes the proud but gives grace to the humble" (James 4:6).

Well, I distinctly remember when I, in childlike faith, asked the Lord to fulfill His promise to baptize me in the Holy spirit. I simply accepted the truth that I would "receive power to witness and live a holy life when the Holy Spirit would come upon me" as we read in Acts 1:8, and the Lord fulfilled His promise.

Oh what joy there is reserved for those who are like "little children," for the kingdom of heaven is theirs!

. . . PRAYER . . .

Lord, teach me to be a little child simply to believe Your Word, and receive the blessings You have in store for me.

. . . TODAY'S THOUGHT . . .

Remember it doesn't matter what your social status is, or your background. God is looking for little children to reveal His eternal riches to, and you qualify to receive them.

—Giulio Gabeli

Pastor, Community Church , Vancouver, BC

July 28

WHERE ARE YOU, GOD?

Yea, though I walk through the valley of the shadow of death, I will fear no evil; For You are with me; Your rod and Your staff, they comfort me. (Psalm 23:4)

It was early on a Monday morning that my phone rang and my mother said, "Son, you had better come quickly. Daddy is going fast. They cannot find a heart beat." Never had I gotten ready so quickly and made the 40-mile trip so swiftly as I did that morning. Upon arrival, I discovered that the struggle of the past year for my dad was over, and he was now with the Lord. Then it hit me—my friend, my daddy was gone, and I was left alone.

During the days that followed, it was difficult to pray and follow the directions of the Word. I hurt; a knot was in my stomach. I accepted the words I had often told my church members to believe God for the needed peace that did not come easily. I found it difficult to accept the reality that although I was walking through a shadow, God was with me. Instead, I was asking, "Where are You, God?"

On Saturday afternoon prior to leaving to return to my pastorate, I stood by my dad's grave still hurting and wondering where God was. Then I looked up and said, "God, I must this day sense Your presence and power, and I am going to stand firm on Your Word that You are with me now."

It was then that the Holy Spirit flooded my soul, and I again discovered that even though I was walking through the valley of the shadow of death, He really was there all the time.

Until you have been there, it will be difficult to fully understand the reality of the words of Psalm 23:4.

. . . PRAYER . . .

God, thank You for Your eternal Word that always shows us where You are. Help us to hold on to the very promise that You are always there for us.

. . . TODAY'S THOUGHT . . .

Just because you know someone is ready to meet the Lord and they will be out of their suffering should they pass away, it is not necessarily easy to accept their going. But when it happens Psalm 23:4 will become real; for God will be there.

—W. F. Waters, Jr.
Pastor, Fairforest, Spartanburg, SC

July 29

WHEN YOU PRAY

So He said to them, "When you pray, say: Our Father . . . (Luke 11:2)

My earliest recollections include Mama's prayers. Every night the family knelt and Mama prayed. She included her family, pastor, neighbors and relatives. She interceded for my father and all the men working in the mines. She never prayed a "bless 'em all" prayer, but called everyone by name and related the details of their needs.

God was very special to her, and she came boldly to the throne of grace. She addressed God as "my heavenly Father," "Father of love," or "merciful Father."

Anyone spending the night would be expected to pray with us. Usually all eight of her children were asleep when she finished. She carried the little ones to their beds and roused the other children and helped them to their beds. On cold winter nights she would warm cloths and wrap our feet. We slept without a care in the world because we were sure that Mama and God were in complete control.

Mama prayed so loudly that one might surmise she believed that God was hard of hearing. I am sure that she never whispered a prayer.

One time, Mama was too busy to drop everything and pray at the moment of need. My sister, Mildred, went into labor and Mama put her philosophy of prayer into action. First, she directed my sister, Lillian, to pray until Mama sent her word. Then, Mildred's husband was sent to a telephone to notify the doctor. Someone else was told to get the sheets and towels that had been boiled to sterilize them. A couple of the neighbor women were summoned to assist with the midwifery. My father was assigned the task of caring for the grandchildren. After the baby arrived and there was no danger to mother or child, Mama prayed. Because of the sound of victory and thanksgiving in her prayer, the neighbors rejoiced and thanked God with her.

. . . PRAYER . . .

Our heavenly Father, let Thy word be a light to our paths and teach us to pray. Help us to find the time—morning, noon, and night—to cease from all other activities, both mental and physical, and to come boldly to Thy throne of grace.

. . . TODAY'S THOUGHT . . .

Jesus did not say, "If you pray, say," but, "When you pray, say. . ."

—Roland McDaniel
Pastor, COG (retired)

July 30

CONFIDENCE FOR LIVING

I can do all things through Christ who strengthens me. (Philippians 4:13)

When I was called to salvation by the convicting power of the Spirit, my response was, "I am unable to live the Christian life." When I faced the overwhelming task of preaching the gospel, pastoring the church, and winning the lost, my response again was human weakness.

Yet, throughout my life, at just the right time, God has dropped into my spirit the assurance of divine enablement. It was the same confidence for living that Paul expressed, ". . . I have learned in whatever state I am, to be content: I know how to be abased, and I know how to abound. Everywhere and in all things I have learned both to be full and to be hungry, both to abound and to suffer need. I can do all things through Christ who strengthens me" (4:11-13).

How can this confidence be realized in the struggle of everyday life? Hold to certain principles to guide you through life's tough places.

Determine to maintain a good attitude regardless of those around you (4:8-9). Everyone fights the battle for the mind, but you can think the best even though life is at its worst. I can experience contentment in any set of circumstances (4:10-12). The last human freedom is the right to choose one's own personal attitude in any given situation. That cannot be taken away. You can't be denied that right. I can learn not to depend on human achievement, but on divine enablement (4:13).

There is power in positive believing. Guard against two extremes: self-sufficiency and human despair. Depend on Christ's all sufficiency. The height of human arrogance is to say, "I can do all things." How absurd! God's word doesn't stop there: "through Christ who strengthens me." It goes beyond human ability to divine sufficiency. That's the secret to confidence for positive living in today's world.

. . . PRAYER . . .

Father, I thank You for the power to cope when the problems of life ultimately cast me back on the bedrock of my faith--the all-sufficiency of Christ.

. . . TODAY'S THOUGHT . . .

It is God's will that I should cast my care on Him each day. He asks me not to cast my confidence away. But, how stupidly I act when taken unaware. I cache away my confidence, and carry all my care.

—Sim A. Wilson

Chairman, World Missions Board, COG

July 31

MERCY AND TRUTH

Mercy and truth have met together; Righteousness and peace have kissed. (Psalm 85:10)

The word *mercy* is translated "loving kindness." Mercy seems to be more flexible and benevolent. The word *truth* is seen as being sturdy and unyielding. It seems impossible for these two words to accomplish God's divine purpose and bring about a spiritual improvement. The psalmist states here: "Mercy and truth are met together. . . ." In all conversions, the Holy Spirit applies these conditions to bring about changes in the lives of people.

One of the more impressive miracles in my ministry occurred during the sickness and death of my older brother. My brother was an excellent musician who spent several years playing nightclubs. He met a nice lady whom he married and settled into a good family life. Unfortunately, he had not accepted Christ into his life. Years later he became very ill and began moving slowly toward death. Circumstances prevented my traveling to the remote area where he lived. In desperation, I prayed for my brother to be saved. The Lord impressed upon me to write him a letter explaining to him the simple plan of salvation. I very carefully framed a letter detailing the simple steps to salvation. I urged him to follow these steps and accept the Lord Jesus Christ into his life. I explained to him that I would call him later in order to consummate the requirements for salvation.

After he read the letter, the Holy Spirit began working in his life. I made the telephone call and ministered to him. During the phone conversation, the Holy Spirit implemented truth and mercy, and he accepted Christ during the telephone conversation. A few days later, he slipped away to be with Christ in that heavenly Kingdom. This was, indeed, a miracle in my ministry.

Mercy and truth! What a team!

. . . PRAYER . . .

Lord, may mercy and truth be combined in our lives.

. . . TODAY'S THOUGHT . . .

The truth is that God is merciful, and God's mercy reveals to us the truth of His plan of salvation.

—Wayne S. Proctor
State Overseer, COG (retired)

August 1

THE GREAT SALVATION

Yes, we had the sentence of death in ourselves, that we should not trust in ourselves but in God who raises the dead, who delivered us from so great a death, and does deliver us; in whom we trust that He will still deliver us, . . (2 Corinthians 1:9-10)

The great Salvation, spiritual deliverance from sin, is the only true remedy for the death sentence brought upon man by Adam's fall. I want to point out the three aspects of this great Salvation that are realities and that are available to all people regardless of the need.

First, salvation is the forgiveness of past sins and transgressions: "delivered us." The sweetest words I heard Him say were "I forgive." I experienced this as a nine-year-old boy in a tent revival, thank God!

Secondly, salvation is a daily experience: "does deliver." Every day as you and I face the adversary of our soul, we are delivered from the power of sin and the devil. Christ ascended and is set down at the right hand of majesty on high to make intercession for us. Hebrews 4:15-16 teaches us the value of this Intercessor, His compassion, His influence with the Father. These words encourage us to come boldly to His throne with our need. I have experienced this for many years and God has always been faithful in times of adversity and heartache. Even in the loss of a child, my wife and I were comforted and sustained. While we do not know what the future holds, we know who holds the future, and that is enough for His grace is sufficient.

Thirdly, salvation is yet to become a reality for us: "in whom we trust that He will still deliver us." Amen! This is our hope and the anchor for our souls. It is steadfast and sure.

The first aspect delivers us from the guilt and stain of sin, the second from the power of sin though surrounded by it. But praise God, the best is yet to come when we will be delivered from the very presence of sin and raptured into glory to dwell forever in the presence of the One who provided so great salvation.

. . . PRAYER . . .

Thank You Heavenly Father for salvation through Christ Jesus.

. . . TODAY'S THOUGHT . . .

We can be confident of this one thing: that God is able to meet whatever need today holds. He inspires in us hope for Eternity.

—Charles E. Prince
State Evangelism Director, COG, TX (retired)

August 2

GOD'S SEASON OF PREPARATION

. . . who, contrary to hope, in hope believed, . . . and being fully convinced that what He had promised He was also able to perform. (Romans 4:18, 21)

The prophet spoke with authority: "I am calling you out of vocational ministry to put you in business. I will prosper, promote, and prepare you for my purposes. In my time I will restore you to full-time ministry." I wept convulsively; I had reluctantly accepted a job in business after dedicating the previous seven years to pastoral preparation and service. But there was hope: it was only for a season.

The weeks, months, years passed. I was indeed being promoted and prospered, but my heart was ravaged with confusion. Seven years of abandon to full-time ministry seemingly had not impressed God. I made the classic mistakes of murmuring like Israel in the wilderness and living for tomorrow instead of seeking God's best for today.

Many have awaited the fulfillment of a promise. Joseph had a dream of rulership; it came to pass only after years of betrayal, false accusations, broken promises and imprisonment in Egypt. Moses was called to deliver Israel from Egyptian bondage, but God first required 40 years of preparation on the backside of the desert. David's anointing to be king came years before he took the throne; in the interim he lived like an outlaw, running for his life. Jesus was Messiah and Savior, but His public ministry was delayed and hidden (from man, not God) for most of His natural life. Paul was called to the nations, but was not allowed to confer with man and went to Arabia for three years.

What does God require to accomplish His purpose? Emptiness, brokenness, being yielded, a crucified life.

Had I known my season of preparation would be 18 years I might have fainted with hopelessness. But God was equipping me with business and personnel skills to lead a Bible college and denomination. Do not be disheartened. Fruit always comes in season (Psalm 1:1-3).

. . . PRAYER . . .

Father, empty me of self and grant me patience during this season of preparation.

. . . TODAY'S THOUGHT . . .

"There is no panic in heaven" (Corrie Ten Boom).

—Jeffery E. Farmer
President, OBSC

August 3

HE IS A MIRACLE-WORKING GOD

But He was wounded for our transgressions, He was bruised for our iniquities; The chastisement for our peace was upon Him, And by His stripes we are healed. (Isaiah 53:5)

"Mr. Jackson, please come to my office immediately." I was teaching 5th grade in 1976 and was being called to the principal's office. Anxiety gripped me. Something was wrong. Upon arriving in the office, I was told that my grandmother had passed away. Devastated, my world turned upside down, God's Spirit intervened.

After the funeral I returned to my classroom. A student I had rescued from emotional abuse had terrorized my substitute teacher and the school. Carmello had been placed in isolation because of his uncontrollable behavior. His support system disappeared when he needed it most. I expressed my dismay at what had happened and assured him of my support. He bit me on the left hand, and I contracted hepatitis. In the hospital for 10 days, my doctors told me I would be isolated for six to eight weeks. More anxiety. My grandmother's death, then hepatitis. What was the Lord saying to me? I asked.

I told my doctor of my belief in the healing power of God. I told him about the God of miracles in whom I believed. The members of my church prayed. My pastor and I continued to believe in the sovereignty of God to heal. By the end of 14 days I was healed and back to work. The hepatitis was gone, and there was no trace of it in my body.

God has completely healed me of the hepatitis and the grief of my grandmother's death. He healed my desperation when I needed Him most. And He still heals today.

. . . PRAYER . . .

Father, we are often overcome by desperate circumstances. It would seem that "when it rains, it pours" in our life. Thank You for understanding and responding in miraculous ways. We are encouraged by Your divine interventions—"being touched with the feelings of our infirmities."

. . . TODAY'S THOUGHT . . .

When anxiety overwhelms and hopelessness seems our preoccupation, there is hope in the Lord Jesus Christ. We can always trust in Him. He is a God of miracles.

—Joseph E. Jackson

Pastor, World Christian Center Ministries, Hartford, CT

August 4

LORD, HELP ME!

Then she came and worshiped Him, saying, "Lord, help me!" (Matthew 15:25)

One of my earliest memories is of falling into a swiftly flowing, flooded, mountain stream at the age of three. Soon after a storm, my brothers and I were walking across a narrow wooden plank bridge. The board began to shake and an awful horror gripped me as I plunged toward the terrifying mixture of debris and racing muddy water. I screamed from the very depths of my soul. The swift current carried me downstream as I began to choke on the cold, bitter, brown water.

As I neared a bend in the creek, a soldier held on to a tree with one hand and reached his other hand toward mine. He had heard my scream as he walked down the road, saw me fall, and raced ahead of me to be there when the current swept me by. Because of the swallowed water, I passed out in his arms. When I awoke my parents were gathered around the bed in the neighbor's house praying. All was OK!

When the Syrophenecian woman came to Jesus, she said, "Lord, help me!" The word she used for help is a picture word that literally means, "Oh, that someone would come running to my screams." She, too, had fallen into the swollen, murky, flooding waters of a stormy life. Her home was ruined. Her daughter was demon-possessed. How can a mother explain such pain to a stranger from another country? All she could do was scream. "Lord, help me." But her heart cried, "Oh, that someone would come running to my screams!"

Jesus heard. He understood. He saw her peril. He came racing to her side. He stretched forth His hand. " O woman, great is your faith! Let it be to you as you desire" (Matthew 15:28).

God understands the screams of our souls when we cry, "Lord, help me!"

. . . PRAYER . . .

Lord, I thank You that as "Abba, Father," You hear the screams of our hearts.

. . . TODAY'S THOUGHT . . .

When life is overwhelming, the Father's hand is outstretched. When we reach for it in faith He will lift us out of the terror that plagues our soul.

—H. Lynn Stone
Administrative Bishop, COG, CA

August 5

A DOUBLE CURE FOR A DOUBLE CURSE

But He was wounded for our transgressions, He was bruised for our iniquities; The chastisement for our peace was upon Him, And by His stripes we are healed. (Isaiah 53:5)

In 1970 when I was in the prime of my life and poised to do great things for God and my family, all seemed to be taken away with one diagnosis. I had noticed over a period of several weeks that I was becoming weaker and had begun to lose weight rapidly. A visit to the doctor delivered a painful blow. I had a severely damaged heart that could not be repaired through medication or surgery.

The next three months were pain-filled as I was completely bedridden and went from my regular weight of 140 lbs. to a dismal 95 lbs. My condition required round-the-clock care, so my devoted wife, Emiline, resigned her job and stayed at home to take care of me.

One evening, five brethren in one accord came to pray for a breakthrough. They confidently claimed the promise of healing in the name of Jesus. One cried out to God saying, "God, I can't come up to You, so I am asking You to come down."

I was too frail for them to lay hands on me, so a proxy knelt by my bed. Through the power of the Holy Spirit, God wrought a miracle and healed my heart. That evening, for the first time in months I was able to call my wife "honey" in one breath. This miracle remains a source of amazement to all those who knew of my critical condition.

The Lord had used me for Kingdom work prior to my healing, but after the healing my ministry reached levels that I had never envisioned. God strengthened me to shepherd a small storefront church in Brooklyn, New York. This congregation grew to be the largest black Church of God in the United States and Canada up until my retirement in 1995—the Church of God of East Flatbush. To God be the glory!

. . . PRAYER . . .

God, grant me Your strength and sustaining grace so that when I need Your healing power, I will find it through Christ's stripes.

. . . TODAY'S THOUGHT . . .

The healing power of God is still working through the lives of ordinary people, doing extraordinary things.

—Peter Gayle
Pastor, COG, Flatbush, NY (retired)

August 6

THE JOY OF THE LORD IS YOUR STRENGTH!

Then he said to them, "Go your way, eat the fat, drink the sweet, and send portions to those for whom nothing is prepared; for this day is holy to our Lord. Do not sorrow, for the joy of the Lord is your strength."
(Nehemiah 8:10)

People often ask me why I believe so strongly that the body of Christ needs a fresh baptism of joy. Just look around and see how many Christians are beaten down in their spirits. They feel disheartened and downtrodden because of church splits and assaults from the secular news media. They feel browbeaten by the troubles and heartaches of life. Many Christians don't have a strong witness for the Lord because they have no joy. I know, because I was a man who had no joy until God's Holy Ghost laughter and joy exploded in my life!

A few years ago, I had sunk to an all-time low as I struggled to keep Oral Roberts University from going down the tubes because of a nearly $50-million debt. I had almost forgotten about Nehemiah 8:10, "The joy of the Lord is your strength." No wonder I felt like I was at the bottom of the barrel. I had not joy of the Lord, which is my strength.

Many Christians today are staggering out onto the battlefield of life, desperately trying to rally for one last stand for Christ. But they'll never be able to stand tall for Jesus without the joy of the Lord, which is their strength.

Isaiah 40:31 declares, "But those who wait on the Lord Shall renew their strength; They shall mount up with wings like eagles, They shall run and not be weary, They shall walk and not faint." But the key to that verse lies in waiting upon the Lord. As you wait upon the Lord, you'll find yourself overflowing with His joy, because in His presence is fullness of joy (Psalm 16:11).

. . . PRAYER . . .

Thank You, Lord Jesus, for a fresh new baptism of Your Holy Ghost joy, which is our strength.

. . . TODAY'S THOUGHT . . .

The bottom line of having the joy of the Lord is a changed heart, a changed life.

—Richard L. Roberts
Oral Roberts University, Tulsa, OK

August 7

A GOOD NEIGHBOR

"'Honor your father and your mother,' and, 'You shall love your neighbor as yourself.'" (Matthew 19:19)

Growing up on a farm in Delaware taught me the value of good neighbors. They were good people who really cared about others. That care made a difference in my life.

It was the neighbors who stopped every Sunday morning to take me to the Methodist church for Sunday school.

It was the neighbors who would spend a day and night after a barn burned to the ground to make sure the flames did not flare up and set fire to other farm buildings.

It was the neighbors who took me to my very first Pentecostal church service.

It was my neighbors who prayed for a 15-year-old boy, and I was born again.

It was my neighbors who prayed with me and I received the baptism of the Holy Ghost on Sunday night, one week after I was saved.

It was the neighbors who sent money to help me attend Lee College and prepare for ministry.

It was the neighbors who planted, cared for and harvested the crops on my dad's farm when he was in the hospital fighting for his life during a period of six months.

It was the neighbors who taught me the greatest commandment: (Mark 12:29-31).

. . . PRAYER . . .

Father, thank You for the good neighbors who have touched my life and helped me to love my neighbors in such a way that they will see the Savior, the Lord Jesus Christ.

. . . TODAY'S THOUGHT . . .

Are neighbors the same in cities as they were on the farm many years ago? Yes, they can be, if you and I apply the second great commandment—"Love your neighbor as yourself."

—W. A. Davis
Administrative Bishop, COG, VA

August 8

THE CENTURY OF THE HOLY SPIRIT

For the promise is to you and to your children, and to all who are afar off, as many as the Lord our God will call. (Acts 2:39)

As Hitler's forces threatened to cross the English Channel to attack London, I, as a foreigner, had to leave the country. My last contact in England was with the great apostle of the faith, Smith Wigglesworth. As warm tears fell from his face and drenched my head, he prophesied that I would see the great move of God that would pale all previous revivals. As we come to the close of this century of Pentecostal outpouring, I know that this sweep of the Spirit is upon us.

This is a century of destiny. Just as God gave the Antediluvians 100 years of Noah's preaching to prepare for the deluge, God is giving our generation 100 years of the Holy Spirit revival to prepare for the Rapture.

The new century was born with Charismatic outpourings. On New Year's Eve, 1900, a great Upper Room experience came to a Bible college in Topeka, Kansas. On April 9, 1906, the Azusa Street Revival broke out in Los Angeles. From these two outpourings, the Pentecostal experience soon flooded the world.

My mother spoke in tongues every day as she carried me in her womb. In 1934, I began going to the nations of the world. In the more than 100 nations I have visited, I have yet to find a place where the move of the Holy Spirit had not preceded me. I have moved with the Latter Rain Movement, the Healing Revival, the Charismatic Revival, and the Word of Faith Movement, and I am now ready for the last outpouring of God on the face of the earth.

What began at Azusa Street will, I believe, end with the return of Jesus for His saints. The move of the Spirit will increase until Jesus comes. This is the latter rain, and I am glad I am a part of it. I challenge you to flow with the Spirit of God into this last mighty outpouring.

. . . PRAYER . . .

Lord, help me not to miss anything that You have in store for Your church!

. . . TODAY'S THOUGHT . . .

Nothing I have ever done and nothing I am doing is nearly as great as what I'm going to do. Reach out with intense expectation of what God is going to do in these last days.

—Lester Sumrall

Pastor, Christian Center Cathedral of Praise, South Bend, IN

August 9

REVEALER AND VINDICATOR OF TRUTH

Now we have received, not the spirit of the world, but the Spirit who is from God, that we might know the things that have been freely given to us by God. (1 Corinthians 2:12)

After a lengthy conversation, the young nurse turned to me with searching eyes and anxious voice, and asked, "Are you a Freudian?"

I answered, "Not really. Sigmund Freud and others have sought unsatisfactorily to explain, if not to excuse, human behavior. I, too, studied them avidly in an effort to avoid or escape God's verdict on the human condition. Now I fully embrace God's Word which declares unequivocally that the basis of the human problem is sin.

"But doesn't it disturb you that an all-powerful God should create people who fall into sin and then judge and condemn them for it?"

"You are laying the liability of God's creating man squarely back on Him. That is normal. We as humans are held responsible for our actions whether or not we are fully conscious of their consequences, so why shouldn't God be held responsible for creating us? But God anticipated that responsibility and accepted it, preparing an antidote for our rebellion. Jesus Christ was slain before the foundation of the world to taste death for every man. In that sacrifice is saving grace. Therefore, God took the risk of creating man.

The Holy Spirit came to convince the world that sin alone is man's problem, but that God accepted the responsibility for His actions in creation and paid in full the terrible penalty for man's rebellion and judgment. But anyone who still resists and rejects such mercy and grace have nothing further to wait for "but a certain fearful expectation of judgment, and fiery indignation which will devour the adversaries" (Hebrews 10:27).

. . . PRAYER . . .

Spirit of God, lead mankind to disillusionment with his own depravity and to hope in the provisions of grace.

. . . TODAY'S THOUGHT . . .

Jesus did not come to judge the world or to blame the sinner. He came to seek and to save all who will come to the Father by Him.

—Margaret Gaines
Missionary, Israel, COG (retired)

August 10

THE CHRISTIAN'S GUARANTEE

In Him you also trusted, after you heard the word of truth, the gospel of your salvation; in whom also, having believed, you were sealed with the Holy Spirit of promise, who is the guarantee of our inheritance until the redemption of the purchased possession, to the praise of His glory. (Ephesians 1:13, 14)

By our measuring line—the prophecies of Scripture—we know that troubles will soon be over for the Christian. We have determined that we are now in shallow water, and day by day we are drawing nearer to the shore of complete deliverance. The Jews have been given their homeland; now they are there. There was a time when we knew nothing of the fire of atomic energy or the pillar of smoke from the blast; but now it has become a common occurrence. There were days when false christs were never heard of; now you constantly hear of someone's calling himself such.

"We also have the prophetic word made more sure, which you do well to heed as a light that shines in a dark place, until the day dawns and the morning star rises in your hearts" (2 Peter 1:19). Events in the Scripture point out the set schedule and timing of the ages. It is by these prophecies that those who are interested in keeping time with the ages can determine our position in God's arranged schedule. It is only by the Scripture that such knowledge can be gained.

Jesus gave two promises before He went away. First He said, "And I will pray the Father, and He will give you another Helper, that He may abide with you forever" (John 14:16). Second, "And if I go and prepare a place for you, I will come again and receive you to Myself; that where I am, there you may be also" (John 14:3). The Holy Spirit has come, and lives are being blessed. Jesus is soon to return, and the church will realize a glorious landing away from the storms of life.

. . . PRAYER . . .

Thank You, Lord, for the assurance You give us of our redemption and entrance into the glories of the Lord.

. . . TODAY'S THOUGHT . . .

The trials of this life are only temporary; our redemption is eternal.

—G. W. Lane (Reprinted from *SpiritWalk: Daily Devotions on the Holy Spirit* by permission of Pathway Press)
General Secretary and Treasurer, COG (former)

August 11

YOUR EVERYDAY, ORDINARY LIFE

I beseech you therefore, brethren, by the mercies of God, that you present your bodies a living sacrifice, holy, acceptable to God, which is your reasonable service. (Romans 12:1)

Instead of trying to escape where God has you—in your station in life, in your marriage, in your education, in your circumstances that have molded who you are—embrace the steps God has ordered for you and the labor He has set before you to do.

Too often people think they must reach some spiritual milestone before they can be used of God. It is your everyday life that God wants consecrated to Him. Once your life is hidden with God in Christ Jesus, everything you do becomes an act of priestly ministration and worship before Him. The world becomes the pavilion of your tabernacle in which you worship Him 24 hours a day.

Allow God to order your steps, and then whatever you do, whenever you do it, will be done in worship to Him. Learn to worship Him in your every breath, because wherever there is true worship, God manifests the tangibility of His presence.

He is yours all the time in whatever you are doing. When you are in the fiery furnace of life's trials, He is there. When you are on the mountain, He is there; when you are in the valley, He is there also. Learn to practice an awareness of God's presence in everything you do.

We worship in spirit and in truth and in the beauty of holiness—separation, sanctification and purpose. Holiness is separation for an intended purpose, and God has an intended purpose for you. It does not matter where your light is supposed to shine. You are a vessel for His glory, and you can make an eternal difference for His kingdom.

. . . PRAYER . . .

Father, we commit to glorify You in every thing we set our hand to today, and we pray You will meet us as we go about our everyday, ordinary lives.

. . . TODAY'S THOUGHT . . .

Wherever you are, whatever you are doing, whenever you are doing it, and however you are doing it—do it all to the glory of God. It will be like a sweet-smelling savor rising to your Father, and your reward will be great in heaven.

—Rodney L. Parsley
Pastor, World Harvest Church, Canton, OH

August 12

A WALK OF FAITH

When my spirit was overwhelmed within me, Then You knew my path. In the way in which I walk They have secretly set a snare for me. (Psalm 142:3)

The words numbed me. Suddenly, I was very warm. Everything became surreal—lymphoma, chemotherapy, radiation, liver biopsy, bone marrow, abdominal surgery. Margaret wept as we sat in stunned silence. Eight-year-old Veronica's hernia was not a hernia. This cannot be happening! There must be some mistake! But there was none.

As a Pentecostal, I had experienced the miraculous power of the Holy Ghost. I knew God could heal, but would He this time? When I was tempted to ask "Why?" the immediate response was "Why not?"

Long days passed, teams of doctors came and went, prayer did not come easily. None of my experiences, sermons, family or friends could comfort me. When I could pray, I did all I had advised others against.

"God, if you'll heal my daughter, I'll do all this for you." You cannot bargain with God with what is already His!

Clearly the Spirit spoke and it was not what I wanted to hear. "Will you do all those things if I don't heal her?" I struggled with the Spirit's question and could not give an immediate response. Agonizingly searing my soul, through tears and brokenness, I was able to respond, "Yes, if I bury her tomorrow I'll keep those pledges and proclaim you are a good God!"

Veronica is grown now, and I learned a valuable lesson. I believe in God's miraculous power. But if we strip everything away from our walk in the Spirit—all the joy, fellowship, power, miracles, signs and wonders, everything—the bottom line is this: *all you have is your faith!* The other things are real, but some time in your life no one and no thing can get you through another day. You either believe or you don't.

. . . PRAYER . . .

Father, thank You for Your faithfulness. You will me nothing but good. Help me to truly believe this and not merely say it.

. . . TODAY'S THOUGHT . . .

When life has no sanity, no one or no thing comforts because they can't. Without any visible rhyme or reason you believe. Whatever the outcome, God is good to you. It's a choice.

—Roger Woodard
Pastor, Family Worship Center, Kings Mountain, NC

August 13

IRON SHOES

Your sandals shall be iron and bronze; As your days, so shall your strength be. (Deuteronomy 33:25)

I had just completed my pastorate at a great church where I had enjoyed the growth and experienced the fulfillment of my greatest vision. I had moved to my new pastorate to be near my ailing father, a pioneer preacher. However, 33 days later I was walking in places, physically, that required extra shoes: ". . . having shod your feet with the preparation of the gospel of peace" (Ephesians 6:15).

I was stricken with spinal meningitis. The words of Moses came up to me out of the pages, "I need iron shoes."

Placed in isolation, I lay at death's door. The next day, I died! But Moses' message kept moving on my behalf. "The eternal God is your refuge, And underneath are the everlasting arms" (Deuteronomy 33:27). When the doctor found there was no life, he signed the death certificate. Then he came out and told the nurse, in the presence of my children, "The man has died, and I am sorry."

Within 10 minutes the death certificate was voided. Within two days I was in a private room. And on the third week, I was home.

The reality of God's restorative power hit me. I wrote to the Disease Control Center in Atlanta, Georgia: "How many categories of diseases are there known to mankind today?" The reply came, "Sir, we have never been asked this question before, but there are only 39 categories of diseases in the world today."

I felt I was able to walk anywhere in my iron shoes because they had placed 39 stripes on His back. I turned to Isaiah 53:5, "But He was wounded for our transgressions, He was bruised for our iniquities; The chastisement for our peace was upon Him, And by His stripes we are healed."

Thirty-nine stripes, and 39 categories of disease.

. . . PRAYER . . .

Father, thanks. You number my steps (Job 14:16) and underneath are the everlasting arms.

. . . TODAY'S THOUGHT . . .

The steps of a good man are ordered by the Lord.

—S. A. Luke, Sr.
Pastor/Evangelist, COG (retired)

August 14

PERFECT PEACE

You will keep him in perfect peace, Whose mind is stayed on You, Because he trusts in You. (Isaiah 26:3)

After many prayers, in a summer revival at the age of 15, I followed the call of God and, with prayer and confession, accepted Christ as my Lord and Savior. God, for Christ's sake, forgave my sins and made me His child. I was freed from bondage and was the happiest person on earth. The next morning while going to the pasture for our milk cow, as the sun came over the eastern horizon, it seemed the clearest and brightest it had ever been. The air was fresher, the bird's sang sweeter, and the breeze seemed to come straight from the throne of God. I was at peace with myself and the world for the first time.

Two years after I was converted, while in a men's prayer meeting, I listened as the leader testified to many answers to prayer including conversions, healings and miracles. These testimonies made me hunger for the infilling of the Holy Ghost. I knelt at the altar and prayed for the Holy Ghost to come into my life. After two hours of prayer and consecration, God filled me with His Spirit. I spoke in tongues for hours as the Spirit gave the utterance. What a wonderful experience!

A few years later I felt a call from God and entered full-time ministry. In my years of ministry, I experienced many wonderful works of the Holy Spirit in many conversions, infillings of the Holy Ghost, healings, and miracles. What blessings!

After retirement from full-time ministry, three major operations and health problems that curtailed my activity faced me. During this time I failed to consecrate properly or to seek God's divine will for my life. When I awakened to this condition, realizing that I needed to know exactly how God saw me, I prayed this . . .

. . . PRAYER . . .

Father, help me to see myself exactly as You see me, and to have the will to do whatever is necessary to feel Your abiding presence.

. . . TODAY'S THOUGHT . . .

God please help me to be more patient. Take out all pride, make me humble, and keep me filled with Your Holy Spirit.

—T. Raymond Morse
Administrative Assistant, World Missions (retired)

August 15

YES, JESUS CARES

Fear not, for I am with you; Be not dismayed, for I am your God. I will strengthen you, Yes, I will help you, I will uphold you with My righteous right hand. (Isaiah 41:10)

The Pentecostal experience was known to me all my life. My grandmother and other family members received the Holy Ghost in the late 1880s. They traveled by horse and wagon to the meetings. Sometimes those in the wagon would be shouting, in trance, speaking in tongues, and singing as they traveled home.

My dad would sit for hours repeating the stories of the Spirit being manifested. For example, a ball of fire hovered over the church one night. People ran in and others ran out. Miracles of healing were given often.

I heard. I saw. I experienced miracles in my own life.

Once, I was half a world away from home. My time with my hosts was coming to an end. So many friends, places, conferences, savory meals, and the Word of God. I was to travel on a plane but, the schedule had to be modified. That night, we had a meeting of Holy Spirit encouragement, peace, and comfort. The next day the plane I was scheduled to be on went down in the ocean with no survivors. Grief was in my heart for the families. I prayed and put it in the hands of God. The Holy Ghost is our guide.

My family and I are grateful for the mercies of God. The pastors in my host country were praying for me as I ministered there. Those at home were praying as well. God knew which plane I should take. To be obedient will bring blessings and miracles on the way.

I believe in miracles. Yes, Jesus cares.

. . . PRAYER . . .

Our heavenly Father, pour out the Holy Spirit upon me that I might hear, see and feel Your power to be true to You.

. . . TODAY'S THOUGHT . . .

Trust in the Lord with all your heart, And lean not on your own understanding (Proverbs 3:5).

—Walter R. Pettitt, Sr.
Director of Evangelism, COG (retired)

August 16

GOD WORKS HARD THROUGH US

To this end I also labor, striving according to His working which works in me mightily. (Colossians 1:29)

A preacher wrote to my father in the 1940s rejecting his offer of a position as an associate in the Philadelphia Church in Chicago. The letter's brutal honesty and self-examination sent a chill up my spine.

He wrote: "I have always admired your vision and aggressive spirit; however, I have found from experience that people who work a little harder, a little faster, and a little more enthusiastically than the average person are often misunderstood, but I believe that there is victory ahead even though the struggle may be hard and long."

So the brother rejected the position and wished Dad well. He couldn't stand the heat, so he refused to enter the kitchen. I'm glad he was honest, but I wonder if he realized what a judgment he proclaimed against himself in those words.

I want to be influenced by people who work a little harder, a little faster, and a little more enthusiastically. That's why I liked being around my father. Often he worked until the wee hours preparing for his preaching. He stayed late because the days were taken up with the people he loved so much. But he still didn't neglect the most important thing, his time with God in the Scriptures and in prayer.

I want to stay on track, prioritize my time and energy according to God's standard, and get the job done I am called to do. I can only do it by His energy working within the power of the Holy Spirit.

Often, working hard means being misunderstood, but I still prefer the company of the giants to the company of those careful for their own comfort and their own comfort zones. I want fire in my belly, vision in my eyes, a cross on my shoulders, and a narrow, disciplined pathway to walk forward on in obedience to the Master.

. . . PRAYER . . .

God, increase my ability to work hard, fast, and enthusiastically through this day . . .this month . . . this year. I want to be energized by You.

. . . TODAY'S THOUGHT . . .

"They vilified me. They crucified me. They even criticized me" (former Chicago mayor, Richard J. Daley).

—Winston Mattsson-Boze

Assemblies of God International Fellowship, San Diego, CA

August 17

INTO GOD'S PRESENCE

Repent. . .so that times of refreshing may come from the presence of the Lord, . . . (Acts 3:;19)

When Jacob was in God's presence at Bethel, he was changed; God blessed him. He held on to God with such tenacity that he received what he needed. Persistence, in which we seek God's presence and are not content until we touch God, is exactly what will change lives today.

A small boy appeared at a church one day while the service was in progress. Upon asking an usher if he could see the pastor, he was told that the pastor was getting ready to preach. The boy persisted: "It's a matter of life and death," he claimed. Directed to one of the pastors, the little boy was asked what he needed. "I need to know if God is here today." "What do you mean?" the pastor asked. "I mean, did God come to church here today?" "Well, we certainly hope so," the pastor replied. "He comes here every day. Why do you ask?" "I've got to know," the boy answered. "The doctor just left our house and mama is dying. The doctor said there is nothing more he could do, that it's up to God now. Can you ask God to help my mama?"

A small boy with a simple request rocked that church. The people fell before God and repented of anything they had done to prevent His presence from the service. The people prayed for the boy's mother. When he returned home, his mother was up, dressed, and preparing him a meal.

Make a decision this day to remove anything in your life that stands between you and God, between you and His Glory. Then you will be more effective in His Kingdom.

. . . PRAYER . . .

Lord, remove from me every hindrance to Your presence. Let me bask in You that I may draw others to Your warm embrace.

. . . TODAY'S THOUGHT . . .

Being in church is not the same as being in God's presence. Being in service is not the same as being God's servant.

—Bob Shattles
Revival Fires Ministries, Inc., Atlanta, GA

August 18

LIVE IN THE SUPERNATURAL

Then the Spirit of the Lord will come upon you, and you will prophesy with them and be turned into another man. (1 Samuel 10:6)

When the Spirit of the Lord came on me in power, I was changed into a different person. I received the Baptism of the Holy Spirit and stepped out of the natural realm into the realm of the supernatural.

A Christian for most of my life, I had never seen a miracle or experienced the supernatural presence and power of God. Through my hunger and search for more of God, He revealed that His purpose for me was that I live and walk in the supernatural. As a "New Creation," old things had passed away and all things had become new. I had a new way of living. No longer was I to live within the limitations of the natural man. He had created me to live and walk in the Spirit.

The moment I received the Baptism in the Holy Spirit, I began to walk in the supernatural. A miracle took place in my mouth as I began to speak in a new language of praise to God. Beginning with the instant and totally healing of my wife Joyce's neck and our son's badly injured finger, miracles have continued in our lives.

We have experienced God's supernatural leading and provision in our lives and have stood in the life-changing glory of his overwhelming presence. We have experienced God's healing power when we have been told that we had cancer in our bodies. I have felt God's power flow into my body and instantly heal me when the doctor said I was going to die. We have experienced the healing power of God flowing through our hands bringing healing to the sick and diseased.

You, too, can experience the joy of living in the supernatural power of God by asking for and receiving the Gift of the Holy Ghost. Or, ask for a fresh filling of His Spirit with all the supernatural gifts of the Holy Ghost operating in your life.

. . . PRAYER . . .

Lord, I ask You to baptize me with Your Holy Spirit. Fill me with the power to live as a daily witness of Your power to save, heal, and deliver. I ask for all of the gifts of the Holy Spirit to flow in my daily life and ministry.

. . . TODAY'S THOUGHT . . .

The Spirit has come upon me in power. I have been changed into a different person. I will live in God's supernatural presence and power.

—A. L. Gill
Gill Ministries, Fawyskin, CA

August 19

PRINCIPLES OF SUCCESS

But wisdom brings success. (Ecclesiastes 10:10)

I am often asked, "What is the secret to success in ministry?" My call to ministry, in 1944, was so definite that I have never wavered in my direction. With Paul, I can say, "Woe is me if I do not preach the gospel." Let me suggest a few principles that have guided me.

Never try to be somebody else. My father was a great preacher and I admired him, but have never tried to imitate him. I had to start where I was and not depend on someone else's position. God knew who I was, my potential, and that the call was peculiarly mine to fulfill.

Handle responsibilities one day at a time. The Lord said, "Do not worry about tomorrow." Although this does not take away the necessity for proper planning, I nevertheless practice the art of taking responsibility for what I can handle at the end of the day and leave unsettled matters for the future. My wife and I sang a song that said, "I am following Jesus one step at a time; I live for the moment in His love divine. Why think of tomorrow, just live for today. I am following Jesus one step at a time."

Leave the past behind. Paul suggests, "forgetting those things which are behind and reaching forward to those things which are ahead." If I erred, I learned. If I sinned, I willingly confessed. But I have never allowed the past to be an albatross around my neck.

Always live in expectation. My father must get the credit for this attitude I adopted years ago. I lay plans in my mind for future accomplishments or joys that may never be experienced, but for the present time are highly motivating. I believe that the steps of the righteous are ordered of the Lord and while I do not hide my head in the sand, I look forward to great things occurring in my life. Jesus' words ring in my ears, "According to your faith (expectations) let it be to you" (Matthew 9:29).

. . . PRAYER . . .

Lord, none of us knows now how successful we have been, but I pray that I have made a contribution to the work of Your Kingdom.

. . . TODAY'S THOUGHT . . .

Be successful today and tomorrow, leaving the past behind.

—Earl P. Paulk, Jr.
Bishop, Cathedral at Chapel Hill, Atlanta, GA

August 20

BE ANXIOUS FOR NOTHING

Be anxious for nothing, but in everything by prayer and supplication, with thanksgiving, let your requests be made known to God. (Philippians 4:6)

Beginning in ministry, we had struggles as all do! I was working diligently for the Lord, raising my family and being a provider. I walked into my house one afternoon, carrying the concerns of ministry, the burdens of providing for my family, and feeling the weight of responsibility as head of my home.

My oldest son was lying on our couch in the cool air-conditioning, eating potato chips. He seemed to be so carefree that it irritated me. I said to myself, "Here I am working, laboring, and believing that all our needs are going to be met, and here my son is not worrying, not concerned how it is going to work out. He just knows that somehow his dad will make things work out."

The Lord stopped me in my tracks. He spoke to my heart so strongly and said, "*Why don't you get on the couch, eat some chips, and trust Me just as your son is trusting you!*"

It was a life-changing word! I began that day to learn to cast my cares upon Him, believing with child-like faith that everything is going to be all right.

. . . PRAYER . . .

Father, today I cast my care upon You, knowing You are a faithful and loving Father and that somehow You will make everything work out for my good and Your glory.

. . . TODAY'S THOUGHT . . .

But as for me, I trust in You, O Lord; I say, "You are my God" (Psalm 31:14).

—Kent Mattox
Kent Mattox Ministries, Lineville, AL

August 21

GOD WILL PROVIDE

You visit the earth and water it, You greatly enrich it; The river of God is full of water; You provide their grain, For so You have prepared it. (Psalm 65:9)

The steaming jungle loomed up on both sides of the river like the walls of a lush green canyon. Our dugout canoe chugged up river. Exhaustion and heat had shut down all conversation among the six passengers seated single-file down the length of the dugout.

We had left in the pre-dawn hours for the thirteen-hour journey from Puerto Bermudez up the Rio Pichis out onto the narrower, swifter Ucayali River and, at last, onto a smaller, unnamed tributary. An Indian guide crouched precariously on the bow of the boat guiding us to a village where some unknown "sickness" had struck. He had come as an emissary to find us at our mission house and plead for help. We agreed to go, but we were all nervous about the dangers of going into an unfamiliar Indian village deep in the jungle. I sent Carlos, my assistant, into Bermudez to buy some cans of tuna as gifts for the village. The Indians loved tuna and the "miracle" of prepared fish always gained us entrée. The Indian guide gestured that his village was just ahead.

"Carlos," I said, "We are nearly there. Get the tuna cans ready."

"Oh, no!" Carlos wailed. "I forgot the tuna!"

I was furious *and* worried. This mistake could get us killed, and I let him know it in no uncertain terms with a tongue-lashing that left Carlos' head bowed and everyone else embarrassed. In an attempt to smooth matters over, I tried to say something religious. "Oh, well, there's no use crying over spilled milk. We'll just have to trust God."

No more than fifty yards up river a huge fish leapt from the river and landed in the boat. The Indian guide crowed with delight, and Carlos peered at me with a smug accusation in his eyes.

There the Lord spoke to me. "Why do you doubt me? I *own* this jungle *and* the river. The fish leap at my command. All you have to do is keep the canoe up river. I will do *all* the rest."

. . . PRAYER . . .

Father, thank You for Your provision and for reminding us that You are God!

. . . TODAY'S THOUGHT . . .

If we obey, God will provide.

—Mark Rutland

President, Southeastern College of the Assemblies of God

August 22

THERE SHALL BE A PERFORMANCE

And blessed is she that believed: for there shall be a performance of those things which were told her from the Lord. (Luke 1:45 KJV)

There is a saying in Nigeria, my country, that when a wife becomes pregnant, the husband becomes pregnant, too. When she goes into the labor room, the husband goes into travail.

Perhaps this was my experience when my wife was pregnant with our first baby. I felt that we were not economically prepared for the baby. There was a long list of things to buy. Occasionally the thought that something could go wrong would flash across my mind.

What if this baby is born deformed? What if this baby doesn't survive? Will my wife survive this pregnancy? Isaiah 66:9 and 1 Timothy 2:15 became my sword each time these terrible thoughts came against me. This mental war continued until I came across Luke 1:45. I knew the story well, but this time it had a different effect on me. There was a new light here that seemed to outshine every other Scripture for the moment. My soul was lifted, joy came, peace took control in the realization that there shall be a performance of the promises given by God and that I am already blessed if I believe!

Hebrews 11:1 says that "faith is the substance of things hoped for, the evidence of things not seen." This means that there is a peace that settles in us once we believe the promises given us. The most important thing in any given situation is to have a word from the Lord. That word will keep you through any darkness or shadow. That word will be your compass and your consolation. Mary believed even though it could cost her life and there was a performance of those things told her.

Not only did God cause that first baby to be born safely, he gave us other children. No other time would have been more perfect. When I held to the revealed word given me, there was peace and an eventual performance of those things told me.

. . . PRAYER . . .

Lord, please help us to see that You are greater than any circumstance. Help us to trust Your unchanging word rather than our doubts!

. . . TODAY'S THOUGHT . . .

Doubt your doubts when they try to replace God's promises.

—John Uga

Pastor, Emuga, Nigeria, Africa

August 23

SAVED AT SEA

On the same day, when evening had come, He said to them, "Let us cross over to the other side." (Mark 4:35)

My brother-in-law and I were both avid blue-water sailors with dozens of years experience between us. We had purchased a 30-foot handmade sailboat in Sweden and sailed to Falmouth, England, for a brief layover for supplies and rest.

Soon it was time to sail on to Lisbon, Portugal, where I had a 45-day speaking tour. We loaded our boat with new supplies, checked her over, and called the weather service for that area. The Bay of Biscay lay ahead, and she was known for instant and extremely dangerous storms.

In order to save time, we decided to sail through the English Channel instead of going around. Although it was risky in a small boat, we were seasoned sailors. But things didn't go as planned. Two days into the voyage, we found ourselves in the middle of an incredible storm with winds gusting to 70 mph and seas in excess of 50 feet.

Over the next seven days, we capsized seven times and lost all food, water, and electric power. Sea water was coming into the boat, so we had to use a small hand pump. We jettisoned our clothes and all personal belongings in order to keep from sinking. I knew I was going to die. We slept in four-hour shifts while the other pumped water out of the boat and watched for freighters. With no lights, we were sitting ducks for those large ships.

I prayed like I had never prayed before; I searched my heart. Water-logged and sinking with no help of rescue in sight, the Lord spoke to me: "I was the One who calmed all of your storms in the past, and I am the One who will bring peace to this storm as well." Within one hour, the seas went from fifty-plus feet to soft swells. Soon, the English Coast Guard rescued us. The boat was lost, but we were saved.

. . . PRAYER . . .

Father, thank You for Your miracle ability to calm all of our storms. No matter what the need, You're the God who can save and change our circumstances by just one Word. Give us grace to trust You no matter what storms we face.

. . . TODAY'S THOUGHT . . .

No matter how bad things seem, I will believe and trust that You are able to deliver me.

—C. Alan Bullock
General Manager, TBN, Mobile, AL

August 24

LEAP OF FAITH

By faith Abraham obeyed when he was called to go out to the place which he would afterward receive as an inheritance. And he went out, not knowing where he was going. (Hebrews 11:8)

One of the hardest lessons to learn is how to trust God in all that He has promised and to learn to live by the principles of faith. The reality of this struggle is realized in the phrases we use to describe it: going from the seen to the unseen, from the known to the unknown, taking the leap of faith, and others.

Abraham trusted God completely and obeyed Him, confident that God would not let him down. Should we not have like faith?

The Lord used a simple, but significant, experience to teach me the basic element of Abraham's faith. I was playing with my son, who was barely one year old, teaching him that all-important lesson of trusting his father. I stood him on the kitchen table and told him, "Jump to Daddy and Daddy will catch you." At first I could see the fear in his eyes, so I came very close to him so that just by leaning forward he would fall into my arms. It wasn't long before he got the idea. He could trust his Daddy to catch him. By the time the experiment was over, he wanted me to stand as far away as possible, knowing I would catch him.

Many times the Lord has taken me back to that day where my son learned he could trust me. The Lord speaks to my heart: "Trust me. I am always at the other end of your leap of faith." As with my son, I have learned to trust in God by taking the short leaps. Many times in the ministry I have had to take the running leaps without seeing with my natural eyes the arms of God on the other side, but He has always been there.

Is it time for you to take your first leap? Start with the short ones; the big ones will come.

. . . PRAYER . . .

Father, teach us to take leaps of faith and to experience the catch of Your loving arms.

. . . TODAY'S THOUGHT . . .

Often the greatest lessons in our walk of faith can be learned in daily occurrences.

—Danny de Leon
Pastor, Templo Calvario

August 25

GOD DOES NOT FORGET

For God is not unjust to forget your work and labor of love which you have shown toward His name, in that you have ministered to the saints, and do minister. (Hebrews 6:10)

God does *not* forget your deeds and acts of kindness, love, and compassion! Paul spoke of the gifts sent to him from the Philippians to Thessalonica as "a sweet-smelling aroma, an acceptable sacrifice, well pleasing to God" (Philippians 4:18) credited to their account (4:17). Mark 4 teaches us to expect some 30, some 60, some 100-fold return on our "investments" in the Kingdom of God. Our investments include our time, labors, assistance to church functions, ushering, helps of any kind, body ministry, favors to fellow Christians, and any "RAK" (Random Acts of Kindness). Therefore, when we do *anything* for the Lord, the Lord will *not* forget.

Best of all, though, is that God waits to *reward* us for our ministry of love to His Body by giving us the desires of our hearts in all areas of our lives. This is the basis of prosperity, success, and abundance in the Christian walk: when we get into God's business, He gets into our business, our needs, and our lives in a big way!

Since the work of the ministry is to be spread between pastor, staff, membership, and volunteers, everyone in the local church has an opportunity to reap the benefits. Many churches put too much emphasis on the paid staff and pulpit ministries. In reality, God sees all acts of love and kindness (or their absence) in all of our lives regardless of our position in the church. If a preacher puts on a show for a television audience and shows little love, respect, and kindness to his church, then he gets less of a real reward than does the usher who shows people these things. It pays to be a real servant of the Lord. God does not look at the position, but at the passion and commitment.

. . . PRAYER . . .

Lord, may the motives and actions of our lives truly reflect the compassion and commitment that You gave for us on Calvary. You gave us an example to follow: greater love has no man than to lay down his life for a friend.

. . . TODAY'S THOUGHT . . .

God remembers us, so remember God! Praise Him and increase the chance of being a blessing and being blessed a hundred-fold.

—Kennard "Buddy" Bell
Ministry of Helps, Tulsa, OK

August 26

GOD USES ADVERSITY TO DEVELOP US

I have been put to death with Christ on his cross, so that it is no longer I who live, but it is Christ who lives in me. (Galatians 2:19-20)

I am a Civil War buff and often stop along the highway to wander through old cemeteries, looking for the distinctive Civil War grave marker. I keep a book with the names of these Americans, North and South, with the companies and regiments each served.

During a recent excursion, I stumbled across the grave of a Confederate chaplain in Washington, Georgia. As I began writing the name in my book, I gasped: Edward McKendree Bounds.

E. M. Bounds.

Yes, the E. M. Bounds whose books on prayer have meant so much to so many Christians. His life of simple, Christ-filled dedication to the ministry in prayer was an example to many men and women of God. He wrote: "Life-giving preaching costs the preacher much—death to self, crucifixion to the world, the travail of his own soul. Only crucified preaching can give life. Crucified preaching can come only from a crucified man."

Twice Bounds was imprisoned: once for being a Confederate sympathizer prior to becoming a chaplain and again after being captured in the battle of Franklin, Tennessee. Hard times. His wife died after eight years of marriage. He remarried and lost two children. More hard times. Such adversity played a significant role in shaping his character. More than that, though, his trusting attitude toward a loving God helped shape a servant heart.

May we not shrink from our duty as Christian soldiers to remain faithful in spite of adversity. May we permit trial and the test to crucify our lives so that we can preach life to the life-seeking masses and demonstrate a true servant's heart toward those we are called to serve.

. . . PRAYER . . .

Lord, allow me to see Your hand at work in my life even when adversity is my lot. Let my heart not become bitter at the hard times, but let me clearly see it is Your Hand at work in my life, developing me for what You have made me.

. . . TODAY'S THOUGHT . . .

Only crucified preaching from a crucified person can give life.

—Dennis L. Kutzner

Executive Director of Calvary Ministries, Inc., Intl, Ft. Wayne, IN

August 27

VICTORIOUS UNDER PRESSURE

Blessed are those who are persecuted for righteousness' sake, For theirs is the kingdom of heaven. (Matthew 5:10)

When you hear about Christians being martyred for their faith, do you think of biblical figures such as Stephen or John the Baptist? If you do, you are out of date by a couple of thousand years. In fact, more Christians have been martyred for their faith in this century alone than in the previous nineteen centuries. In several parts of the world, it costs your life to be a follower of Jesus Christ. For example, some Muslim governments have made it a crime to convert to Christianity—and they enforce this policy brutally.

In spite of severe persecution, the number of believers continues to grow by leaps and bounds. Persecution for Christ's sake is not a mark of defeat, but of victory. Praise God nobody can destroy the Church of Jesus Christ! Jesus, our Chief Cornerstone, said that the gates of Hell will not prevail against the Church (Matthew 16:18). It takes a crucified Church to reach the world with the message of a crucified Christ!

Not long ago in an Islamic country, Bishop Haik Hovsepian, a prominent Christian leader, was brutally murdered for the sake of the Gospel. Prior to his death, he had said, "What a waste to die a normal death." It has been said, "A person that does not have a reason to die for does not have a reason to live for." Through the Bishop's death, thousands of Muslims have come to Christ and the Body of Christ has been strengthened in that part of the world. Although he is in the presence of the Lord, his widow, Takoosh, and four children are faithfully serving the Lord!

. . . PRAYER . . .

Lord, on a daily basis help us to endure hardship unto You like a good soldier of Jesus Christ; always focusing our attention on the end of the journey and the reward You have saved for Your elect who endure to the end.

. . . TODAY'S THOUGHT . . .

Christians in the free world need to keep the suffering church in prayer, to remember those who are willing to pay the ultimate price for their faith, and never to take for granted their freedom.

—Anoosh Bullock
Ladies Conference Speaker, Leader

August 28

I OWE HIM MY LIFE

I can do all things through Christ who strengthens me. (Philippians 4:13)

At the age of one, I contacted an illness which the doctors were unable to deal with because they could not identify it. The medical field declared me incurable, sent me home, and informed my parents that I had only days to live. The next morning my mother and father anointed me with oil and prayed and God performed a miracle. I vomited a malignant tumor and from that day forward began to recover.

I was raised in a pastor's home. I was always faithful to God and the church but I did not desire to be a pastor. But God called me to the ministry and I submitted to Him. This was the moment my mother shared with me the miracle God had performed in me. She had made a pact with the Lord: "Heal my son and I will dedicate him for Your service." Then she felt from God that I would be a pastor.

God has never failed me. He has always been faithful. He has delivered me from death. I've lived a healthy life and He has allowed me to prosper in all things.

Last year I was confronted by a terrible trial. My wife was diagnosed with breast cancer. The first thing that came to my mind was that the God that healed me and restored my life will do the same for her. We both rejoice today with good health. Her doctors have said there is no sign of cancer.

As a child I was taught to pray, read the Bible, fast and be faithful to God. Now as a forty-eight-year-old adult, I continue to pray morning, noon, and night. I read the Bible at least twice a day, fast regularly, and continue to try to be faithful to God. This has given me positive results and I am happy in the Lord.

. . . PRAYER . . .

I praise You, God, for Your mercy and faithfulness toward me. I praise You for manifesting Your healing and protecting power with me. I praise You for hearing my prayer.

. . . TODAY'S THOUGHT . . .

God is the same today. All power in heaven and earth belongs to Him. His promises are faithful and true. Blessed is the man who trusts in Him.

—Efrain Navas
Administrative Bishop, Northeast Hispanic COG

August 29

SEEING THE BIGGER PICTURE

Trust in the Lord, and do good; Dwell in the land, and feed on His faithfulness. Delight yourself also in the Lord, And He shall give you the desires of your heart. (Psalm 37:3-4)

At five, I idolized my father. He could do anything, protect me from evil, leap tall buildings. My greatest joy was resting in his strong arms. Of course, time and reality show us how fallible humans are.

It was a Saturday and my dad had taken me to buy a pair of tennis shoes. How proud I was of these shoes, a symbol of my favor with dad. On this same day, I played Blind Man's Bluff. I was blindfolded and began groping for one of my playmates. I tripped over a garden hose, crashed face first onto jagged bricks, and the blood flowed . . . the worst of it falling on my brand new formerly white shoes. Dad came to my rescue, and no permanent damage was done (except to my shoes). In my father's arms, I asked him the universal question: "Why did this have to happen to me?" Dad (and Heaven) was support but silent.

How often we ask this question when things go wrong. Why do good things happen to bad people and bad things to good people? Are we left to fate or is God involved in our daily lives? The answers are not always easy to find. There seems to be a dynamic tension between the mercy and protection of Almighty God and the capriciousness of the world. Yet, as believers, we ultimately live in hope for the Lord knows the big picture and His plans are never (ultimately) thwarted.

What life attitude is needed to face the White Tennis Shoes of daily existence? Trust in the Lord. Live in the place of service where God plants us, delighting in God and His goodness, with every expectation that life will be precious and fruitful. We are never guaranteed that all will be well in our lives, but the Father's arms are strong enough to comfort and care even when answers are few and far between.

. . . PRAYER . . .

Father, thank You for being with me even when I do not see Your mighty hand. Teach me to trust You while faithfully laboring in Your vineyard until You come.

. . . TODAY'S THOUGHT . . .

The past is there to learn from as preparation for the present and future. All of life is in the hands of our loving God. We can trust Him!

—Dr. Stan E. DeKoven

President, Vision International University, Manteca, CA

August 30

HUNGRY FOR GOD

Blessed are those who hunger and thirst for righteousness, For they shall be filled. (Matthew 5:6)

Many people have shared with me that they are hungry for more of God. But over the years, I have learned that true spiritual hunger signifies much more than what most people realize.

There are some people who come to our meetings with an incredible hunger for more of God's presence and power. Their appetite for a sovereign move of God has been a constant preoccupation. They are tired of the mediocre; they want to see God come down in power. Their thirst for Jesus has not been quenched and their hunger pains have not been satisfied.

The truth is this: A person's desperation for the presence of God will melt all preoccupation with self, notoriety, public image, and social status. His hunger and thirst will drive him to eat and drink. He will be willing to be a fool in the sight of his peers in order to be embraced in the arms of the Lord. He will be willing to wade past all obstacles. His craving for God will crush the enemy's lies. He will get food and nothing will stop him.

A spiritually hungry person desires something deep and lasting. He has tasted from the cup of superficial spirituality and was left with an insatiable thirst. He realizes that only the cup of Living Water and only the true Bread of Life will satisfy the cravings of his heart.

Are you hungry for God? In the impoverished, famine-stricken lands of the world, the truly hungry will stand in line for hours in order to receive nourishment. Are you willing to do anything to have God satisfy your cravings? If you are, then today's verse contains good news. If you go after Him with all your heart, you will be filled!

. . . PRAYER . . .

Lord Jesus, there is a deep yearning in my heart for more of You. My hunger and thirst will drive me to Your side. I will not let anyone or anything keep me from pursuing You.

. . . TODAY'S THOUGHT . . .

True hunger and thirst will drive a spiritual person to eat and drink; nothing can stop him.

—Stephen L. Hill
Evangelist, Brownsville Revival, Brownsville, FL

August 31

GOD—GOOD OR OMNIPOTENT?

I have heard of You by the hearing of the ear, But now my eye sees You. Therefore I abhor myself, And repent in dust and ashes. (Job 42:5-6)

Who had more grounds to question the goodness of God than did Job? He was declared a righteous man, the best in his generation; yet he was required to undergo great suffering. He lost his wealth, health, and closest relationships. Such intense suffering calls into question the goodness of God. As playwright Archibald Macleash puts it in his play, *JB*, either "God is God and is not good, or God is good and is not God." In other words, either God is not good or God is not omnipotent.

Good arguments defending both the goodness and omnipotence of God are not lacking, from Church fathers such as Irenaeus and Augustine to twentieth century theologians such as C. S. Lewis. But in times of suffering, arguments may seem unconvincing. How can a good God allow children to suffer? How can He allow brutality between human beings? Jews ask, Where was God during the Holocaust? We know the argument about human freedom, the fact that life in this world is under judgment and our very environment reflects our fallen state. When the searing pain hits us, though, will the arguments be enough?

Job did not know that he was a test case by which the powers of darkness would ultimately demonstrate the glory a human being can attain in faithfulness to God. Yet when such suffering is experienced, arguments seem empty and our psychology says we have been violated. The greatest battle of faith is maintaining faith in God's goodness and in all His promises when the circumstances do not seem to support it.

The only way to maintain faith is to know God, to experience His presence. Job's questions were put to rest when God revealed Himself. He knew God was good, loving, and omnipotent. The revelation of the Father in Jesus puts our doubts to rest. We know He is good and trustworthy no matter the test. A deep relationship with Jesus will sustain us in all trials. No argument will do without this relationship.

. . . PRAYER . . .

Lord, let us experience You so that all doubt is banished!

. . . TODAY'S THOUGHT . . .

Determine that you will know Him, then you will be victorious.

—Daniel Juster

Tikkun Ministries, Gaithersburg, MD

September 1

ORDERED STEPS

For all the promises of God in Him are Yes, and in Him Amen, to the glory of God through us. (2 Corinthians 1:20)

On my second trip to Mexico, I took my unsaved father-in-law with me. He was a backslidden intellectual with a Ph.D. from Columbia University and no faith in a miraculous God. His only interest in going was to see rural Mexico, "off the beaten path," as he put it. He did!

One night we went to a remote village deep in the mountains near Linares. An interpreter was to meet us but did not show up. Going on without him, I was deflated because this meant that preaching was out. The missionary I was with lacked the language skills to translate, no one in that village spoke English and my *only* Spanish were three phrases I had learned by rote. It had taken me three hard days of practice to learn, "God is love," "Jesus loves you," and "So do I."

At the little village church, the missionary made the pastor understand and we agreed for me to say my three phrases in Spanish and then let the Mexican pastor preach. What other plan was there?

When I finished my little phonetic speech, however, the Lord showed up mightily. I began to think whole Spanish sentences. They came into my head as clearly as English. I preached for thirty minutes in Spanish. When the pastor realized what was happening he shouted to his people, "This man doesn't speak Spanish. It's a miracle!"

I translated the pastor's words for the Americans, then went on preaching . . . in Spanish! I can still speak Spanish, not perfectly, but well enough. I occasionally even dream in Spanish, after twenty years.

My father-in-law, overcome by the miracle, gave his life to God. Many Mexicans were saved and I learned a powerful lesson. God's gifts are works of grace, miraculous manifestations of his goodness and power, *through* us, not *because* of us, to glorify his Holy name.

. . . PRAYER . . .

Heavenly Father, thank You for the miracles You work in us that You may receive glory through us .

. . . TODAY'S THOUGHT . . .

God manifests Himself in us and through us in power and goodness and grace.

—Mark Rutland
President, Southeastern College of the Assemblies of God

September 2

GOD IS FAITHFUL

Train up a child in the way he should go, And when he is old he will not depart from it. (Proverbs 22:6)

There were two daughters and one son born to J. M. and Annie Hart before they were Christians. After their salvation and infilling of the Holy Ghost, they had five sons, of which I am the eldest. Each one of us, at age eight, were brought to the church and dedicated to the Lord to be ministers. Dad was a dedicated minister ordained in 1917 in Hot Springs, Arkansas. His desire was to raise his sons to become preachers of the Gospel.

In 1928, Dad accepted the pastorate of South Side Assembly of God Church in Dallas, Texas. It was there that I met Bonnie Parker and Clyde Barrow. They would come to church with me and then, after the services, I would go with them. The deacons told my father that I would be the next person to go to the electric chair. Dad said, "No! I dedicated him to the Lord to be a minister."

The night I gave my heart to the Lord, Bonnie and Clyde went to church with me. I heard the Lord speak to me: "This is your last opportunity." I turned to them and told them I was going to get saved. They said that they wouldn't go then, but would come later. When I knelt in the altar that night, my Dad laid his hands on my head and prayed: "Lord, I thank you for saving Maurice and making a preacher of him." Sure enough, that prayer was answered. April, 1999, will celebrate 62 years since I totally surrendered to the call of God on my life. My wife, Estelle, and I will also celebrate 62 years of marriage . . . working side by side for the Lord.

The great thing about all of this is that God continues to be faithful to give us health and strength to carry on His work. All five of the Hart brothers became successful ministers and missionaries.

. . . PRAYER . . .

Thank You for parents who wouldn't give up and for Your faithfulness to move in our lives and meet the needs of Your people.

. . . TODAY'S THOUGHT . . .

There is no peace, joy, and contentment greater than knowing you have been obedient to the call of God.

—Dr. Maurice J. Hart
President, Anchor Bay Evangelistic Association, Omaha, NE

September 3

THE GOAL—PERFECTED PRAISE

And He said to them, "It is written, 'My house shall be called a house of prayer,' but you have made it a 'den of thieves'." (Matthew 21:13)

All four Gospel writers record a temple cleansing by Jesus. Obviously, temple cleansing is important or four Scriptural accounts would not have been given.

Besides historical preservation, for what purpose is this event recorded? There must be a spiritual application. 1 Corinthians 3:16 says, "Do you not know that you are the temple of God and that the Spirit of God dwells in you?" If Jesus were to come to my temple, (me) in the flesh, what would He do? Probably as He did in the temple at Jerusalem. Let's follow the progression.

He began by *cleansing* or *purging*. The cleansing is so the temple can become a house of *prayer*. Without purity, there is no genuine prayer. Psalm 66:18 states, "If I regard iniquity in my heart, The Lord will not hear." The prayer out of a pure heart then brings *power*. Matthew 21:14: "Then the blind and the lame came to Him in the temple, and He healed them." This took place after He had cleansed the temple and made it to be a house of prayer. The power then results in *perfected prayer*. Verse 15 describes the *perfected praise* that followed the demonstration of *power* resulting from *prayer* after *purity*.

Jesus quotes Psalm 8:2: "Out of the mouth of babes and nursing infants You have ordained strength. . . ." But Matthew records Him saying, ". . . You have perfected praise" (Matthew 21:16). Did Jesus misquote the Word? Impossible! Jesus *is* the Word (John 1:1). This must be an amplification. *Perfected praise* brings *strength*! God-ordained or -assigned strength to defeat all enemies comes to the person who has developed the area of praise. The progression is simple. 1) Be a pure vessel; 2) Become a praying vessel; 3) Receive the power of the Holy Spirit into your vessel; 4) Allow the Holy Spirit to perfect praise in and through your vessel. Result: God-ordained strength!

. . . PRAYER . . .

I present my being to You so that I may become all that You want me to be.

. . . TODAY'S THOUGHT . . .

If we can *be* what He wants us to *be*, then we can *do* what He wants us to *do*.

—Rich Bowen
Pastor, New Hope, Augusta, GA

September 4

THE SHAPING OF A SPIRITUAL LEADER

And the Lord said to Moses: "Take Joshua the son of Nun with you, a man in whom is the Spirit, and lay your hand on him." (Numbers 27:18)

Moses had come to the final days of his ministry. The crossing of the Red Sea, the manna from heaven, the Ten Commandments, the water from the rock, and the building of the Tabernacle were past. The conquest of the Promised Land lay ahead.

Moses was not permitted to enter Canaan. Joshua, a younger man, gifted with boldness and possessing strong qualities, would take his place. The deciding factor had been "a man in whom [was] the Spirit." This is the secret of godly leadership. Spiritual matters demand Spirit-filled individuals.

God instructed Moses to lay his hand on his successor. Mentoring is often an ingredient of successful leadership. Laying on hands spoke of the continuity of God's redemptive plan. Joshua was not on a solo flight or a Lone Ranger adventure.

Joshua was presented publicly to the congregation. The church is a community of faith. Whatever we do for God as individuals must be done within the corporate body of Christ. God told Moses to transfer his authority to his successor. That was not an easy task. He had talked face-to-face with God; yet he prayed, "Lord, send them a true shepherd."

When Moses died the Lord spoke to Joshua: "Arise, go over this Jordan, you and all this people, to the land which I am giving to them" (Joshua 1:2). Joshua called the people to a renewed covenant with God, crossed the Jordan, took Jericho—and in 10 years had conquered all the Land of Promise.

. . . PRAYER . . .

Lord, give me strength to overcome obstacles, humility in my accomplishments, and the wisdom to give You glory in all things.

. . . TODAY'S THOUGHT . . .

I affirm that God is good. It is only through the anointing of His Holy Spirit that we can succeed in any ministry for Him.

—Loida Camacho (Reprinted from *SpiritWalk: Daily Devotions on the Holy Spirit* by permission of Pathway Press)
Professor, Lee University

September 5

ANOTHER COMFORTER

And I will pray the Father, and He will give you another Helper, that He may abide with you forever. (John 14:16)

I was the youngest of five children born to hard-working parents, Mr. and Mrs. Charlie A. Tuff, Sr. Our mother taught us about Jesus Christ and who He was to her.

One responsibility the children had was to watch out for each other; being the youngest, everyone watched out for me. The major part of this responsibility was bestowed upon my oldest sister, Louise. She really cared for me. Although she was nearly a decade older than me, we grew very close and maintained a closeness into our adult lives.

Eventually, Louise moved to Atlanta, Georgia, because she was diagnosed with ovarian cancer. My oldest brother's health was also failing rapidly. We prayed for them along with friends in various parts of the world. Nevertheless, both of them died within twelve weeks of each other. They had given their lives to the Lord. I was their pastor and was graced by the Lord Jesus Christ to do their eulogies.

It was during this time that I was strongly comforted by the Holy Spirit. Jesus said that He was called alongside to help me. I saw Him during these dark times not only as my Comforter, but also as my Strengthener, my Counselor, my Helper, My Advisor, my Ally, and my Friend. The Lord Jesus sent the Holy Spirit to become everything my family and I needed during these dark times. It is wonderful to know that He is the same in the dark times as in the times of refreshing!

. . . PRAYER . . .

Lord Jesus, thank You for praying to the Father to send me another Comforter. Holy Spirit, thank You that You are by my side to help and strengthen me, to teach me the true course for my life, to comfort me in difficult situations, to intercede in prayer for me, to be a friend, and to remain with me forever!

. . . TODAY'S THOUGHT . . .

The Father sent us the best He had when He sent His Son Jesus. The Father and the Son sent the best they had when they sent the Holy Spirit. Now the Holy Spirit is here to give you the best He has . . . all of Himself. Allow Him!

—Ulysses Tuff

Pastor, The Way, The Truth, and The Life Christian Center, Atlanta, GA

September 6

IS THE HOLY SPIRIT REAL?

Now if anyone does not have the Spirit of Christ, he is not His. (Romans 8:9)

It has been my privilege to flow with the Pentecostal Movement for seventy-five years. The work of the Holy Spirit is four-fold:

1) The Holy Spirit "quickens" us. No person can say that Jesus is Lord but by the Holy Spirit (1 Corinthians 12:3).
2) The Holy Spirit convicts and convinces of sin (John 16:8).
3) The Holy Spirit gives life to believers (Romans 8:10).
4) The Holy Spirit assures us of a resurrection from the dead (Romans 8:11).

Every true believer receives the Holy Spirit (Romans 8:4, John 16:13, John 14:16-17). The Spirit is referred as the:

1) "Spirit of Life" (Romans 8:2).
2) "Spirit" (Romans 8:4-5, 9, 26-27).
3) "Spirit of God" (Romans 8:9, 14).
4) "Spirit of Christ" (Romans 8:9).
5) "Spirit of Adoption" (Romans 8:15).

In the coming of the Holy Spirit, He . . .

1) is the power that raised Jesus from the dead.
2) gives power to put to death the deeds of the flesh (Galatians 5:25).
3) guides the Christian (John 16:13).
4) sets us free from the bondage of fear (Romans 8:15).
5) gives the human spirit a witness, a testimony, and a blessed assurance (Romans 8:16).
6) is a praying Spirit.

. . . PRAYER . . .

Lord, thank You for the Gift of Your wonderful Holy Spirit!

. . . TODAY'S THOUGHT . . .

Jesus sent the Holy Spirit so He could abide in these tabernacles which are made of flesh! We must not talk about receiving an experience like the Baptism in the Holy Spirit until we are aware that we have received the gift of the person of the Holy Spirit.

—Paul E. Paino
Pastor, Calvary Temple Worship Center, Ft. Wayne, IN

September 7

THE HOLY SPIRIT AND YOU

But the Helper, the Holy Spirit, whom the Father will send in My name, He will teach you all things, and bring to your remembrance all things that I said to you. (John 14:26)

Based on the recent exposure to Satanism, New Age, and the Occult, we can surmise that now perhaps more than ever before people are seeking the spiritual realm for answers to life. The Word predicted such a phenomenon would occur: "Now the Spirit expressly says that in latter times some will depart from the faith, giving heed to deceiving spirits and doctrines of demons" (1 Timothy 4:1). But Joel 2:28-29 speaks of another awakening: "And it shall come to pass afterward That I will pour out My Spirit on all flesh; Your sons and your daughters shall prophesy, Your old men shall dream dreams, Your young men shall see visions. And also on My menservants and on My maidservants I will pour out My Spirit in those days." This was fulfilled on the Day of Pentecost in Acts 2 and is being fulfilled today.

In order to combat the deception of the New Age and the Occult, we must understand and know the Holy Spirit. Jesus gives an excellent description of the Holy Spirit in John 14:15-26. He describes the Spirit as "parakletos", "one called in, or called to the side of another to help, aid, give assistance to, and provide guidance." The Spirit comes to us as our personal counselor when we receive Christ as Lord and Savior.

Christ tells us what the Spirit does as our personal counselor:

- *He comforts us*— "I will not leave you as orphans (v. 18). The Holy Spirit is forever with us, our constant companion.
- *He communicates truth to us*—"the Spirit of truth" (v. 17). God's Spirit convicts, develops, and guides us with the Word.
- *He confirms our belonging*—"I am in My Father, and you in Me, and I in you" (v. 20). The Spirit assures us that we belong to God, testifying with our spirit that we are God's children.

. . . PRAYER . . .

Lord, thank You for our personal Counselor, Your Holy Spirit!

. . . TODAY'S THOUGHT . . .

The Spirit must become a living reality to us to combat deception.

—Mark L. Walker

Pastor, Mt. Paran North, Atlanta, GA

September 8

IN EVERYTHING GIVE THANKS

. . . pray without ceasing, in everything give thanks; for this is the will of God in Christ Jesus for you. (1 Thessalonians 5:17-18)

Charles Spurgeon stated, "Prayer is the slender nerve that moveth the muscles of omnipotence."

In 1991, I attended a meeting at which it was decided to sell the Church of God Campground for Pennsylvania and relocate the state headquarters. I wondered how I would share this devastating news with my wife Marion, who is the Founding President of Peniel Drug/Alcohol Program, which had operated for approximately four years at this location.

After I told her, the question of where the ministry would relocate its operations weighed heavily on our hearts. We discussed what was feasible, but our situation looked bleak and our possibilities were limited. Panic, fear, anxieties, and even depression began to creep in and take advantage of our state of uncertainty.

We realized that the answer and direction we needed could only come from God. We began to thank God for our past blessings and pray for our future. God spoke to our hearts out of the Scriptures: "Moreover I will appoint a place for My people Israel, and will plant them, that they may dwell in a place of their own and move no more" (2 Samuel 7:10). Suddenly, we knew that God had heard our prayers. We were confident that God had a plan for the ministry. We were encouraged by God's Word that we could trust Him with our future.

We soon found our permanent home located in Johnstown, Pennsylvania. Once again God had demonstrated His faithfulness!

The wonderful principle of thanksgiving was revealed to us through experiences such as these: 1) *ask* with thanksgiving; 2) *wait* with thanksgiving; 3) *receive* with thanksgiving. Prayer seasoned with thanksgiving is always the proper attitude toward God.

. . . PRAYER . . .

Lord, help me live a life of prayer with thanksgiving no matter my situation!

. . . TODAY'S THOUGHT . . .

Asking and *waiting* with the attitude of thanksgiving is proof that you have faith to believe that God hears and answers your prayers.

—Harold Spellman
Founding President, Peniel Drug/Alcohol Ministries

September 9

PLANTING SEASON

For as the rain comes down, and the snow from heaven, And do not return there, But water the earth, And make it bring forth and bud, That it may give seed to the sower And bread to the eater, So shall My word be that goes forth from My mouth; It shall not return to Me void, But it shall accomplish what I please, And it shall prosper in the thing for which I sent it. (Isaiah 55:10-11)

It was the middle of winter in the hills of Kentucky. If you had not adequately prepared for this season, it was hard on you; sometimes, even if you *had* prepared, it was still a test. I remember overhearing my Daddy talking to my Moma early one morning, "Let me just go down to the cellar and get a couple of those big nice potatoes, Moma. The kids are hungry, and one or two won't matter that much." Then, my Moma said, "But Sam, if we eat the seed, there won't be anything to plant."

Notice the order in which God gives it. Seed to sow, then bread to eat. If we eat our seed, that seed can do no more for us. But if we plant our seed, give it over to the ground, then we can receive a harvest on it. Moma knew those potatoes would do us far more good in the ground at planting time than in our belly!

The anointing is on the seed to reproduce. But that seed cannot reproduce or draw on its anointing as long as it stays in the cellar. When the appointed season comes, that seed has got to get in the ground. The seed is faithful to do what it is supposed to do: die so that it can yield increase. The ground is faithful to protect the seed and give of its nutrients to the seed. As the faithful sowers, we must recognize the seed God gives us to sow and the planting season that He brings into our lives as well.

Colossians 2:7 instructs us to be rooted and built up in Christ. When we are rooted and planted in God, then we will begin to produce fruit. *Hallelujah!*

. . . PRAYER . . .

Father, we thank You right now for Your provision in our lives. Help us to be evermore sensitive to Your leading regarding sowing and reaping.

. . . TODAY'S THOUGHT . . .

When anointed seeds come into covenant with anointed ground, miracle increase occurs!

—Ellen Parsley
Minister, World Harvest Church, Canton, OH

September 10

A THEOLOGY OF THE CROSS

. . . for he is a chosen vessel of Mine to bear My name. . . . I will show him how many things he must suffer for My name's sake. (Acts 9:15-16)

Paul, a chosen vessel of God, suffered many things for the sake of Christ. He confesses: "Are they ministers of Christ?—I speak as a fool—I am more: in labors more abundant, in stripes above measure, in prisons more frequently, in deaths often" (2 Corinthians 11:23). Nevertheless, he concludes: "what comes upon me daily: my deep concern for all the churches" (v. 28). In the midst of unbearable sufferings, Paul's utmost concern was not for his own well being but for that of his church.

In the early years of the Korean Church of God, many congregations suffered for lack of finances. One day, a pastor came to my office to share a plan to raise money. Without a miracle, his church would be closed. He had seen an advertisement in a newspaper wanting to buy an eye for a rich man. He wanted to sell his own eye! He was willing to suffer a tremendous loss out of his deep concern for the church.

I sent him home, assured him that I would come up with a plan, and began to wrestle with God. I struggled, but no new plan came to me. I was the overseer, however, the pastor of pastors, and I felt that I must be willing to embrace the suffering of my pastors . . . so I decided to take the place of the pastor selling his eye.

I went to the surgery room. God began to deal with the doctor who was going to operate on me; somehow, he could not use the scalpel to take out my eye. Leaving the surgery room, he murmured, "What is this awesome presence I feel which does not allow my surgery to proceed?"

Later, the doctor met me in his office and asked about my decision to sell my eye. Hearing the story, he was so moved that he donated the money to keep the local church open! My eye was spared. God had honored the willingness of his servants to suffer for the sake of His church.

. . . PRAYER . . .

Lord, my heart rejoices in the midst of sufferings knowing Your divine presence will keep me and bring about a peaceful close.

. . . TODAY'S THOUGHT . . .

Attaining the glory of resurrection is made possible through the Cross: our willingness to suffer with Christ eventuates a peaceful resolution.

—Yung-Chul Han
President, Bible College, Seoul, S. Korea

September 11

PENTECOST OR FAILURE

"Not by might nor by power, but by My Spirit," Says the Lord of hosts. (Zechariah 4:6)

When E. Stanley Jones reflected on his years of missionary service to India, he wrote: "I came to India with this conviction and the years have done nothing but verify it. It is this: Pentecost is not a spiritual luxury. It is an utter necessity for human living. The human spirit fails unless the Holy Spirit fills. We are shut up to the alternative—Pentecost or failure."

What did he mean, Pentecost or failure? Did he mean that we need to join a Pentecostal denomination or participate in Pentecostal worship or identify ourselves as Pentecostals? Not at all. In essence, he was reiterating the need of the fullness of the Holy Spirit in our lives.

The Holy Spirit is not an impersonal force, spiritual power, or psychic phenomenon. He is God, third member of the triune Godhead, coexistence, coeternal, and coequal with the Father and Son. He is not a new age spirit but a Person, the Divine Guest who takes up residence in our hearts when we confess Christ Jesus as Lord. He is the Comforter (John 14:16), Eternal Spirit (Hebrews 9:14), the Spirit of Adoption (Romans 8:15), the Spirit of Christ (Romans 8:9), the Spirit of Glory (1 Peter 4:14), the Spirit of God (Genesis 1:2), the Spirit of Grace and Supplication (Zechariah 12:10), the Spirit of Holiness (Romans 1:4), the Spirit of Life (Romans 8:2), and the Spirit of the Father (Matthew 10:20).

After Jesus' ascension, the disciples returned to Jerusalem. Ten days later the promise became reality: they were all filled with the Holy Spirit (Acts 2:4). The aftermath was that they turned the world upside down.

. . . PRAYER . . .

Father, I thank You that You sent the Holy Spirit to fill my heart with Your power to live as more than conqueror in this world.

. . . TODAY'S THOUGHT . . .

The Christian life is not lived by good intentions, or through the energy of the flesh, for it's "'Not by might nor by power, but by My Spirit,' Says the Lord of hosts" (Zechariah 4:6).

—David C. Cooper
Pastor, Mt. Paran Central, Atlanta, GA

September 12

ANOTHER COMFORTER

And I will pray the Father, and He will give you another Helper, that He may abide with you forever. (John 14:16)

In John 14:16, Jesus promises that after He goes away He will send "another" Comforter or Helper. In Greek, the word "another" means "another of the same kind." The word "Helper" is a translation of *parakletos*, which literally means "one called alongside to help." Jesus, therefore, promises to send "another" who is just like Himself who will take His place in the lives of His disciples and be everything to them that He would be if present in His physical body.

This truth was made real to me in 1985 shortly after Sue and I had moved to Dallas, Texas. Finances were limited. When the first of the month rolled around, we did not have the money to pay rent. As I went to prayer, I recalled that when Peter needed money to pay his taxes he went to Jesus and Jesus told him where he could get the money. I also remembered that the Holy Spirit who dwells in me is just like Jesus and that I could expect Him to do the same for me. As I prayed, I sensed the Holy Spirit telling me to go to the corporate offices of the company which owned the house and tell them that I wanted financial remuneration for some minor problems in the house.

The house was owned by a large corporation whose national offices were located in a high-rise office building. Having signed our lease at a field office, we had never been there. After talking to two different people, I was finally ushered into a large plush office that belonged to a vice president. He asked me what I needed, and I told him exactly what I had been instructed by the Holy Spirit. I was planning to ask for $300, the amount I needed. Before I asked, however, he said, "Would you be willing to take $500 for your problems?"

Hallelujah! The Comforter/Helper had come through!

. . . PRAYER . . .

Holy Spirit, I acknowledge Your presence with me today and in the name of Jesus I yield to Your wisdom and guidance in my life.

. . . TODAY'S THOUGHT . . .

The Holy Spirit has come and He is here to be everything to me that Jesus would be if He were present in His physical body.

—Eddie Hyatt

Hyatt International Ministries, Inc., Dallas, TX

September 13

SPIRITUAL FITNESS

I beseech you therefore, brethren, by the mercies of God, that you present your bodies a living sacrifice, holy, acceptable to God, which is your reasonable service. (Romans 12:1)

In this world of the "fitness craze," people are spending billions to achieve the "perfect physique." Health clubs and fitness centers are constantly extolling the virtues of proper exercise. We are fascinated and impressed with athletes and their grueling work ethic. We compare and measure ourselves against these famous personalities. We work on becoming just as fit, slender, and attractive. Physical beauty has almost become our number one priority. However, while bodily exercise is an essential component in maintaining good health, the Apostle Paul reminds us to "exercise yourself toward godliness. For bodily exercise profits a little, but godliness is profitable for all things" (1 Timothy 4:7-8).

Paul urged us to present our bodies to God "a living sacrifice." This means that our will is secondary. We are not concerned with conforming to the world's standards. Instead, we are totally committed to God's fitness program. Because we measure ourselves in relation to His requirements, exercise takes on a new meaning. Prayer, fasting, and studying God's Word become our daily work ethic. This workout brings immeasurable present and eternal rewards because we are acting in obedience to God's Word.

As you go through daily living, I challenge you to be a nonconformist. Reject the world's attitudes and standards. Allow the Holy Spirit to transform you to a spiritual "10." Make your sacrifice count for eternity. Allow your life to be one of total surrender to God. With your surrender comes godly acceptance; and with godly acceptance come peace, joy, and abundant living.

. . . PRAYER . . .

Dear Lord, thank You for new mercies each day. Help me to yield myself wholly to You. Take my will and make it Thine, so that You will get the glory out of my life.

. . . TODAY'S THOUGHT . . .

Self-denial is only our reasonable service.

—Michael E. Reid
Pastor, Resurrection Life Fellowship, Delray Beach, FL

September 14

THE SPIRIT'S INTERCESSION

Likewise the Spirit also helps in our weaknesses. For we do not know what we should pray for as we ought, but the Spirit Himself makes intercession for us with groanings which cannot be uttered. (Romans 8:26)

One of the great ministries of the Holy Spirit is intercession. It is important to have the Spirit for intercession, for it is "through Him (Jesus) we both have access by one Spirit to the Father" (Ephesians 2:18).

The Bible lists some great men who interceded in prayer for others. Moses interceded for Israel and Abraham for Lot. Believers today have two divine intercessors. Christ is our intercessor in heaven (Hebrews 7:25). The Holy Spirit is our intercessor within (John 14:16-17).

The Spirit intercedes for our "infirmities" (weakness). We all have weaknesses. It is at this point that the Holy Spirit provides "intercession for us." The Bible does not say that the Spirit removes our weakness. What the Spirit does is to help. This help is effective because the Spirit knows our needs and He knows the will of God.

. . . PRAYER . . .

Heavenly Father, I thank You for the gift of the Holy Ghost. Thank You for the divine help of the Spirit in my times of weakness.

. . . TODAY'S THOUGHT . . .

God's strength is made perfect in weakness.

—Carl E. Maynard
Pastor, Oak Park Decatur, AL

September 15

GIFTED TO BLESS

And He Himself gave some to be apostles, some prophets, some evangelists, and some pastors and teachers, for the equipping of the saints for the work of ministry, for the edifying of the body of Christ. (Ephesians 4:11-12)

A gift is an expression of love and/or appreciation. Gifts are not earned; they are received. Christ's love for His Body is of such magnitude that He has provided gifts in the form of persons whom He has called and whom He has graced for specific spiritual service.

Paul identifies apostles, prophets, evangelists, and pastors/teachers. This list of gifted helpers provided to the Body is not exhaustive, but reminds us that we are not self-sufficient. Spiritual maturity is not the consequence of human ability, but is generated by the Spirit working through people selected and anointed for spiritual ministry.

Paul assures the Ephesians that the leadership needed for them to become spiritually mature is supplied by the Head to the Body. "Perfecting of the saints" (v.12, KJV) does not suggest human perfection, but, rather, describes a process of maturation which Paul elsewhere calls "pressing toward the mark."

Also, the task of these spiritually gifted persons is to tutor others for "the work of ministry." The idea is that of an attendant serving the needs of another. The phrase "work of ministry" describes a servant relationship. Gifted persons give direction and training.

Finally, when those engaged in spiritual warfare find themselves spiritually depleted, they are refreshed and edified by the spiritually gifted placed in the Body. These are not supplied to Christ's Body simply to wear titles, but they are gifted to bless. They give relief and rest to the battle weary. Like a personal trainer, they supervise conditioning and development of the Body for continuation of the work that Christ began "both to do and teach, Until the day in which he was taken up" (Acts 1:1-2).

. . . PRAYER . . .

Lord, I need the careful attention of those gifted to train me for spiritual service.

. . . TODAY'S THOUGHT . . .

Spiritually insufficient in ourselves, we need spiritual supervision to lead us to maturity.

—J. Anthony Lombard
Marketing Department, COG Publishing House

September 16

GOD STILL SPEAKS

When you pass through the waters, I will be with you; And through the rivers, they shall not overflow you. When you walk through the fire, you shall not be burned, Nor shall the flame scorch you. (Isaiah 43:2)

In the midst of more than 600 men on a U.S. Navy warship, I was lonelier than I had ever been. Only eighteen months before I had realized my dream to serve on active duty as a U.S. Navy Chaplain. I had been ordered to a squadron of five ships in San Diego, California, and soon learned my ships were scheduled for a six-month deployment to waters off the coast of North Vietnam. It seemed a terribly long time. My wife, Letha, and I had never been apart for more than a few days in 13 years of marriage, but we believed we could cope with the absence.

The long deployment was a busy and blessed time . . . but the time to return home was always on my mind. But one week before sailing for home, I received shocking news: *My deployment was being extended another six weeks!* A ship of another squadron needed a chaplain. While my shipmates would be home celebrating with their families, I would be thousands of miles away. It didn't seem fair.

I reported to the new ship. Late one night I went onto the open deck. The darkness and the aloneness reflected my feelings. I looked up and saw a clear sky with millions of stars that seemed so near I could almost touch them. Then God broke in. A Scripture came to my mind and God gave me a message of His presence and caring: "When I consider Your heavens, the work of Your fingers, The moon and the stars, which You have ordained, What is man that You are mindful of him, And the son of man that You visit him?" (Psalm 8:3-4).

It was a transforming communication. The weeks of that extended period became times of refreshing and ministry. And the revelation on that ship's deck prepared me for the next 20 years of service. In the dark days of our earthly journey we often fail to see, recognize, and accept the marvelous promises of God. He is there and He cares!

. . . PRAYER . . .

Dear Lord, thank You for the witness of the Holy Spirit that You are always there and .are touched with a feeling of our infirmities.

. . . TODAY'S THOUGHT . . .

In trying times God communicates marvelous messages to us.

—Hugo S. Hammond
Chaplin, United States Navy

September 17

A CURE FOR CARE

Be anxious for nothing, but in everything by prayer and supplication, with thanksgiving, let your requests be made known to God; and the peace of God, which surpasses all understanding, will guard your hearts and minds through Christ Jesus. (Philippians 4:6-7)

Worry, confusion of mind, pressures of daily living, and uncertainty about the future were as common to the Philippians as they are to us today. These cares lead to depression, which is the most common emotional problem in America. Anxiety, as Paul is using the term and as we most often experience it, is the useless, frustrating, debilitating attempt to bear the burdens of life and, especially, of the future alone. Paul's instruction to us in this passage is to take our own past and our own present and our own future with all our shame, all our needs, and all our fears into the presence of God. Stop worrying now!

Paul's solution to worry is prayer coupled with thanksgiving. Prayer is addressed to God as an act of worship and devotion. Do not focus on the problem; rather, focus on God. Remember three things: a) the love of God, which desires only what is best for us; b) the wisdom of God, which knows what is best for us; c) the power of God, which brings to pass that which is best for us. Centering our attention on God in prayer, thanking Him for everything means that we will be full of care for nothing, leaving our care in the safe hands of God. The way to be anxious about nothing is to be prayerful about everything. Take yourself lightly so that "like angels you can fly."

M. R. Vincent said, "peace is the fruit of believing prayer." God's peace, like a sentinel, will mount guard and patrol your heart's door, keeping worry out. Prayer is not words: it is a life; not a service: it is a spirit. We cultivate the capacity to trust through our life of prayer. As our trust expands, our tolerance for uncertainty and ambiguity grows and our anxiety diminishes. "Be careful for nothing; be prayerful for everything; and be thankful for anything."

. . . PRAYER . . .

Lord, in supplication and thanksgiving I turn all my cares over to You.

. . . TODAY'S THOUGHT . . .

Worry is useless; prayer is useful. God will carry our burdens.

—Grey and Linda Robinson
Pastors, COG (retired)

September 18

YOU KNOW HIM

. . . the Spirit of truth, whom the world cannot receive, because it neither sees Him nor knows Him; but you know Him, for He dwells with you and will be in you. (John 14:17)

Many are the significant disturbances that afflict society. Struggles, fretfulness and irritations are characteristic of lives unable to live victoriously under the pressures of living. People are held in bondage with compulsive behaviors that destroy their joy. Unable to deal with their crises, they give up, seek an end and commit suicide.

Jesus told His disciples that He would not leave them helpless or hopeless. He assured them that there would be One who would make them confident and bold, the Holy Spirit. He said that the world does not know Him; consequently, those individuals that do not know the Holy Spirit cannot experience true freedom, ongoing joy, deliverance and unlimited power to endure the pressures of daily living. The Spirit is unnoticed by the world. Those who have no relationship with Christ have no spiritual life. Because of the gift of the Holy Spirit, the apostles enjoyed a relationship with Jesus Christ that was much more intimate and gave them a way to handle the challenging moments of life.

In these difficult times, the Holy Spirit is prodding us, expecting us to grow in our experiential knowledge of Him. As believers knowing Him, we can experience joy in the midst of confusion, uncertainties and death. We avail ourselves of the power to believe, to endure, and to be thankful in spite of the periods of antagonism, persecution and despondency. We learn to be submissive to God and to one another, relating to each other in submission, sure that our new interests, desires and affections will be controlled by the fact that we are to be submitted to each other. When we dwell on the beautiful things of the Spirit, we can experience His wonderful, peaceful presence in the midst of the hustle and bustle of life.

. . . PRAYER . . .

Thank you, Holy Spirit, for working in us and for Your constant indwelling that gives us power to live victorious lives.

. . . TODAY'S THOUGHT . . .

Often the greatest lessons in our walk of faith can be learned in daily occurrences.

—Carlos S. Mòran

Administrative Bishop, Northwest Hispanic COG

September 19

POWER FOR SERVICE?

But you shall receive power when the Holy Spirit has come upon you; and you shall be witnesses to Me in Jerusalem, and in all Judea and Samaria, and to the end of the earth. (Acts 1:8)

The Pentecostal experience described in Acts 1:8 is often described as *power for Christian service.* Many Pentecostals have reduced Spirit baptism to *power to do* the work of God rather than *power to be* the workmanship of God (Ephesians 2:10). But this is not a New Testament understanding of Spirit baptism and empowerment.

In the Old Testament, God foretold our redemptive experiences that were purchased later by Christ. Ezekiel 36: 25-28: "Then I will sprinkle clean water on you, and you shall be clean; I will cleanse you from all your filthiness and from all your idols [*regeneration*]. I will give you a new heart and put a new spirit within you; I will take the heart of stone out of your flesh and give you a heart of flesh [*sanctification/living a life of holiness and spiritual sensitivity*]. I will put My Spirit within you and cause you to walk in My statutes, and you will keep My judgments and do them [*Spirit baptism*]. Then you shall dwell in the land that I gave to your fathers; you shall be My people, and I will be your God [*the goal of living for God*]." We are made holy by Christ's cleansing. We live out that holiness by means of sanctification. Spirit baptism is the power that enables us to live out that sanctified life. We must *be* God's people even as God *is* our God.

The power of *being* a witness is the power of godly character. Without it, one cannot live the sanctified life of holiness. Biblically, there were not Pentecostals and non-Pentecostals. The New Testament Church was Pentecostal; to be Christian was to be Pentecostal.

Beyond confessing your sins and accepting Christ's forgiveness and cleansing (1 John 1:9), your relationship with God is not based on what you do. Rather, you live after the Spirit (Romans 7:6, 8:4).

. . . PRAYER . . .

Lord, I pray that those who have not been filled with Your Spirit will ask and receive.

. . . TODAY'S THOUGHT . . .

See the need for Spirit baptism and the importance of godly character. Your *power in doing* hinges on your willingness *to be empowered.*

—Gerald Scott Ingram

September 20

SPIRITUAL LACK

Then Jesus, looking at him, loved him, and said to him, "One thing you lack" (Mark 10:21).

The "one thing lacking" in the text above keeps many people from ever fully following Jesus. Like the rich young ruler, they come to Him sincerely. But Jesus will not leave them in the state of less-than-full surrender. He demands every disciple to take up the Cross and follow Him. He brings them to the place where Her reveals their spiritual lack. They must die to self or leave sorrowful and unfulfilled.

The last words of Jesus on the Cross were, "It is finished." The victory was secured, the battle won. The problem for us, as humans, is that we are not completely dead yet. We still need the Cross because we are still in the flesh. Crucifixion is an agonizing process, a slow death. It is extremely slow when we are crucifying self. We can never fully die to self as long as we are in this body. So we are commanded to take up our Cross and follow Christ. We carry our Cross with us all the time, and, as needed, crawl upon it and crucify the passions of the flesh that separate us from God. Paul said, "I die daily" (1 Corinthians 15:31).

How do you crucify yourself? You can't. You can, however, get on the Cross, "present your bodies a living sacrifice, holy, acceptable to God" (Romans 12:1). God will finish the process.

Before the Cross, pray. Jesus went to the Garden of Gethsemane the night before He died because He knew the real battle was not in laying down His life, but in combating the forces of hell that would try to keep Him from doing His Father's will. You cannot lay down your life fully until you learn to pray. All of the problems that defeat you can be traced back to a lack of prayer. If you pray, nothing can overcome you.

. . . PRAYER . . .

Father, "not My will, but Yours, be done" (Luke 22:42).

. . . TODAY'S THOUGHT . . .

The act of crucifying the flesh is not nearly as hard as making the decision to do it, as overcoming the lies of the devil that try to convince you that you cannot do it or that the cost will be too great.

—Raymond W. Hardy

September 21

ORDERED STEPS

The steps of a good man are ordered by the Lord, And He delights in his way. Though he fall, he shall not be utterly cast down; For the Lord upholds him with His hand. I have been young, and now am old; Yet I have not seen the righteous forsaken, Nor his descendants begging bread. (Psalm 37:23-25)

In 1945 in a small southeast Missouri town, a young pastor knocked on the door of my parents' home. The door was opened by my grandmother, who was there visiting. The young pastor said, "The Lord has sent me here." He asked, "Is anyone sick in this house?" It was at this point a miracle was set in motion for our family.

My grandmother told the young pastor that her son had been sick for three weeks. The pastor asked if he could pray for him and she asked him to come in. God had truly ordered the steps of this young pastor to our home. A miracle was in store for my father that day. It was because of that visit and prayer that God brought a healing miracle to my father. Dad had been suffering with appendicitis and the doctor had told him he must have surgery or he would die. God completely healed him and to this day he still has his appendix.

After that experience, my parents began attending the Church of God. They reared my sister and me in the church. I was called into the ministry. My wife and I have raised our two children in the Church of God. Our two children have married and now we have a granddaughter being reared in church. My family shall always be grateful to the Lord for ordering the steps of a good man and leading him to my parents' home.

My father has been young and now is old, but he can say as David declared in Psalm 37:25: "Yet I have not seen the righteous forsaken, Nor his descendants begging bread."

. . . PRAYER . . .

Heavenly Father, thank You for the divine direction You give to Your children who trust and obey Your precious word of truth.

. . . TODAY'S THOUGHT . . .

"Though he fall, he shall not be utterly cast down; For the Lord upholds him with His hand" (Psalm 37:24).

—Darrell Mouser
State Evangelism Director, COG, TX

September 22

COME AND DINE

So the people stood afar off, but Moses drew near the thick darkness where God was. (Exodus 20:21)

The people saw the lightning and heard the thunder—and they shrank back in fear. Instead of pursuing His glory, they ran from Him. So the result of their running from holy intimacy was that they died before they entered the promised land. As my friend David Ravenhill would say, "They drank from the river but died in the wilderness." They chose distant respect over intimate relationship.

God is looking for someone who is willing to tie a rope around an ankle and say, "If I perish, I perish; but I am going to see the King. I want to do everything I can to go behind that veil. I'm going to put on the blood, I'm going to repent, I'm going to do everything I can because I'm tired of knowing about Him. I want to know Him. I've got to see His face."

There is much more of God available than we have ever known or imagined, but we have become so satisfied with where we are and what we have that we don't press in for God's best. Yes, God is moving among us and working in our lives, but we have been content to comb the carpet for crumbs as opposed to having the abundant loaves of hot bread God has prepared for us in the ovens of Heaven! He has prepared a great table of His presence in this day, and he is calling to the Church, "Come and dine."

. . . PRAYER . . .

God, help us to always hunger for more of You, to never become complacent but always to seek an intimacy with You far greater than we experienced the day before.

. . . TODAY'S THOUGHT . . .

God desires for His people to move to another level, to reach another plateau far beyond anything they have ever experienced before.

—Tommy Tenney (from *God Chasers*, reprinted by permission)
International Evangelist, Author, Pineville, LA

September 23

ACHIEVING THE IMPOSSIBLE

But Jesus looked at them and said, "With men it is impossible, but not with God; for with God all things are possible." (Mark 10:27)

As a Bible College student around 30 years ago, I heard an experienced missionary speak on the subject of faith. The Rev. David Davids presented a new facet of the word "faith" which impressed me and has remained with me ever since. Faith . . .

- *Believes the Unbelievable.* One clear example of faith in the Bible is that of Abraham (Genesis 12:1-4), who stepped out on the command of God without knowing where he was going, which is something that many of us are reluctant to consider. However, Abraham had a simple faith in God and took Him at His Word (Romans 4:19-22).
- *Sees the Invisible.* In 2 Kings 6 is the story of Elisha in the city of Dothan. His servant was frightened when he saw the Syrian army surrounding the city, but Elisha prayed for God to open his servant's eyes for him to see the host of Heaven that surrounded them. The Holy Spirit opens our eyes to the things of God and reveals the meaning of His Word to us.
- *Knows the Unknowable.* It is amazing that we can know God (2 Timothy 1:12). The "finite" cannot understand the "Infinite." Yet we, through the indwelling of Jesus Christ and by the power of the Holy Spirit, can know the mind of God because we have the mind of Christ in us (1 Corinthians 2:16).
- *Achieves the Impossible.* Faith works in the realm of the impossible. God responds to our faith, not our needs. God cannot lie nor deny Himself. Therefore, He must fulfill what He has promised to do for His children (Galatians 3:20).

. . . PRAYER . . .

Lord, cleanse me through the power of the Holy Spirit of any obstacles in my life, and keep me ever in the center of Your will.

. . . TODAY'S THOUGHT . . .

The operative word of the Scriptures is "believing," the means for every believer to know God's blessing and provision in their lives.

—Graham R. Evans

Co-Director, Emmanuel International Ministries, Wales, UK

September 24

WONDROUS WORKS OF GOD

Stand still and consider the wondrous works of God. (Job 37:14)

"Private Property." "Keep Out." "Do Not Open." These are the words written on three rather ugly, extremely ragged and well-worn cardboard boxes. My children, Micah, Joel, and Bethany, are all collectors of rare and unusual childhood memorabilia. Tucked away as a safe haven of an already cluttered closet rest these possessions. Physical appearance would indicate a meaningless accumulation that should be discarded, no longer useful, having served the purpose.

Ownership may be traced back through preserved footprints of childhood experiences. It was under these ordinary circumstances that the "Life Box" became a vital part of our family history.

Don't be fooled by the outer condition of the "Life Box." Don't be misled by what you think you may see. Inside are revealed the transforming treasures kids are made of—not yet coming to a full realization of purpose, potential, or capacity.

So it is with the Christian life. To novice eyes, it may appear tattered and torn, filled with ashes of what might have been. Potential is found inwardly, though, not outwardly: "For the Lord does not see as man sees; for man looks at the outward appearance, but the Lord looks at the heart" (1 Samuel 16:7). Unexpected difficulties, disturbances, and disappointments may temporarily damage our lives, but the truth remains secure. "Now we have received, not the spirit of the world, but the Spirit who is from God, that we might know the things that have been freely given to us by God" (1 Corinthians 2:12).

God will give grace enough, unconditional love, and constant care. We can depend upon Him for restoration. We are made victorious by the Holy Spirit. "He will guide you into all truth" (John 16:13). He brings comfort and contentment, joy and peace.

. . . PRAYER . . .

Father, may I be reminded daily that sorrow may be turned into joy. May I be reminded that from the ruins of ashes, You will bring forth all Your promises.

. . . TODAY'S THOUGHT . . .

God allows things to happen to us to work His power in us, to flow through us to bless His name.

—Dianne Andrews
Pastor, Rock Mountain Lake, McCalla, AL

September 25

REASSURED BY THE HOLY SPIRIT

"Not by might nor by power, but by My Spirit," Says the Lord of hosts. (Zechariah 4:6)

As a young boy, I prayed a prayer that God answered immediately. To many, this may seem a small thing. For me, however, it left a lasting impression for over 50 years and had become a touchstone in my life. It is not only a well from which to draw water, but also a shelter from the storm and a refuge in a lonely land. When I need strength and help, it is a nail in a sure place.

My thoughts go back to a time when I was only five years old playing outside in late winter. Suddenly, my eyes focused on a beautiful cardinal sitting in a leafless oak tree in our yard. I was fascinated by its brilliant color and very much wanted it for my own. Realizing that I would not catch it, I began to pray and ask God to make this possible. Suddenly, it flew to the ground. I picked it up and carried it into the house.

The bird only lived a few days, yet the answer to that prayer has lived with me all these years as a reminder of what simple faith in our great God can do.

Young David, remembering what God had done, feeling confident facing Goliath in battle, said, "The Lord, who delivered me from the paw of the lion and from the paw of the bear, He will deliver me from the hand of this Philistine" (1 Samuel 17:37).

Through the power of the Holy Spirit, which teaches and brings all things to our remembrance, we can do all things through Christ which strengthens us.

. . . PRAYER . . .

Father, we realize our insufficiency, but the all sufficiency that is in You. Help us day by day through the Spirit to accomplish Your will.

. . . TODAY'S THOUGHT . . .

God still works in mysterious ways, His wonders to perform.

—Roy Bevis

Pastor, Mt. Olive Rd., Birmingham, AL

September 26

THE HEALING WORD

But we all, with unveiled face, beholding as in a mirror the glory of the Lord, are being transformed into the same image from glory to glory, just as by the Spirit of the Lord. (2 Corinthians 3:18)

Serium Hepatitis! The words of the doctor struck me with the force of a thunderbolt. I had just buried a minister friend of mine who died of hepatitis and I knew that unless God intervened quickly for me, this prognosis was equivalent to a death sentence. In a moment of time, I saw thirty-five years of ministry as a Bible college vice president, pastor, and evangelist nearing conclusion.

My wife checked me into a prominent Houston hospital. On the third day, very early in the morning, I awoke with a start. I was crying profusely and speaking in tongues. The room was filled with the awesome presence of God. The Great Physician had entered the room and touched and healed me instantly with His Word. There was a lingering flush of warmth about my person.

The nurse came running into the room and asked excitedly, "What on earth is the matter with you, Reverend?" I tearfully explained to her that God had just healed me and had given me a Scripture. She brought me my Bible and I quickly turned to 2 Corinthians 3:18, the text above, and read the Scripture by which I had been healed.

The doctors tested me thoroughly for verification of healing. Then, they said: "When you came to us three days ago, your infectious enzymes were completely off the chart. Now, much to our amazement, they are absolutely perfect. You are released to go home today."

. . . PRAYER . . .

Thank You, Lord, for Your providential love and care. Healing is always available to those who can say with Paul, "Therefore most gladly I will rather boast in my infirmities, that the power of Christ may rest upon me" (2 Corinthians 12:9).

. . . TODAY'S THOUGHT . . .

As Christians, we should mark well this double paradox of Scriptural life; in ourselves we are weak even when we are strong; in Christ we are strong even when we are weak. Self-sufficiency is insufficiency. Christ-sufficiency is all-sufficiency.

—Dr. Joseph D. Clark
Pastor, Trinity Pentecostal COG, Houston, TX

September 27

LIVING THE BOOK OF ACTS

And they were all filled with the Holy Spirit and began to speak with other tongues, as the Spirit gave them utterance. (Acts 2:4)

In the Old Testament, only those uniquely called or anointed of God received the Spirit. But under the New Covenant, every believer is offered the Promise of the Father (Luke 24:49), the active presence of the Holy Spirit. It is by this activity of the Spirit's fullness in the life of every believer that the ministry of Christ in His Church continues.

In the Acts of the Apostles, we learn to . . .

1. Believe that the power of God comes only by the Holy Spirit. Do not attempt ministry without the Holy Spirit.
2. Seek and receive the Baptism in the Holy Spirit. Continually be refilled with the Spirit to renew regularly your life and ministry. Exercise your prayer language as a part of the Spirit's flow in your life.
3. Expect your Spirit-filled relationship with Jesus to help you speak boldly, with courage and spiritual understanding.
4. Share Jesus boldly. Ask the Spirit to confirm your testimony.

What is meant by "other tongues" in Acts 2:4? Note two things. First, it definitely means foreign languages (see verses 6-13). The disciples were supernaturally witnessing and preaching in the languages of the different nationalities gathering together. Secondly, it may also mean the tongues or ecstatic utterance covered in 1 Corinthians; that is, it may have been what is commonly called the heavenly or prayer language (1 Corinthians 14:2, 14). An ecstatic worship may have been taking place while the disciples were experiencing the infilling of the Holy Spirit. There seems to be some time between the moments of infilling and the crowds arriving to see what caused the explosive sound or noise (v. 2). And there can be no doubt that the disciples were flooded with an ecstatic, worshipful joy.

. . . PRAYER . . .

Lord, help us, please, to live the Book of Acts daily in our lives!

. . . TODAY'S THOUGHT . . .

The New Covenant people of God live the life of the Spirit!

—Wayne Rouse

Pastor, Hunting Ridge, Prattville, AL

September 28

WHEN THE HELPER COMES

But when the Helper comes, whom I shall send to you from the Father, the Spirit of truth who proceeds from the Father, He will testify of Me. (John 15:26)

At some time in our lives we learn the real meaning of the word "Helper" (the Holy Spirit). The word signifies an intercessor, comforter, advocate, counselor.

A few years ago, there was a need for the Holy Spirit to help in my life. Within myself, there were several attempts to resolve a very difficult problem in my life. There were times it seemed that I was succeeding in finding an answer. This went on for some time. Then one day, after all efforts had been tried, the news came: all hope of the answer I was looking for was gone. It was a very dark day indeed.

The promise of the Helper, the Guide, the Teacher, the Holy Spirit, became very important at this time. It was the Holy Spirit who taught me that God's grace is sufficient! It doesn't matter what the needs are, the trials you are facing, the storm that comes up out of no where: "God's grace is sufficient!"

It was a time of praying. I learned to listen to the Holy Spirit speak to my heart through the Word of God. As I opened my Bible, the Spirit guided me to Psalm 37 for my answer, for my promise of assurance that He, the Spirit, was with me. It concludes: "But the salvation of the righteous is from the Lord; He is their strength in the time of trouble. And the Lord shall help them and deliver them; He shall deliver them from the wicked, And save them, Because they trust in Him" (37:39-40). During the days, months, and years, the Holy Spirit has guided my footsteps, taught me of God's grace, and brought peace to my heart in the midst of the storm.

. . . PRAYER . . .

Dear Lord, thank You for sending the Holy Spirit to be our Helper in this life on earth.

. . . TODAY'S THOUGHT . . .

Everyone comes to the place where they need someone to help them get through a difficult problem of life. The Holy Spirit is our Helper.

—Kenneth Northcutt
Oak Hill COG, AL

September 29

DRAW THE LINE

For it is shameful even to speak of those things which are done by them in secret. But all things that are exposed are made manifest by the light, for whatever makes manifest is light. (Ephesians 5:12-13)

The surgeon said that it must be taken out. He was speaking of a small lump under my wife's left arm that had gradually increased from a slight swelling into a noticeable lump during a five-month period.

I waited in the surgical lounge of St. Joseph's Hospital in February, 1987, while my wife was in surgery. When I saw the surgeon emerge from the operating room, I rushed to meet him. He said, "Cancer everywhere, low grade, third stage, every lymph node full of cancer." I leaned against the wall, startled and dazed by the devastating news. My lovely wife of 35 years had cancer.

The Rayburn family began a journey of seeking God for divine intervention. Our four children and I wrapped arms of love and faith around a seriously ill mother and wife. The ministry family and church laity from across Michigan and around the world began a prayer vigil.

During the months after surgery, the surgeon said time after time there was little medical hope for Norma to live. However, prayers were made without ceasing in Norma's behalf. After six months, she continued to live with no evidence of cancer. After one year, the surgeon said to my wife, "Lady, you are indeed a miracle."

Norma has enjoyed a miracle of extended life, free of cancer—a life decreed by our Savior, Jesus Christ the Son of God, who loved us and gave Himself for all who will believe on His name. Nine years from the day a concerned medical surgeon said, "Cancer everywhere, low grade, third stage, every lymph node full. I am sorry, I did all I could do," my wife is living a healthy, cancer-free, vibrant life in Christ.

. . . PRAYER . . .

Lord Jesus, when we have gone to our limit of accomplishment, we thank You that Your divine healing power is available to all who will simply say, "I can do no more; You, Lord, are the healer."

. . . TODAY'S THOUGHT . . .

When you have given your best effort, remember God is available to walk with you the next step.

—Billy J. Rayburn
Director, Cross Cultural Ministries, Cleveland, TN

September 30

THE HOLY SPIRIT AND UNITY

. . . endeavoring to keep the unity of the Spirit in the bond of peace. (Ephesians 4:3)

Unity is necessary for any business to succeed. Confusion causes division, division causes destruction. Unity helps to develop any organism, organization, body, or group.

The Psalmist describes unity as good and pleasant. One of the greatest problems of marriages, churches, and other relationships/ organizations is that each person wants what he/she wants without regard to others. Often we are prone to disagree and want things our way. But, when unity is present, there is the breaking of the will of man to do the will of God and to accept or adjust to others.

It is not wise for some people to dwell together. Amos 3:3 asks, "Can two walk together, except they are agreed?" If there are continual disagreements, as with Abraham and Lot, it may be better for them not to dwell together. The Apostle Paul said, "Do not be unequally yoked together with unbelievers. For what fellowship has righteousness with lawlessness?" (2 Corinthians 6:14). It is better to make sure that "two can walk in agreement" before vowing to "dwell together."

It takes the Spirit of God to produce true unity because it is a characteristic of the Spirit. Uniformity is not necessary, but we must have unity in Christ through the Spirit. Ephesians 4:3 tells us that we are to keep the unity of the Spirit, and the only way to do this is to possess the Spirit. The characteristic of unity is shown in the fruit of the Spirit: love, joy, peace, long-suffering, gentleness, goodness, faith, meekness, and temperance. They are all one unit of fruit.

. . . PRAYER . . .

Dear Father, help Your children to be one in unity as You and our Lord are one. Help us to understand that true unity is not conformity to this world, but to Your will. As the many tiny drops of rain fill the creeks, rivers and oceans, may we fill Your Church around the world with Unity of the Spirit. Amen.

. . . TODAY'S THOUGHT . . .

U - N - I - Together Yielded to the Spirit of God to do the will of God until He comes.

—Tony Pope

Pastor, Northport COG, Tuscaloosa, AL

October 1

THE REFILLING OF THE SPIRIT

. . . but be filled with the Spirit. (Ephesians 5:18)

As we pursue our spiritual journey, it is necessary to be filled with the Spirit, but it is equally as important to be refilled.

The initial outpouring of the Holy Spirit came on the Day of Pentecost. "And they were all filled with the Holy Spirit and began to speak with other tongues, as the Spirit gave them utterance" (Acts 2:4).

On several occasions in the Scripture, there is evidence that people were refilled with the Holy Spirit. Peter and John had been arrested for preaching the Gospel. After they had been released, they went to the home of Mary, John Mark's mother. The saints of God were meeting there for prayer. "And when they had prayed, the place where they were assembled together was shaken; and they were all filled with the Holy Spirit, and they spoke the word of God with boldness" (Acts 4:31). Many of these praying saints had already been filled with the Holy Ghost at Pentecost. After much prayer, they were refilled with the Spirit and received fresh power so they could speak the Word of God with boldness.

There have been many times in my life that it became necessary for me to return to an altar and travail in prayer until a refreshing of the divine Spirit came rushing into my heart. Those times of refilling gave me new courage and new strength and kept me from failing to remain full of the Spirit.

The song, "Fill My Cup Lord," expresses what it means to remain filled with the Spirit: "Fill my cup, Lord, I lift it up, Lord. Come and quench this thirsting of my soul. Bread of Heaven, feed me 'til I want no more; fill my cup, fill it up and make me whole."

. . . PRAYER . . .

Father, help us to stay continually full of the Spirit and to be endued with power that our lives will be a spiritual light to the world.

. . . TODAY'S THOUGHT . . .

It is the will of God and His command for His people everywhere to be both filled and refilled with the Holy Spirit.

—Kenneth Andrews
Pastor, Rock Mountain Lake, McCalla, AL

October 2

SPIRIT-LIFE: AGAPE LOVE!

For it seemed good to the Holy Spirit, and to us, . . (Acts 15:28)

How clearly this Scripture indicates the reality of Spirit-life and the personal relation the first-century Christians enjoyed with the Spirit and with each other! It is evident that these leaders, moved upon by the Spirit, knew Him in a definite, personal way.

A question arose that precipitated the convening of the Jerusalem Council. Apostles, elders, and believers came together to receive an answer from God. The question concerned how Jewish Christians could have fellowship with Gentile Christians who were uncircumcised, ate unacceptable food, and did not keep the Law. Men of God reported God's visitation to the Gentiles. Peter, Paul, and Barnabas addressed the concerns. James gave a word of wisdom that was received by the church. In all their disputing, they gave preeminence to the presence of the third Person of the Trinity among them. The Holy Ghost guided them into truth. Schism was avoided. Then they sent letters telling of their decision. They did not say, "It seemed good to James, Peter, Paul, Barnabas, or the consensus of the church shown by a majority vote." The awareness of the reality of the Holy Ghost pervaded this investigation, discussion, and debate. The Spirit presided and prevailed.

To change the world requires two John 3:16's. We can all quote John 3:16, but what of 1 John 3:16? "By this we know love, because He laid down His life for us. And we also ought to lay down our lives for the brethren." Spirit-life begets divine love. To be convinced of our divine love, the world must see us laying down our lives for each other. Spirit-life enables us to go beyond ourselves, to become concerned with the welfare and well being of our brother. Spirit-life gives us the ability to love automatically and spontaneously without regard to the so-called worldly worth of the person. Spirit-life is an attitude and commitment not to see through each other, but to see each other through.

. . . PRAYER . . .

Spirit, guide us into all Truth and help us do that which seems good to You!

. . . TODAY'S THOUGHT . . .

It seems good to the Holy Ghost and to us to practice 1 John 3:16 as well as to receive the eternal life in John 3:16. Do it today!

—Gerald Johnson
Evangelist, Riverview, FL

October 3

A MIRACLE LEADS FAMILY TO PENTECOST

Is anyone among you sick? Let him call for the elders of the church, and let them pray over him, anointing him with oil in the name of the Lord. And the prayer of faith will save the sick, and the Lord will raise him up. And if he has committed sins, he will be forgiven. (James 5:14-15)

I was reared on a farm in southeast Missouri. My family had no exposure to Pentecost until my maternal grandparents started attending a country church known as Oak Grove Pentecostal Church. We were asked to attend church with them, but my dad would not go. My mother went and, when she returned, my dad told her to stay away from him—he didn't want any of that Pentecostal stuff to get on him. From that time, we began hearing stories about Pentecostal worship and miraculous healings.

My 7-year-old sister became very sick with typhoid fever and pneumonia. After many days of a raging fever and intermittent coma, the doctor told my father she was not going to live. Remembering the miracles associated with the Pentecostal church, Dad called the family together and said, "I don't know if God does things like we have heard about or not, but if He does, it is the only thing that will save my daughter. I am going out to that church and try to find some of those people. If they will come with me, I will ask them to pray for her."

They came and prayed and God miraculously healed her. She came out of the coma, the fever instantly broke, and she sat up in bed and asked for something to eat. She suffered no effects from the illness and today is a great-grandmother whose family is active in church.

We later moved closer to the Oak Grove Church and became a Spirit-filled family. Since that time we have experienced other miracles in our family, including the calling of four Pentecostal preachers. Our God is a God of miracles and the same yesterday, today, and forever.

. . . PRAYER . . .

Father, I thank You for the many manifestations of Your power that I have seen. Help us never to waver.

. . . TODAY'S THOUGHT . . .

Faith in God sees the invisible, believes the incredible, and receives the impossible.

—Oren J. Cloninger
Pastor, COG (retired)

October 4

ARE YOU READY FOR A MIRACLE?

"What then is to be done for her?" And Gehazi answered, "Actually, she has no son, and her husband is old." And he said, "Call her." When he had called her, she stood in the doorway. Then he said, "About this time next year you shall embrace a son." (2 Kings 4: 14-16)

Funny thing about Miracles. . . sometimes they come at you when you least expect it! The book of Amos speaks of a day when the plowman shall overtake the reaper. In other words, by the time we plant the seed, we begin to see the harvest coming in! I believe that time is "Now"!

Miracles are all around us, even the secular media is catching on. TV programs featuring angels or someone's miracle are an everyday occurrence. Yet I wonder, are we really believing for our miracle? If you're not, you need to. I believe your miracle is about to happen. Even if you're not looking for it!

This Shunammite woman was going about her daily business, just like you. With one difference – she gave to a man of God. You've heard it. . . "You can't out-give God." Well, you can't give to His servants without Him taking notice (Luke 6:38).

God knew the desire of her heart. . .and He knows yours! Just remember. . . "Giving is the Key"! It seems that when we are in need, we often forget to give. We become so focused on our needs we fail to see the needs of others. Yes, we need to pray. Yes, we need to believe and Yes, we need to confess a good confession. But we must also be watching for the opportunity to give.

She did what she could do, and then God did for her what she couldn't do for herself. Giving brought her in line for her miracle. Are you ready for Your Miracle?

. . . PRAYER . . .

Lord, give us vision that will enable us to see the opportunities that You have set before us. Allow us to give with a grateful heart, knowing that we can never out-give You!

. . . TODAY'S THOUGHT . . .

Keep your eyes and your heart open for the leading of the Holy Spirit. You never know – today could be the day for your miracle!

—Mike Cox
Pastor, Cornerstone Worship Center, Anniston, AL

October 5

FORGIVEN BY GOD AND BY OURSELVES

. . . how much more shall the blood of Christ, who through the eternal Spirit offered Himself without spot to God, cleanse your conscience from dead works to serve the living God? (Hebrews 9:14)

The ceremonies and sacrifices of the Old Covenant cleansed only the body, the flesh. This allowed humankind to participate in public worship and to escape the punishment of the Law. But the blood of Christ, through the Holy Spirit, enables us to "draw near with a true heart in full assurance of faith, having our hearts sprinkled from an evil conscience and our bodies washed with pure water" (Hebrews 10:22).

We are cleansed from our past sins, but are we *free* from a guilty conscience? As a counselor, I meet many people, both young and old, who carry the load of their past sins with them. They say they believe God has forgiven these sins, but they seem unable to forgive themselves. If we want to be truly freed from guilt, we must give up our arrogance and recognize that our forgiveness is not dependant on us, but rests upon the power of the cleansing blood of Christ. If the holy God of heaven and earth forgives us, who are we to hold on to guilt?

Let us lay aside our unbelief, receive the fact that we are cleansed, and allow Christ through the Spirit to purge our consciences so that we can joyously serve God. The Word admonishes us to forget "those things which are behind" (Philippians 3:13) and to "lay aside every weight, and the sin which so easily ensnares us, and let us run with endurance the race that is set before us, looking unto Jesus" (Hebrews 12:1-2). Like an Olympic runner racing for the prize, we must rid ourselves of the *excess baggage* of guilt lest our failure to appropriate the blood of Christ cause us to lose the race. We are cleansed by the *perfect sacrifice*. Let us go forth in the power of the Spirit to "receive the promise of the eternal inheritance" (Hebrews 9:15).

. . . PRAYER . . .

Father, thank You that I have heard the Gospel. Help me to accept forgiveness and live daily in the knowledge that I am fully cleansed by the blood of Christ.

. . . TODAY'S THOUGHT . . .

Christ's forgiveness frees me and the Holy Spirit empowers me to live joyfully *today*!

—Martha Dismukes
Professor, West Coast Bible College (retired)

October 6

JESUS IN THE FIRE

"Look!" he answered, "I see four men loose, walking in the midst of the fire; and they are not hurt, and the form of the fourth is like the Son of God." (Daniel 3:25)

It was just another Sunday. For me, that meant visiting churches, this time in another state. For my wife, it was juggling the many Sunday responsibilities of a large family. Realizing the risks of being away, I had developed the habit of driving home after an evening service so that there were fewer hours away from home. Just before daylight, I approached our country home, routinely looking for the security light suspended over the house. Seeing none, I presumed a burned-out bulb. Turning into a darkened drive, I found friends waiting to soften the news of a fire that had gutted our home.

Although our family was saved, the guilt of my absence was hard to bear. Sitting down among the rubble a couple of days later, I said to myself, "You drove all those hours just to be home if needed and you still weren't there!"

Certainly, I was thankful. I had walked through the rooms and imagined what the firemen may have found had the Lord been a few minutes later, but I was pained by what seemed to have been the ultimate failure. Then, it seemed, the Lord spoke peace to my mind: "Don't you think I can take care of your family better than you can?" I then envisioned Jesus walking through each bedroom, gently waking the children from their sound sleep. Finally, it dawned on me that I had been so consumed with doing God's things that I had excluded Him from the equation. I was so bothered about failing God, I had failed to trust Him. How is it that in our struggles, oftentimes we fail to see through the pain to the lessons?

. . . PRAYER . . .

Father, grant me the eyes to see Jesus through the flames; to view the lessons, not just the pain; and to return to You, my Creator, the care of my family, knowing that nothing can happen to us that violates Your love for us.

. . . TODAY'S THOUGHT . . .

Finding God's will is a process, not an event. What people or events will come your way that you can use to grow closer to God?

—Clyde M. Hughes
General Overseer, IPCoC

October 7

BECAUSE I LIVE

Because I live, you will live also. (John 14:19)

At the age of 30, the anticipation of graduating from Bible college and the untrodden road of ministry was thrilling. Graduation was special: my parents sat among the 4,000 who assembled, and I was the graduation speaker. Every aspect of the evening transpired as rehearsed. I caught my father's eye as I concluded the sermon. Silent communication passed between us.

During the next few days, my family and I prepared to return home to await ministerial appointment. Prospects were bright and I was in close proximity to my family, seen only intermittently for the last three years.

Two weeks later I sat alone in a tiny church office. Down the short flight of steps in front of the pulpit was a coffin. My father had suffered a heart attack on the trip home and had passed away. In the family conference, I had been asked to preach at his funeral. As the eldest son, I consented, but grief and a sense of inadequacy overwhelmed me.

I thumbed through my father's worn Bible and cried out in desperation. I sensed the awesome presence of the Holy Spirit. With a gentle compassion, the eternal Father held me until my spirit was revived. I was directed to Job 14:14 that Dad had underlined: "If a man dies, shall he live again?" The powerful message of the resurrection of Jesus Christ lifted me. Familiar passages of Scripture flooded my soul with fresh hope.

I did not walk to the pulpit that Mother's Day to open Dad's Bible and begin public ministry in my own strength. The same Spirit who will quicken believers on the day of His coming was the same Spirit who strengthened me to minister. I knew that where His Word went forth in the power of the Spirit, life and liberty would flow.

. . . PRAYER . . .

Father, thank You for the promise of the resurrection and the work of the Holy Spirit to dispel the shadows that Your presence might fill us with light.

. . . TODAY'S THOUGHT . . .

The comfort of the Holy Spirit does not remove the pain of life's disappointments. Instead, He directs us to our Savior and reminds us that His resurrection assures ours.

—Calvin T. Andrews

Pastor, Pentecostal Tabernacle, Cornerbrook, Newfoundland

October 8

STARTING AGAIN

"O house of Israel, can I not do with you as this potter?" says the Lord. (Jeremiah 18:6)

Although I grew up in a Bible-believing evangelical family, I had a highly liberal theological education, even doing a doctorate in liberal theology. I had experienced a call to ministry at the age of twelve and began preaching as a fourteen-year-old boy. I had never been told about the Holy Spirit and, as a theologian, I believed the Spirit ceased activity at the end of the Apostolic Age.

As a young pastor in London, I ministered to West Indian immigrants from the Caribbean Island of Jamaica, many of whom were Pentecostals. When I visited them, they always prayed with me, which my white church members never did, and they prayed as though they actually knew God personally. This was a powerful witness to me.

The day came when everything seemed to go wrong for me. I cried out to the Lord and was filled with the Spirit and everything changed in my personal walk with God and ministry.

Jeremiah's account of his visit to the potter's shop took on a new significance for me (18:1-4). He watched the potter's attempt to fashion a beautiful pot, but the clay would not run in his hands. Eventually he abandoned the hopeless task. He crushed that stubborn bit of clay. Perhaps Jeremiah expected to see him hurl it away into the dust. Instead, he put it back onto the wheel and patiently shaped it into another pot.

Through this incident, God gave a word to the prophet that this is how He treats His people. We all make mistakes and go wrong; but God in His love and mercy never abandons us. He remakes our shattered lives and fashions us into a man or woman in Christ whom He can use in His service and to His glory. "If anyone is in Christ," the apostle Paul says, "he is a new creation" (2 Corinthians 5:17).

. . . PRAYER . . .

Thank You, Father, that in Your great love You never abandon us, but You are always reaching out to save us and to enfold us in Your arms.

. . . TODAY'S THOUGHT . . .

We can never be so far away that we are beyond God's reach. When we go wrong, He patiently starts again to build us up.

—Dr. Clifford Hill
Director, Prophetic Word Ministries

October 9

CONSECRATED!

However, when He, the Spirit of truth, has come, He will guide you into all truth. (John 16:13)

Jesus promised that the Spirit would be sent to the consecrated class of the human family and would abide in the Church. By the Spirit we were begotten and have become heirs of all the exceeding great and precious promises that belong to the consecrated class.

Christ's disciples have crucified the flesh with all its desires and passions and have freely pledged to denounce the appetites of the fallen nature. The apostle Paul admonished us: "If we live in the Spirit, let us also walk in the Spirit" (Galatians 5:25). The Holy Spirit quickens us and perfects us to stand before God on the day of reckoning, but the Spirit can only perfect us if we are willing to walk by His precepts.

Vanity is a terrible sin that hinders the Christian's path. It deconsecrates the soul and leads us into troubles, provoking bickering, bitterness, and envy. But if we walk by the Spirit, leading us into all truth and righteousness, then we will not be vainglorious and haughty; instead, we will be sanctified, humble, meek, and correctable.

Each Christian is spoken of in Scripture as being the temple of the Holy Spirit. Paul asks, "Do you not know that you are the temple of God and that the Spirit of God dwells in you?" (1 Corinthians 3:16). Also, each congregation in worship might be seen as the temple of the Spirit in that he indwells it.

In Scripture, God was represented in the tabernacle by His Shekinah glory. Today, He is represented in all those who are led by the Spirit and walk in harmony with His will. Only the consecrated will be ready for the glories to be bestowed at His appearing. Let us cleanse ourselves so that we "will be a vessel for honor, sanctified and useful for the Master, prepared for every good work" (2 Timothy 2:21).

. . . PRAYER . . .

Holy Spirit, fill us with Your power. Guide our steps and build a fence around us. Indwell us as You did at Pentecost and propel us with power for service..

. . . TODAY'S THOUGHT . . .

Since the constant tendency of the flesh is to look downward, let us reinforce our heavenly desires with daily devotion (Colossians 3:2).

—Fedlyn A. Beason
Superintendent, COG, West Indies

October 10

EQUIPPED TO SERVE

Now when they saw the boldness of Peter and John, and perceived that they were uneducated and untrained men, they marveled. And they realized that they had been with Jesus. (Acts 4:13)

As a very small boy, I had tuberculosis. I left school uneducated and untrained. At age 20, still uneducated and untrained, I converted to Christ. My pastor had talked to me about miracles, so, one day, I said to him, "You talk about miracles. Can God give me an education?" Being a wise man, he pointed me to Acts 4:13.

Two years following my conversion, I was baptized in the Holy Spirit. I felt the power of God go through my being. God called me to be an evangelist with an emphasis on small towns and villages. I was told that I would be unable to attend Bible school because I was uneducated. God did not agree. His fire burned within me. I felt "fire shut up in my bones" (Jeremiah 20:9). Soon I had my first opportunity to preach—ten souls gave their lives to Jesus. I now had my credentials: "the Lord working with them and confirming the word" (Mark 16:20).

Since that time over 40 years ago, I have stood before world leaders, have preached the Gospel of the Kingdom to crowds of up to 40,000 in over 40 nations of the world, and have seen thousands come to Christ and many wonderfully healed. At Cambridge University in England, I spoke one and a half hours on the subject of faith. In different parts of the world, I meet people even now in prominent positions who were there in that meeting and speak of how God met them that day.

There are no limits when we surrender our lives to the Lord Jesus Christ and He gives us His Holy Spirit. In Acts 1:8, the word *dunamis*, "power," can also be translated "ability." The Holy Spirit gives us God's ability to do whatever He has called us to do. We are not limited by our natural ability.

. . . PRAYER . . .

Thank you, Father, for the power of the Holy Spirit that gives us Your ability to do whatever You ask us to do.

. . . TODAY'S THOUGHT . . .

God's power is unlimited and available to us. All is possible with God.

—Don Double
Good News Crusade

October 11

THE INVITATION

Behold, I stand at the door and knock. If anyone hears My voice and opens the door, I will come in to him and dine with him, and he with Me.
(Revelation 3:20)

God created man and woman to worship Him. He didn't need us to do anything for Him. His very nature is all-sufficient, but He chose to create us to fellowship with Him and to love Him. Like us, the creatures He made, he wants to be loved by choice.

Personal ads have become popular ways to seek relationships. If Christ were to put an ad in the newspaper, He could write, "The Fairest Among Ten Thousand, the Prince of Peace, and the only Begotten Son of the Father . . . seeks a relationship with Whosoever will . . . to be His bride, His church, His redeemed . . . has built a home (a mansion, really) to share with His bride . . . and He will be committed to her forever and always, never to be parted, even by death."

Those who answer His call can enjoy a relationship with God in this life and eternally. How do we form a relationship with the Almighty God, who to some seems so far away? By the Holy Spirit, who testifies of the Father and of the Son. He points us to Jesus and shows us His character. He helps us pray in accordance with God's will.

So, to deepen our relationship with God, we must yield to the Spirit. We can only yield as we recognize His voice. This comes by reading the Word, talking to Him, listening to Him, and developing a habit of relating to Him.

. . . PRAYER . . .

Lord, help me to hear Your voice today. As I walk in the Spirit, let me be a witness to others that You are Savior, Lord, and King.

. . . TODAY'S THOUGHT . . .

We're proud of many relationships and talk about them in our daily lives. Do the people with whom you're in contact know of your relationship with God?

—Alisa Coleman
Department of Communications, UTA, Arlington, TX

October 12

A LESSON ON FORGIVENESS

Then Peter came to Him and said, "Lord, how often shall my brother sin against me, and I forgive him? Up to seven times?" Jesus said to him, "I do not say to you, up to seven times, but up to seventy times seven."
(Matthew 18:21-22)

In every crisis is a lesson to be learned. I once learned a lesson through an experience that brought me nearest to emotional, physical, and spiritual collapse in 30 years as a Christian and 20 as a pastor.

Congregational leaders and others were saying and doing things that were damaging to the body and future ministry of the church. I preached a message of correction (2 Timothy 4:1-2). This message stirred so much anger that the church became a boiling cauldron. I had pastored the church for 16 years and had received at least 90% of the people into it, but now it seemed as though everyone was against me.

What could I do to stop this destructive thing from destroying my integrity, the name of the church, and this body of believers? I decided to apologize publicly. I was not convinced that I owed an apology (in hindsight, I should not have apologized), but, to calm the uproar, I stood several weeks later and apologized for the anger in which my corrections were delivered. My statement was: "If I have hurt you, please forgive me." I used the word "if" because I knew I had not offended everyone . . . but the response was, "You said *if*."

All the terrible things said to me and about me were magnified. Anger, bitterness, depression, and much more became my constant companions. I overlooked the lesson of forgiveness I now know.

What is the lesson? Forgiveness is grace we shower upon others. No one is required to ask another for forgiveness in order to be forgiven. According to Matthew 18:21-22, there are no requirements. Simply forgive. It is an act of will. Choose to forgive or not to forgive, but the latter choice leads to our own suffering.

. . . PRAYER . . .

Father, please help us to forgive those who offend us even as we receive forgiveness for our offenses to You.

. . . TODAY'S THOUGHT . . .

Let us today choose to release all unforgiveness from our lives.

—Clyde E. Johns

Pastor, International City, Warner Robbins, GA

October 13

I AM ONE OF THEM

But be doers of the word, and not hearers only, deceiving yourselves. (James 1:22)

While serving as a missionary and superintendent in Latin America, one experience stands out above the rest. The president of Colombia believed the Church of God was a false religion and severely persecuted it. He assigned a group of special police to find Overseer Moreno. He had him arrested and brought to his office, where he was questioned about his "strange religion." Finally, he was told if he did not recant he would be executed.

Brother Moreno refused to obey and told the president he would rather die than give up the Lord Jesus Christ. The president was so amazed that he asked him who was over the church and demanded the overseer come to Colombia to talk to him.

Early Saturday morning I received a call. Brother Moreno advised me of the circumstances and asked if I could come. I told him I would catch the first flight to Colombia. He told me to come praying because he did not know what was going to happen.

When I arrived in Bogota, Colombia, I was met by Brother Moreno and two police officers. We were taken directly to the president's office. He was respectful and asked me about our religion. As I told him about our loving heavenly Father, he began to cry. He said there must be something to this religion that a man would die before recanting. I told him he could go directly to Jesus for forgiveness of his sins. He buried his face in his hands and wept his way to Calvary.

The president sent out orders to every part of the country to cease the persecution of Christians, saying, "I too have received Christ into my heart. Now I am one of them."

. . . PRAYER . . .

I am thankful, Lord, for the timely ministry of the Holy Spirit. He is always there at the right time, to give the right instructions, and to issue the right equipment.

. . . TODAY'S THOUGHT . . .

We must always be ready to practice what we preach. We must be doers of the Word in order to influence the unconverted.

—Vessie D. Hargrave (Reprinted from *SpiritWalk: Daily Devotions on the Holy Spirit* by permission of Pathway Press)
World Missions Director, COG (retired)

October 14

THE HOLY SPIRIT—OUR EARNEST

. . . in whom also, having believed, you were sealed with the Holy Spirit of promise, who is the guarantee of our inheritance until the redemption of the purchased possession, to the praise of His glory. (Ephesians 1:13-14)

The word "guarantee" is translated "earnest" in the King James Version, a very common word in the market-places and in the transactions of buying and selling both today and in the days of the apostle Paul. The "earnest" is money or the portion of something given or done in advance as a pledge to bind a contract between two persons. It is a "down payment."

In Ephesians, the two persons are God and the believer. The earnest is the Holy Spirit. God is the Giver of the Holy Spirit to dwell in our hearts and to guarantee us all the redemptive rights purchased by Christ in His death and resurrection.

The bestowal of the Holy Spirit is God's part-payment of our complete salvation. Our salvation is justification by faith, sanctification by the definite and progressive work of the Holy Spirit; also, we are kept by the power of God and healed by the stripes of Jesus.

The practical side of having the Holy Spirit as an earnest from God is that He will lead us into all truth, teach us to pray, produce in us fruit to the glory of God, and enable us to be an effective witness for Christ. The gift of the earnest of the Holy Spirit to me was the giving of a little taste of Heaven. He was the Witness of my sonship. He was joy unspeakable and full of glory at the beginning of my salvation and continues to lead me into new and ecstatic experiences.

. . . PRAYER . . .

Father, I thank You for the earnest of the Holy Spirit that assures me that I have a mansion in Heaven.

. . . TODAY'S THOUGHT . . .

The presence of the Holy Spirit in us is a foretaste of Heaven and the glory we shall have when Christ comes.

—Cleo Watts
Pastor, COG (retired)

October 15

CONVERSION

For "whoever calls on the name of the Lord shall be saved." (Romans 10:13)

It was a time of revival and it was held in my family's backyard. Under conviction, my heart yearned for something I didn't have. When the preacher preached about eternity, I, being lost, felt lost. The Holy Ghost was convicting me of my sins.

I tried to pray in my own way, but I got nowhere. My mother and father had taught me the way of salvation so I knew that the Lord was dealing with me. I tried to put it out of my mind, but couldn't.

One night, the preacher asked for volunteers to form a prayer chain, each praying an hour a day. Not realizing what I had committed myself to, I volunteered. The next morning I felt good but, the closer my hour of prayer came, the worse I felt. I was to pray from 9:00 to 10:00 a.m. From 9:00 until 3:00, I tried to pray, but seemingly in vain. I was miserable, hurting, and felt like I would die.

My mother's time to pray was 3:00 p.m. I knew that if anyone could get a prayer through to God, she could. I went to her in the garden just before that time. I told her that I had been trying to pray for the last six hours, but that I couldn't. Then I told her that I wanted to get saved. She told me to kneel. There, in the hot sun, I knelt to pray and my mother began praying for me. I felt the forgiveness for my sins; my burden was gone.

In the evening service, I testified what the Lord had done for me. The preacher preached and gave the invitation and I wanted *more* of the Lord. The preacher told me to kneel and pray because what I needed was the Holy Ghost baptism. I started praying and lost sight of who was around me. Soon, the Holy Ghost started speaking through me. The Spirit had come into my life. What a wonderful experience! Everyone may have Him!

. . . PRAYER . . .

Lord, may those hungry for You accept and be filled with Your Spirit!

. . . TODAY'S THOUGHT . . .

". . . if you confess with your mouth the Lord Jesus and believe in your heart that God has raised Him from the dead, you will be saved" (Romans 10:9).

—Ezra K. Waldrop

Superintendent, Home for Children, Sieverville, TN (former)

October 16

HE LEADETH ME

The Lord is my shepherd; I shall not want. He makes me to lie down in green pastures; He leads me beside the still waters. He restores my soul; He leads me in the paths of righteousness For His name's sake. (Psalm 23:1-3)

I don't understand many things about the magnificent work of the Holy Ghost, but I am comforted in God's Word: "I will never leave you nor forsake you" (Hebrews 13:5). I have preached from Psalm 23 on many occasions and have given time and prayer to its study. Little did I realize that one day I would literally live it out.

While ministering in Liberia, West Africa, I was stricken ill. We were experiencing a very successful ministry. Many people were saved and sanctified, receiving the Holy Ghost, and miraculously healed in this ripened harvest. But after much distress, I returned to the United States and was taken to the University Hospital in Augusta, Georgia. I remained there 23 days. My case was very unusual. After several days in critical condition, the doctors diagnosed my case as valsiprin malaria and said that I would never preach again and certainly would never return to Africa. While lying there, though, God spoke to me: "You shall continue the work where unto I have called you."

During all of this, God was with me. He led me back to health and I have made many trips abroad. I still preach and continue to do the work of Missionary Evangelist.

I cannot explain the *why* of all things in the work of the Kingdom, but I am assured that He will finish His work. I am more determined than ever before. There comes a time in each person's life when he should stand aside so that God may use him until the work is finished. Isaiah 40:31 tells it like this: "But those who wait on the Lord shall renew their strength; They shall mount up with wings like eagles, They shall run and not be weary, They shall walk and not faint."

. . . PRAYER . . .

Now therefore, I pray . . . show me now Your way (Exodus 33:13).

. . . TODAY'S THOUGHT . . .

The harvest is not all in, but we will be reapers if we are faithful to the end. "Be faithful until death, and I will give you the crown of life" (Revelation 2:10).

—Ernest C. Moates
Missionary Evangelist COG

October 17

THE PRAYER OF FAITH

Therefore I say to you, whatever things you ask when you pray, believe that you receive them, and you will have them. (Mark 11:24)

My wife and I had been in the ministry several years when our second child, Sandra, was born. She had asthma and was in and out of the hospital many times. We moved to pastor the Boaz Church of God in Alabama, which is on Sand Mountain. Instead of getting better, she grew much worse. We were trusting the Lord: "If you abide in Me, and My words abide in you, you will ask what you desire, and it shall be done for you" (John 15:7).

At seventeen months, she entered the hospital yet again. The doctor informed us that she could not get worse. She might die, but she wouldn't get worse and live. Within the next fifteen hours she would make a change one way or the other. We called many ministers and saints of God to help us pray the prayer of faith according to James 5:15: "And the prayer of faith will save the sick, and the Lord will raise him up."

After seventeen hours, our daughter opened her eyes and told her mother she was hungry.

The doctor advised us to move from Sand Mountain in order for the asthma to get better. We were assigned to the church in Bessemer, Alabama. One Sunday, when Sandra was four years old, a woman whom we had never met told my wife that God was going to heal our Sandra that morning. The woman, my wife, and I laid hands on our daughter at the altar. She was instantly healed of asthma. Sandra is now 50 years of age and has never had another attack of asthma.

. . . PRAYER . . .

Thank You, Lord, for giving us the desire of our heart in the healing of our daughter and for keeping our two sons healthy.

. . . TODAY'S THOUGHT . . .

If we abide in Him and His words abide in us, the prayer of faith will save the sick.

—Dewey W. Smith
Pastor, COG (retired)

October 18

YEAR OF ENCOURAGEMENT

And let us consider one another in order to stir up love and good works, not forsaking the assembling of ourselves together, as is the manner of some, but exhorting one another, and so much the more as you see the Day approaching. (Hebrews 10:24-25)

Each year, through prayer and the direction of the Holy Spirit, the church has a special emphasis. In 1994 it was "The Year of Empowerment." In 1995, "The Year of Coming into His Presence." In 1996, "The Year of Encouragement."

While on a family vacation between Christmas and the New Year with our two sons and their families, our eldest son was skiing with his wife and children when a bad accident occurred. He was struck from behind by a man coming down the slope causing serious injury to his left knee that required three hours of extensive surgery.

Upon returning home for the Watchnight service and sharing in a time of washing feet and communion, my wife took the towels home for washing. We went to bed about 1:30 a.m. and turned off the washing machine. Upon getting up the next morning and stepping into the washroom area I stepped in water. The washing machine had leaked. So New Year's Day we bought a new washer and dryer.

Back to work on Tuesday our youngest son called with the word that he along with fourteen others had been laid-off that day on his job.

Wow! God! The "Year of Encouragement."

I preached the beginning of the series on encouragement. The church was going through a forty-day period of fasting and prayer. The enemy had come in like a flood, but God, we knew, was there with us through all of the trials and problems. It doesn't matter what life brings our way . . . God is greater than the problem. God spoke to me and I shared Psalm 46 with the congregation: in the midst of all the shaking and roaring, "Be still, and know that I am God" (v. 10).

. . . PRAYER . . .

Oh, God, in the midst of life and its experiences, help us not lose sight of Your presence and love.

. . . TODAY'S THOUGHT . . .

Be encouraged by each other, God's Word, and God's Holy Spirit.

—Bob K. Collins

Pastor, Newport News-Denbigh, VA

October 19

SPEAK, LORD, YOUR SERVANT HEARS

Now the Lord came and stood and called as at other times, "Samuel! Samuel!" And Samuel answered, "Speak, for Your servant hears." (1 Samuel 3:10)

The Lord told me to evangelize. I was on my way home from a funeral in Bonham, Texas, thinking of the many things you go through in working for God and His grace that brings you through them all. My wife had been confined to bed for six weeks following a severe heart attack, I had three small children, and I only had $500 to my name. But, it is better to obey and I had heard the Shepherd's voice.

I resigned my pastorate and went to Pasadena, Texas. We looked all over the city for a place to live with no positive results. Some friends knew some people who had a house for sale, but they were asking $1,000 equity. Although I didn't have that kind of money, we went to see the house anyway. As we were getting out of the car the Spirit came on us and we knew that the Lord was working for us. The first thing the owner said after we entered the house was, "My wife and I went to church last night and the Lord said we were to sell this house before the weekend because we are called to preach and we are leaving for Bible college this next week. So we agreed to let you have the house for $300 equity."

With the $200 left over, we bought a stove, refrigerator, bunk beds, table, and chairs. We needed a master bedroom suite, but all I had remaining was $20. We went to our brother's house to help him load his trailer for Bible school. When we filled the trailer, there was no room for his bedroom set. He told me, "Brother Ainsworth, I'm going to give it to you." I told him, "Brother, I have $20 left and I'm going to give it to you!"

So God performed a miracle in order to carry out His will. And, the first month's payment was found in a bank account we thought had been closed for years.

. . . PRAYER . . .

Thank You, Lord, for ordering our steps and then making a way to fulfill them through the power of Your presence.

. . . TODAY'S THOUGHT . . .

Listen to the Lord's voice and obey. He will make a way.

—W. T. Ainsworth
Pastor, COG, Houston, TX

October 20

INTIMACY WITH GOD

. . . that I may know Him and the power of His resurrection, and the fellowship of His sufferings, being conformed to His death. (Philippians 3:10)

The Apostle Paul's cry to know God echoes throughout the centuries and resounds in our time. It is a summons that comes from beyond the body and mind, a pursuit that has its foundation in the heart. It is a deep yearning to experience intimacy with God. His cry should be the quest of every true believer.

In spite of the tremendous ministry, educational abilities, and heritage of this apostle, we find him nearing the close of his ministry still desiring to find intimacy with God. We see the same desire in King David's life: "As the deer pants for the water brooks, So pants my soul for You, O God" (Psalm 42:1). Both men craved to know God.

The Hebrew word for "know" is *yada*, which means to know in an experiential way or to know through relationship. It is not a superficial or intellectual assent to facts. Rather, it is rooted in relationship that is intimate and centered in the heart. Genesis 4:1 illustrates: "Now Adam knew Eve his wife, and she conceived and bore Cain, . . ."

Today, the Holy Spirit beckons us to enter into this knowing as He reveals God to us. The outpouring of the Holy Spirit at Pentecost presented an invitation that is extended to every believer. It is a proposition to experience genuine spiritual union with God, a union that is personal and intimate. When we desire to know God in this way we will truly encounter Him and His fruit will be produced in and through us.

Our longing to experience God should exceed our salvific and sanctifying encounters. Our desire should match that of the Apostle. We should give strength to his cry as we imitate his devotion to know God. It is only when we know God intimately that we can become His transforming agents in this sinful world.

. . . PRAYER . . .

God, forgive me for my superficial desire for You. Please create in me a deep desire to know You intimately.

. . . TODAY'S THOUGHT . . .

The human being can only truly experience God through intimacy.

—Asbury Sellers

Department Executive, COG

October 21

A NEW RELATIONSHIP

. . . for they all shall know Me, from the least of them to the greatest of them, says the Lord. For I will forgive their iniquity, and their sin I will remember no more. (Jeremiah 31:34)

In this text, the prophet gives us the promise of a new relationship: we would "know" the Lord in a way that previously we did not know Him. The Lord sees us in our dilemma, knows our sin, and promises to forgive. He took the initiative to accomplish something for us that we could not accomplish for ourselves. He took the lead in establishing the relationship.

Robert Tuttle told the story about when he was in the third grade and accidentally wet his pants. How humiliating as his classmates would laugh at him and he would become an object of ridicule. But before anyone found out about his accident, a classmate, Susie, approached Robert carrying a fish bowl filled with water and goldfish, stumbled, and spilled the water into Robert's lap. With a lap full of water, no one could tell that he had wet his pants. Should Robert thank Susie or be angry with her? He did not know so he remained silent. The children began to make fun of Susie . . . not of Robert.

Later that day, Robert approached Susie. He had thought about her actions and knew that she had purposely wet him. He asked: "You wet me on purpose, didn't you?" She replied, "Yes." "Why?" Robert asked. Susie said, simply, "I wet my pants one time."

Robert knew Susie in a new way. He could only appreciate what she had done for him because he was not asked: she saw the opportunity and helped him, thereby establishing a new relationship.

God did the same thing when He sent Christ to forgive and restore us to Himself. We, like Robert, are covered with our own mistakes and sin, but Jesus voluntarily shed His blood for us. It fell right into our laps. No more embarrassment or humiliation—Jesus bore it for us.

. . . PRAYER . . .

Jesus, thank You for covering our sin. You provided a new relationship for us through Your sacrifice. I accept that sacrifice for my sin.

. . . TODAY'S THOUGHT . . .

Our relationship with God determines our spiritual strength.

—Gary Osteen
Pastor, Oakwood Gospel Tabernacle, Gainesville, GA

October 22

UNDYING HOPE

. . . looking for the blessed hope and glorious appearing of our great God and Savior Jesus Christ. (Titus 2:13)

The early church was guided and inspired by the hope of Christ's coming. This hope so enlightened them that they were able to live for Jesus in an age when it was just as easy to die for Him. What a powerful thought! A small band of believers who began in a tiny place under intense persecution passed this legacy through dozens of generations and across thousands of miles to the present day. *That's hope!*

These early believers did not receive the promise of Christ's return, but they were able to see it by faith and embrace it. They had a heavenly perspective, so the trials and temptations of their times could not shake them. They were able to confess "this world is not my home; I am just a stranger passing through." No circumstance could block their view of eternity.

In many ways, believers today, especially in America, face different challenges than those of the early Christians . . . *but we must stand firm.* God takes pleasure in giving His people all earthly blessings, but even in the best of times we must understand that this world is not our home. Keep a heavenly perspective. Look every day for the blessed hope of Christ's return and you will pass on to future generations His undying legacy.

No matter what you face today, God is able to make you stable in His purpose, pure in His holiness, and triumphant in your faith. Let the hope of Christ's appearing give you hope for today. Romans 8:24-25 says, "For we were saved in this hope, but hope that is seen is not hope; for why does one still hope for what he sees? But if we hope for what we do not see, we eagerly wait for it with perseverance."

. . . PRAYER . . .

Give me hope that sees beyond the natural world so that I can understand Your purpose and embrace Your eternal promise. No matter what I face, help me to live with expectation for Your return and to share this hope with others.

. . . TODAY'S THOUGHT . . .

Just as Jesus brought light into the world, you are God's minister of hope everywhere you go. Let Jesus radiate from within your heart.

—Eddie Mitchell
Director, Global Missions, The North Church, Carrollton, TX

October 23

A TREE OF LIFE

The kingdom of heaven is like a mustard seed, which a man took and sowed in his field, which indeed is the least of all the seeds; but when it is grown it is greater than the herbs and becomes a tree, so that the birds of the air come and nest in its branches. (Matthew 13:31-32)

The essence of being a Christian is to love God and our fellow human beings. When you first received the love of Jesus, the seed sprouted and started to grow in your heart. That seed grows until it captures every area of your life and reaches out from within you to others. A tree does not simply grow: it changes the atmosphere around it by providing food and medicine in its leaves and fruit, shelter during storms, shade from the heat, and life-giving oxygen to the air. From a small seed to a mighty harvest—*this is how God changes the world.*

The Father sent Jesus to save humanity. Jesus came into a hostile climate and declared the works and words of the Father. *He came to Show and Tell!* This heavenly Seed began to grow a mighty tree that would extend God's kingdom to the Israelites and to anyone else in the world who would believe in Him and receive His love.

You are a branch of the Living Vine. The love of Christ flows within you. Be bold for Christ. Extend His love to others and you will change the spiritual atmosphere. *Guaranteed!* The Lord will work *through you* to bring healing to the sick, food to the hungry, hope to the hurting, and a cool wind to the heated circumstances of life.

Plant a seed in your field and the Lord will grow a mighty tree that will advance His kingdom on earth. Follow Jesus' example of Show and Tell. "Most assuredly, I say to you, the Son can do nothing of Himself, but what He sees the Father do; for whatever He does, the Son also does in like manner. . . . I can of Myself do nothing. . . . I do not seek My own will but the will of the Father who sent Me" (John 5:19, 30).

. . . PRAYER . . .

Dear Lord, make me a mighty tree of righteousness today. Help me to follow You and release the love You have planted in my heart to others.

. . . TODAY'S THOUGHT . . .

Jesus' power within you creates a spiritual atmosphere that is fatal to the devil. Trust God and branch out!

—Dr. Lawrence Kennedy
Pastor, The North Church, Carrollton, TX

October 24

CAST ASIDE THE GARMENTS OF AFFLICTION

And he, casting away his garment, rose, and came to Jesus. (Mark 10:50)

In Biblical days, people wore garments to identify their conditions. The leper carried a bell and rang it whenever anyone approached, calling "unclean" to warn them. The blind carried a garment that identified them as blind so that people could watch for them and not trample them as they rode their horses or run over them with their buggies or wagons.

Bartimaeus was blind and wore such a garment. One day, as he sat by the highway begging, he heard a huge crowd coming his way. He learned that the cause was Jesus of Nazareth. He began to cry out to Jesus, "Jesus, son of David, have mercy on me." While the crowd demanded that he be quiet, he yelled all the more until Jesus heard his cry for mercy.

Notice that when Jesus told Bartimaeus to come to Him that he cast off his garment, arose, and went to Jesus. Such tremendous faith! He believed that when he got to Jesus, he would be healed. He did not think that he would ever need that garment again which identified him as blind. His begging days were over. His world of darkness was past. His sitting by the highway day after day choking on the dust of travelers was mere history.

Whatever your affliction or condition, realize that Jesus is the answer. He made provision for you at Calvary. Cast off your garments of discouragement, bitterness, criticism, darkness, unbelief. Rather than the garment of defeat, put on the garments of victory, joy, peace, healing, and deliverance. Jesus is calling for you to come and let Him bless you.

. . . PRAYER . . .

Deliver us from the garments that bind us, and deliver us from sin, sickness, and addictions. Please help us to put on the garments of praise and worship.

. . . TODAY'S THOUGHT . . .

Let us wear the garments that identify us as belonging to Jesus, the Son of David, as a testimony to what He has done in our lives.

—Robert Kayanja
International Evangelist, Uganda, Africa

October 25

WALKING IN THE FEAR OF GOD

Then the churches throughout all Judea, Galilee, and Samaria had peace and were edified. And walking in the fear of the Lord and in the comfort of the Holy Spirit, they were multiplied. (Acts 9:31)

How can we enjoy the peace of God in our hearts, grow in the knowledge of our Lord Jesus, and prosper in every area of our lives as the first century believers did? In this verse we clearly see the results of the ministry of the Holy Spirit in the church of the first century: peace, edification, and multiplication. What caused such wonderful results? The answer is found in the manner in which the early church walked. They walked in the fear of the Lord and in the comfort of the Holy Spirit.

In the Old Testament, God commanded Israel to fear Him and to keep His commandments (Deuteronomy 6:2). For the Israelites, to fear God meant to revere Him, to stand in awe, to recognize His power and position. The fear of the Lord is the beginning of wisdom (Psalm 111:10). King Solomon defined the fear of God as the hatred of evil, pride, arrogance, the evil way, and the perverse mouth (Proverbs 8:13).

The early church walked in the fear of the Lord because they walked in the comfort of the Holy Spirit. The word *comfort* means a calling alongside to help, to aid, to console, and to encourage. The Holy Spirit reveals evil, pride, arrogance, and perverse talk, around us and also within our hearts. He is the one who knows what is truly evil in God's sight. Without His help, we would be easily deceived.

Psalm 34:11 tells us that the fear of the Lord must be learned. In an age when the Holy Spirit is treated as a dispenser of power, gifts, and blessings, let us remember that the Holy Spirit wants to teach us the fear of God: hating evil, pride, arrogance, the evil way, and the perverse mouth.

. . . PRAYER . . .

Lord, here is a simple prayer: teach me to fear You.

. . . TODAY'S THOUGHT . . .

We can enjoy the peace of God, grow in His knowledge, and prosper in every area of life. The key is to learn the fear of the Lord.

—David J. Greco
Radio Vision Christiana, Wayne, NJ

October 26

CHANGED FOR GOOD

Therefore many of His disciples, when they heard this, said, "This is a hard saying; who can understand it?" . . . From that time many of His disciples went back and walked with Him no more. (John 6:60, 66)

You would think anyone, especially the Jews, who knew Jesus during his time on Earth would be instantly attracted to his teaching. Clearly, He was the long-awaited Messiah foretold by the Prophets. He was the one to restore Israel; the one to change the face of society.

And He did. The problem is, Jesus didn't change things the way the religious leaders expected. They wanted to remain in power. To follow Jesus meant they would lose everything they had worked to obtain. They refused to allow their lives to change.

Many followers enjoyed being in the company of Jesus. They marveled at the sick healed, the blind seeing, the deaf hearing, the demon-possessed delivered, and the dead brought back to life. They saw the multitudes fed, witnessed water turned to wine and the outcast accepted. It wasn't until Jesus wanted to change them that they had second thoughts. As long as Jesus was just the icing on the cake rather than the oven that baked it, things were fine.

It isn't until Jesus begins to chip away at the protected areas of our lives that we find His teaching hard. We don't like others correcting us, telling us what is right or wrong, not even God. Often we struggle in areas that need attention, but we've placed a "Do Not Disturb" sign on the door.

The crowd decided following Jesus required too much change in areas they were not ready to surrender, but the twelve disciples were too committed to turn back (v. 68). They allowed Jesus to enter into the depths of their hearts and make the necessary transformation. The changes Jesus made in them allowed them to change the world.

. . . PRAYER . . .

Lord, help me accept the changes that must be made in my life as You mold me into the person you desire me to become.

. . . TODAY'S THOUGHT . . .

Be one of the committed, not one of the crowd afraid to change!

—Odie Hume

Pastor, Covenant Church, Richardson, TX

October 27

KEEP IN STEP WITH THE SPIRIT

*I say then: Walk in the Spirit, and you shall not fulfill the lust of the flesh. . . .
If we live in the Spirit, let us also walk in the Spirit. (Galatians 5:16, 25)*

The call of the Holy Spirit to become an expatriate missionary implied for me a leap of faith into the unknown. Could I overcome such barriers as language, other world-views, and the needs of another people group? The Knower of my unknown assured me that His enabling and supportive powers far exceeded my relentless questioning.

Knowing that His people would face many unknowns, Jesus promised them the permanent indwelling, enabling, and supportive power of the Spirit in all dimensions and depths of their personal lives. Those who live by the Spirit will participate in the teaching and leading of the Spirit. Forty-three years of active ministry in many countries and cultures have shown me that keeping in step with the Spirit is a life, not a mindset. In every situation, He stirred and strengthened me by His indwelling presence to face and confront all the issues of the unknown.

Consequently, rather than grapple with unanswerable inquiries, I decided to make a life commitment to His guidance as He enabled and led me. Divine guidance began in the hidden laboratory of life, out of which issued the power that molded my will and shaped my character to keep in step with the Spirit.

By stepping into the unknown with the Spirit, an intimate communion sprang forth with Divine Life. What can be more intimate than this living-together-union between the believer and the Spirit? The All Knower, from within me, effectively guided my steps in complete harmony with His will to glorify Christ by fulfilling His unalterable call to "Go into all the world."

. . . PRAYER . . .

Father, I thank You for the assurance that as the Holy Spirit dwelt in Your Son and led Him, so He leads us also with Divine leading.

. . . TODAY'S THOUGHT . . .

He that would keep in step with the Spirit must yield himself to be filled with and controlled by the Spirit. After that, he will exhibit the filling and controlling of the Spirit through a new obedience to the Master's Great Commission.

—William D. Alton
Missionary Superintendent, COG

October 28

I KNOW THE THOUGHTS I HAVE TOWARD YOU

For I know the thoughts that I think toward you, says the Lord, thoughts of peace and not of evil, to give you a future and a hope. Then you will call upon Me and go and pray to Me, and I will listen to you. And you will seek Me and find Me, when you search for Me with all your heart. (Jeremiah 29:11-13)

I wrote a letter to the Lord 20 years ago that changed my life and destiny forever. I was just out of my teen years and although I knew and loved the Lord, there were things in my life that I knew He wasn't pleased with. I was struggling to end a dating relationship with someone I had no business dating in the first place. He wasn't a bad person, but we had different philosophies concerning God, family and church. I knew I must end this relationship no matter how painful it felt. Thus, my letter to the Lord was birthed and in it I poured out my heart to Him. "Lord, I would like to be with you and leave this old world, but what about all the people who don't know you? Take my life and use me. I know with your hand I can be in your perfect will."

I didn't realize the profound impact this letter would have on my life. I gave up the boyfriend and initially felt great loneliness and sadness. However, it was short lived. Little did I know that the Lord had a much better plan, what you may call my destiny. A few months down the road I met a young evangelist who had a heart for God and was destined for purpose in the Kingdom of God. We fell in love, married, set out for ministry, learned hard lessons along the way and now, 18 years and three kids later, have the opportunity to minister and sing to thousands over Christian Television. No, it hasn't always been easy, but God has continually been faithful.

I am so thankful for that letter I wrote the Lord over 20 years ago. The truth is that He's not looking for the best vessel, but for a yielded one. Let me encourage you to make the right decision today for it will change your destiny for tomorrow.

. . . PRAYER . . .

Father, let us put aside our willfulness and seek to please You in all things.

. . . TODAY'S THOUGHT . . .

Jesus said it best: Father, not my will, but Yours be done!

—Joni Lamb
Vice President, DTN, Dallas, TX

October 29

SETTING THE SAIL

And do not be drunk with wine, in which is dissipation; but be filled with the Spirit. (Ephesians 5:18)

After moving to Arizona to pastor, I took a weekend sailing trip in San Diego. Because it was my first trip to San Diego and my first time to sail, it was difficult for me to contain my excitement as we launched out into the bay. I quickly learned to recognize the distinct sound of the wind filling the sail. It was a sound that prepared me for the movement of the boat through the waves. That evening, the peaceful noise of the water and the picturesque sunset on the city provided a relaxing conclusion to a beautiful day.

My wonderful adventure in sailing closely parallels my spiritual life. In sailing, wind is everything. It is the breath of life for the journey. Without wind, sailing is transformed from joy to frustration.

Likewise, my spiritual life is dependent upon the powerful presence of the Spirit, the breath of God, in my life. Too often I have relied upon other sources to propel me to my goals. These sources leave a hollow sense of worth and accomplishment that is akin to the disappointment that comes when you are forced to rely upon a motor in a sailboat. In contrast, when we are filled with the Spirit we experience life with fulfillment that is unequaled.

As believers, we are given the opportunity to receive power and peace from a source that never ends. Will we sail or will we toil? Living a Spirit-filled life requires that we yield to the greatness of God and allow Him to be our Master. Let us discover the Spirit-filled life that is God's way of carrying us safely to our destination.

. . . PRAYER . . .

Almighty God, thank You for the power and peace that comes through Your presence in my life. Help me to surrender to Your sovereignty each day.

. . . TODAY'S THOUGHT . . .

Being filled with the Spirit is like discovering the wind in a sailboat. Be filled with the Spirit and receive God's power and provision for your spiritual journey.

—Paul L. Metler
Doctorial Candidate, Regents University

October 30

A FAITH TO FIGHT FOR

Beloved, while I was very diligent to write to you concerning our common salvation, I found it necessary to write to you exhorting you to contend earnestly for the faith which was once for all delivered to the saints. (Jude 1:3)

I came to the knowledge of what being Pentecostal was at the age of six. As I visited what later became my home church, I sensed there was something different about the church and its people. They sang differently, prayed differently, preached differently, and had fellowship together differently. They were loud, but reverent; zealous, but orderly; and emotional, but purposeful. To a six-year-old, they were frightening at first—like a family member you don't know very well—but they soon became warm and loving. I didn't ever want to leave them.

What was it that made me want to be like them? These people had a faith that was empowered and anointed by the Holy Spirit. They had something so powerful you could feel it when you got around them—something that would draw my brother and me to participate in the prayer lines. It was a power and a faith my brother would describe as "cool waters running all over me."

This is the kind of faith and power for which we must fight. This experience should not die out with any generation, but needs to be passed on from generation to generation. In our zeal to find "other" spiritual experiences, let us be careful to fight for and to hold on to the faith that was delivered to us by those who walked the road of righteousness before us. If our experience with God was worth praying for, receiving, and sharing, surely it is worth fighting off any devil, philosophy, or current trend that endanger our faith from being passed on to our children.

. . . PRAYER . . .

Thank You, Lord, for this glorious faith and experience I have received from You. May I always stay on guard against anything that would threaten its continued presence in my life.

. . . TODAY'S THOUGHT . . .

This faith was meant to be passed on. "For the promise is to you and to your children, and to all who are afar off, as many as the Lord our God will call" (Acts 2:39).

—Paul W. Nolan

October 31

HOPE IN GOD—OUR ANSWER

Why are you cast down, 0 my soul? And why are you disquieted within me? Hope in God, for I shall yet praise Him For the help of His countenance. (Psalm 42:5)

In a moment of bitter disappointment, the devil seemed to whisper behind me, "Does God really do all things well?"

Our first daughter, Judy, a graduate nurse, was on the staff of our church's mission hospital in the western sub-Arctic region of Canada. She met the young assistant pastor of the local church and they fell in love. The wedding date was set. She came home to prepare.

Nine days before the wedding, Judy was rushed to the hospital. Six hours of surgery followed. The next day the surgeon leveled with her mother and me: "You will have to postpone the wedding and she will probably never be able to have any children." That was the instant the devil struck his blow. In that moment of weakness, the thought pierced like an arrow: "Does God really do all things well?"

Parents can take pain and suffering, but it is sometimes more than we can bear when it happens to our children. The happiest time of a radiant young woman's life, the prospect of home and family—all seemed to be slipping away. Her tears tore at our heartstrings.

But in that dark moment, the Spirit reminded us of Psalm 42:5. We clung to that promise and God came forth in fulfillment: the doctor was wrong on both counts. The wedding proceeded as planned and the happy couple has now given us two of our five grandchildren!

Have you entered a dark time when the very foundations of your faith have been shaken and life seems unfair? Don't give up hope. Our unswerving confidence in God will enable us to "yet praise Him."

. . . PRAYER . . .

Father, thank You for the power of hope and confidence in Your love which carries us through every trial.

. . . TODAY'S THOUGHT . . .

God is weaving the pattern of our lives. We can see only the underside, but He sees its beauty. Hope in God!

—Gordon R. Upton
General Secretary and Treasurer (Interim), PAC

November 1

WHERE THE SPIRIT FLOWS

"But you shall receive power when the Holy Spirit has come upon you; and you shall be witnesses to Me in Jerusalem, and in all Judea and Samaria, and to the end of the earth." (Acts 1:8)

Desperately backslidden and suicidally depressed, I knew no place to turn. By Thanksgiving Day 1975, 1 was a hopeless shell of a man. The bitter drought in my own soul was producing its totally predictable fruit in what I brazenly dared to call my ministry. My preaching was of no effect. My prayers were hollow and futile. My marriage was poisoned with rancor. Despair, not thanksgiving, filled my heart that day.

An earlier attempted suicide was followed by a second. I knew that eventually I would succeed. I was afraid of myself and angry at my religion. I believed in Christianity, but it would not work for me.

Then on December 5, 1975, 1 learned about the Holy Spirit. At 4 p.m. that frosty December afternoon, I fell before God and asked for the full blessing of Pentecost. An explosion! An eruption! A tidal wave! I know that different people receive His Spirit in different ways, but He always comes with power!

Power for preaching was suddenly *real* to me. Power to live, to relate, to love, and to give filled our marriage. The power of His presence is a glorious promise. Without the Holy Spirit I am bankrupt and dangerous to myself and others. But where the Spirit flows there is power!

. . . PRAYER . . .

Father, thank You for the blessing of Pentecost and for the power You give me to live victoriously

. . . TODAY'S THOUGHT . . .

For ministry and for life, the promise of power is precious indeed. In a world of striving, laboring self-worshipers, the rested child of God moving in the power of the Spirit is an awesome sight. Ask and you shall receive power.

—Mark Rutland (Reprinted from *SpiritWalk: Daily Devotions on the Holy Spirit* by permission of Pathway Press)
President, Southeastern College of the Assemblies of God

November 2

THE SYCAMORE INCIDENT

And he sought to see who Jesus was, but could not because of the crowd, for he was of short stature. So he ran ahead and climbed up into a sycamore tree to see Him, for He was going to pass that way. (Luke 19:3, 4)

An executive of a well-known financial agency reaped handsome profits with little or no investment on his part. He was quite rich, but his peers were convinced his financial accumulation was obtained through questionable means. Although his face was well known in the city and he was influential in financial circles, few of the movers and shakers met him socially.

When the news was broadcast that a well-publicized celebrity was to visit the city, the executive interrupted his daily routine to see him. Jostling crowds met the popular personality, so the executive sought a viewing position above the throng by climbing a nearby sycamore tree.

As the celebrity arrived, the ludicrously perched executive received the shock of his life. The celebrity, a total stranger, looked up and called him by name, requesting accommodations at his house for the evening. Not only was this shocking to the executive, but also to the attending dignitaries, who viewed such action by the celebrity as totally out of character, especially since the executive was a member of a much-maligned organization.

The executive was a tax collector named Zacchaeus. The celebrity was Jesus of Nazareth, the Christ. Zacchaeus' chance meeting with Jesus, who invited him into a covenant relationship, changed the meaning of his vocation, his associates, and even his enemies.

. . . PRAYER . . .

0 Father, through the Lordship of Your Son and the power of Your Spirit, may our past be redeemed, our present be transformed, and our future be redirected in Your care.

. . . TODAY'S THOUGHT . . .

A New York City construction worker, upon viewing a famous painting titled "The Man of Galilee," stood in awe and adoration. Completely oblivious of the surrounding crowd, he removed his work-stained hat and said, "O Man of Galilee, You can count on me!" May it be so with each of us.

—Edward E. Shoupe
Chaplin, United States Army

November 3

FEAR VERSUS FAITH

But He said to them, "Why are you fearful, O you of little faith?" Then He arose and rebuked the winds and the sea, and there was a great calm. (Matthew 8:26)

When I was World Missions field representative for the Church of God, my wife and I were driving to the Wisconsin camp meeting when a drunk man pulled out of the line of traffic and hit us head on. My wife's arm was broken and she was badly bruised. My pelvis was broken in three places, my knee was shattered, and my lip was split. The pain I suffered was excruciating, indescribable, and unexplainable.

The devil attacked me in a way I had never experienced before. He filled the hospital room and was on my bed. He said, "You know there is no God, and even if there is a God, He does not care about your suffering and does not even love you. If He did, He would not put you in this place of pain and agony." At that moment, a fear came over me I had never felt in all my Christian life. The pain reached the unbearable stage. But, thank God, while I was praying, He gave me grace to withstand the devil.

God spoke to me and said, "Sing a song." A song I had heard years before came sweeping into my mind: "When your enemy assails and your heart begins to fail, Don't forget that God in heaven answers prayer; He will make a way for you, He will see you safely through, Take your burden to the Lord and leave it there."

I sang it twice. Fear was replaced by faith. I rebuked Satan and he left the room immediately. Angels came and sat on the bed with me as I rejoiced in the Lord. I sang the song loudly seven or eight times while doctors, nurses, and visitors came by and looked into my room. I was as happy as I will ever be until I reach my heavenly home. If I live to be 100, I'll never forget that experience.

. . . PRAYER . . .

Thank You, my heavenly Father, for the abundant grace You have given me to have faith regardless of all circumstances.

. . . TODAY'S THOUGHT . . .

Satan never tells us the truth and God never tells us a lie.

—Wade H. Horton
General Overseer, COG, Cleveland, TN (former)

November 4

A LIFE OF PRAYER

Pray without ceasing.(1 Thessalonians 5:17)

Although the Spirit-filled life is replete with miracles and unusual workings of God, there is a deeper aspect of this walk. The greatest miracle to the Spirit-filled believer is the daily fellowship and interaction of God's Holy Spirit on an intimate basis.

Many religions require their adherents to pray. But, none can promise the ever-present comfort, instruction, correction, guidance, and protection which Jesus' followers enjoy through the agency of the Holy Spirit. When we daily commune with God through prayer and Bible study, it's as if the Spirit "goes in front of us" and prepares our way in advance.

A friend once visited me in my office and begged for advice. His life, as he put it, was "falling apart," and he didn't know what to do. Since he was a Christian, I recommended that he significantly increase his daily time with God. Within a short time period, this person reappeared at my office with a markedly changed appearance. Even I was amazed at how God had changed his circumstances for the good.

Through daily prayer and fellowship with God, more is changed than just circumstances. God is allowed to change us into His likeness. And the more we pray, the more dependent we become on that time with God. Our "prayer life" becomes a "life of prayer," as the popular phrase goes. To me, that is one of the greatest joys of my Christian walk – my life with God in prayer.

A good friend and I share prayer requests often. We always seem to end up with the same mutual request: "Pray that I will pray."

. . . PRAYER . . .

Father, may I remember that nothing in Your kingdom is effectual unless founded upon sincere prayer.

. . . TODAY'S THOUGHT . . .

When I'm too busy to pray, then I'm simply too busy.

—Dennis W. Watkins
Director, Legal Services, COG Executive Offices

November 5

WORSHIPPING THROUGH SERVICE

But he who is greatest among you shall be your servant. (Matthew 23:11)

It was a beautiful summer day and several of our church members decided to go to a large Christian gathering. The joy and enthusiasm could be felt throughout the bus as we drove to the event.

Inside the auditorium, the music was grand and our hearts leaped with joy as we joined in the singing and excitement. While singing, I noticed a young mother whose eyes were full of pain and concern. Her young child had become ill and had begun to vomit violently. She leaped up, trying to hold the child's mouth and carry the child out as he dripped down the aisles of the building.

I found a lone maintenance lady. Gracefully, I informed her there was a rather large spill on the floor and the odor had begun to disrupt our worship. "You ought to see the mess in the bathroom," she said. "I am the only one here tonight." Then she reached into her cart and handed me a damp rag. She did not say a word but I knew what that meant. Stunned that she expected me to participate in the cleaning, I nevertheless took the rag (reluctantly) and started back.

I brought plenty of hand towels to share with the believers around me. To my surprise, all those around me, including my church members, did nothing but watch. It took about 15 minutes of intense scrubbing and revisiting the bathroom for more towels to clean up the entire problem. Then, Jesus gracefully whispered to me, "Who do you think is really worshipping—those who sing to Me or those who serve others while they sing?"

. . . PRAYER . . .

Thank You, Lord, for the lesson You taught me on the auditorium floor. Help me to have enough of Your grace to stoop to serve others.

. . . TODAY'S THOUGHT . . .

I learned more on the floor of that event about serving and the carnality of my own heart than I could have ever learned from a sermon. There was something about leaving the safety of my seat and touching something that was unclean that made me see a glimpse of how God often serves us and how we need to serve each other.

—Ricky R. Temple
Pastor, FGC, Savannah, GA

November 6

DIVINE PRESENCE

. . . as I was with Moses, so I will be with you. I will not leave you nor forsake you. (Joshua 1:5)

I was alone in the hospital room. The lights were out. All the family had left for home. "I will be back early in the morning," replied my wife, "Don't worry: I will be here before you go up for surgery." While lying in bed not able to sleep, my mind raced back and forth and questions popped up. Why do I have to go through this surgery? What did I do wrong? Why me?

It is true that I had prayed and fasted for my healing; but it had not happened. Now I faced surgery. The feeling of loneliness during this time was difficult for me to deal with. How could I cope?

During this time of my struggling, the Holy Spirit spoke so clearly to me: "In all of your time of serving the Lord Jesus you have never had to go through a time of real trouble. There have been no deaths in your immediate family and no real sicknesses. You have preached to many that the presence of the Lord and the power of the Holy Spirit would be with them during their time of trouble. After this experience of surgery, you will have a first-hand knowledge of what you say when you tell others that the Lord will be with them."

I will always remember the peace and serenity that came over me at that time. I went to sleep with the assurance that the Holy Spirit would be with me and that I had no need to fear. What a joy to know the same God who told Joshua "as I was with Moses, so I will be with you." Fear and worry were banished. I had the assurance that God would be with me. And when I tell others that the Lord will be with them during their time of trouble, I speak from personal experience.

. . . PRAYER . . .

Thank You, Lord, for the assurance and the presence of Your Holy Spirit that will be with us during our time of trouble.

. . . TODAY'S THOUGHT . . .

This promise was given to Joshua many years ago but it is still relevant for all today.

—Harold L. Jones
State Evangelism Director, COG, North GA

November 7

I NEEDED WHAT THEY HAD

And when they had prayed, the place where they were assembled together was shaken; and they were all filled with the Holy Spirit, and they spoke the word of God with boldness. (Acts 4:31)

My parents spent a lot of time in church and their boys always attended with them. All my life I watched people being filled with the Holy Ghost. Often the preacher would ask, "How many have been baptized in the Holy Ghost?" I always raised my hand along with the saints of the church because I came from a family that was known to be Spirit-filled. But I knew that I had never had a visitation of the Holy Spirit like others and had never spoken in tongues.

Feeling the call to preach, I traveled to Houston to Bible college. Everyone there was full of the Holy Ghost with evidence of speaking in other tongues. I knew that what they had was real and that in order to become a Pentecostal preacher, I must also be baptized in the Holy Spirit.

One night I sneaked off to the prayer chapel. I said to God and myself, "I won't leave until I am baptized in the Holy Spirit." I cried, prayed, praised, walked, knelt, and stood. Then suddenly the excitement of the Spirit flooded my soul and my lips began to speak words I did not understand. The strange words and my tears of joy let me know that God had baptized me in His Spirit. The influx of new spiritual strength made me certain I had advanced another step toward receiving all God's promises to me. I knew I wouldn't need to lie anymore: I had received what was needed.

The experience I felt that night has never left me. In travels around the world in ministry, it has helped me with a boldness to live many, many spiritual experiences.

. . . PRAYER . . .

Thank You, Lord, for giving Your Spirit to everyone who asks. You know just how to make life more enjoyable.

. . . TODAY'S THOUGHT . . .

God's blessings are available to everyone. People receive in different ways, but the same Spirit is always available. Never stop seeking.

—Robert W. Boyle
Pastor, COGoAF, Ramona, OK

November 8

GOD REALLY DOES CARE

Now when Moses went into the tabernacle of meeting to speak with Him, he heard the voice of One speaking to him from above the mercy seat that was on the ark of the Testimony, from between the two cherubim; thus He spoke to him. (Numbers 7:89)

One of the miracles in the lives of my wife and myself extends over a number of years. We were both employed in full time secular jobs and also led a Bible study. A young couple came to the study and prophesied that we would go into the ministry. We disagreed. We were comfortable doing the Lord's work where we were. Soon after, though, I found myself unemployed. We left for greener pastures.

We became involved in a small church. Again, I was laid off. At a church service, the speaker said that God's hand was upon Abraham to leave Ur, then to leave Haran until he went to Shechem. He said that God's hand was upon someone there that night. My wife and I both felt God speaking to us, so we said, "Speak Lord, for your servants listen."

We listed our house for sale. Because of many layoffs, the town was overloaded with houses for sale. We said, though, that if God wants us to go into the ministry, we would merely put a sign on the lawn. Our neighbour laughed at us, saying that it was a waste of time.

In December, I contacted the Bible college to attend spring semester even though the deadline was past. A few days later, the school president phoned to tell me to send the application immediately and that I would be accepted even though they did not know me.

We went to the city to look for a three-bedroom apartment. We had no success. Searching one last time, my wife felt the urge to contact a specific place even though it was closed. The superintendent was there, though, and agreed to wait for us. The apartment was exactly what we needed. Our house was sold within the week. Praise God!

. . . PRAYER . . .

Thank You, Lord, for being a compassionate, loving God, who is always attentive to our everyday human needs.

. . . TODAY'S THOUGHT . . .

As humans, we experience pain, sorrow, troubles and heartaches. But Jesus is the answer to all our needs. He cares. He really does.

—Berkley E. Nurse
Pastor, OBSCC, Wetaskawin, Alberta

November 9

WALKING FROM "THIS" TO "THAT"

Therefore be imitators of God as dear children. (Ephesians 5:1)

To walk in power we must know who we are in God. Find what the mind of the Lord is concerning you and follow Him.

God has something greater for us if we will be faithful. If God doesn't hold out the hope of greater things ahead, we will wallow in the hog pen when we could be living in the palace. The prodigal son left the hog pen when he determined, "If I can only get back to my father, I'll be better off."

You'll never leave "this" for "that" until you know "that" is better than "this." As long as you think "this" is all there is, you'll never let go and move to "that." If you're trapped in the middle of "this" and someone preaches to you about "that," all of a sudden you understand "that" is better than "this" and you'll leave "this" and run after "that."

When you walk with God, you are changed. Enoch walked with God, and was not (Genesis 5:24). When he started walking with God, he was. When the woman at the well met Jesus, she was an adulterer; as she continued with Him, she left adultery and became an evangelist.

God is a moving God. When God brought Israel out, they went from slaves to sons overnight. That's what happens when you get saved. Overnight you go from where you are to being a child of God. With every step, you get a little farther from what you used to be. The farther you walk, the farther away Egypt becomes.

Psalm 37:23 says, "The steps of a good man are ordered by the Lord, And He delights in his way." God will direct your steps if you'll walk with Him. He'll change you from glory to glory and from faith to faith and bring you out from "this" to "that."

. . . PRAYER . . .

Father, thank You for helping me say goodbye to the past so that I can follow You for all of my tomorrows.

. . . TODAY'S THOUGHT . . .

God is still working in my life. I choose to follow Him. I give up "this" for "that." I will come out of my situation if I keep walking with God.

—Mike Purkey
Pastor, AG, Lenexa, KS

November 10

UNEXPECTED

For the Son of Man has come to seek and to save that which was lost. (Luke 19:10)

It had been another of many Saturday nights at the smoke-filled barn dance. Alcohol flowed and couples danced the jitterbug to the blaring music of the local country band. At approximately 4:30 a.m., I staggered up the walkway of my parents' home, little knowing the drastic change that would occur in my life in the next 12 hours.

My newly converted father and sainted mother attended church services as I slept off a terrible hangover. They returned saying guests, including the pastor, were coming to lunch. I jumped out of bed and tried to look presentable enough to keep from embarrassing my parents.

As I finished lunch, the guests sang "When the Roll Is Called Up Yonder." The pastor engaged me in a conversation that led to spiritual things. Just then my "barn dance" friends drove into the driveway, so I went outside to visit with them. When they learned that a pastor was in the house, one commented, "I'm going to tell him where you were last night." I responded, "Come on in. He was just talking to me about the Lord." Hurriedly, the driver sped away and I returned to the house.

The conversation continued where we had left off earlier. Soon, the pastor asked if I would pray with him. Since he was a guest and preachers are supposed to pray, I agreed without a thought of praying myself. He prayed; he had others to pray; and suddenly and unexpectedly, I found myself praying. Tears of sorrow and guilt were flowing and I cried out, "Lord, save me!" He knew what I meant. He forgave my sins and delivered me from alcohol. The tears continued, but now they were tears of joy.

For more than 42 years, God's grace has sustained the relationship that began when an unexpected guest introduced me to my Savior.

. . . PRAYER . . .

Thank You, Lord, for people who are sensitive to Your Spirit and are willing to share Your love at unexpected times.

. . . TODAY'S THOUGHT . . .

Some unexpected happenings bring happiness; others sadness. In either, our Lord is present to accept our thanks or our petitions.

—Elwood Matthews
Director, Voice of Salvation, COGOP (retired)

November 11

JUST SAY, "YES, LORD."

But our God is in heaven; He does whatever He pleases. (Psalm 115:3)

I was sitting in a train in Washington, D.C., looking through a foggy window. For many years I had sensed a call on my life for ministry, but had put off answering it. I was now in my junior year of studies in business management and economics. I was 21 years old and on my way home to Charleston, West Virginia, from a discouraging eye examination in Baltimore, Maryland. I had always had poor vision, and now the word had come: "You have a hole in your retina." I was scheduled to see the finest retina surgeon in the world at Johns Hopkins Hospital.

There, sitting in that train car, I said, "Lord, if You will heal me, I will go to seminary and prepare for the ministry." Immediately I knew I was wrong. "I should be willing to go whether You heal me or not." At that instant the course of my life changed.

After unsuccessful eye surgery at Johns Hopkins, I began to take steps to obey God's call, finishing my business degree and eventually graduating from seminary and entering the pastoral ministry. Though I have experienced many miracles in my life, God did not heal my eyes.

Many times in life we come to points of confrontation with the will of a sovereign God. At these times we are tempted to try to strike a deal with God. It is much better simply to say "Yes, Lord." We simply need to obey God. We may not understand or even agree with God, but He knows the plan He has for us. It may be that He will not do what we want Him to do in the way we want Him to do it. But He is God. He has a right to rule and He loves us.

Since that day on the train, I have seen God directing my life as again and again I have come to times of decision. I have learned that I, as well as all of us, can trust Him!

. . . PRAYER . . .

To Your name be glory. You are the sovereign God. Thank You for Your love. Today, we say, "Yes, Lord."

. . . TODAY'S THOUGHT . . .

Our God is in heaven. He does whatever He pleases. It pleases Him to love and direct us.

—L. Dayton Reynolds
General Overseer, Elim Fellowship, Lima, NY

November 12

BE STRONG AND OF GOOD COURAGE

Have I not commanded you? Be strong and of good courage; do not be afraid, nor be dismayed, for the Lord your God is with you wherever you go. (Joshua 1:9)

My wife and I had faced many pressures and spiritual attacks for several months. A spirit of division had gotten hold of one of our dearest families. The pressures from the church, our radio ministry, and hard economic situations were really pounding our minds and hearts. One day we received letters from three listeners from three different cities. Each of them gave us the same Scripture to encourage us—Joshua 1:9: "Have I not commanded you? Be strong and of good courage; do not be afraid, nor be dismayed, for the LORD your God is with you wherever you go." These words were a clear message from God to us at a very critical time.

The command given to Joshua is filled with lessons for the Christian today. It is also a great promise that can be attained with His help. Just as Joshua had to expel the enemies from the land he was to possess, we must expel one of the greatest enemies of our soul: the spirit of fear. By doing so, we can attain spiritual victories. Getting to this place of victory is not easy, but it can be accomplished by living in obedience to God and His Word.

As we stay in His Word and obey Him, we will not be dismayed or live in fear. Fear is not God's will for His children. He has not given us a spirit of fear. God's command is to have courage because He is always with us. God will fulfill His promises in His time, which is always the best and right time.

. . . PRAYER . . .

Father, thank You for Your strength that is ours. Thank You because Your promises are for now and forever. You always make us triumph in Christ Jesus. I bless Your name!

. . . TODAY'S THOUGHT . . .

God's Word encourages us: "Fear not, for I am with you; Be not dismayed, for I am your God. I will strengthen you, Yes, I will help you, I will uphold you with My righteous right hand" (Isaiah 41:10). Be strong. He is with you today and always.

—Jose A. Reyes, Sr.
Spanish Voice of Salvation, COGOP

November 13

DON'T FIGHT THE BEES

So Samson went down to Timnah . . . and . . . a young lion came roaring against him. And the Spirit of the LORD came mightily upon him, and he tore the lion apart. . . . After some time, when he returned . . , he turned aside to see the carcass of the lion. And behold, a swarm of bees and honey were in the carcass. (Judges 14:5, 6, 8)

On his way to Timnah, Samson faced a lion *and* conquered it. When the time came for him to return and he passed by the place where he had met the lion, nothing remained but a skeleton. When Samson walked over to the carcass, he found a swarm of bees with honey.

Can you see a picture of your situation here? Your past contains only the skeletons of the hurts and failures you have experienced. The young lion that roared against you is only a skeleton if you have allowed the Spirit of God to come upon you and you have conquered it. Yesterday's mistakes are only skeletons today. They can't hurt you anymore.

The devil wants you to fear the future because of past failures, but he is a liar. Not only does God annihilate the young lions that attack and attempt to destroy you, but He also puts something sweet in the carcass for you.

Don't be afraid to look back. When God forgives you, covers your sins, and restores you, His Spirit will come mightily upon you. After you have ripped the lion apart, you can walk back and look the carcass in the face. You may have some places in your past you need to pass by and put into perspective. Don't be bluffed by the enemy and run in fear. Let go of the past and give it to God. He will turn your failures and hurts into something sweet.

. . . PRAYER . . .

Father, thank You for helping me conquering the lions of the past. Help me to face the future with faith, looking for the sweetness in the carcasses of yesterday.

. . . TODAY'S THOUGHT . . .

Don't fight the bees. They are going to bring something sweet into your life. Reach in and sweep out the honey. Let God bring good out of your bad situation.

—C. Herschel Gammill
Pastor, Cathedral of Life, Canton, OH

November 14

CHOOSING NOT TO GRIEVE

In this you greatly rejoice, though now for a little while, if need be, you have been grieved by various trials. (I Peter 1:6)

For some eighteen months beginning in January, 1992, my soul suffered grievously. During these months, I experienced the greatest weakness of my entire ministry. Having to contend with several leaders who viciously attacked my ministry left me feeling rejected, humiliated, and embarrassed. Grief overwhelmed me and daily I felt the pain of David in Psalm 32:4: "For day and night Your hand was heavy upon me; My vitality was turned into the drought of summer."

In utter despair I cried out to God for His healing power. But the Spirit spoke to me: "I cannot heal your grief." Shocked, I cried, "What do you mean You can't heal me of my grief? You can heal anything."

Gently, He spoke again: "Grieving is a choice of your will. When you choose to stop grieving, I will heal your pain." Instantly I arose and began to praise God as peace flooded my soul. Strength began to flow into my spirit and body as I obeyed His Word to me.

Shortly after this experience, God poured out His Spirit on our church and a citywide revival began and continued for seven weeks. On Halloween Sunday, 1993, more than 4,000 people of all faiths gathered in the Civic Center in Toledo, Ohio, and hundreds were saved by the blood of Jesus.

Often the choice of our will causes us to struggle and become weary. Grief, anger, doubt and worry are all choices of our will. Likewise, we can choose grace, peace, faith and trust.

Once David said, "I am weak, yet anointed." Though grieving for his son, he remembered the source of his strength.

. . . PRAYER . . .

0, Father, help me to be full of Your Spirit that I may with Your wisdom always choose Your good, pleasing, and perfect will.

. . . TODAY'S THOUGHT . . .

God's power in our lives is often limited by the unwise choices of our will. Understanding the difference between good choices and bad choices will often protect us from unnecessary pain.

—Tony Scott
Pastor, Cathedral of Praise, Toledo, OH

November 15

THANKSGIVING IN ADVERSITY

And do not be drunk with wine, in which is dissipation; but be filled with the Spirit, speaking to one another in psalms and hymns and spiritual songs, singing and making melody in your heart to the Lord, giving thanks always for all things to God the Father in the name of our Lord Jesus Christ. (Ephesians 5:18-20)

We pulled into the driveway and our son, David, jumped out of the van, onto his bicycle, and rode off singing, "Thank You, Lord, for Your blessings on me." His mother, Diana, and I stood with tears flowing as I asked, "How can he do it?" The doctor had just told us all that David's leukemia, which had been in remission, was evident again. But we knew how David could be so positive: The same God who sustained us, sustained him. David's faith was firmly fixed on the All-Powerful, All-Wise God. With the certainty of the painful and sickening regimen of treatments to begin the next morning, David was not singing a mournful "Why me, Lord?" but a melody of praise and thanksgiving.

Precedent is set in the Word for response to adversity. Paul and Silas were hurting from a fierce beating. They had been falsely accused and thrust into the inner prison. Their feet were securely fastened in the stocks. Yet they prayed and sang praises! Acts 16:25 states, "But at midnight Paul and Silas were praying and singing hymns to God, . . ."

Among the results of the Spirit-filled life are "singing and making melody in your heart to the Lord, giving thanks always for all things to God" (Ephesians 5:19, 20).

From his confident trust in God, David could sing thanksgiving to the Lord even in adversity. By God's grace, you can too!

. . . PRAYER . . .

God, regardless of the circumstances, we are secure in You. Please help us not to lose sight of Your oversight and abundant provisions when we are suffering. From a heart enabled by Your Spirit, we desire to keep on thanking and praising You.

. . . TODAY'S THOUGHT . . .

God has not promised that the circumstances will bring happiness every day, but He enables us to give thanks anyway because we know He is at work for our good and His glory!

—John A. Lombard, Jr.
Professor, Lee University

November 16

HANDFULS ON PURPOSE

Also let some grain from the bundles fall purposely for her; leave it that she may glean, and do not rebuke her. (Ruth 2:16)

In less than six verses in the Book of Ruth, three men have died and three widows are left to decide, "What do we do now?" A childless widow named Naomi and her two daughters-in-law must determine their destiny. Orpah kissed Naomi good-bye while Ruth held to her, rejected her own past and journeyed into an uncertain yet bright future.

Returned to Bethlehem, Naomi maintained a home while Ruth found employment in a harvest field that belonged to a man named Boaz. One day, Boaz noticed Ruth. Having a desire to see her succeed, he instructed his men to leave a larger portion of grain for her to reap as she worked the field. Boaz called these portions "handfuls of purpose."

Our Father has placed in our fields special "handfuls" of blessing, hope and love. God never works by accident so these measured blessings of God come to us at specific times to meet specific needs.

Once while in prayer, I asked the Father to send me a reminder that He had indeed directed me to a particular pastorate. It had been a difficult time and I was looking for a little reassurance.

After I returned to my office, I found a cake sitting on my desk, baked and brought by a sweet elderly lady in the congregation. A card she had written and placed within the box relayed this message, "Pastor, we love you. Please never doubt that God sent you to us."

The cake was my handful and I never doubted my assignment again. Your handful may come in the form of a song, a letter from a friend, a smile or a dramatic healing. Handfuls of God's care come in different sizes and shapes but they do come. He knows what field you're working in and He will be faithful to strategically place your next blessing where you need it most.

. . . PRAYER . . .

Father, please help me to work faithfully in the harvest and patiently await the next gift from Your hand.

. . . TODAY'S THOUGHT . . .

While some make it one day at a time, I have found that for many it's one handful to the next.

—Tim Hill

Administrative Bishop, COG in Southern OH

November 17

THE LIGHT OF THE LORD

For you were once darkness, but now you are light in the Lord. Walk as children of light (for the fruit of the Spirit is in all goodness, righteousness, and truth). (Ephesians 5:8, 9)

After Robin came home from school that Thursday, Wanda and I were able to enjoy one of those increasingly rare trips to the mall with our daughter accompanying us. While Robin and Wanda looked for clothing from store to store, I walked the mall.

I spotted the young man who had preached in our most recent youth rally. I stopped to have a chat with him, but the chat developed into a deeper Christian sharing. While we were talking, the place where we were standing suddenly became daylight bright. I immediately looked up to see what had happened. I discovered myself looking straight at the sun through the skylight. Bright sunshine! What a rare sight over Lynchburg skies during that past week! The young brother said, "I thought someone had turned a spotlight on us."

I began thinking afterward that God frequently uses light in His dealings with man. To make the earth habitable for man, God said, "'Let there be light'; and there was light" (Genesis 1:3). Psalm 119:105 says, "Your word is a lamp to my feet and a light to my path." And we think of judgment in terms of the white light of God's judgment. Thank God, our conversation was holy. That bright sunbeam was a quick reminder that God is up there!

. . . PRAYER . . .

Father I praise You for the marvelous light of Your love that shines upon us daily!

. . . TODAY'S THOUGHT . . .

"Let your light so shine before men, that they may see your good works and glorify your Father in heaven" (Matthew 5:16).

—Mack A. Shires (Reprinted from *SpiritWalk: Daily Devotions on the Holy Spirit* by permission of Pathway Press)
Pastor, Saxophonist, Bible Teacher

November 18

SPIRIT OF THE HOLY GOD

. . . I know that the Spirit of the Holy God is in you. . . (Daniel 4:9)

Daniel was a favorite character of my childhood. Although impressed by his prayer life, I especially liked how he survived the lions' den. Little did I realize the impact he would have on my later life. During a time of personal crisis, I rediscovered Daniel's secret.

Speaking to Daniel, King Nebuchadnezzar proclaimed, "the Spirit of the Holy God is in you." As crises plagued the Babylonian kingdom, God lifted up the prophet Daniel in the midst of chaos. God knew Daniel and His Spirit was in him.

Crises plague us today: the world, the church, the ministry, the laity . . . . all are in crisis. These crises, too, must be met with prophetic fervor by men and women in whom the Spirit of the Holy God lives. The need for Pentecostal prophets is greater today than ever before.

In *Fire From Heaven*, Harvey Cox reminded me that Pentecostalism offers a vital hope and an alternative vision of what the world should be and can be through Jesus Christ and the power of the Spirit. He pointed out that our Pentecostal foreparents were prophets of holiness and hope. This knowledge rekindled my passion for being a prophetic Pentecostal. From many outpourings, God's Spirit has moved across this nation from the mountains in the east to the coasts of the west, from the cotton mills of the south to the factories of the north, and ultimately to the nations of the world.

Our world, dominated by crises and chaos, cries out for hope. Souls are hungry for a new hope. Although I was ashamed to be called a Pentecostal during my teenage years, God has now placed within my heart a desire to be one of the many needed Pentecostal prophets of hope who will rise up and take their rightful place in today's society through Jesus Christ and the power of the Holy Spirit.

. . . PRAYER . . .

Lord, help us as Pentecostals to arise with prophetic fervor through the power of the Spirit of the Holy God that is in us.

. . . TODAY'S THOUGHT . . .

As Pentecostals, we must take our rightful place in today's society as beacons of hope in the darkness of sin, despair and hopelessness.

—Robert D. McCall
Coordinator, Missions Publications, COG

November 19

ASSURANCE

I will say of the Lord, "He is my refuge and my fortress; My God, in Him I will trust." (Psalms 91:2)

The knot in my neck had become quite large and irritated. Habitually, I would rub it throughout the day. Finally, out of increasing concern, I visited my doctor. He responded that a diagnosis could not yet be made and that I would need to see a surgeon and have a biopsy taken. It could then be determined if the knot was malignant or benign and a decision could be made. I took the information but, for some reason, could not seem to bring myself to make an appointment.

Several weeks passed and I was alone in the sanctuary of the church that I was pastoring, praying about the services for the weekend. I had been in prayer for some time when suddenly the enemy came in and whispered, “You have cancer and are going to die.” Immediately I felt fear such as I have never known. I seemed to be frozen by fear. I continued in prayer thinking I would “pray through” the situation and find peace. However, it seemed my prayers were now getting no higher than my head. At once I felt compelled to rebuke the enemy. I told him I knew who he was and from whence he came. I continued by telling him that I knew he had the power to afflict my body but that he did not have the power to take my life, for that power alone was in the hands of God. Suddenly a boldness came over me and I continued by telling him, “I may die, but this one thing I know: I am not going to die until God says it is enough.” Instantly I felt peace and victory sweep over me and I continued in a time of rejoicing and thanksgiving.

I was not instantly healed. Several weeks went by and, as I arose one morning and reached up to rub the knot, it was gone! Was it cancer? I do not know. I *do* know that God assured me He is very much in control. My life is in His hands: “Surely He shall deliver you from the snare of the fowler And from the perilous pestilence. He shall cover you with His feathers, And under His wings you shall take refuge; His truth shall be your shield and buckler” (Psalm 91:3-4).

. . . PRAYER . . .

Thank You Father that in You 1 have nothing to fear.

. . . TODAY’S THOUGHT . . .

He is able to keep that which is His.

—Ron Martin

Administrative Bishop, Rocky Mountain Region, COG

November 20

HELP IN DISCOURAGING TIMES

Now the Lord spoke to Paul in the night by a vision, "Do not be afraid, but speak, and do not keep silent; for I am with you, and no one will attack you to hurt you; for I have many people in this city." (Acts 18:9, 10)

It was a tough day. My world felt like it was coming apart. I prayed for God to send a ministering angel to me to help me through a very difficult time. He spoke to my heart through the Scripture and reminded me that in discouraging times God gives us the following.

Peace. "Do not be afraid." He is the peacemaker. Jesus said, "Peace I leave with you, My peace I give to you; not as the world gives do I give to you. Let not your heart be troubled, neither let it be afraid" (John 14:27). He is the peace that passes all understanding.

Proclamation. "But speak." He encouraged me to continue doing what I was doing. Satan tries to hinder the work of God by discouraging us, but we must keep on keeping on.

Promise. "For I am with you." What consolation to know that even in the heat of the battle, He is there. He will not leave us nor forsake us. God is on our side.

Protection. "No one will attack you to hurt you." God assured me that He was my protection from the dangers and hurts of life. He will quench the fiery darts of the wicked. He is my refuge.

Partnership. "For I have many people in this city." The Holy Spirit lifted my spirit and reminded me of the strength that is in the fellowship of my brothers and sisters in the Lord. I was made aware of the importance of true fellowship more than ever before.

The Lord taught me that day always to look up because one can depend on God to give help in discouraging times. He is the true Savior.

. . . PRAYER . . .

Father, thank You for being our source of courage in difficult times. You are always there.

. . . TODAY'S THOUGHT . . .

One writer said it so well when he said, "Tough times don't last, but tough people do.

—Jerry A. Smith
Director, Home For Children, Raleigh, NC (former)

November 21

GOD'S HEALING TOUCH

Then Moses and the children of Israel sang this song to the Lord, and spoke, saying: "I will sing to the Lord, For He has triumphed gloriously! The horse and its rider He has thrown into the sea! (Exodus 15:1)

As a young pastor in my twenties, I experienced life-threatening consequences of what should have been a normal surgery. Ten days following the surgery, it was discovered that my abdomen was full of infection; at one point, I was told that I had only 90 minutes to live. The surgeon performed another emergency surgery in an effort to save my life. For the next several days my life was in the balance.

My parents, Pastor and Mrs. Watson Argue, were traveling as missionary evangelists at that time. Several hundred miles away from me, they received a phone call from a man in the church I was pastoring. He told them that they must come quickly if they wanted to see their son alive.

My mother's habit was to take critical needs like this to the Lord in intercessory prayer. During an intense time of prayer, the Lord spoke and gave to her the text above: "The horse and its rider He has thrown into the sea!" My mother knew that this was God's promise.

She obtained space on the next flight and within hours was at the hospital. For fear of further infection, I was kept in isolation. She entered my room wearing the protective clothes required. Although I was in a semi-conscious condition, I sensed a presence in the room. She walked to my bedside and whispered: "This is your mother. I've prayed through and God has given me the assurance of your well being." She then quoted to me the Scripture above and continued: "This is also the song that the saints are going to sing around the throne of God as promised in the book of Revelation. This is God's assurance for you."

From that moment, healing, strength and restoration were mine. I am a testimony of the promise, "He sent his Word and healed them."

. . . PRAYER . . .

Thank You, Lord, for your promises that are true and your power that is great.

. . . TODAY'S THOUGHT . . .

Dire circumstances provide yet another opportunity for God's power to be shown and victory to be won.

—Don Argue
President, National Association of Evangelicals

November 22

RECOVERY

"Now David was greatly distressed, for the people spoke of stoning him, because the soul of all the people was grieved, every man for his sons and his daughters. But David strengthened himself in the Lord his God."
(1 Samuel 30:6)

While David and his men were away, the Amalekites invaded Ziklag and burned the city. They took away as captives the wives, sons, and daughters of David and his men.

Today the enemy has attacked our families and has taken many of our family members captive. We need to do as David did: we need to strengthen ourselves in the Lord our God.

God's message to us who have suffered loss is to pursue. We must not stop praying for and talking to our loved ones whom the enemy has captured. "So David inquired of the Lord, saying, 'Shall I pursue this troop? Shall I overtake them?' And He answered him, 'Pursue, for you shall surely overtake them and without fail recover all'" (1 Samuel 30:8). What a wonderful promise to David and his men who had suffered such tremendous loss.

Today the enemy is beating up on ministers and their companions for the children who have gone astray. The same God who blessed David to recover his family will do the same for us. 1 Samuel 30:19 says, "And nothing of theirs was lacking, either small or great, sons or daughters, spoil or anything which they had taken from them; David recovered all."

You, too, can have a revival of recovery. The Scripture said David wept until he had no more power to weep. Perhaps you have wept for your family members in the same fashion. Encourage yourself and receive strength from God. The God that answered David's desperate need can and will meet your needs as well.

. . . PRAYER . . .

Dear Lord, strengthen me and help me to have faith for my family members who are unsaved.

. . . TODAY'S THOUGHT . . .

Jesus said to him, "If you can believe, all things are possible to him who believes" (Mark 9:23).

—Orville Hagan
Director, International Evangelism Department, COG

November 23

THE LORD, MY SUFFICIENY

And He said to me, "My grace is sufficient for you, for My strength is made perfect in weakness." Therefore most gladly I will rather boast in my infirmities, that the power of Christ may rest upon me. (2 Corinthians 12:9)

Sometimes we preachers feel the need to defend our position—our "apostolic authority." Paul defended his apostolic authority in 2 Corinthians 11:5; and there have been times when I have had to dig my heels in and defend my authority as a God-ordained minister of Christ's gospel. Such times are never pleasant; in fact, for me such times are a last resort. After 47 years in the ministry, I am certain of this: the gospel ministry is no place for the faint hearted, timid man or woman. As Paul reminded young Timothy, "God has not given us a spirit of fear" (2 Timothy 1:7).

The ministry is no place for the individual afraid to face tough times; tough times simply come with the territory. Paul knew well about tough times, much more so than most preachers today. But Paul also knew something else and that "something else" is what sustains a God-called minister in tough times. In the midst of all his tests, tribulations, and tough times, Paul cried out to God for deliverance. It was then that he heard the assuring voice of the Lord, "My grace is sufficient for you, for My strength is made perfect in weakness."

When Paul later spoke of glorying in his weakness, he was not speaking of weakness as we commonly think of it. Rather, he was boasting of the total sufficiency of his Christ. He fully understood what our Lord meant when he said, "Without Me you can do nothing" (John 15:5*)*. He also knew by personal experience what he would one day write to the Roman believers, "Yet in all these things we are more than conquerors through Him who loved us" (Romans 8:37).

. . . PRAYER . . .

Lord Jesus, thank You today for the total sufficiency of Your grace.

. . . TODAY'S THOUGHT . . .

Today, I confess with Paul: "I can do all things through Christ who strengthens me" (Philippians 4:13).

—Herman L. Smith
Pastor, Desert View, Tucson, AZ

November 24

NEVER TOO LATE!

He who calls you is faithful, who also will do it. (1 Thessalonians 5:24)

"Gordon, it's for you!" My wife, Jacqueline, stood in the doorway with a surprised look on her face. The phone had rung as we were packing our last few belongings onto a rented U-Haul truck. "Who is it?" I shouted back while I squeezed on the last remaining boxes. "I don't know; they are calling from some place in Nova Scotia."

I had finished three years of ministry training at Eastern Bible College in Peterborough, Ontario, along with a year at Trent University. I felt I had done all I could to prepare for the pastorate, yet nothing had opened for us. Seven years earlier God had called me at the ripe old age of 30 to prepare for pastoral ministry. "But God," I argued, "I'm too old to go back to school. Can't I serve you as a Christian businessman?" The call got stronger and stronger.

After three years of intense struggling, I finally submitted. My wife and I sold our business and home in Sussex, New Brunswick. With our two small children, Monica and Tim, we moved a thousand miles away to the lovely city of Peterborough. As my wife worked to support us, I gave myself to full-time study. God marvelously met our needs—often in the nick of time.

Now, in the spring of 1981, I had given up hope of full-time ministry. I decided to return home to pick up where I left off. But God had different plans! At the last minute, the phone rang. On the other end of the line was the chairman of the deacon board of the Lockeport Pentecostal Church in Nova Scotia. From fifteen hundred miles away came the invitation: "Would you come and preach for a call?" The next Sunday, my family and I received a unanimous vote to be the pastor of my first church. A week later we were unpacking the U-Haul truck at our new parsonage. Oh, the faithfulness of God, who is never too late!

. . . PRAYER . . .

Thank You, Lord, for Your faithfulness. You always come through in the nick of time.

. . . TODAY'S THOUGHT . . .

Don't be anxious. God hasn't forgotten you. The answer to your prayer is already on the way. Do your part and He will do His.

—Gordon B. Henry
Pastor, Eathurst, New Brunswick, FGCC

November 25

THE MIRACLE OF PERFECT LOVE

There is no fear in love; but perfect love casts out fear, because fear involves torment. (1 John 4:18)

Anxiety can debilitate our spirit and body so easily. While lying in a Fort Worth, Texas hospital a few years ago, anticipating a heart angiogram, I was overwhelmed with fear.

For a few hours the fear that I was experiencing was very real. The fear that gripped me caused me to dread the night which seemed to be moving unusually slowly. Suddenly the Spirit brought a Scripture to my mind. "There is no fear in love; but perfect love casts out fear" (1 John 4:18).

Realizing God was endeavoring to grant me peace in a time of crisis, I made an altar in the hospital room. In prayer, I experienced something I had never experienced before. I experienced an inexpressible peace.

The joy and peace of mind I received drove out the fear. I slept peacefully the entire night.

The medical procedure went smoothly the next day and the doctor's report was excellent. There was no heart disease.

Thank God!

. . . PRAYER . . .

God, grant to us the wisdom and sensitivity to hear Your voice in times of crisis when fear seems to be overpowering us. Then, we shall receive peace from You.

. . . TODAY'S THOUGHT . . .

Today's problems cannot be greater than God's blessed promise to keep us in all things. For if God be for us, who or what can be against us.

—Bob Bohannon
Pastor, COG, Lubbock, TX

November 26

GOD'S REMEDY FOR TROUBLESOME TIMES

And the Lord God of their fathers sent warnings to them by His messengers, rising up early and sending them, because He had compassion on His people and on His dwelling place. But they mocked the messengers of God, despised His words, and scoffed at His prophets, until the wrath of the Lord arose against His people, till there was no remedy. (2 Chronicles 36:15-16)

Growing up in the South is an experience every one should have. Mom, Dad and five children made up our household.

Occasionally, one of the children would get sick. That's when Mom and Dad sprang into action. To prevent colds and influenza, we wore medicated cloths on our chests. For cuts, a piece of fatback was placed on it and the injured spot was wrapped with cloth. If we stepped on a nail or a sharp object, the punctured area was washed, beaten with a paddle, fat-backed and wrapped. The grand finale for us was castor oil that was taken twice a year as a cure-all for whatever was wrong.

If remedies were used as a cure-all for whatever ailed us, and if the home-prescribed medication made us well again, how much more will God's remedy relieve us from our troubles. The Psalmist said, "This poor man cried out, and the Lord heard him, And saved him out of all his troubles" (Psalm 34:6).

The world was in trouble. Sin was the order of the day. Many remedies were brought forth: the blood of bulls, the ashes of heifers, sheep and lambs, oxen and rams, pigeons and doves, meal, and the fruit of the ground—but all these were a shadow of the remedy that was to come.

What the Law could not do, because it was weak through the flesh, God accomplished by sending his own Son in the likeness of sinful flesh. He condemned sin and Jesus became its remedy.

. . . PRAYER . . .

Our Heavenly Father, thank You for sending Your best remedy, Your Son, Jesus Christ, who became the propitiation for our sins, and not for ours only, but for the sins of the whole world

. . . TODAY'S THOUGHT . . .

Accept God's remedy today that fulfills His plan of salvation for your life.

—Wallace J. Sibley
Director, Cross Cultural Ministries, Cleveland, TN

November 27

GOD'S CHOICE IS BEST

Who is the man that fears the Lord? Him shall He teach in the way He chooses. (Psalm 25:12)

It was a Sunday night in 1980. My pastor finished his message by saying, "If you are frustrated because you don't see God answering a prayer or solving a problem, come forward for prayer." So I went forward. After praying, I returned to the piano. We then sang a chorus:

Not what I wish to be or where I wish to go.
For who am I to choose my way?
The Lord shall choose for me, 'tis better far I know.
So let Him bid me go or stay.

As the song ended, the Lord spoke to me: "Are you willing to go?" My heart answered, "Lord, You choose." I knew that He was waiting to see if I would choose what he had chosen for me. I was to be ready to go.

My husband and I had lived in this community for almost twenty years. He had pastored two churches, but now was in business for himself and away from the church. I had a great teaching job at a nearby university. What did "go" mean? Was I to go to another university? Was Paul to leave his business? Where were we to go? What were we to do if we left? So much was going through my mind. Like Mary, I pondered these things in my heart and told no one.

Nothing seemed to change for months, but God was working. The business world was losing its charm for Paul. God sent three ministers into his life to minister to him. All three had a part in our "going," even though none of us recognized it at the time. In less than a year, Paul had recommitted his life to the Lord. Through a series of miraculous works, he was back in the ministry and pastoring a church. God provided a position for me in a university in the new town to which we moved.

I think of that song often. God wonderfully prepared my heart to make the right choice as I sang it that night. I can say that going has been "far better" for both my husband and myself.

. . . PRAYER . . .

Lord, I know that when I commit it to You, You will guide my choices and me.

. . . TODAY'S THOUGHT . . .

God always works for my best. If I am willing to listen, He will guide me in my choices so that my choices coincide with His.

—Alvis T. Harthern

Pastor, Grace Covenant Church, Carrollton, GA

November 28

BEYOND MY DREAMS

And it shall come to pass in the last days, says God, That I will pour out of My Spirit on all flesh; Your sons and your daughters shall prophesy, Your young men shall see visions, Your old men shall dream dreams. (Acts 2:17)

I heard the Gospel as a teenager and found Christ as my Savior. My parents were not born again Christians and they did not encourage me in my new-found faith, but neither did they hinder me. So life was a mixture of the reality of Christ's love and the dreams and illusions of a teenager wrestling with all the temptations teenagers struggled with then and today.

I reckoned that if it was the job of the Holy Spirit to glorify Jesus, I needed more of the Holy Spirit. So I began to seek the Lord. One day I began to sing in a language I had never heard and never spoken before. I had never been to a Pentecostal church!

I am now privileged to lead one of the larger New Churches just outside London and a network of churches that contains more than 10,000 people. Along with my colleagues Roger Forster and Lynn Green, God planted a seed that created a dream to see millions marching for Jesus across the world, praying for revival of Pentecostal Christianity. "March for Jesus" was born and is already a part of our history.

We cannot be committed to Christ unless we are committed to the things to which He is committed. Christ is committed to His Word, to the Gospel, to the very rich and to the terribly poor. Whenever the Gospel is lost to a nation or to a people group, it is always lost to the movers and shakers and disenfranchised. We must pray for revival, but we must also prepare for revival. It is a preparation of heart, of mind and of relationships to accommodate God's future in the earth.

. . . PRAYER . . .

Thank You for dreams that can be purged of pretense and unreality and that can be filled with Christ's love and power for the people around us and for the nations of the world.

. . . TODAY'S THOUGHT . . .

The key to turning dreams and aspirations into fulfilled achievements is development. God grant us the gifts, friendships and encouragement to develop our dreams for Jesus Christ.

—Gerald Coates
Pioneer, Surrey, England, UK

November 29

PENTECOSTAL HERITAGE: HELPING THE HURTING

These things I have written to you who believe in the name of the Son of God, that you may know that you have eternal life. (1 John 5:13)

In an effort to fulfill the Pentecostal commands of Christ in Acts 1:8, I contact thousands of sick, lonely, and hurting people each year in hospitals, dwellings and nursing homes. I encounter many people who have been so inadequately discipled and so poorly established in the Word that they are often overwhelmed with an almost complete lack of sound biblical assurance of their salvation.

No one has sufficiently taught these spiritually suffering Christians that (1) God "desires all men [*none excluded*] to be saved and to come to the knowledge of the truth (1 Timothy 2:4); that (2) "The Lord is . . . not willing that any should perish but that all [*all*] should come to repentance" (2 Peter 3:9); and that (3) "there is no other name [*no church, no ritual, no organizations—just the Lord Jesus*] under heaven given among men by which we must be saved" (Acts 4:12).

These distressed believers have not been clearly and emphatically informed that (1) every time they come to the Lord in prayer, they are responding to a drawing of God's Holy Spirit (John 6:44); that (2) Jesus draws "all peoples [*none excepted*] to Myself [*Jesus Himself*]" (John 12:32); that (3) He, Jesus, promised never, ever to reject anyone who comes to Him (John 6:37); and that (4) all one has to do to be saved is to call "on the name of the Lord" (Romans 10:13), confess and repent of his or her sins (1 John 1:9, 2:1-2; Luke 13:3-5). Jesus never made it difficult for anyone to be saved (Luke 18:10-14; Luke 19:7-10, John 8:3-11; Luke 23:39-43).

. . . PRAYER . . .

Lord, thank You that we can all receive Your salvation as easily as this tax collector! "And the tax collector . . beat his breast, saying, 'God, be merciful to me a sinner!' I [Jesus, "Emmanuel . . . God with us" (Matthew 1:23)] tell you, this man went down to his house justified [saved from sin]" (Luke 18:13,14).

. . . TODAY'S THOUGHT . . .

One's Pentecostal witnessing for Christ, confessing that "Jesus is the Lord" and that "Jesus is the Son of God," confirms the indwelling of God the Father and God the Holy Ghost (1 Corinthians 12:3; 1 John 4:15).

—Dr. Charles R. Beach
Professor, Lee University

November 30

A MAGNIFICENT OBSESSION

That I may know Him and the power of His resurrection, and the fellowship of His sufferings, being conformed to His death, if, by any means, I may attain to the resurrection from the dead. (Philippians 3:10-11)

Nowhere else in Paul's writings does he express such joy in knowing Christ as in the Philippian letter. What was the secret of this man? He knew what it was to be in union with Christ in death, burial and resurrection.

Ultimately, Christianity is the ability to react to any situation in life as Jesus Christ would react. Though in prison when he wrote, Paul was living in triumph. He was living above circumstances. He saw from God's standpoint. As a man often at the pulpit, serving as pastor of an active, growing church, and meeting publication and appointment deadlines, I want to know Paul's secret!

Paul's secret is found in his knowledge. Paul had knowledge of Christ Jesus: "that I may know Him." Not know *about* Him, but *know Him*. Paul had knowledge of the might of the Man: "and the power of His resurrection." Resurrection power is power wrought in Christ when He was raised from the dead. Paul had knowledge of His mission: "the fellowship of His sufferings." Not suffering *for* sin or *for* Christ, but suffering *with* Christ, being identified with the heartthrob of the Son of God for a lost world. Jesus died not simply to save us from suffering, but that our suffering may be like His.

How can we be conformed like this? By getting a personal knowledge of the Man, His might, and His mission to a suffering world. This is personal faith appropriating the principle of dying with Him to be raised to show the Man, His power and His mission.

A magnificent obsession is the answer to victory in the life of the believer!

. . . PRAYER . . .

Father, empower me by Your Spirit to show You, Your might, and Your mission to those I come in contact with each day.

. . . TODAY'S THOUGHT . . .

The way to triumphant living is found through a personal knowledge of Christ.

—Herbert F. Carter
Academic Dean, Heritage Bible College

December 1

PERSEVERANCE

Indeed we count them blessed who endure. (James 5:11)

One of the greatest lessons that I have learned in life is *perseverance.* Webster's Dictionary defines it as, "To persevere even with obstacles." However, I define it simply as, "Don't give up."

If you don't give up, you can't be defeated. Winners don't quit, and quitters don't win. That reminds me of such Scriptures as Matthew 24:13: "But he who endures to the end shall be saved"; and Ephesians 6:13: ". . . and having done all, to stand"; and 1 Timothy 6:12: "Fight the good fight of faith, . . ."

It is extremely important that you persevere over the right things at the right time. Both are important. This is where being led by the Spirit and walking in God's will are so vital. If you know that what you are attempting is God's will, then keep on keeping on no matter what it looks like. Why? Because God knows what it looks like on the other side. "He who promised is faithful" (Hebrews 10:23). Where God guides, He provides.

But there is a difference between a "good thing" and a "God thing." Sometimes it is not wise to continue on with something that is not working even though it may be a good thing. Only if you know that God has led you to do it do you persevere beyond circumstances. In other words, you can't force something to be God's will. For major decisions, you must have a *rhema* word from God!

Then there is timing. God's plan not only involves persons, places, and things, but also timing. God has a perfect time and it is up to you to find out what that time is. Sometimes you are too early or too late. Then, you must remember that discretion is the better part of valor. Know when to fight and when to back off.

Finally, when you persevere and fight, be led by the Spirit. Recharge your spiritual battery by getting into His presence.

. . . PRAYER . . .

Lord, help us to follow your will and to persevere to the end.

. . . TODAY'S THOUGHT . . .

The combination of perseverance and the anointing of the Holy Spirit can help you do great things for the kingdom of God!

—Marcus D. Lamb
President, DTN Dallas, TX

December 2

MEEKNESS IS NOT WEAKNESS

But the meek shall inherit the earth, And shall delight themselves in the abundance of peace. (Psalm 37:11)

"Life isn't what happens to you, but how you respond to it!" "If life gives you lemons, make lemonade!" Although these statements are generally good, many times responding in a Christian manner is very difficult. People, even Christians, can be cruel to us. Our loved ones can be abused. We can be persecuted and have lies and gossip spread about us. Under such circumstances, it is difficult to respond meekly.

We misunderstand meekness when we define it as weakness, as *allowing anyone who comes against us to abuse us.* We have often done great harm to our families and to other Christians when we expect them to accept abuse. Jesus was meek, but never weak. He became angry. He drove out the money lenders. He stood His ground against those who sought to subvert His work.

Jesus was meek, but powerful. He submitted to the Father's will in meekness, but he effected the Father's will in power. True power (and, thus, true meekness) is the ability to be God's servant and to effect God's will. True power requires God: it is victorious, purposeful living found only in and brought about only by the Lord.

Meekness is not denying that we are angry or that abuse has not occurred. That is deceit. It *is*, however, constantly critiquing ourselves and our attitudes, constantly asking ourselves if our motives are pure, constantly questioning whether we are responding with the attitude of Christ and in the power of the Holy Spirit. It means that love is our standard and that nothing less than love is sufficient. It means that we submit our pride and stubbornness to God and allow Him to transform them into humility and self-giving. It means that we allow God to respond in us and through us so that in the worst of circumstances God can receive glory and honor.

. . . PRAYER . . .

Father, help me to respond to evil with a Christian attitude and in the power of the Holy Spirit.

. . . TODAY'S THOUGHT . . .

Don't confuse meekness with weakness. The meek resist evil through the power of God, resisting the spirit of vengeance.

—Vardaman W. White

Director, Pentecostal Research Center (former), Cleveland, TN

December 3

FROM BARRENNESS TO FRUITFULNESS

So you shall serve the Lord your God, and He will bless your bread and your water. And I will take sickness away from the midst of you. No one shall suffer miscarriage or be barren in your land; I will fulfill the number of your days. (Exodus 23:25-26)

God wants to bless you. He is not the author of barrenness, which is part of the curse.

The Old Testament records the story of Rachel. She was barren. To be barren was the worst curse that could befall a woman. What was her response? She cried out in Genesis 30:1, "Give me children, or else I die!" Such should be the response of anyone who is barren. "Give me children, or else I die!" Such should be the response of the Church today. "Give me souls, or else I die!" Such should be the response of Christians everywhere. "Make us fruitful or else we die!"

God can bring from barrenness amazing fruit. From Manoah's barrenness came the great judge Samson and from Elizabeth's barrenness came John the Baptist, the forerunner of Christ. From barrenness God brings world changers!

As humans, we often embrace barrenness. We claim it as our own. That is the *opposite* of what we should do. "Sing, O barren, You who have not borne! Break forth into singing, and cry aloud" (Isaiah 54:1).

Are you barren? Then sing. Rejoice. Praise God. Have a party. Expect a miracle. Do everything *but* accept the barrenness! In fact, in Isaiah 54:2 God tells the barren to "Enlarge the place of your tent, . . ."

In the movie *Field of Dreams*, the famous phrase is, "If you build it, they will come." Let us rephrase that: "If you prepare for a miracle, it will come." If you enlarge your tent, the children will come. If you expect fruit, the fruit will come. If you believe that God will turn your barren desert into a garden, then get ready to pick the fruit off the trees!

. . . PRAYER . . .

Lord, let us reject barrenness, expect fruitfulness, and praise you at all times!

. . . TODAY'S THOUGHT . . .

God desires to bless us. Desire fruitfulness, worship God in every circumstance, and prepare for the blessings God is about to perform.

—Jentezen Franklin
Pastor, Free Chapel Worship Center, Gainesville, GA

December 4

WE CAN

Then Caleb quieted the people before Moses, and said, "Let us go up at once and take possession, for we are well able to overcome it." (Numbers 13:30)

Such simple words: We Can. Yet how many are unable to say the words without adding "'t" to it?

The Israelites camped on the edge of the Promised Land. All they had to do was go in and take it; simply trust God to do as He had promised and possess the land.

But they added "'t" to "we can." They turned a positive into a negative.

Twelve men went into Canaan to check it out. Upon returning to the camp, the people gathered around to hear their report. It was an amazing land, flowing with milk and honey, rich and fertile. Can you hear the "oohs" and "ahs" of the people? Can you see their smiles? The excitement in their eyes?

But then came the rest of the report: the cities are walled and well fortified; the inhabitants are huge, making us seem as grasshoppers in comparison! In short: *we can't!*

One of the twelve, Caleb, spoke. "We can." We can take the land. We can trust the Lord. We can possess what God has given us.

Why did most say "we can't" and Caleb say "we can"? They all saw the same things, but their attitudes were different. Caleb (and Joshua) were positive; the others were negative. The two saw opportunity; the ten saw obstacles. The two had set their direction: "Let us go up at once and take possession. . . ."; the ten were content to stay where they were. The two were focused; the ten were split between desire and fear. The two said "we can." The ten added "'t."

Caleb and Joshua did not give up. Forty years later, after the doubters had died in the wilderness, the two entered the Promised Land. The others could, but didn't. The two could, and did.

. . . PRAYER . . .

Lord, thank You that when You say we can, we can!

. . . TODAY'S THOUGHT . . .

Accept the promises of God, trust the Lord, and be positive.

—Jack A. McClure
Pastor, COG (former)

December 5

BREATH PRAYER

But those who wait on the Lord Shall renew their strength; They shall mount up with wings like eagles, They shall run and not be weary, They shall walk and not faint. (Isaiah 40:31)

While majoring in spiritual formation pursuing a D.Min. at Asbury Seminary, I was required to have a spiritual director. My director was Ron DelBene, an Episcopal priest. Although he is one of the most respected and sought after leaders in the spiritual formation movement, my response was: "What can an Episcopal priest teach a Pentecostal about spirituality?" But Ron was asking the Lord "why," too. Ron is truly a spiritual person and he raised my spiritual awareness acutely.

One lesson he taught me was the ministry of breath prayer. Now I share it with you. First, how do you address God? Father? Lord? Jesus? Another name? Consider your address, then write it on a 3x5 note card. Next, if God were standing before you and asked you what *one* thing He could give you, what would you answer? Your *first impression* is what is from your heart. Write this answer down on the note card, too. Now, carry this note card with you at all times. Look at it throughout the day. Pray the prayer. I have found it helpful to place reminders in strategic places. A useful method is to peel off the sticky colored dots you can buy at an office supply store and place them on the telephone, refrigerator, microwave, mirror, speedometer, computer, or wherever you would easily encounter them. When you see the dots, pray your prayer. For example, when the phone rings, pray first, then answer the phone. Or before you open the refrigerator for a snack, pray.

Prayer becomes breath prayer when you look at the prayer reminder and pray without saying, "I have to pray." When you breathe, you do not say, "Breathe in, breathe out"; you breathe naturally. Prayer should become as natural to every child of God.

This exercise will revolutionize your prayer life, as it did mine.

. . . PRAYER . . .

Lord, we humans often take the wind of the Spirit for granted. Help us to breathe more perfectly in harmony with the Spirit that we may breathe out Your inspiration to others!

. . . TODAY'S THOUGHT . . .

Use breath prayer to slow down and seek first God's kingdom.

—G. Charles Satterwhite

Pastor, First Methodist Church, Brewton, AL

December 6

SPIRIT BAPTISM: A CRISIS EXPERIENCE

He said to them, "Did you receive the Holy Spirit when you believed?" And they said to him, "We have not so much as heard whether there is a Holy Spirit." (Acts 19:2)

I take no issue with my Christian brethren who do not have the same understanding of the person and work of the Holy Spirit as I and other Pentecostals do. However, I'll never forget my experience of receiving the Baptism.

I was around 14 years old when my dear old grandmother, Agnes Crouch, in her long black dress with white starched cuffs and gleaming blue eyes, literally made me get on my knees to seek the Baptism. She said, "Son, you've just got to receive the baptism in the Holy Spirit with the evidence of speaking in tongues."

Just a young boy, I wasn't nearly as excited about receiving the baptism in the Holy Spirit as she was about my receiving it. But that precious saint of God prayed for me until she prayed the "glory" down. I'll never forget as long as I live that night when I received the enduement of power from on high.

I call it a crisis experience, because it is a crisis of the will. One must yield oneself completely. It is also a crisis of faith. One receives the baptism in the Holy Spirit by faith, not by intellectual reasoning.

Finally, it is a crisis of commitment. One is endued with power for service in the kingdom of God.

The pertinent question to ask yourself today is, "Have I received the Holy Spirit since I believed?"

. . . PRAYER . . .

Heavenly Father help me today to submit my will completely to Your will and by faith claim the promises of Your Word.

. . . TODAY'S THOUGHT . . .

The first step in knowing God's will is being willing to accept it, whatever it might be.

—Paul Crouch (Reprinted from *SpiritWalk: Daily Devotions on the Holy Spirit* by permission of Pathway Press)
President, TBN

December 7

NEVER GIVE UP

". . .He cried with a loud voice, Lazarus, come forth. And he who had died came out. . . (John 11:43-44)

The family of Lazarus thought they would not see him again on earth. He was dead and buried. There are families today whose unsaved loved ones seem as unreachable as Lazarus was to Mary and Martha.

Lazarus and unsaved loved ones share many things in common. Lazarus was beyond the voice of his family. Many unsaved loved ones have no contact with their families. Lazarus was in bondage (bound with grave clothes) and blind (his face was bound with a napkin). Unsaved loved ones are in bondage to Satan and he has blinded them to the truth of the Gospel (2 Corinthians 4:4). The family of Lazarus was grieving for him. Families with unsaved loved ones grieve for the lost.

Prayer to the Father is often the only thing that links a family to an unsaved loved one. Never Give Up praying and thanking God for the gift of salvation. Just as Lazarus responded to the voice of Jesus, lost loved ones can still respond to His voice today. The voice of the Spirit can penetrate their spirits. And just as Lazarus was restored to his earthly family, unsaved loved ones can be restored to their earthly families if they choose to respond to the voice of the Holy Spirit.

Remember Jesus' words to Martha: "I am the resurrection and the life. He who believes in Me, though he may die, he shall live" (John 11:25). Jesus assured her that if she would believe, she would see God's glory (John 11:40); so today God hears the prayers of the saints for their unsaved loved ones and assures them that "whatever things you ask when you pray, believe that you receive them, and you will have them (Mark 11:24). It is God's desire that all men be saved and come to the knowledge of the truth (1 Timothy 2:4). Never Give Up.

. . . PRAYER . . .

Father, thank You for raising up the Lazarus' we are holding up in prayer and restoring them to everlasting life. Speak to the hearts of our unsaved loved ones. We believe they will choose Your gift of salvation and we thank You.

. . . TODAY'S THOUGHT . . .

Never Give Up. Pray believing that you receive and then thank the Lord continually for the answer. The repentance of your loved one will bring joy not only to you, but also to the angels of God.

—Diane E. Willcocks-Owens
Co-Director, Life Through Faith Ministries Intl, Dawsonville, GA

December 8

OIL FOR A MIDNIGHT CRISIS

"And at midnight a cry was heard: 'Behold, the bridegroom is coming; go out to meet him!' Then all those virgins arose and trimmed their lamps. And the foolish said to the wise, 'Give us some of your oil, for our lamps are going out.'" (Matthew 25:6-8)

Crisis situations are simply a part of human experience. Regardless of how we may plan to avoid emergency, there will still be times in which we will find ourselves cornered and in need of divine assistance, needing what I call "a mid-crisis anointing."

In Scripture, oil was often used to illustrate the influence and activity of the Holy Spirit. In the Old Testament things were anointed as a symbol that they were being set aside for the purpose of God.

The parable of the ten virgins deals with the mindsets and conditions that shall surround the return of Christ. The ten experience a midnight crisis hour as the bridegroom returns. Although all had lamps, access to oil, and the knowledge that the bridegroom was soon to come, five were prepared and five were not. The difference between success and failure is that the five wise virgins had oil in their lamps, which caused their lamps to burn. They had oil for a midnight crisis.

Holy Spirit anointing is not just for great services when we soar from one mountain of splendor to the next. It is not just a euphoric feeling to dance under and to make us feel good. No, the anointing is also to help us through the crisis hour. It can make the difference in determining whether we burn out or burn on. My experience shows me that the anointing is even greater during the crisis hour.

The anointing is like time-release multivitamins stored in the body until there is stress, then arising when needed. If you are going through a midnight crisis today, may that anointing God has placed in you provide new strength today. May you have "Oil for a Midnight Crisis."

. . . PRAYER . . .

Lord, anoint me with fresh oil until the storm passes over.

. . . TODAY'S THOUGHT . . .

"It shall come to pass in that day That his burden will be taken away from your shoulder, And his yoke from your neck, And the yoke will be destroyed because of the anointing oil" (Isaiah 10:27).

—William A. Lee, Jr.

National Evangelist, COG, Cleveland, TN

December 9

FRIENDS IN HIGH PLACES

"Then Jacob awoke from his sleep and said, 'Surely the Lord is in this place, and I did not know it.'" (Genesis 28:16)

To each new generation God must reveal His plan. In Jacob's case, this was not so easy. He was smothered and mothered at home. His own brother was so mad at him he wanted to kill him. Jacob's own father wanted him to leave home and go live with a relative. All this was God's way to get Jacob just where He wanted him to be.

After leaving home, Jacob had the ground for his bed, a stone for his pillow, and the heavens for his room. Jacob found out that every lonely spot is God's house filled with angels. It was in this difficult situation that Jacob discovered he had Friends in high places. There's a new song entitled "Friends in High Places." It says: "I was in need and I needed a Friend. I was alone and I needed a hand. I was going down but someone rescued me. I walk by faith and not by sight. If things go wrong it'll be all right. Cause someone greater is watching over me."

As Jacob lay upon the ground, he had a dream in which he saw a ladder that reached from earth to heaven. At the top of this ladder, he saw the Lord standing above watching over all things concerning his life and future. Someone greater is watching over us all. Someone greater is interested in every detail of our lives, including yours.

The next morning Jacob went on his journey. First, though, he made a vow to God and named the place Bethel, or "House of God." The heaviness of leaving home had lifted. The uncertainty of his future had been answered. The presence of God had raised his spirits.

The Psalmist said of the Lord, "But You, O Lord, are a shield for me, My glory and the One who lifts up my head" (Psalm 3:3). Right now make that your confession.

. . . PRAYER . . .

Regardless of my situation, I have a friend who will never leave me nor forsake me.

. . . TODAY'S THOUGHT . . .

Even if things are going wrong, everything will be all right, because Someone greater is watching over you.

—Buddy Barron
Evangelist, Gainesville, GA

December 10

A SINNER'S PRAYER

And whatever things you ask in prayer, believing, you will receive.
(Matthew 21:22)

My search ended in 1978. It took me through drugs, elicit sex, Mormonism and the occult, until one day our family was invited to a small Pentecostal church in the hills of Grass Valley, California, to watch a "Christmas Program."

My father warned us about "Holy Rollers," which naturally meant that I had to find out more about it. The Christmas play needed a lot of work, yet somehow God used it to draw me to Him. In that building there was much more than four walls. The tangible presence of the Holy Spirit filled that place and for the first time in my life, I felt love; not a love that tried to get anything from me, but a love that came to give.

Six months later I went down to the altar and prayed this prayer: "God, if you are real, than save me." It was not a prayer dripping with faith or a prayer with a great understanding of doctrine. It was a real prayer to a real God and a real sinner was transformed that day.

Three months later I saw my first "Holy Roller": my mother, filled with the Holy Spirit. Soon after, I received the infilling with other tongues. In that moment I realized that the presence I felt in that room was now in me. Love, pure love, is a power that causes men to do great exploits for God.

The next few years I saw a great Charismatic revival. Baptist, Methodist, Catholic, Church of God, Assembly of God, Church of Christ and others came together in unity to follow hard after God. Those are days that I look back on for strength. However, we have a promise that future events will be even greater than those of yesterday.

All I did was ask and God reached down, pulled me out of darkness and filled me with His love. That's all you must do, ask and you shall receive.

. . . PRAYER . . .

Lord, thank You for the salvation you provide when we ask.

. . . TODAY'S THOUGHT . . .

"Ask, and it will be given to you; seek, and you will find; knock, and it will be opened to you" (Matthew 7:7).

—Rev. Charlie Fultz II
Pastor, Northside COG, Gainesville, GA

December 11

GOD HAS A PLAN

The angel of the Lord encamps all around those who fear Him, And delivers them. (Psalm 34:7)

I was tired; no, exhausted. Body and mind. Struggling to stay awake. Driving. Only a few more miles back to the parsonage. Sleep.

My car went under the left side of a tractor-trailer. The truck tore the top of my car off on the passenger side. The car bounced off the truck's rear tires, rolled backwards and landed in the median. I was hanging out of the car with my left hand dragging the ground, my body held in by my seatbelt.

I escaped without serious injury.

Several days later I visited the garage where they had taken my car. I was walking around it observing the total damage. A stranger standing nearby asked, "Who was killed in that wreck?"

I replied, "No one. I was driving alone."

He said, "Man, if I were you, I'd be in church Sunday."

The Lord allowed my life to be spared because He had a specific purpose in mind for me. 2 Timothy 1:9 says that God has called us according to His own purpose. God had a plan for my life. Only ten months later, He revealed the ministry opportunity he had planned.

God's promise of protection became evident to me as I read Psalm 91:11: "For He shall give His angels charge over you, To keep you in all your ways." Psalm 121:8 reveals God's promise of preservation: "The Lord shall preserve your going out and your coming in From this time forth, and even forevermore." God acts in our lives so that we may fulfill His marvelous plans!

. . . PRAYER . . .

Thank You, Lord, for Your merciful kindness and for being a very present help in trouble.

. . . TODAY'S THOUGHT . . .

We may become weak, weary, and worried, but God's promise to us will never fail. His protection will always be sure and His purpose for us will be fulfilled.

—Bobby G. Ross
Pastor, Eastway COG, Charlotte, NC

December 12

JESUS' NAME

And heal the sick there, and say to them "The kingdom of God has come near to you." (Luke 10:9)

We were 12 hours up the Amazon River deep in the jungle of Peru. I marveled at the beautiful jungle vegetation, but beneath its beauty lurked death. The medical ship that we traveled on made its first landing of the day. As a missionary nurse, I was anxious to get started to do the work the Lord had sent us to do.

Within minutes of docking the ship, a ten-year-old girl was bitten by a highly venomous pit viper. The "fer-de-lance" is the second-most venomous snake in Peru and the culprit in many deaths from snakebite. The child's mother had summoned the village "curandero" or witch-doctor. He would use herbs on the child and sing to the snake's spirit to try and gain favor and thus save the child from certain death.

Each time we go to the mission field we must be prepared to do spiritual warfare. We persuaded the mother to bring the child to the ship instead of to the curandero. We had no anti-venom but we had the power of the Holy Spirit. Jesus commanded that we "Go into all the world and preach the gospel to every creature. . . . And these signs will follow those who believe: In My name they will cast out demons; they will speak with new tongues; they will take up serpents; and if they drink anything deadly, it will by no means hurt them; they will lay hands on the sick, and they will recover"(Mark 16:15, 17-18).

We took the Kingdom of God to that village in the jungle of Peru. In the name of Jesus by the power of the Holy Spirit, that little girl recovered from a deadly snake bite.

. . . PRAYER . . .

Lord Jesus, thank You for the gift of the Holy Spirit that enables us to go to all the world to preach Your gospel. Thank You for the power of Your Spirit that heals the sick.

. . . TODAY'S THOUGHT . . .

Every day we must surrender to the will of the Father so that we may be conformed to the image of Christ. We must submit to the Holy Spirit; and as we do, we are true servants, vessels made and used by God. We should expect and anticipate with assurance and confidence that His Glory will be manifested in our lives.

—Sharon L. Smith

Medical Missionary, Free Chapel Worship Center, Gainesville, GA

December 13

A LOVED ONE IS SLEEPING

"O Death, where is your sting?" (1 Corinthians 15:55)

A loved one now is sleeping,
Just gone on before;
another link to bind us
To that eternal shore.

The Waters threatened deep,
And, seeming widely rolled;
But weary limbs and tired feet
Soon pressed the sands of Gold.

We loved thee well 'tis true,
But Jesus loved thee best;
So lay thy tired head upon
Thy Savior's loving breast.

World's trials and temptations
Thy soul again shall never test;
Beyond their power victor,
Thou hast entered into rest.

Over death and grave a conqueror,
A victor's crown is thine
While we around thy memory
A laurel wreath will twine.

Now looking for the Savior,
With those who've gone before,
To come again rejoicing
We'll meet to part no more.

United then a family
To sing His praise, His name adore;
Joining tender thoughts and memories
Of these then happy days of yore.

. . . PRAYER . . .

In faith, our God, we commend our present life and our future beyond it to Your loving care.

. . . TODAY'S THOUGHT . . .

In Christ is total victory, power to live abundantly and victory over death, hell and the grave.

—poem by Charles W. Parham (at the death of a friend)
A Founding Father of the Assemblies of God

December 14

NEW LIFE, NEW DIRECTIONS

For in Christ Jesus neither circumcision nor uncircumcision avails anything, but a new creation. (Galatians 6:15)

God laid His claim on my life with something like a net rather than a bolt of lightning. In late April 1938,1 began to feel deep disquiet about my aims and purpose in life. During this time I knew that something vital was missing from a life that consisted mainly of tutored studies, research and creative writing. So, I left my writing project and went in search of spiritual life instead.

On Monday morning, May 1, 1939, I took a streetcar to Atlanta for two conferences with noted preachers, both of which included discussion, counsel, and prayer. But my emptiness and dissatisfaction remained. Disappointed, I took a streetcar back home, eight miles outside Atlanta. At 11:30 a.m. the trolley stopped on a sidetrack in a wooded area where the cars could pass each other. I was the only passenger, so I sat in silent prayer. "God, I've prayed but I don't feel anything. So I'm going to read your Bible and do everything it says. Then I'll leave it to you to do with me as you will."

At that resolve, my heart was filled with cleansing joy and peace that abruptly made me sensitive to the colors of spring, the sound of the birds and the goodness of life. I knew that Jesus Christ had received, possessed and indwelt me, an assurance that has remained unshaken for 61 years. In the euphoric days that followed, I received the baptism of the Holy Spirit and hastened into the new life and new directions that God willed for me.

. . . PRAYER . . .

Thank You, Father, for the promise of life in this world and for life with You forever.

. . . TODAY'S THOUGHT . . .

All men need new life in Christ—respected gentlemen fully as much as the most objectionable sinners.

—Charles W. Conn
Historian, Author, Former General Overseer COG

December 15

THE LORD CARES

Therefore humble yourselves under the mighty hand of God, that He may exalt you in due time, casting all your care upon Him, for He cares for you. (1 Peter 5:6,7)

Jesus told us that in this world we would have tribulation. However, we should be of good cheer for He has overcome the world (John 16:33).

What comfort! What peace of mind! What consolation we find in these beautiful words of our Savior!

God understood from the beginning that as His children we would face adversities that would deflate us, causing anxious times in our lives. To deliver us from these situations and circumstances, the Lord has given us the privilege of casting (thrusting) these cares upon Him, allowing Him to handle them.

Why? Because he cares for us.

We can find consolation in knowing that we have the Lord who cares for us as our personal Savior, Friend and Deliverer.

. . . PRAYER . . .

Thank You, Lord, for preserving, supporting and delivering us. We are sustained all the day long because our cares are borne by You.

. . . TODAY'S THOUGHT . . .

"Be anxious for nothing, but in everything by prayer and supplication, with thanksgiving, let your requests be made known to God" (Philippians 4:6). Our Lord will deliver us from every anxiety as we give it to Him.

—Aston D. Miller
Pastor, Grace Temple COGC, Washington, MD

December 16

GOD OF THE IMPOSSIBLE

For with God nothing will be impossible. (Luke 1:37)

As a child, I learned to believe all things are possible if you can only believe. My personal experience with the Lord as an adult reinforced my belief that God intervenes in our daily lives with his miracle-working power. Shortly after pioneering my first church, I had a unique experience which reminded me that God still works in the midst of His people.

On a Wednesday night, as service was beginning, a young lady walked into the sanctuary and seated herself on the back pew. As I gave the invitation that night, I said, "If you have a need, God is here to meet that need." The young lady rose from where she was seated and made her way to the altar. Her first words to me were, "Will God meet my need?" We exchanged a few words and I felt impressed of the Spirit to pray. I said, "In the name of Jesus, heal and make whole." After the service, the young lady left before I had time to speak with her.

On Sunday morning I noticed the same young lady sifting in the back of the sanctuary. I felt impressed to ask if anyone had a testimony they wanted to share. The young lady rose timidly and, in a whisper so soft you could hardly hear, simply said, "Wednesday night God healed me of cancer." She then quickly sat down.

After the service, the woman told my wife and me that she had recently been diagnosed with cancer—the final stages. But on Wednesday when we prayed for her, she felt a warmth come over her body like nothing she had ever experienced before. The next day she went to see her doctor. He could find no trace of the cancer!

Today, she is working in her local church and continuously reminding everyone that nothing is impossible to those who believe. Each time I see her, I am reminded that God uses the prayers of individuals like you and me to demonstrate His miracle-working power.

. . . PRAYER . . .

God, help me to believe You for the impossible each time I pray.

. . . TODAY'S THOUGHT . . .

The eyes of the Lord go to and fro, looking to meet my needs.

—Tommie Shook

Pastor, North Anchorage, Anchorage, AK

December 17

BY MY SPIRIT

So he answered and said to me: "This is the word of the Lord to Zerubbabel: 'Not by might nor by power, but by My Spirit,' Says the Lord of hosts." (Zechariah 4:6)

The stress seemed almost as great as the faith. Pressures were mounting. Demands were overwhelming. Going to the office was more difficult than going for a root canal.

This was a new feeling for me. I had never been where I wanted to run. I had always enjoyed challenges. But this time was different. My strength was gone, my sleep disturbed, my nerves on edge. I could neither think straight nor pray with passion. Lately, prayer consisted only of begging God to give me a break. Something had to give.

And then it happened. The voice that I had come to know and love so dearly was now speaking to me again. I had always heard that God will come through just in time. It had happened for me. That gentle, compassionate, longed for, needed voice spoke: "Son, you cannot do in the flesh what can only be done in the Spirit."

That was my answer. I had taken a $2,500,000 building project on myself and had assumed total responsibility for success of the ministry. How foolish could I have been? Battles are not won in the flesh. The success of God's Kingdom does not hinge upon my success. The battle is not mine, but is the Lord's. That simple phrase meant so much to me!

Are you going through a struggle? Are you feeling overwhelmed? With so many pressures vying for our attention and demands upon us that seem inhuman, it is easy to become lost in the maze of every day stress. But God says to all of us, "Remember, it is not by might nor by power, but by My Spirit." The battle is not yours, but the Lord's!

. . . PRAYER . . .

Our Father, thank you today for Your faithfulness at all times. Thank You for the gentle reminder that we are Yours and all that concerns us is Your concern as well. Keep us at peace with you.

. . . TODAY'S THOUGHT . . .

The Lord has promised victory through our trust in Him. Remember, you are not in this alone. God is there for you. He is faithful. You can count on Him.

—Darrell W. Waller
Pastor, COG, Winchester, VA

December 18

THE UNITY OF PENTECOST

When the Day of Pentecost had fully come, they were all with one accord in one place. . . . And they were all filled with the Holy Spirit and began to speak with other tongues, as the Spirit gave them utterance. (Acts 2:1, 4)

Found in these verses are four *unities* that were present on the Day of Pentecost and should accompany every revival. The first was unity of place. All who received were in one place: the Upper Room. I remember the place I received the outpouring of the Holy Spirit as a 15-year-old boy more than 50 years ago. My dad heard of a place where people were meeting God and my heart was hungry for the Holy Spirit baptism. He loaded our family into the car and drove halfway across Texas to that place. We went expecting to meet God.

The second unity was unity of purpose. They were all in one accord. We had only one reason for driving to that distant place. We wanted to meet with God. I remember that my dad asked for prayer and said, "These boys came here wanting to receive the Holy Spirit before they go home." They prayed and we received. We had to drive well into the night for my dad to be back home to go to work Monday morning, but we had a purpose.

The third unity was unity of power. They were all filled with the Holy Spirit. Jesus said, "But you shall receive power when the Holy Spirit has come upon you" (Acts 1:8). I have never doubted that I received power that night.

The fourth unity was unity of praise. They heard them praising God for His wonderful works (Acts 2:11). Praise accompanies the Pentecostal baptism. I remember riding home that dark night and not wanting to stop praising God. For hours, I kept praising God. Since that night I have grown in my understanding and appreciation of my personal union with the Holy Spirit.

. . . PRAYER . . .

0 God, let the Pentecostal power fall afresh in Your church as Your people live in unity.

. . . TODAY'S THOUGHT . . .

When God's people come together in the unity of place with a unity of purpose, they will experience a unity of power and live in a unity of praise.

—Daryl R. Merrill
International Board Member, FGFCM

December 19

THE GARDEN OF GOD

A garden enclosed is my sister, my spouse, A spring shut up, A fountain sealed. . . . Let my beloved come to his garden And eat its pleasant fruits. (Song of Solomon 4:12, 16).

One of my favorite places is the flower garden. I am astounded at God's creativity exhibited in the garden. The explosion of color, the aroma of scent, and the feel of the lush and multi-textured plants reflect the glory of God's handiwork.

From the very beginning, gardens have also held a special place in the heart of God. In Genesis He lovingly created the Garden of Eden and placed mankind within to dress and keep it. The first Adam failed in his endeavors, yet thousands of years later the last Adam would succeed in His struggle for obedience in the Garden of Gethsemane.

Now, instead of man being in the garden, God has placed the garden in man. God is the "husbandman," the tender of this garden growing the spiritual fruit of love, joy, peace, longsuffering, gentleness, goodness, faith, meekness, and temperance.

In the Song of Solomon, the bridegroom describes his bride as "a garden enclosed" and inaccessible to him. She responds with "let my beloved come to his garden and eat its pleasant fruits." Christ is our bridegroom; we are His bride.

At the entrance of our spiritual gardens is a gate that swings freely. We choose to open the gate or to keep it closed. Let us not be closed off from His presence, but let us experience the intimacy of a relationship that only He offers. It is time to open our gates and welcome the divine husbandman into His garden. God is the One who will tend our garden, plant His righteous seed and bring forth everlasting fruit.

. . . PRAYER . . .

Dear Lord, as my bridegroom, friend, and lover of my soul, I choose to open my garden gate to You. I invite Your presence into my innermost being. May I experience the fullness of Your love and express the joy of being Your bride.

. . . TODAY'S THOUGHT . . .

In the intimate times with Him, God plants the precious seeds of promise in our hearts, minds, and spirits. With time, they grow into a beautiful garden that He displays to the world.

—Pamela Palagyi

December 20

LIVING WATER: HOLY GHOST

On the last day, that great day of the feast, Jesus stood and cried out, saying "If anyone thirsts, let him come to Me and drink. He who believes in Me, as the Scripture has said, out of his heart will flow rivers of living water." But this He spoke concerning the Spirit, whom those believing in Him would receive; for the Holy Spirit was not yet given, because Jesus was not yet glorified. (John 7:37-39)

It was January 18, 1960. I went to revival services at the Loudon Church of God with Reverend Randall Geren as the evangelist. Sitting there as a nineteen-year-old backslider, I began to realize that, in the words of Jeremiah speaking of the potter and clay, the Lord wanted to make me "again into another vessel, as it seemed good to the potter to make" (Jeremiah 18:4).

A potter mixes the clay with water, thus making it manageable. I see now, looking back on that cold January night, that the Living Water of the Holy Spirit made me manageable so that the Master Potter could mold me and make me into a vessel of honor for His use. Just as water is used in softening clay for the potter, so God uses His Holy Spirit as the softening agent of a hard heart. Jesus, the Master Potter, took a young backslider that night long ago and molded him into the vessel he needed to be.

When a man is thirsty and desperate, Jesus is the only one who can meet that need. Abundant living will be the result of rivers of living water flowing out. "I have come that they may have life, and that they may have it more abundantly" (John 10:10).

Two years after that blessed service, I received my call to the ministry. The vessel made that night has been blessed beyond the vessel's ability to contain it.

. . . PRAYER . . .

Thank You, Lord, for making me a vessel fit for the Master's use.

. . . TODAY'S THOUGHT . . .

Only the person who believes in Jesus Christ can receive the living water of the Holy Spirit.

—Bobby G. Scott
State Evangelism Director of TN, COG

December 21

FIRST INSTALLMENT

In Him you also trusted, after you heard the word of truth, the gospel of your salvation; in whom also, having believed, you were sealed with the Holy Spirit of promise, who is the guarantee of our inheritance until the redemption of the purchased possession, to the praise of His glory. (Ephesians 1:13-14)

December 26, 1987. It was cool and had just begun to rain. The joy and excitement of the holiday season still lingered. Three brothers in Christ and myself journeyed to the nearest mall to take advantage of the end of the year bargains.

The crowd of people was overwhelming. We parked, pressed our way into the mall and began our shopping spree. We enjoyed both the fellowship and the sight of the mad frenzy of people pushing and shoving over saving a few dollars. After lunch, it was time to go home.

Driving home, we reflected on the goodness of God. Three of us had been saved a year earlier. We were all hungry and on fire for God. God had done an awesome work in our lives in a year's time. The other two received the baptism of the Holy Spirit, but I was yet to be filled.

The presence of Jesus filled the car to the extent that we had to pull over on the side of the road. We wept and worshipped for the next 45 minutes. As the presence of God became stronger, I began to sense a rumbling in my spirit. Not fully understanding, I continued to worship God. Then rumbling rushed upward and came out of my mouth and I began to speak in tongues. The next hour was literally heaven on earth. We jumped out of the car, shouting, dancing and praising God.

Ephesians 1:13-14 states that we are sealed with the Holy Spirit of promise which is the earnest of our inheritance. The word "earnest" means a down payment or an installment. To ensure that God will come through on all of His promises, He has made a down payment by giving us the Holy Spirit. His indwelling presence is a guarantee that God will consummate all of His promises to us.

. . . PRAYER . . .

Holy Spirit, please indwell and empower; be in us and on us in power.

. . . TODAY'S THOUGHT . . .

"Though every believer has the Holy Spirit, the Holy Spirit does not have every believer" (A.W. Tozer).

—Greg Gober

Minister, Free Chapel Worship Center, Gainesville, GA

December 22

GOD IS A FORGIVING GOD

This is a faithful saying and worthy of all acceptance, that Christ Jesus came into the world to save sinners, of whom I am chief. (1 Timothy 1:15)

For most of my early teenage years, I wrestled with the thought of God being forgiving and merciful. Sitting in a revival, the preacher said to repent and be saved. I could not comprehend that a loving God could cleanse and make me whole despite my past sins. Night after night, I asked God to forgive me, yet always left with the feeling of unworthiness and the sense of being eternally doomed.

Many people doubt God's forgiveness. The Bible says, "My people are destroyed for lack of knowledge" (Hosea 4:6). As a part of our prayer and devotion, we must consider the following:

1. God will always be faithful to His Word and will speedily forgive the repentant heart (1 John 1:9).
2. No one is perfect or without fault (Romans 3:23).
3. Salvation is not measured by our goodness, but by God's grace (Ephesians 2:9).
4. The death of Christ was a complete work that wrought our redemption (John 3:16).
5. As God forgives us, we must be willing to accept God's forgiveness and forgive ourselves (Philippians 3:13-14).
6. God will continually perfect you until He returns (Philippians 1:6).

God's Word speaks to us Truth. We can go boldly into the throne of grace because we are made righteous and whole through the sacrifice of our Savior Jesus Christ. Romans 5:1 "Therefore, having been justified by faith, we have peace with God through our Lord Jesus Christ." "Amazing grace, how sweet the Sound that saved a wretch like me. I once was lost but now am found, I was blind but now I see.".

. . . PRAYER . . .

God I thank You because You sacrificed Your life so that I might have eternal life.

. . . TODAY'S THOUGHT . . .

God promised that He would forgive us (1 John 1:9). His Word remains true.

—Dr. Jonathan Ramsey, Jr.
Administrative Bishop, COG, Southern NE

December 23

HIS MERCY ENDURES FOREVER

Let us therefore come boldly to the throne of grace, that we may obtain mercy and find grace to help in time of need. (Hebrews 4:16)

Preaching in a conference, I sensed in my spirit a great urgency to go home: something was wrong. Arriving home, I was relieved to discover that my wife and children were fine. Wondering why the Lord had spoken to me as He did, I began to unwind after a long day.

Then the phone rang. I was alarmed to hear the distressed voice of my father-in-law, Pastor John Osteen. "Gary" he said, "could you come over and be with me? I'm not feeling well and I'd like you to be here."

"Absolutely," I responded. "I'll be right there!"

Daddy Osteen was sitting on the couch in the living room when I arrived. He was very sick and was having difficulty breathing. Immediately, I sat down beside him and began praying in the Spirit.

"Gary," he said, "These are the darkest days that Dodie and I have ever walked through. The pain and the suffering are so great."

I tried to make him comfortable on the couch, but lying down made breathing more difficult. I moved him to his recliner and encouraged him to try and sleep sitting up. He wanted me to lie down on the couch, but if he had to sleep sitting up, I was going to do the same. So I turned off the light and sat down in the recliner next to him.

In that very quiet and intimate moment, he and I in the darkness of that room, there was a question I knew I had to ask. "Daddy, do you ever wonder where God is in the midst of all this suffering?"

"Well," he said, in a soft, frail voice. The two-second pause seemed like an eternity. "Sometimes." But then be spoke with such authority and power, boldness and conviction, that I recognized the anointing. "But His mercy endures forever!" And there in my arms, God in His mercy received Daddy Osteen into glory, never to suffer again.

. . . PRAYER . . .

Dear Lord, when we've done all that we know to do, help us to trust that You know better. We simply ask, have mercy on us, O Lord.

. . . TODAY'S THOUGHT . . .

Suffering is always difficult, but God's mercy is always extended. God cares for you and will always answer your cry for deliverance.

—Gary Simons

Pastor, High Point Church, Arlington, TX

December 24

THE GLORIOUS HOLY SPIRIT

"Stand up and bless the Lord your God forever and ever Blessed be Your glorious name, which is exalted above all blessing and praise!" (Nehemiah 9:5)

My father passed away when I was quite young, and my family did not have many material possessions. We were not totally devoid of spiritual influence, however, for we had a godly grandmother.

I was a rebellious child. I got into any mischief I could find; I even bootlegged whiskey for a while in Atlanta and spent one night in jail. The Holy Spirit often convicted me of the life I lived. When I thought of my grandmother's prayers, it seemed that with each step I took away from God, I felt her tears slosh in my shoes.

One Sunday afternoon at the corner of Humphrey and Hightower Streets in Atlanta, I was led of the Spirit to enter an old-fashioned brush arbor building. The floor was sawdust strewn over the hard-packed ground. The preacher rolled his Bible in his hand, paced up and down the aisles, and preached a "hell fire and brimstone" message.

My sinner's heart trembled as God made me conscious of my need to give Him my heart and life. I "hit the sawdust trail" and fell into the altar. A dear sister named Anna Belle, whose husband was a prize fighter—a lady who loved to dance and rejoice before the Lord—prayed with me.

Oh, what a glorious experience it was to be saved! Heaven and earth came together with a smack and I was right in the middle of it all! Not only was I saved, but I also received the baptism in the Holy Spirit that same afternoon.

The glorious Holy Spirit has been so wonderful to me through the years.

. . . PRAYER . . .

Sweet Holy Spirit, let us never become so big or so important that we fail to hear You when You speak. Guide and direct us in all things.

. . . TODAY'S THOUGHT . . .

The Holy Spirit echoes softly in our minds the sounds of a mother or grandmother at prayer. Like the aromas from the kitchens of our childhood, they draw us back home and eventually into the arms of Jesus.

—John Thomas "Jake" Roberts (Reprinted from *SpiritWalk: Daily Devotions on the Holy Spirit* by permission of Pathway Press)
State Overseer/Church Leader, FL (former)

December 25

THE GIFT

And the Word became flesh and dwelt among us . . . (John 1:14)

In the dim morning light she brought it to me—the first present ever she picked out herself. Smudged. Wrinkled. Taped and re-taped over the precious paper with her very own drawings. Handmade just for me.

Her little hands carefully nestled this special package that contained its unique treasure that was given to me by my little daughter. Years will pass. The innocence will fade. Womanhood will overtake her. More sophisticated gifts will replace the childish handmade present. Store-bought ties and sweaters and expensive colognes in exquisite decanters, perhaps. But none will ever match this early morning visit with the first gift ever given from her heart. To me, it was packaged to perfection.

But how do you package love? Will it fit in a box or a sack or a stocking hanging by the fireplace? God used a stable. Love came wrapped in straw and the beauty of a virgin mother's smile.

The Word was God. And the reason He was called "Word" was because He expressed all the marvelous things God wanted to express to us. He expressed the love, the patience, the long-suffering, the forgiveness, and family relationship of God, our Father.

When we receive His Word into our hearts the wonderful event happens again. The Word becomes flesh—in us. His coming had a greater impact upon the world than all the other events of history combined. His coming into your life will be far greater than all the rest of your life, too. And it lasts forever.

. . . PRAYER . . .

Father God, thank You for the gift of Your only Son, Jesus Christ. We receive Him anew in the quietness of this moment with abiding faith that the Word, indeed, becomes flesh in us.

. . . TODAY'S THOUGHT . . .

If we were not able to give anything else to those about us this Christmas, we could give them nothing more precious than our love; the love that Christ has put in us.

—Carl H. Richardson
Carl Richardson Ministries, Brandon, FL

December 26

PEACE ON EARTH?

"Glory to God in the highest, And on earth peace, goodwill toward men!" (Luke 2:14)

We were both cloaked in heavy coats and scarves as we strode along together, the skies above filled with winking stars etched into the inky backdrop of space. Christy, our youngest daughter—a junior high school student—was with me as we enjoyed one of our frequent walks. She was talking, her remarks initiated by the fact that a friend's house had recently been broken into and robbed.

"Ya know, Dad, it really makes me afra—well, not afraid, but it kinda bothers me when . . . ya know . . . all the stuff that's on the news . . . and when bad things happen, like . . . well, robberies and killings and . . . you know, all that stuff." Then, punctuated by a sudden waving of arms: "You know what I mean? I wish everything would be peaceful!"

I do know what she meant. We get tired of living in a weary world worn by sin and death. A thousand manifestations of those two factors surround us, but the end analysis is always the same: The root is sin and the fruit is death. Sin kills joy, hope, love, trust, peace, people.

"Sometimes I think it would be so-o-o nice to live somewhere like Chippewa Falls" (where her cousins live in Wisconsin).

"Chris," I began. "When you visited Amy and David in Chippewa Falls, were there any police cars there?" She got the point. I went on: "There's no place in the world you can go to find peacefulness because there's no place in the world to get away from people who hurt and who hate. Peace isn't what's around you, but what's inside you."

We talked more and she understood and was satisfied. For peace is knowing 1) you are right with God, 2) you are right in your relationships, and 3) you are living in God's will.

. . . PRAYER . . .

Lord Jesus, bring peace to hearts as they accept Your grace.

. . . TODAY'S THOUGHT . . .

The angels' message, "Peace on earth," is not a tease or a taunt where open hearts will let peace work its wonder. And that peace will guard the heart that continues in confident surrender to the Father's Will and Way (Philippians 4:6-7).

—Jack Hayford

Pastor, Church On The Way, Van Nuys, CA

December 27

DESPAIR OR HOPE?

. . . that by two immutable things, in which it is impossible for God to lie, we might have strong consolation, who have fled for refuge to lay hold of the hope set before us. (Hebrews 6:18)

In my last few years of being a pastor, I have been compelled to observe the despair and lack of hope in both young and old. According to religious pollster George Barna, many local churches are barely surviving and approximately 3,000-4,000 of them close their doors every year. In a news letter dated August 1998, one of the mega-ministries in the United States stated the following: "We estimate that approximately 1,500 pastors leave their assignments each month due to moral failure, spiritual burnout or contention within their local congregations."

Winston Churchill said shortly before his death, "Our problems are beyond us. We are a generation staggering around the rim of hell." Amidst this sense of hopelessness and helplessness, as believers we can stand on the solid rock of God's Word. We can take great hope and comfort in knowing that our past is as a shining light that shines more and more unto a perfect day.

Regardless of one's eschatological belief, we all have the blessed hope of our Lord's return. In our occupation of the King's business we can bring hope to the hopeless, light to those in darkness, and life to those in death.

Let us, who name the Name of Christ, increase our hope in the true and living God, the Almighty God who works all things after the counsel of His own will. We are a part of His will and purpose. Hope!

. . . PRAYER . . .

Our Father, You are our hope. Help us to increase and grow in our hope in the years to come.

. . . TODAY'S THOUGHT . . .

Lost hope is the devil's best friend.

—Paul Harthern

Pastor, Grace Covenant Church, Carrollton, GA

December 28

WALK IN THE SPIRIT

If we live in the Spirit, let us also walk in the Spirit. (Galatians 5:25)

The young Christian sat with his pastor before a fireplace on a wintry morning.

"Pastor, I am confused. I hear that the Holy Spirit should be in me, and that I should be in the Spirit. How can both be true?"

The pastor quietly picked up the poker, went to the fireplace, and placed the end in the flames. Soon, the poker became fiery red. "Now," asked the pastor, "is the poker in the fire, or is the fire in the poker?"

To be filled with the Spirit and live continually in His presence is the desire of many people. However, the Lord wants more from His children than merely a passive experience or relationship. It is vital that we live in the presence and influence of the Holy Spirit, but it is also vital that we walk in the Spirit—actively follow a course of obedience to His commands.

To walk in the Spirit is to walk in paths of service to our Lord; this more than simply responding to events around us. It is the active pursuit of His will—the aggressive following of His lead. Living in the Spirit is the vital beginning point of our relationship with God, but it is in the obedience of walking that we influence others and do God's highest will.

When we walk in the Spirit, we know the fellowship of the Comforter—the Walker alongside—who guides our steps and enables our witness. It is our walking in the Spirit which best accomplishes God's will in us.

. . . PRAYER . . .

Thank You, Lord, for the Holy Spirit who furnishes not only a sacred atmosphere for my living but also makes a path for my footsteps to follow. Help me to walk that path of obedience and service.

. . . TODAY'S THOUGHT . . .

The joy we find in the presence of the Holy Spirit is multiplied when we step out in obedience to His guidance.

—Dr. Aaron M. Wilson
Editor, Pentecostal Messenger, PCOG

December 29

LIVING ON THE EDGE OF A MIRACLE

And there are also many other things that Jesus did, which if they were written one by one, I suppose that even the world itself could not contain the books that would be written. Amen. (John 21:25)

It was 5:00 a.m. as a friend and I crossed the park in Quesaltenango planning to take the bus to Guatemala City to catch a plane to the United States. To our surprise we saw the bus leaving the station early. Since we were four hours from the city, the situation looked hopeless. My friend said to me, "I believe you live on the edge of a crisis." After thinking about his words, I responded, "No, I live on the edge of a miracle." We walked back across the park and saw another bus. I asked the driver where he was going and if he had seats available. He said, "Guatemala City. I have two seats left." We arrived 30 minutes earlier than the bus we were planning to take.

Where are you living today? On the edge of a crisis or the edge of a miracle? Did Noah, while building the ark, live on the edge of a crisis or miracle? Did Moses, when confronting the Red Sea, live on the edge of a crisis or miracle? Did Joshua, when confronting the Jordan river, live on the edge of a crisis or the edge of a miracle?

Many people discount the possibility of miracles today. I write with authority, however, since I am a modern-day miracle. When I was born, the doctor told my dad that I was born dead. My dad said, "No, my son shall live and preach the gospel." Crisis or miracle? At four years of age my parents were again told I could not live. At seven and fifteen they were told the same. I am now 69 and have experienced 44 years of missionary work in 66 countries and traveled approximately 3 million miles. I have lived through five years of revolution in Cuba, been in perils of robbers, perils of the heathen, perils of the wilderness, perils in the sea, perils in the air, perils in storms, perils in the cities and perils in health. But through it all I have learned to trust in God.

. . . PRAYER . . .

Father, help us to believe and expect your miracles today!

. . . TODAY'S THOUGHT . . .

Thousands live on the edge of a miracle every day and experience miracles as they believe and act on God's promises. Receive your miracle today. "Jesus Christ is the same yesterday, today and forever."

—Hugh Skelton

Director of Missions, Free Chapel Worship Center, Gainesville, GA

December 30

GOD'S SUFFICIENT GRACE

My grace is sufficient for you, for My strength is made perfect in weakness. (2 Corinthians 12:9)

As a seminary student, my life entered a series of difficulties that pressured me in several areas of life: the pressure pastoring a church, of working to support my family, and of being a seminary student. I was on the verge of giving up and withdrawing from school. I vividly remember saying to God, "Lord, you called me to this ministry and opened this door for me to come to Bible school." Through the tears and frustration and feeling of defeat, I cried out to God, "Where are You now!" I was on the verge of ministerial burn out.

Suddenly, God spoke a word of comfort and release to my troubled soul. "For I know the thoughts that I think toward you, says the Lord, thoughts of peace and not of evil, to give you a future and a hope. Then you will call upon Me and go and pray to Me, and I will listen to you. And you will seek Me and find Me, when you search for Me with all your heart (Jeremiah 29:11-13).

I learned valuable lessons that day:

1. God has purposes, plans and promises for our lives.
2. God is constantly aware of our circumstances and situations.
3. We must never give up in searching for Him.

Perhaps you have experienced some difficult struggles in life. Know that:

1. Even in our hurt, there is healing.
2. Even in our fears, there is faith.
3. Even in our complaints, there is comfort.

. . . PRAYER . . .

Thank You, Lord, for giving us Comfort and Assurance in difficult times.

. . . TODAY'S THOUGHT . . .

He is a present help in the time of trouble.

—Timothy McGahee
Pastor, Bountiful Blessings, Sebring, FL

December 31

LIFE IN THE NEW YEAR

For what is your life? It is even a vapor that appears for a little time and then vanishes away. (James 4:14)

For the ancient peoples of Tibet, the New Year begins on February 9. The holiday is celebrated with seven festival days of feasting, drinking, dancing, and making merry. The main meal on New Year's Day begins with a soup of "dumplings." The dumplings are made carefully and little pieces of dough are folded over an object that may or may not be edible.

The entrée has a symbolic meaning. Supposedly, it reveals your personality or predicts the coming year for you. If you bite into your morsel and it contains yak butter, you are a sweet, congenial person. If it has meat, a kind of chili, you are rude. If it contains a piece of wood, you are lazy. Salt is good and indicates you are a good person. A white stone means that you will live a long life.

In truth, no one can predict what kind of year the next 12 months will be. No one can predict what your life will be like; not a psychic, crystal-gazer, palm reader, or tantalizing New Age enticement.

Of one thing we can be sure: the eternal God knows and controls the future. And we know that He can control the things of life for us. In the words of William Cullen Bryant's immortal "Thanatopsis":

So live that when thy summons comes to join
The innumerable caravan which moves
To that mysterious realm where each shall take
His chamber in the silent halls of death,
Thou goest not, like the quarry-laden slave at night,
Scourged to his dungeon, but sustained and soothed
By an unfaltering trust, approach thy grave
Like one that wraps the drapery of his couch
About him, and lies down to pleasant dreams.

. . . PRAYER . . .

Father, teach me to trust You completely. I want to know that You are guiding by day and watching over me by night. Keep me in peace.

. . . TODAY'S THOUGHT . . .

. . . when He, the Spirit of truth, has come, He will guide you into all truth (John 16:13).

—Marcus V. Hand
Editor-at-Large, Publishing House, Cleveland, TN

CONTRIBUTING AUTHORS

Life in the Spirit has been a work of joy and has covered a span of over four years. It is now a part of ushering in the new millennium. *Life in the Spirit* celebrates the accomplishments of the Holy spirit during this last century and points to the future millennium with great anticipation. A few of the contributing authors have changed ministry responsibilities, going on to greater things for God. However, with few exceptions, the titles and positions will be used at the time the compilation of *Life in the Spirit* began.

Some of the greatest men and women in the history of Christianity are contributing authors in this book. A few have already accomplished the work God has called them to do and have gone on to receive their crowns. Most of those in *Life in the Spirit* are among those who now are making the greatest impact, and **will** make the greatest impact in the future, upon the world for Christ as they are empowered by the Holy Spirit.

SYMBOLS USED TO IDENTIFY DENOMINATIONS AND ORGANIZATIONS

AG	Assemblies of God
AGIF	Assemblies of God International Fellowship
CHC	Congregational Holiness Church
COG	Church of God
COGC	Church of God in Christ
COGMA	Church of God, Mountain Assembly
COGoAF	Church of God of Apostolic Faith
COGOP	Church of God of Prophecy
COGOPC	Church of God of Prophecy of Canada
DTN	Daystar Television Network
EF	Elim Fellowship
FGC	Foursquare Gospel Church
FGCC	Foursquare Gospel Church of Canada
FGCOG	Full Gospel Church of God
FGFCM	Full Gospel Fellowship of Churches and Ministers
ICFG	International Church of the Foursquare Gospel
IF	Ichthus Fellowship
IPCC	Italian Pentecostal Church of Canada
IPCoC	International Pentecostal Church of Christ
IPHC	International Pentecostal Holiness Church
OBFFC	Open Bible Faith Fellowship of Canada
OBSC	Open Bible Standard Churches
OBSCC	Open Bible Standard Churches of Canada
PAC	Pentecostal Assemblies of Canada
PAN	Pentecostal Assemblies of Newfoundland
PCOG	Pentecostal Church of God
PFWB	Pentecostal Free Will Baptist
TBN	Trinity Broadcasting Network

ABOUT THE AUTHOR / COMPILER

Dr. Robert White, a Christian since age fourteen and a preacher since age eighteen, has served in many capacities during his forty-seven year ministry: Pastor, Evangelist, Bible Teacher, Conference Speaker, World Missions Director, Seminary President, Presiding Bishop of his denomination, and much more. With a passion for knowledge and education, he attended Lee University (Cleveland, Tennessee) and received a B.A. from Rocky Mountain College (Billings, Montana), an M.A. from Arizona State University (Tempe, Arizona), and a D.Min. from Hamma School of Theology (Springfield, Ohio).

But his passion has always been and remains winning souls for Christ, bringing unity within the Body of Christ and bringing reconciliation and harmony to the races and cultures that make up the Body of Christ. His zeal has led him to preach crusades, conferences, seminars and special services in over fifty-four countries; and it has been the force behind many of his decisions as a denominational leader, the books he has authored or compiled (*Circle of Love, Soaring Above the World with Your Feet on the Ground*, *SpiritWalk*), and the preaching he loves to do in his current role as International Evangelist.

Life In The Spirit holds a special place in his heart. He loves the Pentecostal/Charismatic Movement, the people who comprise it and, especially, the Lord who has empowered His people "To preach the gospel to the poor; . . . to heal the brokenhearted, To proclaim liberty to the captives And recovery of sight to the blind, To set at liberty those who are oppressed" (Luke 4:18). He considers it not merely a duty, but a privilege, to serve the One who has made his life so rich.

Dr. White's wife, Kathy, is his partner in ministry and is also an author and speaker. Together they travel as they always have, spreading the Gospel of their beloved Lord.